THE GREAT AMERICAN HOUSING BUBBLE

THE
GREAT AMERICAN
HOUSING BUBBLE

What Went Wrong and How We Can
Protect Ourselves in the Future

Adam J. Levitin

Susan M. Wachter

Harvard University Press

Cambridge, Massachusetts
London, England
2020

To Sarah—A.J.L.

To Michael—S.M.W.

Who make our houses our homes.

First printing

Library of Congress Cataloging-in-Publication Data

Names: Levitin, Adam Jeremiah, author. | Wachter, Susan M., author.
Title: The great American housing bubble : what went wrong and how we can protect
ourselves in the future / Adam J. Levitin, Susan M. Wachter.
Description: Cambridge, Massachusetts : Harvard University Press, 2020. | Includes
bibliographical references and index.
Identifiers: LCCN 2019046762 | ISBN 9780674979659 (cloth)
Subjects: LCSH: Freddie Mac (Firm) | Federal National Mortgage Association. |
Mortgage loans—United States—History. | Housing—United States—
Finance—History. | Global Financial Crisis, 2008–2009.
Classification: LCC HG2040.5.U5 L48 2020 | DDC 332.7/20973090511—dc23
LC record available at https://lccn.loc.gov/2019046762

Contents

Preface

We're an odd couple. We're a law professor and a real estate economist separated by a generation and, on a good day, about two hours on the Acela Express. We've been collaborating on scholarship and policy work since 2008, and we owe our acquaintance to the financial crisis that followed the collapse of the Great American Housing Bubble.

In September 2008, when the entire US economy appeared to be imploding, we both found ourselves participating in a number of conference calls as part of "brain trusts" to which members of Congress were turning for ideas on how to help bail out not just banks but also beleaguered homeowners. We recognized in the course of those calls that we could do a lot more together than we could separately. Adam knew something about the mechanics of securitization and foreclosures, and Susan knew quite a bit more about real estate economics. We realized that by putting these pieces together we could articulate a much more coherent critique of what went wrong—and a much sharper formula for how to fix it—than we could individually. Over the years we have batted ideas back and forth and educated each other, while working through our thinking on housing finance in a series of articles, book chapters, congressional testimonies, and policy briefs. This book is the culmination of our efforts.

Our immodest goal in this book is to provide the definitive account of the creation and collapse of the Great American Housing Bubble and to set forth tangible principles and metrics to guide housing finance reform.

Put differently, this book is about what went wrong in housing finance and how to fix it. Astonishingly, over a decade after the bubble burst, no definitive account yet exists of the bubble, which brought on the greatest destruction of wealth in modern memory, culminating in the financial crisis of 2008. While there are numerous accounts of the financial crisis of 2008, the events of the fall of 2008 are very much an epilogue to the story of the bubble. The question that concerns us is what went wrong in the housing finance market such that there was a bubble in the first place.

As of our writing, in the beginning of 2020, the housing finance system in the United States remains broken. The bubble drove home prices in some parts of the country to record highs. The collapse of the bubble triggered the worst financial crisis since the Great Depression. It also left a legacy of over 7 million homes sold in foreclosure—one in every nineteen housing units in the United States, with millions of families displaced and many others trapped in houses that they could not sell without taking a loss. More than a decade later, the effects of the collapse still linger in the form of depressed interest rates. Although the housing finance system is currently stable, it remains on government life support and is, incredibly, still in limbo.

Understanding what caused the bubble is paramount for preventing a recurrence and for ensuring a stable housing finance system going forward. If we don't understand what caused the Great American Housing Bubble that destroyed trillions of dollars of wealth, destabilized numerous communities, precipitated millions of home foreclosures, and played a key role in tectonic shifts in global financial markets, how can we ever hope to prevent future bubbles?

We believe it is important to understand what happened in the housing market not only for its own sake, but also because of the lessons it holds for rebuilding the housing finance market. Given the far-reaching effects of housing finance in consumers' lives (where and how we live), in the economy ($11 trillion of mortgage debt, financed through $9.5 trillion of various mortgage-related securities), and ultimately even in the political system (homeownership affects civic participation), it is imperative the housing finance system ensure Americans have access to affordable, stable, and fair housing finance.

The story we tell is not about people directly, or at least it does not feature individuals. You will not meet colorful stock characters from the bubble years like the charlatan mortgage broker, the wily house flipper, the hapless subprime borrower, the do-nothing regulator, the Cassandra professor, the unctuous lobbyist, the smarmy politician, the rube asset manager, the eccentric genius investor, or the rapacious Wall Street financier.

They make great fodder for journalistic accounts, and we love reading about them, but their personality quirks are a distraction from the search for what went wrong; more importantly, these synecdoches, although helpful for casual discussion, offer no help in figuring out how to fix the market.

Instead, ours is a story of two intertwined markets—the housing market and the housing finance market—that are populated by institutions, financial products, and regulations. These markets are indelibly connected for a simple reason: most Americans purchase their homes on credit; without mortgage credit, our housing stock and our whole way of life in America would look radically different. Ours is a tale of the possibilities—and limits—of markets, and the complicated role of government in markets. Ultimately it is a story about what sort of country we live in and what sort of country we will leave to our children and grandchildren: can we bequeath them a country with a strong homeownership culture, stable neighborhoods, and sources of retirement savings, and fair access to adequate credit? The question of who can get housing financing and on what terms affects consumer behavior, community makeup, local democracy, and the economy as a whole.

These lofty points aside, every story needs a protagonist, and we have one. The hero of our story is the thirty-year fixed-rate mortgage (FRM) or "30-year fixed"—the "American Mortgage," a uniquely American financial product that has unusual benefits for consumers and market stability. The American Mortgage only emerged following World War II. It is the product of substantial regulatory interventions in the mortgage market and requires a certain institutional and regulatory environment to thrive. The story of the American Mortgage is one of enormous social benefits resulting from government interventions in the market.

A good story also needs an antagonist, and we have one of those too. The tale we tell of the housing bubble is a tale of the temporary eclipse of the American Mortgage and the return of a modern form of the "bullet loans" that prevailed before the New Deal. Bullet loans were short-term, interest-only loans with a "bullet" of principal that was due at maturity. The interest-only structure kept monthly payments lower than they would be on an amortized loan that has payments of interest and principal. The expectation was that borrowers would generally refinance bullet loans as they approached maturity, so they would never have to make the bullet payment.

During the bubble years, a variety of nontraditional mortgage products proliferated that shared some of the key characteristics of bullet loans. Some nontraditional mortgage products were interest-only or partially amortized loans, while others had initial low-rate teaser periods. All of these loans offered lower initial payments, which enabled borrowers to buy more house because the loans were underwritten based on the borrower's ability to afford the initial payments, not the maximum possible payment. A larger "bullet" payment always loomed. Moreover, most nontraditional loans were low- or no-documentation loans that were underwritten without verifying the borrower's ability to make even the initial teaser payments.

Nontraditional mortgage products thus enabled borrowers to bid up home prices beyond what would have been possible with the 30-year fixed. The shift in mortgage products eased credit constraints on borrowers, but this easing was not sustainable because the nontraditional mortgage products relied on the borrower's ability to refinance before monthly payments increased and the "bullet" hit. Refinancing, however, is not possible if a borrower's credit quality has declined, the collateral property's value has declined, or the markets are in turmoil.

The return of bullet loans was possible only because of a shift in the way mortgages were financed. The 30-year fixed is a product cultivated by three unique financial institutions that are the linchpin of the postwar American housing finance market: Fannie Mae, Freddie Mac, and Ginnie Mae. These institutions are granted special privileges in exchange for facilitating housing finance in the United States, and they are subject to a particular set of regulations. Most importantly, Fannie, Freddie, and Ginnie bear the credit risk—the risk of nonpayment—on all the mortgages they finance, but they generally pass along the interest rate risk—the risk that the mortgages are at a below-market interest rate or will be refinanced—to investors.

Fannie, Freddie, and Ginnie provided the financing that made the American Mortgage the dominant housing finance product for decades. They did so in part through securitization. Securitization is a financing technique that transforms various types of assets into securities. In the case of mortgages, securitization involves the issuance of debt securities collateralized by pools of mortgage loans. (Other types of assets are also securitized, but mortgages are the dominant asset class in the securitization market.) Mortgage securitization thus links consumer borrowers with capital market investors, who indirectly fund the consumers' mortgages. Securitization is important to the 30-year fixed because banks eschew funding long-term mortgages with short-term liabilities such as deposits. This is because banks risk insolvency if they fund long-term, fixed-rate assets with short-term, fixed-rate liabilities: the bank will lose money if the interest rate it pays on the deposits rises above the rate it earns on the mortgages.

Starting around 2003, the American Mortgage was displaced from its dominant position in the US housing market as the mortgage finance market shifted away from securitization by Fannie, Freddie, and Ginnie (collectively, "agency securitization") toward what is known as "private-label securitization" (PLS), meaning securitization undertaken by Wall Street banks. PLS differed substantially from agency securitization in that investors in private-label mortgage-backed securities bore not just the interest rate risk on the mortgages but also the credit risk.

The PLS investor base included virtually all major financial institutions— banks, insurance companies, hedge funds, pension plans, money market mutual funds, and so on. PLS investors were more willing to finance riskier products (bullet loans) than were Fannie, Freddie, and Ginnie. These investors did so at rates that did not reflect the systemic risk that the mortgages generated because of the correlated nature of home prices. When the bullet loans exploded, the losses fell on the broad swath of PLS investors. This started a chain reaction within the financial system because of the uncertainty over the extent of the losses and where they lay within the system. The uncertainty meant that the solvency of all parties within the financial system was suspect, which resulted in a system-wide contraction of credit that was, of course, self-fueling, because concerns about insolvency resulted in illiquidity, which in turn begat actual insolvency.

The story of the bubble, then, is this: the shift from regulated agency securitization to unregulated PLS produced an oversupply of underpriced mortgage finance in the form of bullet loans. These loans enabled previously credit-constrained borrowers to bid up housing prices. This set off an arms race in which otherwise unconstrained buyers were compelled to borrow more in order to compete to purchase a limited supply of housing. The result was a rapid increase in housing prices. PLS was the high-octane fuel that powered the housing bubble. At the same time, PLS and the modern bullet loans it financed all but ensured that the boom in housing prices— and the enormous borrowing predicated on it—would be unsustainable.

We thus lay the blame for the bubble, in the first instance, on PLS and the bullet loans it financed. We are not the first or only ones to point to bullet loans and PLS as essential to the housing bubble, although we marshal new and powerful evidence for that point. But merely identifying bullet loans and PLS as the culprit leaves many questions unanswered.

Our work here is to unravel the full mystery: How did it happen? Why did the market shift from agency securitization to PLS, and why did it do so when it did? PLS, after all, was not a novel financing technique; PLS dates back to 1977 but remained a fringe part of the economy until 2003, when it took off like a rocket. Why did the market fail to price in the risk posed by the growth of bullet loans? Why did credit rating agencies, short investors, and credit-sensitive subordinated debt investors all fail to price against the growth in risk in the housing market? Why is housing uniquely threatened by "innovative" lending products and not other assets? You'll have to read further to find the answers, but here's what you can expect—a summary tour of the book.

The introduction presents an argument in favor of homeownership. The policy goal of expanding homeownership has come under frequent criticism since the 2008 financial crisis. We argue that this criticism is misplaced and fails to understand some of the critical value of homeownership, both to homeowners in the form of a hedge against rent increases and to society generally because of the stability of housing tenure engendered by ownership.

The introduction explains how housing markets have become indelibly linked with financial markets because most homes are purchased on credit. It also shows that this linkage is problematic owing to three unique features of housing markets: the correlated nature of home prices, the feedback loop (endogeneity) between home prices and credit terms, and the difficulty for investors in shorting housing. These three features make housing markets uniquely prone to credit-fueled bubbles.

Chapters 1 through 4 provide an overview of the US housing market at the end of the twentieth century and the history of the US housing finance system in that century. These chapters provide the institutional context for understanding the housing bubble that emerged in the twenty-first century. Bubbles and busts in real estate have happened many times before, so a historical perspective is important. These chapters also present an extended analysis of the development of the 30-year fixed. The advent of the American Mortgage provided the backdrop for a historic and sustained expansion of homeownership in the United States in the post–World War II period. Nonetheless, the 30-year fixed has come under attack recently as a less-than-ideal product because of the interest rate risk it places on lenders and its mismatch with actual housing tenures. We present a defense of the 30-year fixed, which we believe is a well-designed product that benefits consumers and lenders alike and is necessary for stable homeownership.

Chapter 5 relates the denouement of the housing bubble: why the bubble collapsed, how the bubble connected with and sparked the financial crisis, and how the aftereffects still reverberate. During the bubble, housing-related assets became an important component of financial institutions' highly leveraged balance sheets, while their liabilities were frequently short-term and flighty, meaning that spooked creditors could often demand immediate repayment. This meant that any perceived impairment in the value of the housing-related assets risked triggering a liquidity crisis for financial institutions because they were unable to roll over their own borrowings in the repo and swaps markets. We also explain how housing as an asset class is uniquely vulnerable to downward price spirals, just as it is to bubbles, and how foreclosures further depressed housing prices and exacerbated the collapse of the bubble.

Chapter 6 turns to the question of identifying the bubble. While there is broad agreement that there was a bubble in the housing market, there is far less agreement about when it began and ended, or even how to define it. We argue that the bubble began quite late—only in 2003–2004—and that the increase in housing prices in 2001–2002 was driven by changes in economic "fundamentals," namely historically low interest rates that made home purchases more affordable relative to rentals and the expanded use of automated underwriting technology. Locating the beginning of the bubble is particularly important to identifying its causes; any explanation of the bubble must be able to explain its timing.

Chapters 7 and 8 address existing theories of the bubble. In Chapter 7, we demonstrate empirically that the housing bubble was, in the first instance, a supply-side rather than demand-side phenomenon, as the supply of mortgage financing increased and its price dropped even as risk was rising. This is consistent only with the bubble being predominantly a mortgage debt supply-side phenomenon, which means that demand-side theories that point exclusively to irrational borrower exuberance, local housing supply constraints, or low-income housing needs do not explain most of the bubble. This is not to say that we deny the basic claims of these theories, but rather that we do not believe they are capable of explaining the bubble overall. Instead, we believe that the bubble was set off by an expansion of the mortgage-financing supply that enabled previously credit-constrained borrowers across income groups to bid up home prices. Otherwise unconstrained borrowers responded with their own increased borrowing in order to remain competitive in the home purchase market. As a result, mortgage debt increased across the credit spectrum, not just for subprime borrowers. Mortgage suppliers more than met this demand increase, by churning out increasing amounts of debt that was poorly underwritten and not priced for the risk.

In Chapter 8, we turn to an examination of supply-side theories of the bubble. What caused the expansion of the mortgage supply in the 2000s? We first show that supply-side theories pointing to affordable housing policy and monetary policy fail to match the timing of the bubble or to explain developments in other related markets, such as that for commercial real estate. We then explore the "global savings glut" theory propounded by former Federal Reserve Board chairman Ben Bernanke, which argues that the bubble was the result of a surplus of international savings seeking "safe," AAA-rated assets. The excessive demand for AAA-rated PLS drove down the cost of mortgage credit, as investors were willing to accept less yield relative to risk. We show that Bernanke's global savings glut theory is incomplete because it fails to account both for the workings of PLS, which was the financing channel for the housing bubble, and for the division of the globe into bubble and no-bubble countries.

In Chapter 9, we probe the source of the increase in supply in mortgage financing and present our theory of the bubble. We show that the bubble was a supply-side phenomenon driven by nontraditional mortgages financed by PLS, but that the growth in the PLS-financing channel was possible only because of the emergence of a new type of investment vehicle, called the collateralized debt obligation (CDO). PLS could be marketable only given a demand for both the AAA-rated tranches and the lower-rated tranches. Traditionally, these lower-rated tranches had been purchased by savvy credit risk investors, but during the bubble years they were outbid by CDOs, which had a set of misaligned incentives that encouraged investment in lower-rated PLS tranches irrespective of risk. As a result, rather than pricing adversely in response to the rising risk on US mortgages, CDOs' conflict-ridden underpricing of risk on PLS resulted in the flooding of the mortgage market with underpriced mortgage financing. This underpriced financing enabled previously credit constrained borrowers to enter the home purchase market or to make larger bids for homes, which in turn pressured previously unconstrained borrowers to borrow up to their constraints as part of a mortgage arms race. The result of the credit expansion was that borrowers bid up home prices beyond fundamental values, resulting in a bubble. Because the mortgages financing these purchases were poorly underwritten, they were not sustainable, and the bubble burst.

In Chapter 10, we turn to the question of why the market did not recognize the bubble. We show that it was not possible for the market to identify a bubble in the US housing market in real time because of the heterogeneity and opaqueness of PLS and because housing prices continued rising. A bubble can be identified when there is a rise in prices that cannot be explained by fundamentals coupled with a compression of credit spreads with rising risk. This combination indicates an underpricing of risk. Credit spread compression must be calculated on a risk-adjusted basis, but PLS heterogeneity and opacity frustrated the analysis of risk. As a result, the mortgage market underpriced two imbedded options in mortgages—a default "put" option and a leverage "call" option—with the effect that the market was substantially riskier than anyone was able to recognize. Investors could not observe the universe of data necessary to evaluate credit spread compression in real time. Informational problems delayed the recognition of a bubble in real time. Once the smart money in the market finally caught on to the bubble, it was already too late.

The smart money did catch on to the bubble, but it faced a problem of how to go short. The illiquid nature of housing means that it cannot be directly shorted. Instead, housing can be shorted only through derivatives, but as Chapter 11 explains, the move to credit default swaps in particular as the method for shorting housing necessarily increased the housing-based leverage in the financial system and exacerbated the effect of the bubble's collapse. While the shift to PLS produced the expansion of the mortgage finance that fueled the bubble, an inability to recognize and effectively short an overpriced market was the fundamental failure that enabled the bubble.

Chapter 11 turns to the regulatory and market developments in the wake of the bubble's collapse. It covers regulatory responses to the bubble, such as the Qualified Mortgage (QM) Rule promulgated by the Consumer Financial Protection Bureau (CFPB) and the Regulation AB II reforms enacted by the Securities and Exchange Commission (SEC). It also presents a set of critical market developments: the reduction of Fannie Mae and Freddie Mac's investment portfolios, the advent of Fannie Mae and Freddie Mac credit risk transfer transactions, and the use of increasingly fine-grained risk-based pricing for mortgages.

Chapter 12 takes up the question of housing finance reform. The financial system has, in the decade since the crisis, already experienced both a massive regulatory reform and a subsequent partial regulatory rollback. Housing finance reform, in contrast, remains largely unaddressed. Various legislative proposals have all withered in Congress. Housing finance is one of the most politically intractable issues, in no small part because of continued disagreement over what caused the bubble, an issue we hope to put to rest.

The collapse of the housing finance system in 2008 presents an opportunity for rational reform and improvement. American housing finance has never been a rationally designed system. It has been formed by extemporized reactions to crises, rather than designed *ab initio*. Indeed, the problems that emerged during the bubble occurred in no small part because the system developed to rely on informal regulation of the market by Fannie Mae and Freddie Mac through their duopolist market position, rather than direct government command-and-control regulation. This system worked well enough as long as Fannie and Freddie maintained their duopoly power and did not themselves compete for market share in risky products—but instead confined their competition to the provision of service to the lenders from which they purchased loans. When Fannie and Freddie lost their market power with the growth of PLS, the informal regulatory structure failed.

Today, however, it is possible to engage in a rational ground-up redesign of the system. In Chapter 12, we identify the key issues that need to be addressed in a reform of the housing financing system and the trade-offs and dilemmas involved. In particular, we focus on the tension between wanting private capital to hold the risks in the housing finance system and the reality that when housing prices spiral up and down and crash the system, there are inevitably enormous negative spillover effects on households and the economy.

In this chapter, we also identify a set of detailed and tangible principles for any housing finance system. Our overriding goal is a system that produces a stable housing finance market and ensures the availability of affordable housing finance to all Americans. Doing so requires addressing the market failure we identify in Chapter 10. We argue that the information part of the market failure is best addressed by ensuring a high degree of primary and secondary market product standardization because homogeneity makes it possible to observe compressions in credit spreads in close to real time. Enabling closer observation of credit spreads would enable lenders to better price the embedded default "put" option that exists in all US mortgages, which encourages borrowers to pursue additional leverage.

We also argue that the overriding goal of any housing finance system should be to produce stable and financially sustainable access to mortgage lending. The widespread availability of the 30-year fixed as the standard product achieves this (although it does not preclude carefully underwritten adjustable-rate mortgages or shorter-term fixed-rate mortgages as options). The 30-year fixed is not only a product particularly well suited for fostering financial stability; it is also one that ensures deep and sustainable affordability. The 30-year fixed is not a naturally occurring product. Ensuring its widespread availability requires active intervention in housing markets, particularly narrowly cabining competition in the housing finance system, lest it produce a short-termist race to the bottom in standards and products as competitors underprice each other to gain market share.

Standardizing markets around the 30-year fixed would help ameliorate the information failures that plague the mortgage market. Likewise, we advocate for a repeal of an obscure statutory provision that prevents lenders from controlling the combined loan-to-value ratio on their properties by prohibiting junior mortgages. This prohibition is a unique feature of American mortgage regulation that imbeds a leverage "call" option in all mortgages, enabling borrowers to increase their leverage without the consent of existing mortgagees. A relic of congressional attempts to address 1970s inflation, the prohibition on junior mortgage limitations had little importance until the rise of second mortgage lending during the housing bubble. We argue that homeowners should not have the unlimited right to increase leverage on their properties because leverage creates externalities on other lenders and borrowers. Instead, mortgages should contain specifically enforceable, but waivable, negative pledge clauses, which would allow the first mortgage lender to limit encumbrance through junior mortgages and, more importantly, ensure that lenders are aware of the extent of junior mortgages.

We also aim to address the incompleteness of housing markets. Because housing cannot be shorted directly, it is necessary to have firm regulatory control over credit standards, coupled with adequate information about credit spreads for lenders. But regulators can still benefit from market signals. We argue that this can be provided through a market in synthetic credit risk transfers reflecting the entire mortgage market. This derivative market would enable the pricing of overall credit risk. A liquid market in synthetic credit risk transfers will provide valuable market feedback for regulation.

We go a step further, however. Any housing finance system must address the unique nature of housing as an asset: home values are correlated geographically and serially and are tied to the particular credit terms available to borrowers. One's home may be one's castle, but it turns out that the castle's walls are shared with other castles, such that a breach in one wall is a breach in all.

Consider the unique price correlation in housing: whereas the value of your neighbor's car has no effect on the value of your car, the value of your neighbor's home affects the value of your home. Likewise, whereas the value of a car yesterday does not affect the value of an identical car today, the sale price of a home yesterday affects the price of a similar home today. And whereas the interest rate that your neighbor pays on a car loan does not affect the value of your identical car, the interest rate and terms that your neighbor pays for his or her mortgage can affect the value of your house, which will in turn affect how much lenders will lend prospective buyers of your house. Housing is unique as an asset class in that property values are tied together and to the mortgage market. Housing is, in a sense, a communitarian asset.

The indelibly connected nature of home prices and credit terms means that a stable housing finance market cannot be subject to the volatility of continuous risk-based pricing; that is, the price of credit will adjust along a spectrum according to the borrower's risk profile. Risk-based pricing will, by definition, go to extremes whenever there is an increase in the risk of a disaster. A market with risk-based pricing will be self-fulfilling in terms of its risk predictions. As the market prices adversely to risk, it increases risk, not just for the adversely priced borrower, but for all borrowers by depressing home prices. Thus, risk-based pricing will actually result in more expensive mortgages, because the instability generated by risk-based pricing will itself be priced.

Accordingly, it is imperative that a reformed housing finance system eschew the increased risk-based pricing that has emerged since the 2008 financial crisis in favor of a pricing of credit risk that is sustainable over the cycle. This means having countercyclical pricing and the accumulation of reserves in good times against future losses. Such sustainability will limit housing price volatility and make homeownership less risky and more affordable. The effect will be to enlarge the pool of mortgages, which will make them more liquid while simultaneously reducing systemic instability and amplifying the social benefits of homeownership. This ultimately benefits *all* borrowers because it produces a more stable and sustainable housing finance market, enabling all borrowers to avoid a volatility premium and society to avoid systemic crises. In Chapter 12 we explain the sort of system design features necessary to prevent pro-cyclical risk-based pricing.

The book's final chapter, Chapter 13, builds on the previously identified principles and design features to succinctly present our proposal for a reformed housing finance system: a federally regulated securitization utility (or possibly utilities) that we call Franny Meg, which would replace Fannie Mae and Freddie Mac. Franny Meg would issue standardized mortgage-backed securities on which it would guaranty the timely payment of principal and interest. That structure would shift interest risk to capital market investors. Credit risk would be allocated in layers among Franny Meg's own private capital, capital market investors in credit-linked notes (synthetic risk transfers) that reference Franny's entire book of business, and an explicit and paid-for line of credit with the US Treasury. Franny Meg would thus prevent the problem of socialized losses and privatized gains.

Critically, the spreads on credit-linked notes that reference the entire US housing market would inherently internalize the externalities created by correlated housing prices. This means that the spreads on the credit-linked notes would indicate to Franny Meg's regulator the state of risk in the mortgage market overall, such that rising spreads would signal the need to curtail Franny Meg's payment dividends and for Franny Meg to build up reserves through retained earnings.

The Franny Meg utility structure would complete housing markets by creating both a source of information about the level of risk in mortgage lending and home prices, and a liquid, tradable vehicle for investors to express long and short positions on housing. Franny Meg would enable markets to price interest rate risk and credit risk, while maintaining lending standards over the cycle and preventing the races to the bottom that have marked competition in securitization. The Franny Meg vehicle would thus harness the power of the market to ensure systemic stability, affordability, and continued access to homeownership for American families.

Introduction

In Praise of Homeownership

Let's face it: housing finance isn't exactly sexy. It's hard to get excited about mortgages. Talk of the "mort-gage" or "death pledge" is a surefire conversation killer at most cocktail parties. "I study housing finance," is not a great pickup line (or so we're told). And yet the housing finance system is a topic society ignores at its own peril.

It is hard to overstate the importance of housing finance in modern life and in the modern economy. The type of housing finance system we have determines our built environment and the nature and quality of our lives as individuals. It determines where and how we live. It determines who among us can become homeowners, and it determines what kind of houses, what kind of neighborhoods, and what kind of communities we live in. It affects the stability of the economy and the level of economic equality. And it even affects our ability to participate fully as citizens in our local communities. Some of these effects are direct and tangible; others are indirect and diffuse, but important nonetheless.

Some commentators have suggested that the collapse of the bubble should cause us to rethink long-standing public policies to encourage homeownership.[1] We think this is entirely the wrong lesson to take from the bubble. Instead, the lesson is a reminder of just how valuable homeownership is to society and the need to build a strong and durable housing finance system that can support broad and sustainable homeownership going forward.

This introduction sets forth the importance of homeownership, and by necessity housing finance, in virtually every aspect of American life. Our purpose in starting with this paean to homeownership is simple: we want to convince you of the importance of understanding the housing finance system, why we need to understand what went wrong with it during the housing bubble, and what needs to be done to reform it, and that is all about the importance of promoting homeownership.

Homeownership's Benefits for Consumers

Let's start with a simple observation: everyone needs shelter. Yet few people can afford to buy a home outright, or at least one in which they want to live. The reality of American economic life is that median household's pretax income in 2018 was around $60,000.[2] Part of this income is used to pay taxes and basic consumption expenses, leaving the median household with perhaps $45,000 in annual disposable income. Over the last quarter-century, the average household has generally saved only around 6 to 7 percent of its annual disposable income.[3] That means that a median household might save around $3,000 per year *if* its savings rate is near average. Many households, of course, do not consistently save at this level.

If households had to purchase homes out of their accrued savings, their ability to purchase homes would be nearly impossible. Few households would be able to cobble together more than several thousand dollars of savings for a home purchase, even after a few years of average savings. Imagine what sort of homes one might be able to purchase solely out of accrued savings. Would they have garages? Central air conditioning? Indoor plumbing? It's not likely. If Americans had to rely solely on accrued savings for home purchases, homeownership would have to be postponed long beyond the usual age for family formation, many fewer households would be homeowners, and our homes would look more like third-world dwellings.

Because of the limitations on accrued savings, most home purchases are financed with loans, and the house is pledged as collateral under a mortgage to secure repayment of the loan. Mortgage finance facilitates the smoothing of income over the borrower's lifetime by enabling him or her to telescope future anticipated income into the purchase price. This enables borrowers to become homeowners at the time of household formation, rather than having to save up for years, while facing high, rising, or uncertain rents.[4] Without mortgage finance, Americans would live in substantially different and inferior homes. Housing finance—whether for owner-occupants or for landlords of multi-family housing—makes possible the construction and maintenance of our communities.

Housing is critical as shelter, but it is not only shelter. It also provides access to community services, education, utilities, and jobs. Owner-occupied homeownership also helps build good communities, as homeowners are more civically engaged than renters.[5]

Housing is also a financial asset. Home equity is the largest financial asset for most American families and is often the centerpiece of a household's retirement savings.[6] Not only does home equity provide a source of retirement savings, but once a home is paid off, it keeps expenses for shelter in check and offers a source of collateral for subsequent borrowing, through a home equity loan or a reverse mortgage. Indeed, when a home is purchased with an amortizing mortgage—a mortgage on which the principal is reduced with every installment payment—the home becomes a savings commitment device. Every mortgage payment is an accrual of savings (in the form of home equity) that can be used in the future, and once the mortgage is paid off, the family's housing expenses are drastically reduced, effectively producing on-going savings.

A large body of commentary exists on whether homeownership is a good investment relative to a diversified portfolio of equities.[7] Some studies, including a recent comprehensive study that covers many countries and provides results over many time periods, show returns similar to those of stock markets.[8] Other studies find that in a strict horse-race contest, renting plus stock market investments often results in higher wealth accumulation than an investment in a home.[9] This result, however, is contingent on the renter reinvesting any rental savings.[10] Many renting households lack the ability to do so, so the forced savings commitment of an amortizing mortgage results in homeownership generating greater wealth accumulation for homeowners.[11]

Simply comparing the returns on an investment in a home versus in equities misses what may be the most important value of the home as a financial asset: it is a hedge against the risks of renting. Specifically, homeownership is a hedge against gentrification, inflation, and unequal economic growth.[12] If a neighborhood gentrifies or improves in any way, home prices—and rents—will go up. Homeowners reap the benefit of such neighborhood improvement; renters end up paying more and risk being priced out of their own neighborhoods. Likewise, homeowners are shielded from inflation, even if they are mortgaged. A fixed-rate mortgage is, obviously, fixed, and adjustable-rate mortgages are tied to index rates that do not necessarily track inflation. Renters, however, get squeezed by inflation.

Most rental contracts are short-term (one-year) contracts, allowing the rent to be regularly repriced, absent rent controls. Economic growth in general is also threatening to renters, particularly if wages do not keep pace with economic growth, as they have failed to do for the last generation in the United States. Homeownership thus provides an important set of hedges that protect homeowners against risks associated with their cost of shelter.[13]

Homeownership is also generally cheaper than renting for comparable properties. For the mobile household, renting makes sense, because the transaction costs involved in buying a home are far higher than for renting. But otherwise, in general, homeownership is cheaper. This is not only because homeownership has a built-in hedge against rising rents, but also because rental markets involve a so-called renter externality. All else being equal, rents are higher than homeownership costs because of the difficulty of monitoring renter behavior and the natural tendency to take better care of what we own. The higher costs are passed on to renters in general.[14] Landlords generally offer the same terms to all tenants, but they cannot prospectively distinguish between good tenants, who will pay on time and care for the property, and bad tenants, who will pay late or damage the property. Accordingly, landlords offer terms (rent, security deposit, etc.) that reflect the expected mix of good and bad tenants and the extent of the damage from bad tenants.[15] All tenants pay higher rent because of the costs imposed by bad tenants, whereas homeowners do not have to pay for this renter externality.

Homeownership also offers a better cushion than renting against temporary disruption to income.[16] When considering the benefits of homeownership, it is also worthwhile considering the life of a renter. Renters, particularly low-income renters, live with the threat of eviction hovering over them. Eviction is the story of many low-income renters' lives,[17] and with the displacement from eviction come a host of negative social spillovers. Any disruption in income that results in a month's missed rental payment can be the trigger for an eviction. Every state allows for landlords to terminate a lease within 30 days of non-payment. Few landlords with a standard twelve-month lease will wait for the rent to be more than 30 days late before terminating a lease and commencing an eviction action. In contrast, a mortgage lender is forbidden from commencing a foreclosure to terminate the mortgage and force the sale of the collateral property until the borrower is 120 days delinquent on the loan.[18] This means that a homeowner has a much longer cushion than a renter for recovering from temporary disruptions to income.[19]

Homeownership's Connection with the Financial and Real Economy

Housing debt is a significant factor on consumer balance sheets. The home mortgage is often the largest financial obligation of a household.[20] In aggregate, American home mortgage debt amounts to an enormous market measured in *trillions*, not millions or billions. As of summer 2019, there was nearly $11 trillion in home mortgage debt outstanding in the United States,[21] accounting for almost 70 percent of all consumer debts in the economy.[22] By way of comparison, also as of summer 2019, corporate debt of nonfinancial firms was less than $10 trillion.[23]

Mortgage debt alone, however, is not the full measure of the housing finance system. Mortgage debt gets amplified by secondary market borrowings used to fund it, such as the $9 trillion in securities of various sorts issued by Fannie Mae, Freddie Mac, the Federal Home Loan Banks, and Ginnie Mae that were outstanding as of 2019. The US mortgage securities market is the largest single debt market in the world. It is a larger market than that for either US Treasury securities or corporate bonds. Much of this debt is owned, directly or indirectly, by US consumers, often through retirement funds. Thus, housing finance appears on both sides of the household balance sheet: as debt in the form of mortgage debt, and as an asset in the form of mortgage investments and home equity. Housing finance ties the lives of real people to the financial system; it is the key link between Elm Street and Wall Street.

Housing also provides a key link between the consumers and Main Street businesses. Housing finance is one of the key engines of the economy, not just because of the scale of the housing market itself, but also because it affects other sectors such as home building and home furnishings, as well as the property taxes that finance many local government services. While housing itself has generally had around a 16 percent share of gross domestic product over the last several decades, it exerts a multiplier effect by supporting jobs for construction, realtors, and home furnishers, such that every two home sales indirectly support one to two new jobs.[24]

Accordingly, because most homes are purchased on credit, housing finance is one of the major channels of monetary policy transmission. Lower interest rates make home purchases more affordable, and loosened credit constraints on consumers encourage greater purchase activity and ultimately economic growth, because of the multiplier effect. Housing is the single largest connector between consumer balance sheets and the rest of the economy, and no financial asset class is more deeply embedded in the real economy than housing.

There is a flip side to the multiplier effect, however. When housing prices fall, the effects also reverberate negatively through the economy. They do so through four transmission mechanisms: the balance sheet channel, the construction channel, the collateral channel, and the housing supply channel.

First, lower home prices reduce the value of assets on household balance sheets, which results in consumers, who feel poorer, cutting back on spending and borrowing.[25] Second, when home prices fall, construction activity halts, so the related jobs disappear. Third, declining home prices are often accompanied by mortgage defaults, which erode the financial system's capital and willingness to lend generally. This last transmission mechanism can be recursive, for as financial institutions curtail lending, home prices fall further, and so on.[26]

Finally, residential mortgage defaults can trigger their own downward spiral. The distinguishing characteristic of owner-occupied housing is that foreclosure results in the borrower being put out of the home, thereby increasing the supply of housing available for sale without a concomitant increase in the demand for homeownership, because the foreclosed resident will generally not have the credit quality to buy a home. The excess supply can be significant given the slow growth in demand. Thus, the excess supply weighs down housing prices, causing further foreclosures in an ongoing spiral.[27] Price declines usually increase demand, resulting in a new market clearing price, but in housing, downward price movements increase supply through foreclosure, which leads to a vexing spiral of further price declines.

In contrast, defaults on commercial real estate mortgages do not create such an upheaval because ownership is separate from residency. If a commercial property's landlord defaults on its mortgage, the property might be sold in foreclosure, but there will typically not be evictions of paying tenants and thus an increase in the supply of available rental properties.

All of these factors—from the direct effects of declining house prices to the indirect effects of panic and the self-fulfilling dynamic—depress consumer confidence and reinforce growing expectations of negative growth. Weak consumer confidence, therefore, became its own self-fulfilling prophecy, potentially setting off another vicious cycle, with the potential of a growing shadow inventory plus the large number of homeowners who are underwater. Thus, the dynamic of falling prices increasing demand and decreasing supply—the normal path to equilibrium—does not hold.

Residential real estate is also unique in its ability to cause systemic disruptions. No other asset class has such a potentially far-reaching and destabilizing effect on the economy. This is again because of the financialization of housing. The links between housing markets and financial markets run both ways. Housing, like bank deposits, is an essential store of wealth for consumers. Just as consumers cannot effectively monitor banks against the risk of failure, so too are they unable to effectively protect themselves from the risk of home price declines. Homeowners are unlikely to be able to identify a bubble; it is difficult even for financial specialists to do so. Rather, homeowners are likely to believe that nominal home prices will continue to rise. But even if they could identify a bubble, there is not much that homeowners can do about it. They cannot sell their home to others in the expectation that they will buy their specific home back in the bust; houses cannot be sold short.[28] Because the financial sector is heavily exposed through mortgages to the housing sector, it too is at risk.

The lesson from the housing bubble is that a failure of the housing sector means a failure of the financial sector and massive macroeconomic consequences. This does not counsel for a retreat from policies meant to support homeownership, however. Attempting to avoid systemic risk by backing away from homeownership is to throw away the baby with the bathwater. As we argue in the following section, homeownership has tremendous societal benefits that should be encouraged. The fact that housing is financialized means that it is a locus of systemic risk, but this merely counsels for renewed attention to designing a stable, resilient housing finance system that can produce stable, affordable homeownership for all households that wish to be homeowners.

Social Benefits of Homeownership

Homeownership affects not only consumers themselves and the economic system, but also society more broadly. Homeownership has major positive spillover effects—"externalities," to use the economics jargon—that benefit society. These positive externalities come in the form of more stable communities, deeper civic engagement, lower crime rates, better health and educational achievement, lower reliance on public assistance, and better care and maintenance of properties.

Conversely, declines in homeownership in the form of foreclosures have strong negative social externalities. Unlike other assets, including commercial real estate, a mortgage default often requires the eviction of the owner-occupant. Evictions from foreclosures strain communities and families, exacerbating unemployment, inequality, and even public health.[29]

There is obviously a strong correlation between homeownership and factors such as income, education, age, and marital status, among other factors. The scholarly literature on homeownership benefits, however, has striven to isolate the effect of homeownership itself and has found that homeownership has benefits in terms of community stability, educational achievement, crime reduction,[30] civic engagement, and property maintenance and improvement. Homeownership benefits community stability. Renters move nearly five times as often as homeowners, in large part as the result of eviction.[31]

Residential stability strengthens community ties because it allows for the building of long-term relationships.[32] The benefit of stability, however, requires a long-term fixed-rate mortgage, because adjustable-rate mortgages leave households vulnerable to being priced out of neighborhoods when interest rates rise.

Homeownership also appears to relate to educational achievement. There is a correlation between homeownership and higher high school graduation rates,[33] as well as reading and math performance.[34] Conversely, changing schools, which is associated with moving and thus more closely associated with renting, has a negative impact on low-income and minority educational attainment.[35] It is unclear whether the causal factor for improved educational outcomes is homeownership, housing stability, or favorable neighborhood conditions that make extended residence attractive. One study found that neighborhood stability beyond homeownership improves educational outcomes,[36] but given that homeownership contributes to neighborhood stability, it too may contribute to improved educational outcomes.

Homeowners' greater financial stake in a community and their higher transaction costs of selling and moving also incentivize them to be more active in the political process to protect the value of their property.[37] Homeowners are more politically active than renters,[38] vote at much higher rates,[39] and have greater awareness of the local political scene, as well as involvement in voluntary civic organizations and organized religion.[40] Indeed, to the extent that civic engagement results in an improvement in a community, it will also result in an increase in property values. This benefits homeowners but harms renters, who will be faced with higher rents.

Civic engagement may well be a product of long-term residency rather than homeownership *per se*. Homeownership achieves stability of residency, as does renting if rents are controlled or long-term, such as through public housing or rent controls. Generally, however, rents are not controlled, and rental contracts are short-term. That means that unlike homeowners, many renters can be readily priced out of a community or simply not have their leases renewed if the property owner wishes to use the property otherwise.

Not surprisingly, homeownership is associated with better maintenance and improvements of properties. Because rental contracts are typically short-term, renters have little incentive to spend their own funds on property improvements or even maintenance, just as no one buys new tires for or washes a rental car. Conversely, owner-occupants maintain their homes better than landlords because of pride of ownership.[41] Moreover, because landlords cannot distinguish between renters who will maintain the property and those who will cause damage, they charge rents accordingly based on the expected (blended) level of care. As a result, consumers who plan to care for their dwellings are motivated to purchase homes rather than pay rents that are inflated to reflect the risk of lack of care.[42] The better maintenance and improvement of properties by homeowners redounds to the benefit of the property value of neighboring properties, and because many communities are zoned such that owner-occupied properties are clustered together separately from rental properties, the positive property value externality of homeownership is captured primarily by other homeowners. Similarly, factors such as better educational achievement and lower crime rates benefit property values, and those benefits are captured by homeowners, not renters, who instead bear the cost of higher rents when property values increase.

All in all, renters are not only exposed to different set of risks than homeowners, but renters are also missing out on economic gains that accrue to homeowners. Since the 1990s, returns to investment in housing have been a growing share of gross domestic income (see Figure I.1). In other words, an ever-larger slice of the economic pie is going to homeowners. Indeed, while there has been a growing recognition of the inequality in the distribution of income between labor and capital,[43] the long-term rise in the share of capital income has consisted exclusively of the rise in the return on housing.[44] The rate of return on nonhousing capital has remained stable.[45] The increase in income from housing has accrued to homeowners, not renters, and is likely to have implications for intergenerational wealth distribution.[46]

The divide between renters and homeowners is not as neat as it might seem. Most Americans will, at some point in their lifetime, be homeowners. While homeownership at any moment in time has never risen much above two-thirds of households, renters tend to be concentrated among both younger households—which have not accumulated the capital necessary for a home purchase or lack the career stability for a home purchase to make sense—and older households that have moved into rental retirement housing. In this sense, even though there is always a large minority of households that are renters, homeownership remains the American Dream,

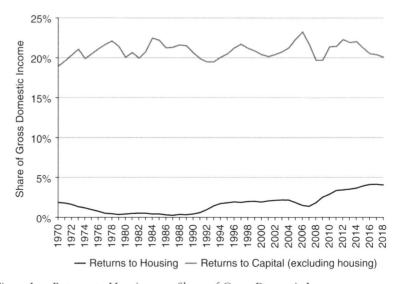

Figure I.1. Returns to Housing as a Share of Gross Domestic Income, 1970–2018

Data source: US Bureau of Economic Analysis. Returns to housing are calculated as the quotient of the sum of (a) net housing value added: net operating surplus: rental income of persons with capital consumption adjustment (series B1035C1A027NBEA); (b) net housing value added: corporate profits with inventory valuation and capital consumption adjustments (series B1036C1A027NBEA); and (c) net housing value added: net operating surplus: proprietors' income with inventory valuation and capital consumption adjustments (series B1034C1A027NBEA) over (d) gross domestic income: net operating surplus: private enterprises (series W260RC1A027NBEA). Returns to capital (excluding housing) are calculated as the quotient of gross domestic income: net operating surplus: private enterprises (series W260RC1A027NBEA) over gross domestic income: net operating surplus: private enterprises (series W260RC1A027NBEA).

a point of financial and lifestyle stability to which most households aspire for at least part of their lives. In the aftermath of the crisis, however, homeownership rates have decreased, particularly for Millennials, not just relative to their older sisters and brothers who became homeowners during the bubble, but relative to their parents' generation. Abating recent decreases in the accessibility of homeownership will require a robust financial system that is not yet in place.

For all the positive spillover benefits that are associated with homeownership, there is one that we believe trumps them all: homeownership is the bedrock of modern American democracy. Homeownership not only gives a household a financial stake in the quality of its local community, but lack of homeownership deprives households of full civic participation. Consider what happens when a renter successfully advocates for better schools in the neighborhood: home prices—and rents—go up. The homeowners benefit from this increase in property values, but the renter gets priced out of the neighborhood. While there are obviously many examples of civically engaged renters, homeownership ensures that one can enjoy the fruits of one's civic labors. The renter's civic engagement will always suffer from the free riding of the homeowner. Accordingly, we believe that homeownership is fundamental to American participatory democracy, particularly as practiced on a local scale.[47]

Given the enormous social benefits of homeownership, we believe it is imperative to have a housing finance system that supports wide and deep homeownership. By this we mean not only a high level of homeownership, but also *sustainable* homeownership—homeownership financed by affordable mortgages that do not themselves create instability in consumers' financial lives. The mortgage products that are offered determine whether sustainable homeownership is possible, and which products are offered depends on the structure of the housing finance system. Why this is so and what is needed beyond markets to preserve stability comprise the subject of this book.

Incomplete and Inefficient Markets

We are a pair of academics who study markets because we are fascinated by their power—markets generally work and do a good job setting prices. This is an amazing phenomenon, akin to the laws of physics or nature. So, what are we doing here making a full-throated argument in favor of a housing finance system that goes beyond market forces?

To understand why, it is necessary to recognize that housing markets are not like other markets. Housing is an inherently incomplete and inefficient market with enormous externalities. Some are negative externalities, such as spillover effects from foreclosures. Others are positive externalities, however. For example, the dominance of the 30-year fixed and the pricing cross-subsidy among borrowers inherent in Fannie Mae and Freddie Mac underwriting (see Chapter 12) both produce positive systemic stability externalities that not only benefit all homeowners financially, but also ultimately promote American democratic capitalism.

Housing is different from other assets in many ways. First, housing markets are incomplete markets because housing cannot be shorted, at least directly, because housing is insufficiently commoditized and liquid. One house (even in a Levittown-type community) is not interchangeable with another. Differences in location, construction, and condition matter, such that law has long treated contracts for the sale of real property as unique, enabling buyers to demand specific performance of the contract in the event of a breach by the seller, rather than the usual remedy of monetary damages.

Contrast this with a publicly traded stock, which is highly liquid. If you think the value of IBM stock will rise in the future from 100 to 110, you can go and buy shares on the market, perhaps for 101. And if you think the value of IBM stock will fall in the future from 100 to 90, you can go and sell IBM stock short, meaning you can sell the stock today (without yet owning it) at, say, 95 (to a very happy buyer) for delivery to the buyer on a future date. If IBM stock indeed falls to 90, you can buy the stock at 90 in time to meet your delivery obligation. You will have sold the stock for 95 and only paid 90 for it, pocketing the difference in prices as your profit.

Alternatively, you might go short on the IBM stock by buying a put option, which would give you the right to sell the stock at a particular price on a future date. If you think the stock will fall from its current price of 100 to 90 and you buy a put option to sell it at 97, you can wait until the stock price falls, buy it at 90, and exercise the put option to then sell it for 97, with the difference in prices again serving as your profit.

With housing, however, neither method of shorting is possible. Investors who think that prices of property in a neighborhood are going to go up can express this view by buying the properties in the neighborhood. While any particular property might not be available for sale, some properties are likely to be available. Investors who think that a property's price is going to fall, however, cannot readily express this view by selling property in the neighborhood because they do not own it. Thus, if you think that the value of your neighbor's house is going to fall in the future, you can't sell it short the way you would the IBM because there is no way you can meet your delivery obligation to your buyer—you don't own your neighbor's house, and your neighbor isn't selling it. Similarly, you can't buy a put option on your neighbor's house because you won't ever be able to meet the delivery obligation on the option unless your neighbor is willing to sell. This means that there is only long (that is, upward) pressure on home prices. There are no shorts in the residential real estate market, so long pressure is not offset by short (that is, downward) pressure.

Second, and relatedly, housing is not a liquid asset. In part this is because housing is not standardized: the split-level located a block off the interstate and the colonial overlooking the lake aren't interchangeable. It is also in part because there are high transaction costs in the sale and purchase of housing. Closings are expensive and cannot be done immediately, especially if the purchase is financed.[48] But another reason is simply that homeowners are not looking to buy and sell all the time. This is because houses are not just a financial asset. Homeowners do not generally sell when their home price moves. Instead, they sell because of reasons relating to their lives—new jobs, growing or shrinking families, marriage or divorce, or changes in their finances. This means that home prices are slow to adjust up or down compared to, say, the market for IBM stock.

Third, home prices are correlated geographically and serially. The value of my house affects the value of neighboring houses, and vice versa. This is geographic correlation. For example, if you leave a rusting car up on cinderblocks on your front lawn, it will diminish the value of your neighbor's house (for who wants such an unattractive vista?), whereas if you plant a beautiful garden, it will increase the value of your neighbor's home. Similarly, if your house goes into foreclosure, it will push down the value of neighboring homes. Indeed, one study found that pricing spillovers from foreclosures accounted for a third of the total decline in property values in 2007–2009.[49] In contrast, the value of your car does not affect the value of your neighbor's car. If you don't wash your car, it has no impact on the value of your neighbor's car, and if you trick out your ride with a new stereo system, the value of your neighbor's car also won't budge.

Likewise, home pricing is correlated serially. Most homes are purchased on credit,[50] and the amount of credit lenders will make available depends on the lender's valuation of the house, because lenders will only loan up to a specified loan-to-value (LTV) ratio. Valuations are based on appraisals, and appraisals are generally based on the sale prices of comparable properties. So, if housing prices have been rising for a type of property—say, split-levels in the neighborhood—then appraisals will also go up, and lenders will make more credit available while holding the LTV constant. The result is that the prospective buyer will bid up the house price, thus making home prices serially correlated.[51]

Finally, housing is different because the value of your house (and hence your neighbor's house, given the geographic correlation) depends in part on the credit terms you receive. It is hard to overemphasize the importance of the circular connection between housing prices and mortgage credit terms. The terms of mortgage credit are based in part on housing prices—in the form of collateral valuations—and an expectation of relative stability of those valuations. Yet housing prices are themselves dependent on the terms of mortgage credit, because easier credit enables buyers to bid up prices, and the reverse is true as well. This means there is an endogeneity between the mortgage market and the housing market, such that the terms on which one lender will lend may affect housing prices, and thus the risk on *other* lenders' loans. No lender has an underwriting model capable of accounting for this endogeneity of risk. Because most homes are purchased on credit, the interplay between credit terms and housing prices is critical for addressing the stability of the housing and housing finance markets.

Because of these differences, housing finance markets cannot be expected to function like normal markets. If credit terms are tightened due to an exogenous shock, housing prices will fall, but slowly. The fall is predictable and ongoing, and housing finance markets will respond by curtailing credit, further destabilizing the market. Lender X does not care what its lending terms do to the value of a home that is collateral for lender Y. More generally, neither lender X nor lender Y cares about the systemic risk externality that results from its own overly risky lending practices, and even if X cared about the externality from Y's easy credit standards, there is little it could do to protect itself short of not lending.

The interlinked housing and housing finance markets are incomplete and involve asset price correlations and connections to the credit market on a scale not exhibited by other markets. The implication from this is that the housing finance market cannot be expected to set prices in a socially efficient fashion. Just letting laissez-faire markets price the financing for housing will lead to mispricing because of the massive negative externalities. Markets cannot and will not take into account the correlated nature of home prices; while we know of such correlations, they cannot be readily translated into pricing models.

As we have seen, there are also enormous positive social benefits from stable homeownership, yet terms set by the market will not account for those positive externalities either. This means there is a strong public interest in ensuring that the terms of housing finance are those that maximize the positive social externalities.[52] A stable housing finance system requires using the tools of regulation to harness and channel market power constructively.

The social nature of housing means that we are really all interconnected. Our home prices are tied together because of geographic and serial price correlation. Ensuring that any future reforms of housing finance ensures that the system's stability is of the highest order of importance. It is important not just for the stability of the housing finance system, but also for the well-being, financial and political, of the American middle class, and with it, American democratic capitalism. Stability in the housing finance system bolsters American democracy by bolstering homeownership, and thus civic involvement. A nation of homeowners is a modern translation of the Jeffersonian ideal of yeomen farmers.

A century ago, the real estate industry promoted homeownership as an antidote to Bolshevism and anarchism, saying, "Homeowners don't riot."

Our concern is not a Red Menace, but rather a deep change in American society, the full consequences of which are hard to predict, but one that leans toward greater inequality and perhaps political extremism. A nation of homeowners is a nation in which all households share in the prosperity that has generally gone with homeownership and in which all households are protected from the risk faced by renters—the risk of being priced out of one's own community by gentrification, inflation, and economic growth.

Maintaining broad access to homeownership is thus critical for preserving the broad economic equality that is necessary for the preservation of American democratic capitalism. Nothing less than that is at stake with the future of housing finance reform. So, while the technical details of housing markets may not be the stuff of blockbuster films, it is a topic that we ignore to our own peril as a society. Establishing and maintaining a stable housing finance system is vital for ensuring social and economic prosperity across America for generations to come. That is the world we want for our children and grandchildren. That is why we wrote this book.

Welcome home.

CHAPTER ONE

Housing Finance before the New Deal

THE MODERN AMERICAN housing finance system is built on a New Deal foundation. The products and institutions that shape today's market originated in the New Deal's response to the collapse of the housing finance system during the Depression. To understand these products and institutions and the problems they were designed to address, we need to go back and examine the state of the housing finance market before the New Deal.

There is limited material on housing finance before the Great Depression. No comprehensive history exists. Primary sources, to the extent they exist, provide only an atomistic view of the market, and the available data are often spotty and of questionable reliability. With these caveats, however, a clear picture of the pre–New Deal mortgage market nevertheless emerges.

Before the New Deal, America had low homeownership rates and smaller, but more expensive, housing with far fewer amenities. Pre–New Deal housing markets were local, not national. Housing finance was scarce, and rates varied substantially among regions. Short-term, nonamortizing loans with high down payments were the standard loan product. Noninstitutional lenders were a substantial portion of the market—that is, many loans were made by individuals. There were virtually no secondary markets, and there was no federal governmental involvement in the housing finance market outside of a brief intercession during World War I.

Homeownership before the New Deal

The most salient feature of the pre–New Deal housing finance market is a substantially lower homeownership rate than today. (See Figure 1.1.) Renting, rather than owning, was the pre–New Deal norm. The first US Census Bureau study of homeownership, from 1890, put homeownership rates at 48 percent.[1] Homeownership rates hovered in that range until 1930, when they declined during the Depression. There were large variations in homeownership rate by state, ranging from 29 percent in South Carolina to 78 percent in North Dakota.[2] Homeownership also varied considerably by race. While white homeownership rates were 51 percent in 1890, just 17 percent of black households were homeowners.[3]

Among homeowners in 1890, most (72 percent) owned their homes free and clear, meaning that only 13 percent of the total population had a mortgage.[4] White homeowners were much more likely to have mortgages than black homeowners, with 29 percent of white homeowners having a mortgage, compared with just 11 percent of black homeowners, a situation reflecting racial disparities in access to credit.[5] Likewise, there were substantial regional disparities in mortgage finance. Nearly half the homes and farms in the Central Plains were mortgaged, and the northeastern states

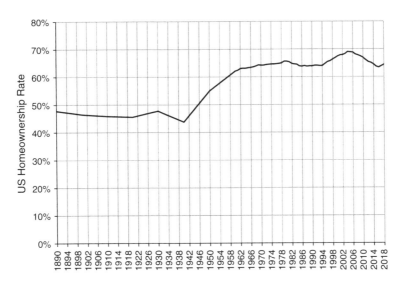

Figure 1.1. US Homeownership Rates, 1890–2018

Data source: US Census Bureau, "Current Population Survey/Housing Vacancy Survey," Series H-111 Reports; US Census Bureau, "Historical Census of Housing Tables, Homeownership"; US Census Bureau, *Report on Farms and Homes: Proprietorship and Indebtedness in the United States*, at 19, tbl. 7 (1890).

also had a high rate of mortgage finance, but less than 10 percent of homes and farms in the South were mortgaged.[6] Despite these variations, a mortgage was the exception rather than the rule in pre–New Deal homeownership, so consumers' ability to purchase housing was generally constrained to current income and savings.

Prior to World War I, the United States was predominantly a rural nation, with much of the population engaged in agriculture. As a result, farms were an important part of the US housing stock, but they differed substantially from other housing by virtue of being income-generating properties. The large percentage of the population living on farms also meant that farm finance was, in part, housing finance, and farm policy was housing policy. Homeownership was much higher on farms (66 percent) than for houses generally (36 percent), and especially as compared to urban areas (22 percent in large cities).[7] Again, there were huge regional disparities, with farm tenancy being much higher in the South than elsewhere.[8]

Housing before the New Deal

Simply comparing homeownership rates does not tell the full story of the pre–New Deal housing market. Home type, amenities, and size were also considerably different from today. Single-family detached housing has remained at around 60 percent of the housing stock since 1900, but there has been a shift in the nature of multifamily housing. Multifamily buildings were, historically, primarily two- to four-family units; they have been increasingly replaced by large, multiunit buildings.[9]

Likewise, home amenities were substantially different in pre–New Deal America. In 1920, only 1 percent of US homes had both electricity and indoor plumbing.[10] Even in 1940, 45 percent of homes lacked complete indoor plumbing (hot and cold piped water, a bathtub or shower, and a flush toilet).[11]

Historically, houses were also considerably more crowded. The average home size was smaller, and it contained more people than today. At the beginning of the twentieth century, the average *new* home had 700–1,200 square feet of living space.[12] In contrast, the average new home completed in 2018 had 2,588 square feet of living space.[13] In 1890, there were, on average, five people per housing unit, a number that has dropped to approximately two today.[14] Thus, real population density in homes has declined something around tenfold over the past century, substantially changing the nature of people's interactions and expectations of privacy.

While pre–New Deal housing was more modest than today's, housing costs, relative to income, were higher. In 1900, the average home price was around $5,275. This was at a time when median household income was around $750, making the median home price about seven times the median income. In 2018, median household income was $63,179,[15] while the median existing home sold in July 2018 for around $269,600, or over four times the median income.[16]

Thus, not only was homeownership substantially lower before the New Deal, but it was ownership of less house and cost much more.

The Pre–New Deal Mortgage

An important reason why homeownership rates were lower in pre–New Deal America is because the availability of mortgage finance was limited. Some of the limitations on mortgage financing were a function of the characteristics of the pre–New Deal mortgage, which were heavily shaped by the institutional nature of lenders and legal constraints on lending.

What little data that exist on the pre–New Deal housing finance market all indicate that the standard loan was a "bullet loan"—a fixed-rate, interest-only, short-term loan with the principal due in a "bullet" payment at maturity.[17] Most mortgaged homeowners did not have the cash to pay off the balance at maturity, however, so they would refinance, or "roll over," the loan. The refinancing would often be from the same lender, thus effectively extending the term of the original loan, but giving the lender the opportunity to adjust the interest rate or decline to continue to lend based on changed market or borrower conditions.

In terms of specific maturity lengths, an 1894 study found an average loan lifespan of 4.81 years.[18] This is consistent with a study of the 1925 Chicago real estate market that found that 93 percent of residential mortgages had terms of five years or less (with 81 percent having five-year terms),[19] and only 2 percent had terms over ten years.[20] There appears to have been some variance, however, based on type of lending institution; savings and loan associations extended longer-term credit, with contract lengths averaging around ten years. (See Figure 1.2.)

Loan-to-value (LTV) ratios on pre–New Deal mortgages were also relatively low, meaning a high down payment (or junior mortgage) was required for a purchase. (See Figure 1.3.) A multistate 1893 study found the average LTV on home mortgages to be 42 percent,[21] while an 1894 study found an average LTV between 35 and 40 percent.[22] LTVs might have gone up over time, however, as in Chicago in 1925, the average LTV on first-lien loans

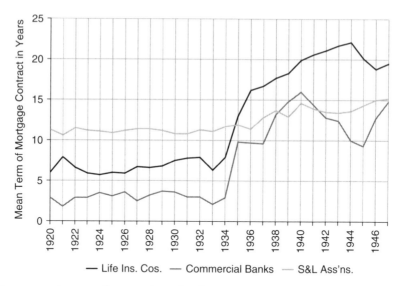

Figure 1.2. Average Contract Length of Mortgages on 1–4 Family Residences, 1920–1947

Data source: Leo Grebler *et al.*, *Capital Formation in Residential Real Estate: Trends and Prospects* 234, tbl. 67 (1956).

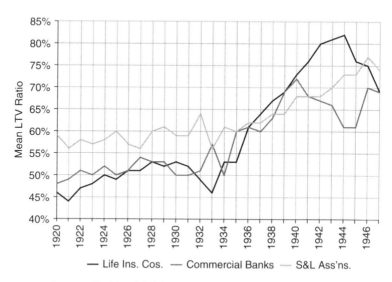

Figure 1.3. Average Residential Mortgage Loan-to-Value Ratio, 1920–1947

Data source: Leo Grebler *et al.*, *Capital Formation in Residential Real Estate: Trends and Prospects* 503, tbl. O-6 (1956).

was 50.5 percent,[23] in keeping with what contemporary scholars called "the conventional 50 percent first-lien" loan.[24]

While first-lien LTVs were low, they were not the whole story. Second mortgages were very common in pre–New Deal America. In Chicago in 1925, roughly half of properties had second lien mortgages.[25] Those properties with a second lien typically had combined LTVs of 65 percent, with first-lien LTVs of 41 percent.[26]

The pre–New Deal mortgage was also typically nonamortized—that is, it was an interest-only obligation.[27] To be sure, there were institutions, namely building and loan societies and certain life insurance companies, that offered somewhat longer-term and amortizing first-lien mortgages.[28] Indeed, the amortized mortgage became a hallmark of building and loan association lending, as amortization was "an adaptation of the concept of a continuing savings plan."[29] Paying down principal meant building up savings in the form of home equity. From its beginning, the amortizing mortgage was an alternative savings product—an alternative to the deposit account as a safe place for consumer savings. Long-term, amortized mortgages were a niche product in the pre–New Deal market,[30] however, perhaps because they cost 80 to 100 basis points more than bullet loans, consistent with the increased interest rate risk borne by the lender.[31]

Not only were interest rates higher on amortized loans, but because of amortization, so too were the periodic payment burdens. The bullet loan structure made periodic mortgage payments more affordable for borrowers. Yet because the bullet loan was designed to be rolled over into a new loan, it always carried the risk that refinancing would not be possible. Not surprisingly, foreclosure rates were substantially higher on nonamortized or partially amortized loans.[32] (See Figure 1.4.)

There was very limited credit reporting in pre–New Deal America, so mortgage lenders lacked standardized metrics or data sources for consumer creditworthiness. Instead, loans were made based on individualized evaluations. (This lack of standardized underwriting data and reliance on in-person borrower evaluation contributed to discriminatory lending, an issue discussed in subsequent chapters.)

In the era before credit scoring, LTVs providing critical credit protection; loans were asset- rather than income-based. Although the homeowner might default due to a decline in income or disruption to cash flow or inability to refinance, there was likely to be a significant equity cushion in the property that would limit the lender's losses in the event of a foreclosure. Pre–New Deal foreclosure rates were quite low; they were around 0.3 percent in 1929,[33] compared with an average of around 1 percent between 1978 and 2007.[34]

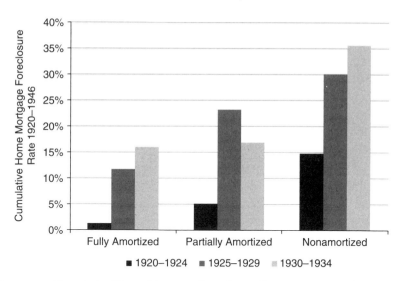

Figure 1.4. Cumulative Home Mortgage Foreclosure Rates 1920–1934 by Amortization and Loan Origination Year

Data source: Raymond J. Saulnier, *Urban Mortgage Lending by Life Insurance Companies* 140, tbl. B11 (1950).

On the other hand, in the event of a severe market downturn, such as the Great Depression, borrowers could find themselves with a depleted equity cushion, such that they would not be able to refinance. In such a case, the borrowers would be faced with having to make the large balloon payment out of pocket, and would likely default. Moreover, because many loans were adjustable rate, a sudden increase in rates could leave many borrowers unable to afford their monthly payments. Borrower exposure to interest rate risk increased lender exposure to credit risk. The default risk engendered by short-term mortgages in a volatile monetary environment offset some of the protection of low LTV ratios.

Sources of Mortgage Finance

The design of the pre–New Deal mortgage discouraged homeownership. Another factor limiting homeownership in pre–New Deal America was the restricted sources of mortgage finance. The United States lacked a fully integrated capital market prior to the Depression. There were pre–New Deal advances toward the creation of a national capital market—the creation of the Federal Reserve System, the development of a national commercial paper market, and the rediscounting of bank notes[35]—but regional capital disparities remained, particularly for housing finance.

In a fully integrated capital market, investment capital is transferred to the most attractive investments regardless of location.[36] In the pre–New Deal United States, however, legal, transactional, and informational barriers kept capital—especially mortgage capital—regionally segmented, and resulted in an inevitable misallocation of capital.

The pre–New Deal housing finance market was intensely local. As one of the earliest scholarly works on the mortgage market noted in 1894, "in America the making of a mortgage loan is essentially a local transaction."[37] There was substantial variation in terms of the institutions lending in any given community. For example, some communities had well-established building and loan associations, which often had a significant impact on homeownership rates, whereas building and loan associations did not exist in other communities.[38] Even within communities, however, there were also bifurcated lending markets—many financial institutions would simply not lend to borrowers of color or various immigrant populations. While some minority-owned institutions emerged, such as black life insurance companies, black building and loan associations, and various ethnically or religiously associated benevolent societies, institutional mortgage lending was highly constrained within minority communities.

The fact that the United States was a predominantly rural nation prior to the First World War contributed to the localized nature of the housing finance market.[39] Lending against rural properties poses particular challenges in terms of property valuations, because of a lack of appropriate comparables, because of the expense and difficulty in getting appraisers to travel to rural properties, and because many rural properties are essentially commercial properties—farms—with a residential unit attached.[40] These valuation difficulties are especially problematic for nonlocal lenders, who have limited knowledge of local conditions.

The pre–New Deal housing market was vulnerable to national economic conditions, such as the seasonal flows of capital from money centers to the interior in conjunction with the harvest. Even so, interest rates and the availability of financing varied significantly by locality and region. There was much greater mortgage availability in capital-rich regions like the East than in capital-poor regions like the South and West.[41] Moreover, the pre–New Deal economy as a whole was much more localized, and consumer credit was more sensitive to local economic conditions. The result was that mortgage financing was highly cyclical and geographically based. The local nature of the pre–New Deal lender base was the major factor in the local variation in mortgage financing availability and terms.

Individuals were a major source of mortgage finance well into the 1950s. As of the 1890s, over half of mortgages by dollar amount were held by

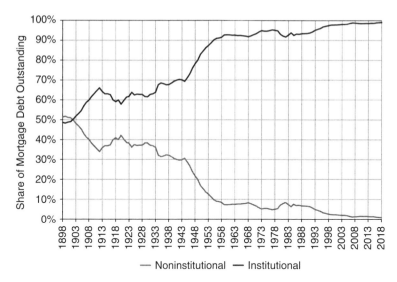

Figure 1.5. Share of Mortgage Debt Held by Financial Institutions, 1896–2018

Data source: Bd. of Governors of the Fed. Reserve Sys., Statistical Release Z.1, Financial Accounts of the United States, tbl. L.218 (difference of line 5, series FL893065101, and the sum of lines 6 through 8, series FL153065103, FL103065105, and FL113065103) (data for years 1945–2018); Leo Grebler et al., Capital Formation in Residential Real Estate: Trends and Prospects 468–471, tbl. N-2 (1956) (data for 1896–1944).

individuals.[42] (See Figure 1.5.) Even as late as 1939, individuals still held a third of all mortgage debt.[43] Second mortgages, in particular, were often seller financed, meaning that they were made by individuals. In Chicago in 1925, one study found that 78 percent of second mortgages were seller financed.[44] Most individual lenders were unlikely to lend outside of their local area.[45] The prevalence of individuals as a source of mortgage finance meant that a major source of mortgage capital remained local.

A broad range of financial institutions participated in the pre–New Deal mortgage market: banks, savings institutions (savings and loans, building and loans, mutual savings banks, stock savings banks, credit unions), insurance companies, and mortgage banks.[46] (See Figure 1.6.) A variety of legal restrictions on operations generally or on mortgage lending in particular applied to different institutional lenders. These restrictions limited the geographic movement of mortgage capital, as well as the size and terms of loans.

Depository institutions were legally restricted in their ability to operate outside limited local or regional markets. Most states had some form of branch banking restrictions that limited banks to operating branches solely within the state, or even within single counties.[47] This had the effect of localizing mortgage credit.

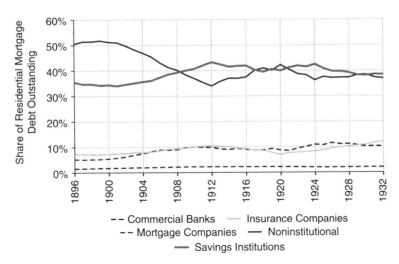

Figure 1.6. Share of Residential Mortgage Debt Outstanding, 1896–1932

Data source: Leo Grebler *et al.*, *Capital Formation in Residential Real Estate: Trends and Prospects* 468–471, tbl. N-2 (1956).

Some institutions, like life insurance companies and mutual savings banks, did lend interregionally via loan correspondents—mortgage companies—that originated and serviced the loans on their behalf.[48] The life insurance companies and mutual savings banks, however, never comprised more than a limited part of the market. Their ability to form capital was limited, and correspondent lending posed the additional risk of thinly capitalized correspondents taking advantage of informational asymmetries with the ultimate lenders to sell shoddy loans. As a result, mortgage capital remained primarily local.

There were also legal restrictions specific to mortgage lending. Some banks ("national banks") have their corporate charters from the federal government, while others have their charters from state governments. Prior to 1913, national banks were forbidden to originate any real estate mortgage loans.[49] They were permitted to take real estate mortgages as security for or in satisfaction of existing debts, but the mortgages could be for no more than five years.[50] In 1913, the restrictions were relaxed in regard to originating farmland mortgages,[51] but national banks were not permitted to make loans on non-income-producing residential real estate until 1927, and even then loans were limited to 50 percent LTV and five-year terms and could not, in the aggregate, exceed 25 percent of bank capital.[52] It was not until 1983 that restrictions on national banks' real estate lending were completely lifted,[53] and not until 1994 that interstate branch banking restrictions were eased.[54]

There were also major limitations on mortgage lending by state-chartered banks. State-chartered banking institutions were often prohibited from purchasing out-of-state loans[55] and were limited by regulation in the percentage of assets they could deploy in mortgage loans,[56] in the LTV ratios for individual loans,[57] or in the maturities of their real estate loans.[58]

Similarly, state-licensed insurance companies were subject to a variety of restrictions. Some were limited to investing in mortgages only within the state of their licensure or neighboring states.[59] Life insurance company mortgages were also generally subject to LTV limitations.[60] Other limitations on insurance company mortgage holding included loan size restrictions and requirements that the property be improved or income-producing and the security be a first lien.[61]

Restrictions of financial institutions' mortgage lending were shaped by safety and soundness concerns. As far back as 1790, Treasury secretary Alexander Hamilton had warned against mixing commercial banking and real estate lending.[62] Land speculation, the original American pastime, had been implicated in most of the busts of the nineteenth century, including the failure of the Second Bank of the United States,[63] and the American passion for real estate speculation was sufficiently well-known that it was satirized by the likes of James Fenimore Cooper, Mark Twain, and Charles Dickens.[64] It was a hard-learned lesson that the potential volatility in land values (against which there was no complete hedge) combined with real estate's illiquidity to make real estate lending fundamentally incompatible with safe and sound deposit taking or insurance activity.

Limited Secondary Markets

Before the New Deal there was no national secondary home mortgage market. This meant that housing was not financialized—there was not a widely tradable asset class based on housing. While individual lenders could contract to sell mortgage loans to private investors, the norm was for originators to retain mortgages on their books. As a nineteenth-century study noted, "American mortgages are not available securities, and usually remain all their life the property of the mortgagees themselves."[65] This meant that originators bore a liquidity risk, even if it was mitigated by the short duration of the loans. Keeping the mortgages on the books also limited originators' lending capacity; funds that were tied up in a mortgage could not be redeployed. The problems of liquidity and lending capacity were particularly acute for lenders such as banks that financed themselves through short-term liabilities such as demand deposits, because a run on the bank would leave a balance-sheet-solvent institution unable to cover its liabilities as they came due.

A closer look at the contemporaneous international scene places US market developments in context. By the mid-nineteenth century, deep secondary mortgage markets were well-established in both France (the state-chartered joint stock monopoly *Crédit Foncier*) and the German states (cooperative borrowers' associations called *Landschaften* and private joint stock banks in Prussia and Bavaria). As economic historian Kenneth Snowden has observed, "By 1900 the French and German market for mortgage-backed securities was larger than the corporate bond market and comparable in size to markets for government debt."[66] Although there were significant design differences in the European systems, they all operated on a basic principal—securities were issued by dedicated mortgage origination entities. Investors therefore assumed the credit risk of the origination entities. Because these entities' assets were primarily mortgages, the real credit risk assumed by the investors was that on the mortgages.

Secondary market transfers of credit risk can pose what economist George Akerlof has termed a "lemons" problem.[67] In Akerlof's lemons model, sellers have informational advantages over buyers. As a result, sellers snooker buyers by selling them "lemons"—substandard products priced as quality products. Lemons markets are inherently unsustainable. Once buyers recognize that a market is a lemons market, they retreat from it, resulting in its collapse.

Secondary mortgage markets necessarily have informational asymmetries between sellers and buyers. Unless such asymmetries are held in check, these markets are not sustainable. Instead, mortgage- and bond-underwriting standards will necessarily decay to enable mortgage originators and bond sellers to take advantage of the investors' overestimation of the quality of the mortgages, and thus the bonds. Avoiding the lemons problem is a central challenge for any secondary mortgage market.

The European systems avoided the lemons problem through two mechanisms that protected investors from credit risk. First, there were close links between the mortgage origination entities that issued the securities and the state. Mortgage investors thus believed there to be an implicit state guaranty of payment on the securities they held. Second, and relatedly, the state required heavy regulation of the mortgage market entities, including underwriting standards, overcollateralization of securities, capital requirements, dedicated sinking funds, auditing, and management qualifications.[68] These regulatory safeguards and the implicit state guaranty kept the secondary market lemons problem at bay in European systems.

The story played out differently in the United States. In the United States, no secondary residential mortgage market emerged before the New Deal. But there were secondary markets for farm and commercial mortgages that developed—and collapsed—during the late nineteenth and early twentieth centuries. Every one of these failed secondary markets played out Akerlof's lemons script. This history is instructional for understanding what happened in the housing bubble in the 2000s and the issues confronting a reform of the housing finance system.

A secondary commercial mortgage market first appeared in the United States in the 1870s.[69] It was an attempt to import the *Crédit Foncier* model, as eastern mortgage companies formed to finance western city building, such as the reconstruction of Chicago after the Great Fire.[70] This system attempted to link eastern capital to western development needs. The eastern mortgage companies used local loan correspondents to originate and service loans that they purchased. The eastern companies then financed the loans by issuing bonds. When the loans provided by correspondents were found to be of poor quality, however, the eastern companies, which were affiliated with the leading eastern financial houses, ceased underwriting the mortgage bonds because of concerns for their reputation.[71]

A second attempt at developing a secondary market emerged in the 1880s. This time, western mortgage companies formed to finance farms along the frontier, as national banks and many state banks were prohibited from making real estate loans.[72] The western companies originated and serviced the loans and assigned the ownership of the loans to trust accounts in eastern banks. The western companies then issued debentures using the trust accounts as collateral. The companies did not pledge their own capital as well.[73] This resulted in a process quite similar to modern securitization, as "the debentures were issued in series backed by specific mortgage pools."[74]

In 1893, however, the western land boom collapsed, and most of the western mortgage companies failed.[75] The companies had been thinly regulated by state government in the eastern markets (primarily New York, Connecticut, and Massachusetts) where they sold the debentures.[76] Regulatory postmortems of the mortgage companies revealed that they often violated their stated underwriting standards and securitized only the lowest-quality collateral. This should not be surprising, as there was neither incentive alignment through capital at risk nor regulatory oversight.

Despite these early debacles, within a couple of decades another secondary commercial mortgage market emerged, this time for residential multifamily housing. Prior to 1900 the financing of apartments was primarily by savings banks and insurance companies.[77] A 1904 New York law permitted title guaranty companies, which traditionally insured only good title to a property—a business with very low loss correlation—to also insure payments of bonds and mortgages—a business with high loss correlations.[78] This enabled a type of private mortgage insurance industry called the "mortgage investment guaranty."[79] A further amendment of New York law, in 1911, permitted title companies "to invest in, to purchase, and to sell with guaranty of interest and principal or with guaranty of title, such bonds and mortgages as were legal for insurance companies."[80] This permitted title companies to originate mortgage loans, insure them, and then sell debt securities backed by the mortgages. The favored form of securities was the participation certificate, which allocated the cash flow from the underlying mortgage pool in proportionate shares, much like later Fannie Mae/Freddie Mac Pass-Thru Certificates.[81] These participation certificates thus created a sort of secondary market in mortgages. The purchasers of the participation certificates believed that they were assuming the credit risk of the title company that insured the mortgages rather than the borrower, so they were not particularly concerned with the quality of the mortgage underwriting.

As defaults in the housing market rose in 1928–1934, the guarantied participation certificate market collapsed. Poor regulation and malfeasance by the title companies made it impossible to weather a market downturn. The title companies were required to reserve a percentage of their capital, rather than a percentage of their commitments, against losses.[82] Title insurance companies had historically incurred only negligible and uncorrelated losses, and they were still regulated as if their business were primarily in title insurance.[83] Thus, many of the companies' commitments far outstripped their capital. New York required a maximum LTV ratio of 50 percent but regulators did not conduct their own appraisals, so the LTV limit merely encouraged overly high property appraisals.[84] The companies also routinely violated their underwriting standards, used unregulated subsidiaries to hold defaulted assets,[85] and served as their own trustees and depositaries and swapped collateral among insured pools to cover losses.[86]

The collapse of the housing market led New York to take over forty-seven mortgage guaranty companies in 1934.[87] Massachusetts, New Jersey, and California also took other companies into receivership.[88] In response, New York and other states prohibited mortgage guaranty insurance.[89] Private insurance of mortgage loans was thus not possible until 1957, when the Wisconsin State Insurance Department passed an administrative rule permitting the insurance of mortgages,[90] which led to the emergence of today's private mortgage insurance market.

In addition to the participation certificates, in the 1920s another type of secondary market instrument emerged, the single-property real estate bond.

Whereas participation certificates were issued against a pool of mortgages, single-property real estate bonds were backed by a single building, a distinction roughly analogous to that between securitization and project finance.[91] Single-property real estate bonds were used to finance large construction projects, such as the skyscrapers of New York and Chicago, including the Chrysler building, the Wrigley building, and the Tribune Tower.[92] In a single-property real estate bond, the owner of the property would execute a deed of trust pledging interests in the land and all improvements as security for payment on the debt owed to the trust.[93] The borrower would also agree to make periodic payments to a trustee for bondholders, as well as to a sinking fund.[94] The borrower would then issue bonds that entitled the holder to a pro rata share in the cash flow from the loan.[95] The bonds carried the same default risk as the loan made against the deed of trust—that of the property owner.[96] There were no additional credit enhancements.

Real estate bonds revolved around real estate bond houses that would originate and service the loans, underwrite and distribute the bonds, and serve as the bonds' trustee.[97] Although the bonds were rated by rating agencies,[98] their marketability was established via the underwriter, the real estate bond house.[99] As economic historian Kenneth Snowden has observed, "All bonds distributed by a given house tended to trade at a single yield that did not vary with characteristics of the specific borrower. This indicates that investors evaluated the quality of the bonds according to the reputation of the issuer even though it had accepted no formal liability."[100]

Although there was no formal liability for the real estate bond house, it did have reputational liability, and real estate bond houses generally agreed to buy the securities.[101] The bonds were treated as separate assets classes by the name of the bond house—Strauss bonds, Miller bonds, Greenebaum bonds, and so forth—rather than by the specific properties that backed them.[102] The real estate bond houses did nothing to correct this impression; they advertised the bonds as under their own name first and that of the borrowers' secondarily.[103]

In the 1920s boom market, reputation was the bond houses' primary constraint, but their position as trustees for the bonds allowed them to control information flowing to bondholders, as well as to cover up defaults. Investors had to rely on the bond houses in their underwriter roles to properly price the bonds, which involved a valuation of the underlying collateral. By the late 1920s, the bonds were often issued on properties that were under construction, making valuation very difficult.[104] Moreover, although each bond issuance was backed by a separate collateral property, the real estate bond houses treated the collateral as a common trust and mingled the accounts of all outstanding securities, enabling them to cover up defaults with sinking fund payments on other loans.[105]

As long as the public was willing to continue purchasing the bonds, the system worked, even as underwriting standards declined.[106] This meant that single-purpose real estate bonds turned into little more than a Ponzi scheme.[107] By the Depression, the real estate bond houses had all collapsed. Over half their bonds defaulted, and recovery rates were only 50 percent.[108]

The 1920s real estate bond market had attempted to use sellers' reputation and claims about past bond performance to assure bond buyers of the quality of the bonds, but this reputational assurance was only good while it lasted. Once the bond houses began to fail, the reputational assurances and performance history were worthless. The single-property real estate bonds left as their enduring legacy some of America's most iconic buildings and also the major federal securities law protecting bondholders, the Trust Indenture Act of 1939,[109] which imposed postdefault duties on indenture trustees and limited the ability of majority bondholders to force amendments of payment terms on minority bondholders.

What we see, then, is that every iteration of failed secondary mortgage markets in the United States fit with Akerlof's lemons problem. These early American secondary mortgage markets shared several commonalities. First, all were purely private enterprises; there was no government involvement whatsoever. Second, none was conceived of as an attempt to create a planned secondary market. Rather, they were created out of expediency. In the 1870s, eastern capital was looking for an outlet, and the correspondent system was the only practical way to deploy it in western markets. Similarly, in the 1880s, the western mortgage companies lacked sufficient capital to finance frontier farm development themselves and needed a means of funding their origination operations. Neither of these episodes envisioned using secondary markets as a means of implementing any sort of policy goals; they were simply means of deploying or obtaining capital. Third, they were virtually unregulated, and what regulation existed was wholly inadequate to ensure prudent operations. Fourth, they all suffered from an inability to maintain underwriting standards, because the loan originators had no capital at risk in the mortgages themselves, because regulation was scant, and because investors in the mortgage-backed bonds lacked the ability to monitor the origination process or the collateral. In light of investors' informational disadvantages, there was ample opportunity for originators and bond underwriters to engage in fraud. And fifth, they all failed, an outcome closely related to the lack of government involvement, lack of regulation, and inability to maintain underwriting standards (itself a symptom of lack of government involvement and regulation). In contrast, successful European structures, "were either publicly financed or sponsored and were subject to intense regulatory scrutiny."[110] France's *Crédit Foncier*, for example, had a monopoly on the mortgage market, so there were no competitive pressures on underwriting. Sustainable secondary mortgage markets have always required significant government oversight and involvement in order to ensure against decays in underwriting standards; even so, there are strong political pressures against the government holding the line on such standards.

Negligible Federal Government Involvement in Housing Policy

The final notable characteristic of the pre–New Deal housing finance market is the absence of federal government involvement, including a lack of enforceable antidiscrimination laws. The contrast with the post–New Deal world is enormous. Today there is a substantial federal role in housing and in housing finance markets. Yet with two exceptions, for the century and a half preceding the New Deal, the federal government never played a direct role in any part of the housing market.[111]

One exception was the pre–New Deal farm finance system. Farms are not just commercial units, but also include residences. The farm finance system, however (which is discussed in Appendix A), was never conceived of as a housing finance system. The other exception was the short-lived, but intense, government involvement with housing during World War I.

Addressing World War I Labor Unrest

World War I placed huge demands on American industrial production, particularly shipbuilding. The United States had significant shipping needs for transporting and supplying an expeditionary force in Europe, as well as supplying its European allies. Meanwhile the German U-boat campaign was decimating the American merchant marine fleet.

The federal government responded by authorizing the US Shipping Board, the newly created regulator of the merchant marine fleet, to create a subsidiary Emergency Fleet Corporation to manage the nation's merchant shipbuilding program. The wartime boom in shipbuilding resulted in enormous labor market migrations. The merchant shipbuilding industry grew from 50,000 workers in 1916 to 380,000 workers in 1918.[112] These workers were concentrated in a limited number of communities with shipyards. The huge influx of labor to shipyard communities placed pressure on those communities' housing stock.

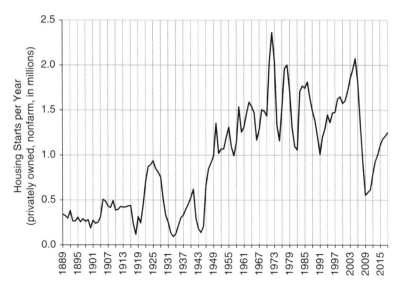

Figure 1.7. Housing Starts, 1889–2018

Data source: *Historical Statistics of the United States, New Residential Construction*, Series Dc510 (Susan B. Carter, *et al.*, ed., 2006) (1889–1958 data); US Census Bureau and US Department of Housing and Urban Development, "Housing Starts: Total: New Privately Owned Housing Units Started [HOUST]," retrieved from FRED, Federal Reserve Bank of St. Louis, *at* https://fred.stlouisfed.org/series/HOUST (1959–2018 data).

At the same time, home-building activity ground to a halt because of the war effort's demand for construction materials, labor, and capital. (See Figure 1.7). Indeed, these effects were felt even before America's entry into the war because home-building activity was displaced by the demand for materials, labor, and capital from war-related exports.

The result was America's first housing crisis. The poor and expensive housing conditions faced by shipyard workers contributed to labor turnover and unrest,[113] including strikes that threatened the war effort.[114]

Congress responded in March 1918 by authorizing the Emergency Fleet Corporation to acquire, build, or finance housing,[115] and ultimately appropriated $75 million (around $1.33 billion in 2018 dollars) for it to do so.[116] While the Emergency Fleet Corporation acquired or built housing in a few cases, typically it made loans to shipyards, which would form subsidiary realty companies to buy or build housing that would secure the loans.[117] The Emergency Fleet Corporation, however, controlled sales, rents, and property restrictions on the housing until six months after the war's end and limited shipyards' dividends until its mortgages were paid off.[118] The Emergency Fleet Corporation ended up financing housing for 30,000 shipyard workers plus their families, for a total of perhaps 60,000 people.[119]

There were concerns, including from Franklin Roosevelt, then assistant secretary of the navy, that the Emergency Fleet Corporation's activities were inadequate to address the housing needs of US war industries.[120] Thus, in June and July 1918, Congress appropriated $100 million (around $1.67 billion in 2018 dollars):

> for the purposes of providing housing, local transportation, and other general community utilities for such industrial workers as are engaged in arsenals and navy yards of the United States and industries connected with an essential to the nation defense, and their families . . . only during the continuation of the existing war.[121]

To carry out this task, a Bureau of Industrial Housing and Transportation was created within the Department of Labor, which then created a government corporation called the United States Housing Corporation, "to administer all government housing for industrial workers."[122] The US Housing Corporation purchased land (including through eminent domain), planned residential communities, and built and managed them.[123]

The armistice was signed before the US Housing Corporation could complete its projects, and after the war, Congress required the units that were built to be privatized.[124] The properties of the Emergency Fleet Corporation were also privatized,[125] although there was interest, including from President Woodrow Wilson, in preserving them as model industrial communities.[126] The programs produced some nascent calls for a more permanent federal government role in housing, but these urgings went unheeded until the crisis of the Depression.[127]

The Emergency Fleet Corporation and the US Housing Corporation represented different approaches to the housing problem. The Emergency Fleet Corporation provided financing, but did not build or act as a landlord. In contrast, the US Housing Corporation directly provided housing.

Neither effort, however, was the result of reformist goals. Instead, both were motivated by the need to maximize industrial output for the war effort. They were purely instrumental engagements that did not reflect general housing policy concerns.[128] They were also collectively very modest endeavors, reflecting less than 1 percent of US World War I expenditures.[129] Nonetheless, the Emergency Fleet Corporation and the US Housing Corporation created a precedent for federal government involvement in housing finance as a response to market failures—namely, the failure of the market to respond in a timely fashion to the housing needs of a geographically shifting labor market. Moreover, many of the individuals involved in the World War I housing effort "reentered government service and worked for New Deal agencies" when the federal government again became involved in housing.[130]

More importantly perhaps, the federal intervention in housing markets during World War I was an implicit recognition of the importance of housing within the social fabric of the nation. Policy makers began to recognize that housing was not just about a place to live. Although housing was not yet financialized as it is today, they began to recognize housing's strong connection with the economy as a whole.

Homeownership as a Defense against Bolshevism

Historically, developments in the housing market have been inextricably linked to the sociopolitical atmosphere of the era. The World War I interventions had been motivated in no small part by concerns over the disruptive effects of labor unrest on the war effort. Post–World War I America was haunted by the specter of labor radicalism, particularly in light of the experience of the Bolshevik Revolution in Russia and failed communist revolutions in Bavaria and Hungary. Some observers directly tied homeownership to the fight against the Red Menace. The chairman of the Board of the Federal Reserve Bank of Cleveland proclaimed that "the home is the savior of the nation, and men who own their own homes do not think of Bolshevism, I.W.W.'ism and kindred diseases spreading over the country."[131] Similar sentiments were expressed in the *American Building Association News*: "Every home erected in this land means one more powerful argument against Socialism, Bolshevism, Anarchy."[132] As a speaker at the American Bankers' Association's Convention observed, "It is impossible to associate radicalism with home-ownership—and home-ownership is the only known insurance against these "isms."[133] The United States League—the trade association of savings and loan associations—even adopted the slogan, "The American Home—the Safeguard of American Liberties."[134]

Homeownership offered workers a stake in the established order—and also reduced labor mobility, and thus labor's bargaining power. There was an undeniable logic to the belief that homeowners do not riot. Still, the mortgage industry's appeal to the colors matched its own financial interests, irrespective of the real threat of revolution, as the industry stood to gain from increases in homeownership. Notably, however, the mortgage industry did not call for continued government intercession in the market in order to boost homeownership. Homeownership was to be promoted, but privately.

Concerns over working-class radicalism also fueled calls for urban renewal and mediation of slum and tenement conditions. As Frederick Law Olmsted, Jr., wrote, it was "self-respecting home life upon which the security of our democracy rests."[135] Olmsted argued that "the country must come to recognize the house problem as a national problem of the most vital importance to the security of our democracy."[136] This required dealing with poor housing conditions for the working class, he explained, as "there is probably no other activity in the nation which does more to fix the conditions that determine the health and mold the character of our people than housing."[137] Indeed, the post–World War I housing shortage was perceived as a public health issue.[138]

While the proponents of the mortgage industry and others strongly promoted homeownership, there was little interest in improving the conditions of renters in urban slums, and the industry opposed legislation that would "multiply the evils of renting tenantry." Renting was seen by the mortgage industry as nothing less than anti-American. Instead of ameliorating the conditions of renters, the only hope was to transform them into homeowners, as an editorial in the *American Building Association News* explained:

> It is certain that a rent-paying tenant misses many of the vital factors that go to make up . . . The dangerous and destructive doctrines [of the "Wobblies," anarchists, and Bolsheviks] were never formulated around the firesides of any American home, but they have been hatched out in the fetid slums of our great cities and have been incubated around the camp fires of wandering, hopeless, homeless hoboes. No man ever waved the red flag of anarchy over a home of his own which sheltered himself, his wife and his children.[139]

Despite the belief that homeownership was "an antidote for Bolshevism"[140] and the recognition that housing conditions affect public health, and social and labor stability, the Red Scare did not result in government intervention in the housing market. While the Department of Labor and later the Department of Commerce sponsored the "Own Your Own Home" public messaging campaigns promoted by the National Association of Real Estate Brokers,[141] there was no substantive federal government involvement in the post–World War I housing or housing finance markets. Postwar efforts to have the federal government support greater home construction and ownership went nowhere. A bill proposing a Federal Home Loan Bank—a reserve bank system for the savings and loan industry—was introduced in Congress in 1919 but failed to get out of committee.[142]

State and local governments as well did little in this period to improve housing conditions.[143] Indeed, even during World War I, few states attempted to regulate rents, in sharp contrast to other countries' wartime approach.[144] There were some small attempts to draw more capital into housing by making mortgages a legal investment for different types of financial institutions or providing tax exemption,[145] but little happened on the local or national levels.

World War I did not result in an enduring federal government involvement in housing markets and did not entail any federal participation in housing finance, but it did create a precedent for later federal intervention in housing markets in pursuit of public policy and the use of government-owned corporations as vehicles for state action.

The aftermath of the war presented the United States with its first real housing crisis because of the standstill in home construction during the war as well as increasing urbanization. Between 1919 and 1922, there was an acute national housing shortage, as the construction loan and mortgage finance markets suffered from lack of capital.[146] The real estate certificates and bonds "had withered to one-half of [their] former volume."[147]

The housing capital shortage appears to have been due to several factors. Changes to the new federal income tax along with high yields offered on short-term securities and the tax-free bond market led to a flight of capital from mortgage investments.[148] Moreover, the building and loans, institutions that made up about 40 percent of the mortgage market (as shown in Figure 1.6), relied on financing from commercial banks, but commercial banks did not want to loan to the building and loans against their mortgage assets because mortgage collateral was ineligible for rediscounting at Federal Reserve Banks.[149]

The postwar housing shortage rapidly became a housing boom, as war-repressed demand became a flurry of construction (as shown in Figure 1.7).[150] The factors contributing to the boom have not been well explored by the scholarly literature, but the effects of unleashing previously repressed housing demand appears to have been spurred on by easy monetary policy, greater confidence in market stability under the new Federal Reserve System, the emergence of real estate bonds, and what may have been a decline in lending standards.[151] The postwar housing boom peaked in 1925, well before the 1929 stock market crash that ushered in the Great Depression, but the precipitous drop in prices and in housing starts did not occur until 1929, when financial markets froze, cutting off financing for construction.

The pre–New Deal housing finance system was a highly localized world in which individual, noninstitutional lenders played an enormous role and in which there were no real secondary markets. Many Americans financed their home purchases, but housing was not yet financialized. No widely traded asset class based on housing had yet developed. While there were glimmers of products and financing structures that would eventually come to define the American housing finance system,[152] pre–New Deal housing finance was largely built around short-term, nonamortizing products, which were a recipe for disaster when the Great Depression hit. The federal government's response to the crisis completely reshaped the American housing finance market, as we shall explain in the next chapter.

CHAPTER TWO

The New Deal Mortgage

AMERICAN HOUSING FINANCE was completely transformed during the New Deal. The New Deal created a host of institutions that remain central to US housing markets and collectively gave birth to the crown jewel of American housing finance: the 30-year fixed-rate mortgage, or the American Mortgage.

None of this was planned beforehand, however. The New Deal reforms were ad hoc responses to different exigencies and interest groups, rather than part of an overall plan for the reform of housing finance. Nonetheless, these reforms created a system of governmental and quasi-governmental institutions that functioned as a type of "public option" for the secondary housing finance and insurance markets. In the New Deal era, the public option was primarily through mortgage and deposit insurance provided by the government; any secondary market operations by the government were extremely limited.

The story of the New Deal reforms begins with the housing crisis caused by the Great Depression. The economic contraction during the Depression brought with it a sharp rise in foreclosures, a decline in home construction, and a precipitous drop in mortgage finance availability due to the failure and retrenchment of financial institutions.

As unemployment soared, many homeowners found themselves struggling to make mortgage payments. The predominant interest-only bullet loan structure only exacerbated the situation. Even if a homeowner could

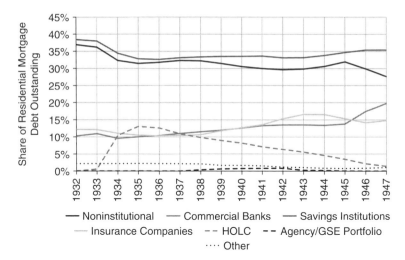

Figure 2.1. Residential Mortgage Market Share by Institution Type, 1932–1947

Data source: Leo Grebler *et al.*, *Capital Formation in Residential Real Estate: Trends and Prospects* 468–71, tbl. N-2 (1956).

still make the periodic interest payments, the bullet payment of principal loomed. Before the Depression, homeowners would simply roll over or refinance the loan upon maturity. But the decline in housing prices fueled by defaults—as much as 50 percent in some areas[1]—meant that homeowners were often underwater and unable to refinance. Even though loan-to-value ratios (LTVs) were relatively low on first mortgages, many homeowners had second mortgages, which pushed combined LTVs upward. As a result, some homeowners found themselves without equity in their homes and unable to refinance the bullet loan before maturity. Even when homeowners were not underwater, however, refinancing was not always possible because of the Depression's credit contraction.

The pre–New Deal funding channels for the American housing market were particularly vulnerable to a credit contraction. In 1932, around 40 percent of mortgage debt was held by individuals,[2] with another 40 percent held by various types of thrift institutions—savings banks and building and loans.[3] (See Figure 2.1.) While all funding sources for mortgage finance cut back on lending during the Depression, individuals and thrifts were especially hard-hit because of their lack of diversification, vulnerability to disintermediation, and lack of federal liquidity support.

Individual mortgage lenders had limited funding capacity to begin with and were vulnerable to their own unemployment. In addition, they were extremely undiversified, as they would make only a few loans at a time, all in a single geographic area, with loans that were large relative to their assets.

In an uncertain market, it was only natural that individuals would pull back on lending.

The same was true for savings institutions, or "thrifts," such as savings and loans (S&Ls). Many of the thrifts' mortgage loan assets were in default, while their deposit base evaporated with bank runs and, prior to the institution of deposit insurance, a large shift in deposits to the federal Postal Savings System, which functioned as a type of ersatz deposit insurance.[4] Between 1929 and 1934, there was a 28 percent decline in S&L deposits,[5] and many more thrifts prohibited withdrawals until loan repayments came in,[6] meaning that the decline in *lendable* deposits was substantially greater. The contraction in the thrift deposit base was accompanied by a 77 percent contraction in S&L mortgage lending.[7] The disintermediation of deposits to the Postal Savings System was particularly devastating for thrift institutions because this system could not relend to them, only to commercial banks.[8]

Whereas commercial banks—which accounted for around 10 percent of the mortgage market—had had, since 1913, the possibility of emergency liquidity support from the Federal Reserve through the Fed's discount window, there was no such liquidity source for thrifts. Thrifts could not borrow at the Fed's discount window, and the Fed was not yet permitted to make advances against mortgage collateral.[9] Instead, thrifts seeking liquidity had to look to commercial banks for loans,[10] but this was a runny source of funds. Whenever there were adverse economic conditions, commercial banks called their loans, and this was very much true after 1929.[11]

Thus, the bullet loan mortgage structure that predominated before the New Deal left homeowners dangerously exposed to macroeconomic risk, which, by its very nature, is likely to produce large, correlated losses, which in turn further macroeconomic downturns. While no mortgage structure can protect against unemployment and price declines, the long-term, fixed-rate, amortized mortgages would not have exposed borrowers to the refinancing risks of underwater homes and frozen markets and would not have so badly decimated financial institutions in turn.

The combination of bullet loans, unemployment, declining home prices, and frozen finance markets meant that half of all residential urban mortgages were in default at the beginning of 1934.[12] Foreclosure starts soared, although many were not completed, in part because of extraordinary state and federal foreclosure prevention measures.[13] Indeed, completed foreclosures remained relatively rare, topping out at 1.33 percent of nonfarm properties in 1933, although this was roughly three times historical levels.[14] The delayed and avoided foreclosures helped mitigate the immediate social impact

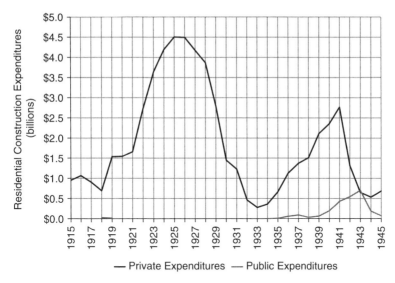

Figure 2.2. Residential Construction Expenditures, 1915–1945

Data source: *Historical Statistics of the United States, 1789–1945* (1949), Series H 4, 14.

of high mortgage default rates, but may have contributed to the length of the crisis by preventing the housing market from clearing, which involves achieving a supply-demand equilibrium such that there is no longer excess supply or unmet demand.

The collapse in housing prices produced a vicious cycle with employment. As housing prices fell, so too did construction. New housing starts dropped 90 percent from their peak in 1925 to 1933,[15] and residential construction expenditures fell by 94 percent during the same period.[16] (See Figure 2.2; also refer back to Figure 1.7.) The sharp contraction in home building contributed to unemployment in home-building and related industries, which in turn created a downward spiral of unemployment, declines in home prices, foreclosures, and construction contraction.

The New Deal response to this crisis was for the federal government to directly assist in the provision of adequate housing for Americans in order to spur economic recovery by encouraging the residential construction industry and to rejuvenate financial institutions by improving their balance sheets and easing cash flows to enable them to make more loans. As part of this massive societal reconstruction, the Franklin Roosevelt administration also undertook an overhaul of the housing finance system by building, initially, on work done by a blue ribbon commission convened by the Herbert Hoover administration.[17]

There were four key pieces of the initial New Deal overhaul of housing finance.[18] The initial two components were responses to immediate Depression exigencies, while the latter two were responses to the problems created by the first two components.

Federal Home Loan Bank System and Federal Savings and Loan Insurance Corporation

First, in 1932, under President Hoover, Congress created the Federal Home Loan Bank (FHLB) system, a credit reserve system modeled after the Federal Reserve, with twelve regional FHLBs mutually owned by their member institutions and a central Federal Home Loan Bank Board (FHLBB) to regulate the system.[19] The idea of an FHLB system was not new—it was expressly modeled on the Federal Reserve System and the Federal Farm Loan Bank System. Indeed, legislation for a federal building loan bank had been proposed after World War I.[20]

The regional FHLBs were authorized to make both short-term unsecured advances to member institutions as well as long-term advances against mortgage collateral. Membership in the regional FHLBs was initially limited to safe and sound S&Ls, building and loan associations, savings banks, and insurance companies that were in the business of making long-term loans.[21] This limitation meant that the FHLBs only supported institutionalized mortgage lending; there was no support for individual lenders, including incorporated firms that were not structured (and regulated) as thrifts, banks, or insurance companies.

FHLB membership was obtained through a subscription of stock in a regional FHLB. The FHLBs were initially capitalized with a stock subscription from the US Treasury.[22] They were also authorized to borrow, including by issuing tax-exempt bonds[23] with joint and several liability among the twelve regional banks.[24] The FHLBs' debt was explicitly not backed by the federal government.[25] Figure 2.3 presents a contemporary illustration of the FHLB system as a type of Hoover Dam, holding a "reservoir of capital" pooled from three separate funding streams—sale of debentures, paid-in capital, and the deposits of member institutions—that could be used to power the mortgage industry.

The FHLB system provided a liquidity backstop for the thrift industry by making advances to thrifts that were secured by the thrifts' mortgage loans. Thrifts could borrow against their loan holdings via the FHLB system, which thus freed thrift associations from relying on commercial banks for credit. Not surprisingly, the FHLB system was met with strong opposition

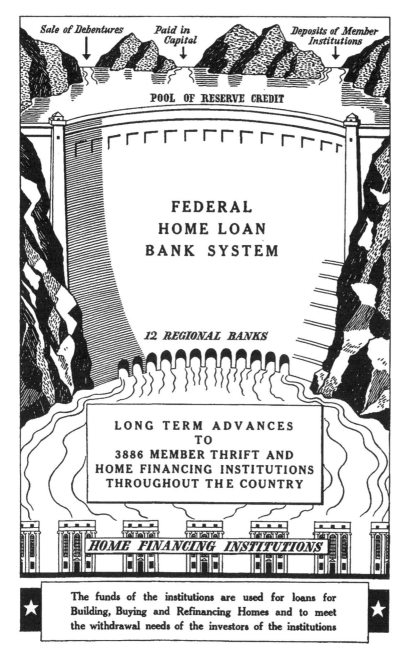

Figure 2.3. The FHLB System as Hoover Dam

Source: Federal Home Loan Bank Board, *Fifth Annual Report, 1936–37*, 10 (1937).

from commercial banks, which lost a captive market, but was supported by the thrift industry, which gained a funding source. FHLB rediscounting made mortgages overall a more liquid asset,[26] although that liquidity was constrained by the resources in the FHLB system and the statutory limits on FHLB advances.

Initially, the FHLBs were permitted to make advances only on loans with a maturity of no more than fifteen years and a size under $20,000 and that were no more than six months delinquent.[27] The size of the advance, however, depended on the terms of the mortgage. If the loan was an amortized loan with a term of at least eight years, then advances could be as large as 60 percent of the principal of the loan, capped at 40 percent LTV. All other loans were eligible for advances of only 50 percent, capped at 30 percent LTV.[28] These terms were later liberalized.[29] The advances to any member were limited to twelve times the amount of its paid-in stock.[30] The FHLBs were also permitted to make short-term unsecured advances (for no longer than a year) of up to 5 percent of a member's assets.[31] The FHLBs were additionally initially permitted to be a direct lender of last resort to consumers.[32]

The FHLBs were subject to a variety of regulations. They were supervised and subject to examination by the FHLBB. Their capital was regulated; they were required to maintain reserves of 100 percent of their paid-in capital, augmented with 5 percent of their net earnings semiannually, an obligation that ranked as senior to any payments to their shareholders.[33] The FHLBs also had their rate of return limited by statute. The maximum rate permitted on their debentures was 5.5 percent, and the maximum margin was 1.5 percent.[34] This effectively limited the terms on which the FHLBs could advance funds, and that in turn reduced the rate that lenders who funded themselves through FHLB advances could charge borrowers. Additionally, all loans made by FHLB member institutions, whether or not used as collateral for advances, were also subject to state usury laws or, if no usury law applied, an 8 percent all-in cost cap.[35] The rate of return and rate cap regulation meant that the FHLBs were disincentivized from taking on risky mortgages because the risk premium they could charge was capped.

Starting in 1933, the FHLB system also assumed regulatory oversight of the new federal S&Ls authorized by the Home Owners' Loan Act of 1933.[36] This new type of lending institution was designed to promote mutual savings and mortgage lending. The Home Owners' Loan Act limited federal S&L lending activity: all lending had to be against real estate, and loans beyond 15 percent of total assets had to be secured by first liens on properties located within fifty miles of the S&L's home office and with a property value cap.[37]

Oversight authority over the federal S&Ls included resolution authority for failed institutions.[38] Resolution authority was bolstered in 1934 with the creation of the Federal Savings and Loan Insurance Corporation (FSLIC).[39] FSLIC provided deposit insurance for S&Ls, just as the Federal Deposit Insurance Corporation (FDIC), created in 1932, provided for commercial banks. Federal deposit insurance for S&Ls increased their attractiveness to savers and helped make them competitive with commercial banks for deposit gathering.[40]

While the S&L industry did not witness a boom in the 1930s, the creation of the FHLB system, the federal thrift charter, and FSLIC insurance set the stage for the later ascendance of the S&L industry in mortgage lending from the 1950s to the 1980s.

Home Owners' Loan Corporation

The FHLBs had originally been given temporary mortgage origination authority,[41] but it was only as a direct mortgage lender of last resort when no other source would lend. The FHLBs made scant use of this authority;[42] the requirement that no other lender be available meant that FHLB's direct loan applicants were inherently poor risks.

Faced with a growing problem of mortgage defaults, Congress responded in 1933 by authorizing the FHLBB to create the Home Owners' Loan Corporation (HOLC), a US government corporation initially capitalized via a stock subscription by the US Treasury,[43] which was authorized to refinance troubled mortgages. The creation of the HOLC ended the need for FHLB direct lending, and the authority for it was repealed.[44]

The HOLC purchased defaulted mortgages from both financial institutions and noninstitutional lenders in exchange for tax-exempt 4 percent eighteen-year bonds.[45] The financial institutions had to consent to a haircut on the refinancing, as the HOLC would loan up to the lesser of 80 percent of LTV (but using a generous appraisal standard) or $14,000.[46] The HOLC then restructured the mortgages into fifteen-year, fixed-rate, fully amortized obligations at 5 percent interest rates (or 4.5 percent after 1939), which significantly reduced mortgage payments by allowing borrowers to pay off the mortgages over a longer term.[47] The HOLC originated and serviced all its mortgages in-house.

The HOLC received applications from 40 percent of residential mortgagors in its first year of operation and refinanced half of them.[48] The HOLC resulted in a sudden and massive government entrance into the mortgage market—within a year it owned over 10 percent of all mortgages. When its lending authority expired in 1936, it still held over 10 percent of the mortgages in the United States, having restructured over a million mortgages.[49] Yet "it was well understood that in the HOLC no permanent socialization of mortgage lending was intended and no attempt to preserve home ownership irrespective of public cost."[50] The HOLC was pitched only as a one-off, crisis-driven intervention in the market. Therefore, it "did not serve to divide opinion on any fundamental issues. Creditors were relieved of a crushing weight of frozen assets in a time of great stress, and debtors obtained more favorable credit terms than had ever before prevailed in this country."[51]

Because the HOLC would not refinance loans at 100 percent LTV, its refinancings required consent of the existing mortgagee. At first, the federal government guaranteed only the timely payment of interest on HOLC securities, but not repayment of principal. Lenders were reluctant to accept HOLC refinancing, as they were both taking an instant loss and assuming the credit risk of the HOLC, whose assets were, by definition, a bunch of distressed loans.[52] Therefore, in order to facilitate HOLC refinancings, the federal government began to guaranty the principal on HOLC securities too,[53] and these securities eventually traded at par.[54]

The HOLC had wound down by 1951, but it had accomplished three major feats. First, it had turned a large pool of mortgages into marketable securities.[55] Thus, the HOLC demonstrated the viability of a government-backed mortgage securities market. Second, it had set the long-term, fully amortized, fixed-rate mortgage as the federal government standard and demonstrated its feasibility.[56] The HOLC's use of the long-term, fully amortized, fixed-rate mortgage, along with the creation of the FHLB system, marked the government's commitment to supporting "the practice of the savings and loan associations of making long-term amortized first mortgage loans with relatively small down payments and modest monthly payments."[57] As Marc A. Weiss has noted, the HOLC, along with "other New Deal programs[,] adapted the S&L model and vastly extended it to a large number and wide range of financial institutions, increasing the length of first mortgage loans from 3 to 30 years, decreasing the down payments from 50% to 10% or less, and significantly lowering interest rates."[58]

Third, the HOLC standardized many mortgage lending procedures, including standardized national appraisal methods, use of credit reports, mortgage forms, and origination, foreclosure, and REO management processes.[59] In particular, it pioneered an appraisal process that used an equally weighted formula of (1) the estimated current market price, (2) the cost of purchasing a similar lot plus constructing a similar building, minus depreciation, and (3) capitalization of the last decade's worth of imputed rental income.[60] Many appraisers became trained in HOLC methodology, and its methodology was subsequently adopted and spread by the Federal Housing Administration (FHA) as part of its mortgage insurance requirements.

The HOLC's legacy, however, has been marred by its association with redlining, that is, the refusal to lend in certain geographic areas because of that area's racial makeup.[61] The term comes from the practice of lenders and insurers literally drawing a red line on a map around areas they would not serve.[62] The practice of redlining seems to have predated the HOLC,[63] and the HOLC itself did not engage in redlining in its own refinancings.[64] But starting in 1936, after most HOLC lending was complete, the HOLC created a set of residential security maps that assigned areas one of four grades, which corresponded to a color on the map. The grading was not solely a reflection of neighborhoods' racial makeup,[65] but also the condition of housing.[66]

While the HOLC's maps do not appear to have been widely available to private lenders, they were available to the FHA,[67] which went on to undertake its own residential security mapping project,[68] and a property's residential security coding was a factor in FHA underwriting guidelines.[69] Because lenders wanted FHA insurance (and the liquidity such insurance gave their loans), FHA residential security maps translated into redlining by lenders. Redlining not only affected minorities, it also operated to discourage the creation of racially integrated neighborhoods, as the FHA would not insure mortgages of white borrowers who lived too close to black neighborhoods absent some clear physical barrier between the neighborhoods, such as Detroit's infamous Eight Mile Wall.[70]

Federal Housing Administration Insurance

Mortgage insurance was the third piece of the housing finance overhaul, and it came in the form of federal mortgage insurance from the FHA. The HOLC was designed to deal with existing mortgages. It helped financial institutions move illiquid, nonperforming assets off their books in exchange for liquid, government-guarantied assets. The HOLC, however, was limited in its ability to inject new funds into the economy to stimulate mortgage lending or home building, and as urban historian Kenneth T. Jackson has noted, President Roosevelt wanted to "stimulate building without government spending and that would rely instead on private enterprise."[71] For this goal, a more ambitious apparatus needed to be created. It was laid out in the 1934 National Housing Act.[72]

The National Housing Act created the FHA, a government agency, to provide ongoing encouragement of mortgage lending and homebuilding.

The FHA partially insures payment of principal and interest on mortgages in exchange for a small insurance premium charged to the originator and passed on to the borrower. FHA insurance settlements are paid out either in cash or in FHA debentures with maturities linked to the maturity date of the loan.[73] FHA debentures are guarantied by the US Treasury.[74] Originally, the Treasury guaranty of the debentures was intended to be a "strictly temporary measure to insure early adoption" of the FHA mortgage, and were to lapse in 1937.[75] In 1938, however, the insurance was made permanent to assist in the creation of a secondary market for FHA-insured loans.[76]

Because of the credit risk assumed by FHA, FHA insurance was available only for loans meeting certain characteristics. The maximum interest rate permitted on FHA-insured mortgages (exclusive of the insurance premium) was originally 5 percent.[77] FHA was also willing to insure long-term and (for the first time) high-LTV mortgages. At first, FHA would insure loans with terms up to twenty years and 80 percent LTV, but after the 1937 recession, terms were liberalized to provide construction stimulus.[78] FHA also required that mortgages be fixed-rate and fully amortized.[79] These terms were modeled on the terms of HOLC refinanced mortgages but were later liberalized. Eventually FHA was willing to insure up to 97 percent LTV and thirty-year terms (and even forty years on certain property types).[80]

As with FHLB membership, FHA insurance was only available for institutional lenders, not individuals.[81] The long-term impact of the FHA's exclusion of noninstitutional lenders was to almost fully institutionalize the mortgage market.[82]

Because of the credit risk it assumed, FHA had to continue the work of HOLC in developing standard national procedures for appraisal and property management.[83] The methods that FHA developed acquired widespread acceptance in the mortgage industry as a whole.[84]

FHA-insured loans were designed to assist in improving housing affordability for the middle class. They were not, however, designed to expand homeownership for the poor. The New Deal exhibited tensions between those who sought to regenerate the old economic system and those who wanted to create a new, more socialized economic system. In the housing sphere, this reflected itself in the question of federal involvement in public housing. When FHA was created, it was not intended to be in the public housing business;[85] its goal was, instead, to reinvigorate the collapsed mortgage finance sector by acting as "a mutual mortgage insurance system to which all mortgage lenders had access, the expenses and liabilities of which were to be covered by insurance premiums collected by the lenders from the borrowers."[86]

The National Housing Act had a small set-aside for low-income housing, but the major New Deal push to create public housing was instead tasked to the United States Housing Agency, a 1937 creation that financed slum clearance and the building of low-income housing units. Eventually FHA picked up the role tasked to the United States Housing Agency, but FHA was not originally meant to insure low-income housing.

Instead, FHA-insured loans were a middle-class affordability product. Low down payment requirements and long terms more than offset the impact of full amortization on monthly payments, and rate caps further ensured affordability even if they rationed credit. The government's assumption of credit risk created a cross-subsidy among riskier and less risky borrowers, but the government's ability to diversify credit risk across the insurance pool likely resulted in lower mortgage costs as well.[87]

Although FHA-insured loans were geared toward affordability, they offered benefits to both borrowers and lenders. Borrowers were insulated against mortgage payment risk since rates would not be impacted by market shocks, while lenders were protected against default risk because of the government guaranty.

In order to ensure the realization of the affordability benefits of FHA-insured mortgages, it was necessary to free financial institutions from legal restrictions on their lending activities. Thus, FHA-insured loans made by national banks were exempt from the LTV and maturity restrictions of the National Bank Act.[88] The FHA also embarked on a successful campaign to get all forty-eight state legislatures to amend their banking and insurance regulations in order to permit state-chartered institutions to originate and hold all FHA-insurable loans.[89]

Notably, the removal of state mortgage lending restrictions was done in concert with the creation of federal restrictions and standards. Thus, the Home Owners' Loan Act's exemption of federally chartered thrifts from state usury laws must be seen in the context of the FHA insurance interest rate cap and FHLB member rate cap.[90] The FHA interest rate cap served as a federal usury law for mortgages. It directly limited rates on FHA-insured loans,[91] and it indirectly limited rates on conventional loans through competition between FHA and conventional products.

The creation of FHA changed the institutional balance in mortgage lending. The FHA and the National Housing Act had been strongly supported by commercial banks and insurance companies because it removed restrictions on their urban mortgage lending and made mortgages a more economically feasible investment by providing liquidity.[92] Not surprisingly, FHA was opposed by the S&L industry. S&Ls had just gotten the FHLB system for their exclusive use in 1932, a major improvement in their position from their prior dependence on commercial bank credit. Moreover, S&Ls were local institutions and not particularly interested in free national capital movement.[93] The FHA increased competition for the S&Ls in their core mortgage lending business from insurance companies and commercial banks, not just locally, but also from out of state.[94] The S&Ls were also at a disadvantage in this competition because the dividends they paid on their depositors' shares were at higher rates than the interest commercial banks paid on time deposits. Accordingly, S&Ls made a smaller spread on FHA-insured mortgages than commercial banks.[95]

The FHA insurance system was a response to several problems. First, it was a reaction to the government finding itself a major mortgagee as the result of the HOLC refinancings. The government hoped to be able to sell the HOLC refinanced mortgages to private investors, but no investors would take the credit risk on the HOLC mortgages. Offering a credit guaranty of the mortgages was the only way to move them off the governments' books as a whole.

Second, the government was hoping to attract more capital into the battered mortgage sector. The FHLB system and FSLIC insurance encouraged S&L mortgage lending, but to encourage commercial bank capital deployment in the mortgage sector, more was needed. Commercial banks were reluctant to become deeply committed to mortgages not least because of the illiquidity of mortgage assets.

FHA insurance had the effect of standardizing the credit risk on insured mortgages. Standardization via FHA insurance was intended to transform mortgages into more liquid assets. Notably, FHA insurance was not originally intended as a long-term intervention in the housing market—hence the original temporary duration of the Treasury guaranty of FHA debentures. Instead, FHA was intended to deal with the problem of unloading the pool of HOLC mortgages and jump-starting the housing sector. Only when it became apparent that the sector needed longer-term care did FHA evolve into an ongoing guaranty program to ensure greater housing affordability going forward.

When FHA was created, private mortgage insurance did not exist. There had been a mortgage insurance industry of sorts at the beginning of the twentieth century, but it faltered and collapsed in scandal during the Depression.[96] States only began to allow insurance companies to insure mortgages starting in 1957.[97] Thus, when the FHA was created, it was not competing against private insurance.

Like the HOLC, the FHA was a response of expediency to a problem, rather than a systematically planned housing finance structure. The FHA insurance system developed as a parallel, rather than a complement, to the

FHLB system. As political scientist David French explained, the FHLBB aimed to "unite the strength of local credit *institutions* in a national system bulwarked by central reserve facilities, standardized national charters, and share insurance. The Federal Housing plan, on the other hand, attempts to unify, not the lending institutions themselves, but the form and security of the *mortgage loans* they make."[98]

Accordingly, the FHLBB plan appealed to S&Ls, which were local and did not have access to a national supply of credit or discount window access, while the FHA plan appealed to life insurance companies and banks, which wanted guarantied loan returns. The New Deal interventions in the mortgage market were not meant to be permanent, nor were they particularly coordinated. Instead, they represented simultaneous programs for different interest groups: the FHLBB system for the savings banks and the FHA for the banks and life insurance companies.

Despite its haphazard origins, FHA insurance, along with HOLC refinancings, played a major role in standardizing mortgage terms. The importance of standardization cannot be overstated because it was the precondition for the development of a national secondary mortgage market. Secondary markets are built around liquidity, and nonstandard instruments are not liquid because each individual instrument must be examined, which adds transaction costs.

FHA insurance also supplied a second precondition for a secondary market. A secondary mortgage market cannot function unless credit risk is perceived as negligible or monitorable. Elimination, or at least the standardization of credit risk, is itself part of standardizing the instruments to trade in a secondary market; as long as there is heterogeneous credit risk among mortgages, secondary market liquidity will be impaired. As economic historian Kenneth Snowden has observed:

> The key to successful securitization is to issue marketable assets only on the default-free cash flow implicit in the underlying mortgage pool—for uninformed investors will be unwilling to share any of the risk associated with default. Broad and thick secondary markets arise for mortgage-backed securities like these, and they trade at yields comparable to government bonds. Secondary markets are much thinner, on the other hand, when the entire cash flow from the underlying mortgage is securitized or when the default insurance component is only partially split off. In the extreme, mortgage-backed securities that carry default risk may not be marketable at all.[99]

Thus, in earlier secondary market experiments, credit risk on the mortgages, which investors could not easily ascertain, was perceived as being eliminated via sureties, as with the mortgage guaranty participation certificates or the single-property real estate bond houses. As early as 1943, Paul Matthew Stoner, the FHA's assistant director for Statistics and Research had recognized this. He argued that FHA insurance was necessary to replace the discredited mortgage guaranty certificate system.[100] For capital markets to fund mortgages, credit risk had to be neutralized (or at least perceived as such).

FHA mortgages were sufficiently standardized in their terms and credit risk to allow for an institutional market supporting them.[101] Thus, as economists Leo Grebler, David Blank, and Louis Winnick noted:

> Government insurance of residential mortgage loans has created a debt instrument that can be shifted easily from one lender to another. From the lender's point of view, government insurance endows mortgage loans with greater uniformity of quality that has ever been the case before, and it reduces the necessity for detailed examination that usually accompanies the transfer of loans from one mortgagee to another. As a result, an active "secondary market" for FHA and VA [(Veterans Administration)] loans has developed, which in turn has widened the geographical scope of the market for mortgage loans and given it some of the characteristics of national capital markets.[102]

FHA insurance alone, however, was not sufficient for a secondary mortgage market to develop.[103] For that, the final New Deal innovation was required.

Fannie Mae: The Federal National Mortgage Association

Investors had little appetite for buying individual mortgages in the secondary market, even if the mortgages were insured, because of the liquidity and interest rate risk involved, as well as the transaction costs of diligencing individual mortgages. Therefore, the National Housing Act of 1934 also contained the fourth element of the housing finance overhaul. It provided for a federal charter for "national mortgage associations" that would purchase these insured mortgages at par and thus create a secondary mortgage market.[104] The goal was to create a secondary market that would encourage mortgage originators to make new loans by allowing them to capitalize on future cash flows through a sale of the mortgages to the national mortgage associations, which would fund themselves by issuing long-term fixed-rate debt with maturities similar to those of the mortgages.

There were no applications for a federal national mortgage association charter, however. Therefore, the Reconstruction Finance Corporation (RFC), the so-called "fourth branch" of government during the New Deal, a government corporation that was active in many areas of the market as a financier because of the unwillingness of private institutions to lend, created a subsidiary, the Reconstruction Finance Corporation Mortgage Company, a Maryland state corporation. The RFC Mortgage Company purchased FHA-insured mortgages, but only on existing properties.[105] The reasons for this limitation in activity are not clear. When no applications for a federal national mortgage association charter were forthcoming even by 1938, the RFC created another subsidiary under the federal charter provisions, the Federal National Mortgage Association of Washington (later the Federal National Mortgage Association, and now Fannie Mae).[106] Fannie Mae was originally a wholly owned subsidiary of the RFC, itself a US government corporation. Unlike the RFC Mortgage Company, Fannie Mae originally purchased FHA-insured mortgages on new construction.[107]

As Figure 2.4 shows, Fannie purchased mortgages from financial institutions in exchange for its debt securities, which were backed (at this time) by the full faith and credit of the United States government. Fannie would either keep the mortgage loans in its own portfolio, against which it issued bonds (which it used to fund its operations), or resell the loans whole to private investors. This meant that Fannie was able to pass on some of the interest rate risk on the mortgages to its bondholders, as their bonds had fixed-rate coupons. Neither the Fannie bondholders nor the lenders that sold mortgages to Fannie in exchange for its debt securities assumed any credit risk, however, because Fannie was a government corporation.

Fannie's activities before World War II were limited. Fannie Mae's prewar activity peak was in 1939, when it purchased $88 million in mortgages,[108]

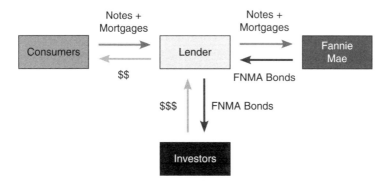

Figure 2.4. Fannie Mae Funding of Mortgages through Corporate Debt
Original creation by the authors.

or 3 percent of the $2.9 billion in originations that year.[109] Not until a decade later did Fannie surpass this level of activity.[110]

During World War II Fannie Mae largely ceased purchase operations. In 1942, the RFC Mortgage Company and Fannie seem to have assumed the same (limited) activities. The US mortgage market was moribund during the war and did not need government support because the wartime demand for mortgage finance was extremely limited and private investors were eager for wartime outlets.[111] Fannie purchased almost no mortgages between 1943 and 1947 (and none in 1944) and let its holdings dwindle to almost nothing.[112]

Fannie Mae's prewar accumulation of mortgages (as well as those of the RFC Mortgage Company) "were expected to decrease as soon as the FHA type mortgage had proved itself."[113] The RFC Mortgage Company was even dissolved in 1947.[114] Lack of wartime construction created an acute postwar housing shortage, but the immediate postwar period was also flush with long pent-up funds that could finance construction and mortgages.[115] By 1948, however, other, more attractive investment outlets had become available, and the mortgage market was strapped for funds.[116]

In 1944, aiming to make housing more affordable to discharged servicemen, Congress had authorized the Veterans Administration to guaranty mortgages for veterans. The VA would originally guaranty up to 50 percent of the loan, required no down payment, and capped interest rates at a level equal to or below FHA insurance eligibility caps.[117]

VA mortgages were fixed-rate, fully amortized loans with terms of as long as 30-years.[118] The increase in the amortization period from 15 years to 20, then 25, and finally 30 years made housing even more affordable to servicemen by reducing monthly payments, which were spread out over a longer time period. The FHA soon adopted the 30-year fixed as its standard as well, which spread to private lenders too.

FHA and VA loans accounted for over 40 percent of mortgage dollars outstanding by the 1950s. (See Figure 2.5.) Thus, by the end of the 1950s, most mortgages were 30-year fixed with down payments of 20 percent.[119] This mortgage, a 30-year, fixed-rate, fully amortized, fully prepayable mortgage with 20 percent down established itself as the standard product in the US mortgage market, *the* American Mortgage.

Fannie Mae was virtually reborn in 1948, when Congress amended its charter to authorize the purchase of VA-guarantied mortgages.[120] Fannie Mae entered the VA-guarantied market in force. From June 30, 1948 to June 30, 1949, Fannie Mae's holdings increased 809 percent, as the agency extended advance purchase commitments in order to stimulate the construction market.[121]

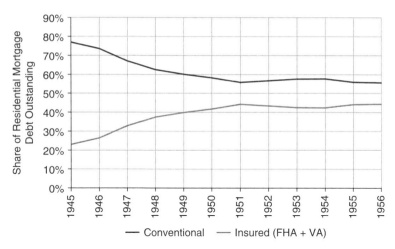

Figure 2.5. Conventional and Insured Mortgage Shares of the Residential Mortgage Market, 1945–1956

Data source: Saul B. Klaman, *The Volume of Mortgage Debt in the Postwar Decade* 38, tbl. 1 (1958).

In its first decades, Fannie Mae accomplished five key things. First, Fannie created a secondary market for FHA and VA mortgages. By 1950, a third of FHA-insured loans and a quarter of VA-guaranteed loans had been acquired by their holders through a secondary market purchase rather than origination, compared with only 11 percent of conventional loans.[122] This secondary market provided liquidity for mortgage originators by linking capital market investors to mortgage lenders (and ultimately to mortgage borrowers).

Second, the Fannie Mae secondary market reduced regional discrepancies in interest rates and financing availability.[123] Fannie was able to harness investor capital from capital-rich regions to purchase or invest in mortgages from capital-poor regions. This helped smooth out the impact of regional economic booms and busts on the housing sector.

Third, the secondary market created by Fannie Mae enabled geographic diversification for investors in the housing market, which provided a form of insurance for regions that were hit by temporary economic dislocation. Borrowers gained from the stability and lower interest rates that would result from this geographical diversification.[124]

Fourth, Fannie Mae provided stability to the housing market by serving as a buyer of last resort through its portfolio operations. As mortgage interest rates rose during 1949 to 1951, the supply of credit for VA-guaranteed loans, which bore a maximum interest rate of 4 percent, shrank. Fannie Mae responded by stepping up its purchases of VA loans to help maintain the supply of low-cost VA loans.[125] Fannie was thus able to support the market by expanding or shrinking its investment portfolio like an accordion.

Fannie's "accordion" portfolio provided an important countercyclical balance in the housing sector. As housing economist Jack Guttentag has observed, Fannie's secondary market operations mitigated fluctuations in residential construction activity because Fannie "maintained fixed or 'sticky' mortgage purchase prices."[126] Fannie's holdings rose more rapidly with declining construction and falling mortgage prices. The agency thus had a countercyclical effect on the housing construction market.[127] From time to time, Congress also passed special legislation to enhance Fannie's countercyclical impact on the mortgage market. For example, in 1949–1950 and again in 1958, Congress authorized Fannie to make extra purchases at an above-market price.[128]

Fannie increased its purchases during the late 1940s and early 1950s through the issuance of advance commitments to purchase any and all FHA or VA mortgages at par. These advance commitments let mortgage lenders originate loans with a guarantied resale market. Lenders were thus relieved of both liquidity risk and interest rate risk. While most originators of FHA and VA mortgages would hold the mortgages on their books, Fannie Mae's advance commitment gave them the option to convert the long-term payment stream of a mortgage into immediate cash via a sale to the agency. Moreover, if interest rates rose, originators could avoid holding assets that yielded less than market rates by selling them at par, rather than at a discount, to Fannie. Fannie thus assumed the interest rate risk on mortgages under its advance commitment program. Ultimately, Fannie's advance commitment program encouraged the growth of mortgage banks with this originate-to-distribute model.[129]

Fannie kept the advance commitment offer in place during most of the period from 1948 to 1954.[130] The Housing Act of 1954 required that Fannie Mae acquire mortgages under its principal program at market prices,[131] but even after 1954, Fannie Mae tended to lag behind the market in price adjustment.[132]

Finally, Fannie continued the work of the HOLC in establishing the 20 percent down, self-amortizing, 30-year fixed-rate mortgage as the national standard. The subsidized cost of funds for the 30-year fixed due to Fannie's government backing helped crowd out other mortgage products. In contrast, outside the United States the long-term fixed-rate mortgage was and remains a rarity.

The Housing Act of 1954 rechartered Fannie Mae with a structure that envisioned a gradual quasi-privatization, but without any timeline specified. Under the new charter, Fannie would have both nonvoting preferred stock and nonvoting common stock. Treasury would provide the original subscription for the preferred stock, which was to be retired over time, but without any deadline.[133] Until the preferred stock was retired, Treasury was allowed to purchase debt obligations that Fannie has issued to support its secondary market operations and to issue full faith and credit debt to do so.[134] Sellers of mortgages to Fannie were required to purchase the common stock in amounts equal to 3 percent of the unpaid principal amount on the mortgages.[135] Thus, eventually, Fannie Mae would end up having solely private capital. While the common stock was freely transferrable, it had no governance rights: the charter provided that Fannie's board of directors would be made up of government appointees, even after Treasury's preferred stock was retired.[136] While the rechartered Fannie Mae was initially prohibited from making advance purchase commitments,[137] this restriction was subsequently rescinded in 1956, giving Fannie an important tool for providing liquidity to the market.[138]

The rechartered Fannie was given two main tasks. First, it was charged with providing a secondary market facility for FHA and VA loans to ensure their liquidity. Fannie was directed that it should have purchase standards equivalent to those of private investors, price its loan purchases to "prevent excessive use" of its facilities (that is, slightly above competitive market rates), and ensure that it was self-supporting.[139] Fannie was authorized to issue debt to finance its secondary market operations, but it was required to clearly indicate that its debt issuances were not obligations of the US government, but only of Fannie itself.[140]

Second, Fannie was tasked with providing "special assistance" to the US mortgage market. The legislation gave the president the power to temporarily authorize Fannie to purchase any sort of mortgage, not only insured loans, as part of a "special assistance function"; that is, to stabilize the housing market or provide funding for "segments of the population unable to obtain adequate housing under established home financing programs."[141] Treasury was authorized to purchase Fannie's debt securities to support the special assistance even if its preferred stock had been retired.[142]

On the one hand, the legislation's goal was for Fannie Mae to be "financed by private capital to the maximum extent feasible," and to this end, it was to be gradually privatized, and its debt obligations would not bear the eagle. On the other hand, the government maintained complete control over Fannie's governance, and the special assistance power meant that the government could use Fannie as a policy instrument at will, exposing the mandated private risk capital to risks that private capital had, by definition, shunned. The Fannie Mae rechartering was an attempt for the government to have its cake and eat it too. The result was that Fannie transformed into a government-controlled, mixed-ownership corporation. While Fannie shifted to private risk capital, the government still called the shots.

Regulation of the Post–New Deal Mortgage Market

Coming out of the New Deal, the primary mode of regulation of the US housing finance system was through the insurance market, rather than the secondary market. Fannie Mae's holdings in the postwar years were minimal.[143] Fannie's importance at the time lay in providing a put option for mortgage lenders, rather than its actual operations. FHA and VA, however, insured or guarantied a sizable percentage of the market, peaking at 45 percent for combined share. (Refer back to Figure 2.4.) While FHA and VA loans were never a majority of the market, they set the standard there. The American Mortgage prevailed,[144] whether insured by the FHA and VA or originated by S&Ls without insurance.

There were differences, to be sure, between FHA and VA products and conventional loans. FHA/VA products were the lower down payment/ higher-LTV option, but at higher cost. Moreover, lending standards evolved and differed between FHA/VA and conventional loans, most particularly in regard to alleged redlining. FHA/VA redlining ended in the late 1960s, as the agencies reversed course and began launching high-LTV urban lending initiatives.[145] S&L lending patterns shifted later in response to antidiscrimination legislation like the Fair Housing Act of 1968,[146] the Equal Credit Opportunity Act of 1974,[147] and the Home Mortgage Disclosure Act of 1975,[148] as well as in response to the Community Reinvestment Act of 1977, which encouraged insured depositories to lend in their communities.[149]

The basic contours of the American Mortgage, however, permeated the entire market because of the influence of FHA/VA standards. While S&Ls, the dominant mortgage origination institution, eschewed FHA lending (but not VA lending),[150] there was competition between S&Ls and FHA/VA originators, such as mortgage banks (which often then resold the loans to life insurance companies) and commercial banks. Among the S&Ls themselves, competition was more limited both because of regulatory restrictions on the rate of return they could pay depositors[151] and the local nature of the institutions.[152] Because of consumer demand for the 30-year fixed, competition among different origination channels pushed the entire market toward the American Mortgage, even for non-FHA/VA lenders.

Regulation also played a significant role in the prevalence of the American Mortgage. Most importantly, federal thrifts and national banks were prohibited from making adjustable-rate loans,[153] and some states prohibited all lenders from making adjustable-rate loans.[154] Federal thrifts and national banks were restricted in the LTV[155] and geographic scope of their lending[156] and required to make amortizing or partially amortizing loans, with greater LTVs allowed for amortizing loans.[157] In addition, mortgage underwriting was impacted by what FHA/VA would insure and what Fannie Mae would buy or the mortgage collateral against which the FHLBs would advance funds. Prior to 1982, the FHLBs were restricted by statute in terms of the mortgage collateral against which they could make advances.[158] These restrictions pressured the S&Ls to adopt the American Mortgage, as the FHLBs were the primary source of liquidity for S&Ls, and the FHLBs were permitted to make larger advances against amortizing loans with minimum term lengths.

Originally, the FHLBs were permitted to advance up to 60 percent of the amount of the mortgage loan (capped at 40 percent of the appraised value of the collateral property) for amortizing, first-lien, one- to four-family mortgages with terms of at least eight years but no longer than fifteen years.[159] Advances on all other mortgages were capped at the lower of 50 percent of the loan or 30 percent of the appraised value of the property.[160] Mortgages with terms of over fifteen years were ineligible as collateral for advances.[161]

The statutory restrictions on FHLB advances were amended several times, keeping pace with changes in FHA and VA term limits.[162] Eventually the terms of advances settled at limits of 90 percent for FHA/VA loans and 65 percent of amount and 60 percent of appraised value for conventional amortizing, first-lien, one- to four-family mortgages with terms of at least six years, but no longer than thirty years.[163] Advances on other loans were limited to 50 percent of the loan or 40 percent of appraised value, and the maximum term permitted was thirty years.[164] The effect of these tiered limitations on advances was to favor longer-term, amortizing mortgages over nonamortizing or shorter-term mortgages. Thus, the terms of FHLB advances helped established the American Mortgage outside the FHA/VA market.

While it was formally possible for lenders to make loans other than the American Mortgage, there was no secondary market for these loans and more limited liquidity provision against them. Lenders were therefore generally unwilling to assume the risks on these loans themselves. Thus, the federal government was able to effectively regulate the mortgage market through the domination of the insurance market by a public option—public provision of services that competed with private-market providers—as well as through traditional command-and-control prohibitions on adjustable-rate loans, limitations on the interest rates paid to depositors, and restrictions on FHLB advances. In combination, the public option and command-and-control regulation constrained the products and rates on offer, which limited risk in the market, even though it did limit credit availability at the margins.

A Snapshot of the Postwar Housing Market

Following World War II there was an explosion in the US housing market. The affordable, self-amortizing, long-term mortgages provided by the new mortgage institutions enabled a dramatic rise in homeownership that has persisted for most of the post–World War II period. As Figure 2.1 shows, the HOLC assumed substantial market share between 1933 and 1935, but thereafter its portfolio gradually wound down as its mortgage purchases were curtailed. Savings institutions and noninstitutional lenders dominated the market, but the role of noninstitutional lenders was gradually diminishing and would rapidly fade post–World War II. Commercial banks and life insurance companies were the other major players in the market, but they occupied a decidedly smaller space than savings institutions. Finally, Fannie Mae played a very limited role in the market. At this juncture, the main value provided by Fannie Mae was the *possibility* of liquidity for insured loans, rather than serving as the actual financing channel for a significant volume of mortgage lending.

The key development in the postwar mortgage market was less in terms of the type of lending institution shifts and more in terms of the loan product terms—full amortization over a longer amortization period and higher LTV tolerances. These product shifts were facilitated by changes in the governmental backing of the mortgage market and were largely responsible for the increase in homeownership, most dramatically seen among young households, which could afford homeownership earlier than otherwise.[165] (See Figure 2.6.) The increase in homeownership was accompanied by a movement to the newly built suburbs. The New Deal mortgage institutions transformed the United States from a nation of renters to a nation of homeowners. The new financing institutions, along with the invention of the automobile and the building of circumferential highways, created the suburbs, as returning servicemen moved to the new Levittowns, which were then in construction. The postwar American middle class resides in a housing market made possible by massive government intervention in mortgage design.

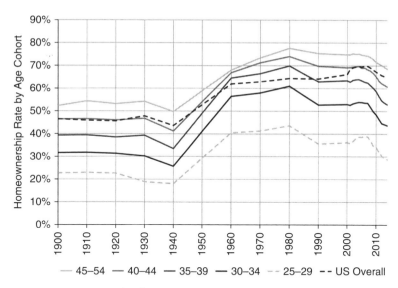

Figure 2.6. Homeownership by Age Group, 1900–2014

Data source: Daniel K. Fetter, "How Do Mortgage Subsidies Affect Home Ownership? Evidence from the Mid-Century GI Bills," 5 Am. Econ. J: Econ. Pol'y. 111, 144 (2013).

The postwar years also saw a boom in home building, which had been limited during the Depression and again during the war. It exploded in the postwar years as GIs returned home and started new lives and families. (Refer back to Figure 1.7.) Suburban development boomed, encouraged by the development of highway systems. In addition to the wide availability of housing finance through FHA and VA, the lower cost of land and newly built housing in the suburbs enabled affordable homeownership. Typical housing quality also improved significantly. Crowding fell substantially from 1940 to 1970, dropping from 20 percent of units classified as crowded (more than one person per room) to just 8 percent,[166] with severe crowding declining from 9 percent to 2 percent.[167] During the same period the percentage of housing units with complete plumbing went from nearly 55 percent to over 93 percent.[168] Not surprisingly, the median home price (in constant dollars) more than doubled from 1940 to 1970.[169]

Despite these gains in quality of housing, it is important to recognize that the postwar housing market did not serve everyone. While the Civil Rights Act of 1866 prohibited housing discrimination on the basis of race,[170] it did not provide for federal enforcement. Federal law did not prohibit discrimination on the basis of race, religion, or national origin in home sales, rentals, or mortgage lending until 1968. The Supreme Court prohibited racially based zoning in 1917,[171] but private deed restrictions and restrictive covenants effectively prevented racial, religious, and ethnic minorities from purchasing in many neighborhoods. These covenants and deed restrictions ceased to be legally enforceable as of 1948,[172] but they continued to be unofficially encouraged by the FHA's underwriting manual until 1968 and were used to signal who was welcome in a neighborhood. Realtors also discouraged blacks from buying into white neighborhoods or blocks, or simply refused to show blacks properties there.[173]

In addition, Americans of color often found themselves excluded from the institutional housing finance market. While FHA would insure loans to black borrowers, FHA redlining made it difficult for blacks to obtain housing credit from institutional lenders, particularly in the cities to which they were migrating after World War II.[174] When black buyers were able to obtain institutional loans, they often had to pay the lender a high up-front commissions in addition to an interest rate. These commissions ranged from 15 to 35 percent, compared to 3 to 6 percent for whites.[175] Instead, much of black homeownership was financed by private lenders.[176]

These lenders often used an abusive financing instrument called a "contract for deed," rather than a straight mortgage or deed of trust. A contract for deed is essentially a rent-to-own arrangement, in which the borrower only gets title to the property after repaying the entire loan. That means that the borrower does not have any equity in the property until the entire loan is paid off, so if the borrower defaults, then all the borrower's payments will be forfeited, no matter the value of the property.

Thus, while there were sources of mortgage credit for blacks, they were decidedly more limited than for whites and on less favorable terms.[177] The result was that black homeownership substantially lagged behind white homeownership, even though both rose significantly in the postwar years. (See Figures 2.7 and 2.8.)

Black homeownership was stymied not only by discrimination in the housing market, but also by discrimination in the employment market. Employment discrimination made it more difficult for black families to save up for down payments without FHA assistance, and they often had to show better credit quality for the same loan.[178] Because the black population lacked capital for down payments, it was largely a population of renters. Discrimination was more likely to exist in the rental market because of the ongoing relationship between landlord and tenant that does not exist in the seller-buyer relationship. The supply of rental housing available for blacks was inadequate, resulting in overcrowding and higher rents. While the black population was around 9.7 percent in 1950, only 6.5 percent of housing units were available to them.[179] As a result, black

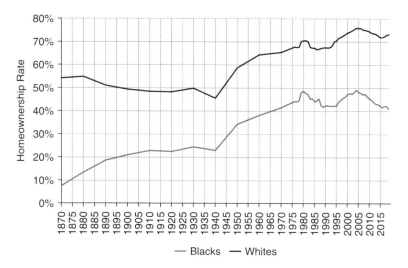

Figure 2.7. Black and White Homeownership Rates, 1870–2019

Data source: William J. Collins & Robert A. Margo, "Race and Home Ownership from the End of the Civil War to the Present," 101 *Am. Econ. Rev.* 355 (2011), online appendix, *at* https://assets.aeaweb.org/asset-server/articles-attachments/aer/data/may2011/P2011_3441_app.pdf, at 7, tbl. 2 (data for 1870–1970); Urban Institute, *Nine Charts about Wealth Inequality in America (Updated)*, Oct. 5, 2017, *at* https://apps.urban.org/features/wealth-inequality-charts/data/Homeownership.xlsx (data for 1976–1993); US Census Bureau, Homeownership Rate for the United States: Black or African American Alone [BOAAAHORUSQ156N], retrieved from FRED, Federal Reserve Bank of St. Louis, *at* https://fred.stlouisfed.org/series/BOAAAHORUSQ156N (data for 1994–2018); US Census Bureau, Homeownership Rate for the United States: Non-Hispanic White Alone [NHWAHORUSQ156N], retrieved from FRED, Federal Reserve Bank of St. Louis, *at* https://fred.stlouisfed.org/series/NHWAHORUSQ156N (data for 1994–2018).

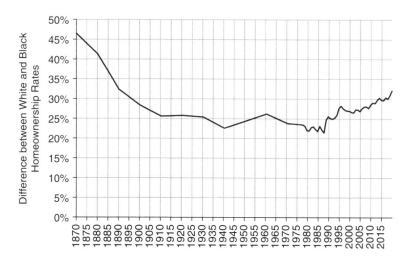

Figure 2.8. Black-White Homeownership Rate Gap, 1870–2019

Data source: William J. Collins & Robert A. Margo, "Race and Home Ownership from the End of the Civil War to the Present," 101 *Am. Econ. Rev.* 355 (2011), online appendix, *at* https://assets.aeaweb.org/asset-server/articles-attachments/aer/data/may2011/P2011_3441_app.pdf, at 7, tbl. 2 (data for 1870–1970); Urban Institute, *Nine Charts about Wealth Inequality in America (Updated)*, Oct. 5, 2017, *at* https://apps.urban.org/features/wealth-inequality-charts/data/Homeownership.xlsx (data for 1976–1993); US Census Bureau, Homeownership Rate for the United States: Black or African American Alone [BOAAAHORUSQ156N], retrieved from FRED, Federal Reserve Bank of St. Louis, *at* https://fred.stlouisfed.org/series/BOAAAHORUSQ156N (data for 1994–2018); US Census Bureau, Homeownership Rate for the United States: Non-Hispanic White Alone [NHWAHORUSQ156N], retrieved from FRED, Federal Reserve Bank of St. Louis, *at* https://fred.stlouisfed.org/series/NHWAHORUSQ156N (data for 1994–2018).

households ended up paying roughly 50 percent more than white immigrant communities for housing in worse condition.[180]

Upper- and middle-class blacks were often interested in buying homes, but private builders generally did not build new housing stock in black neighborhoods.[181] Instead, blacks wishing to buy had to do so in transitioning neighborhoods, where there was often limited housing stock available to them, and often only properties in need of renovation.[182] As a result, the sale price was often an above-market price.[183] The high sale price also meant that many buyers would struggle to maintain the obsolescent properties because they had committed a large proportion of earnings to the home purchase.[184]

Discriminatory lending marred the postwar housing finance market. Yet the basic institutional structure of the market, built on the rock of the 30-year fixed-rate mortgage and a set of federally endorsed institutions, enabled a tremendous expansion in homeownership and was a model of stability until the interest rates shocks of the 1960s and 1970s, which the next chapter explores.

CHAPTER THREE

The Rise of Securitization

Limitations on Depositary Funding of Fixed-Rate Mortgages

Homeownership massively expanded in the three decades following World War II, with the homeownership rate rising from 44 percent in 1940 to nearly 66 percent in 1980. (Refer back to Figure 1.1.) This expansion of homeownership was the dividend from the New Deal reforms that produced the American Mortgage and marked a substantial transformation of American society, as it accompanied the suburbanization of America. While discrimination remained a scourge in the housing market, homeownership expanded, not just for whites, but for all groups, such that by 1980 white homeownership was at 71 percent, while black homeownership was at 49 percent. (Refer back to Figure 2.7.)

In the 1980s, however, homeownership rates stalled and declined slightly as interest rates rose. The historic rise in inflation in the 1970s sent the mortgage industry into turmoil because of the vulnerability of the S&Ls—the leading institution in the postwar mortgage market—to inflation.

S&Ls ruled the postwar US mortgage market until the mid-1980s. (See Figure 3.1.) But the S&Ls had a particular vulnerability built into their method of financing mortgages. S&Ls, along with the other major institutional players in the mortgage market, commercial banks, and insurance companies, all financed mortgage loans through their balance sheets. This

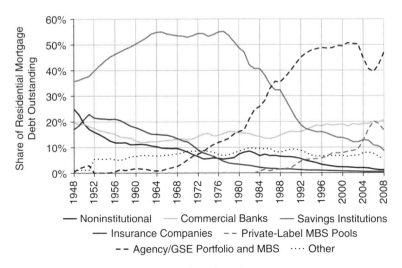

Figure 3.1. Residential Mortgage Market Share by Institution Type, 1948–2008

Data source: Bd. of Governors of the Fed. Reserve Sys., *Statistical Release Z.1, Financial Accounts of the United States*, tbls. L.218–219 (providing data for 1952–present); Leo Grebler *et al.*, *Capital Formation in Residential Real Estate: Trends and Prospects* 468–71, tbl.N-2 (1956) (data for 1948–1951).

means that these firms took consumer or business deposits (or insurance premia) and invested them by making mortgage loans. The mortgage loans remained on the institutions' books. The funding sources for S&Ls, commercial banks, and insurance companies were all potentially flighty, however. Deposits are often withdrawable on demand, and insurance policies can be canceled at will. If depositors or policyholders are concerned about an institution's solvency or can get a better deal elsewhere, they can readily move their business. This mismatch between the duration of these institutions' assets (long-term mortgages) and the duration of their liabilities (demand deposits and redeemable life insurance policies) meant that these institutions could readily find themselves in a bind whereby they lack the liquid funds to satisfy withdrawal and redemption requests.

As the United States experienced economic turmoil in the 1960s and 1970s, it became increasingly clear that the intermediation of housing finance through depository and insurance company balance sheets was vulnerable to disruption, which ultimately materialized in the S&L crisis of the 1980s. The increasing strains on the S&L industry from a mismatch between asset and liability durations set the stage for one of the most important developments in housing finance: securitization, a financing technique that enables securities markets, rather than bank deposits and insurance premia, to be the source of funding for mortgages. Securitizations are complicated transactions, and we will explore them in more detail in this chapter, but for now, it is only necessary to understand that they involve the issuance of bonds, the repayment of which comes from the payments on a discrete pool of mortgage loans.

Several distinct types of securitization emerged in the US housing finance market: Ginnie Mae, Fannie Mae, Freddie Mac, and "private-label" securitization. The differences are extremely important in our story, and we will delve into them in some detail. But from a big-picture view, it is also important to keep sight of the commonalities of securitization, namely, its potential benefits and risks.

There are three substantial benefits from securitization relative to balance-sheet financing. First, securitization potentially facilitates a much greater diversification of investment. Whereas an S&L is intensely exposed to the housing market in the local community in which it lends, a securitization can be backed by a diversified, nationwide pool of mortgages. Second, the funds invested in a securitization are locked in and not redeemable, so there is no risk of a mismatch between asset and liability durations. Third, securitization is amenable to "structuring," which is the allocation of risks to investors on something other than a pro-rated basis. Whereas all depositors rank equally with each other in terms of a claim on an S&L's assets, a securitization can be structured to give the claims of some investors priority over others (who are presumably compensated with a higher yield). This sort of structuring allows securitizations to capitalize on distinctions in investors' risk appetites.

At the same time, securitization poses a different set of risks than balance-sheet lending. Two of these risks are particularly important. First, securitizations are not diversified in terms of asset classes. Whereas a depository, even an S&L, would not make *solely* mortgage loans, a mortgage securitization is concentrated on a single asset class. Second, securitization is more heavily intermediated than balance-sheet lending, which opens the door to information asymmetries between the investors (who bear the risk) and the intermediaries. Intermediaries may attempt to capitalize on this information asymmetry to undercompensate investors for the risks they assume. Put another way, securitization is susceptible to moral hazard, as the intermediaries who arrange the securitization do not bear the risk of the performance of the securitization, unless they separately choose to guaranty it.

The remainder of this chapter explains how securitization evolved and replaced S&L balance-sheet lending as the dominant form of US mortgage finance. That transformation began in 1966, when the United States encountered its first postwar credit crisis.[1] The economy was expanding more rapidly than the Federal Reserve Board believed to be prudent, so the Fed took a series of actions that had the effect of raising market interest rates.[2] The problem was that prior to 1980, the interest rate that depository institutions could pay on all types of deposit accounts was also regulated by a Federal Reserve regulation (Reg Q).[3] Reg Q was designed to protect depositories from an interest rate mismatch between their short-term and demand deposit liabilities and their holdings of long-term fixed-rate mortgages by preventing them from competing on rates for deposits. Despite Reg Q, the innovation of money market mutual funds, which invested in commercial paper and competed for funds by offering higher interest rates, meant that an asset-liability mismatch for depositories was inevitable if the depositories were not to lose their deposit base.

The Fed refused to raise the Reg Q ceiling on interest rates payable by depositories on deposits to keep pace with the unregulated interest rates on commercial paper and Treasury securities.[4] As a result, capital flowed out from depository institutions into Treasury bonds ("Treasuries") and commercial paper, creating a capital shortage in the private market financed by bank loans.[5] This capital shortage in depositories hit large ticket items, like mortgage loans, the hardest, and mortgage originators found themselves without the resources to make new loans. As a later Federal Reserve chair noted, the "tightening of monetary policy in 1966 contributed to a 23% decline in residential construction between the first quarter of 1966 and the first quarter of 1967."[6] With global inflation, the banking industry's colloquial "3-6-3 rule"—"borrow from depositors at 3 percent, lend at 6 percent, and golf at 3 o'clock"—could no longer work, as money market funds offered rates far higher than 6 percent.

Despite the credit crunch, Fannie Mae continued to buy FHA/VA mortgages, which helped stabilize the housing market. Fannie's market share soared as a result, but its profitability suffered, and concerns arose about its future viability. In 1968, the Lyndon B. Johnson administration, which was eager to make room in the federal budget for Great Society spending and the Vietnam War,[7] split Fannie Mae into two entities.[8]

One entity, which continued to bear the name Fannie Mae (or Fanny May, as it was often called at the time), was privatized.[9] The newly privatized Fannie Mae continued to conduct secondary market activities, but at first it continued to buy only FHA/VA mortgages. The new Fannie Mae, under a revised federal charter, was privately capitalized but under government regulation, and with a third of its board of directors appointed by the president of the United States.[10] At the time, the Department of Housing and Urban Development (HUD) had to approve Fannie's securities issuance, and the HUD secretary had the authority to require Fannie to engage in mortgage purchases "related to the national goal of providing adequate housing for low and moderate income families, but with reasonable economic return to the corporation."[11] Thus, even while privatized, the federal government maintained a substantial degree of control over Fannie Mae.

Ginnie Mae and the Advent of Securitization

The other entity remained government-owned and was christened the Government National Mortgage Association, or "Ginnie Mae."[12] Ginnie Mae's mission was restricted to guarantying securities backed by FHA-insured and VA-guarantied mortgages.[13]

As noted above, the issuance of securities backed by discrete pools of assets is the essence of the financing technique known as securitization. Securitization is centered around segregating selected cash-flow-producing assets of a firm from the firm's liabilities and other assets. The separation of select cash-flow-producing assets enables investment based solely on the risks inherent in the selected cash flows, rather than in the total package of the firm's assets and liabilities.

This type of financing is often advantageous for both investors and borrowers. Investors can invest in a more targeted, bespoke package of risks than when investing in an operating firm, and, through securitization, borrowers may be able to raise capital at a lower cost than if they borrowed directly. For example, a firm with high-quality cash flows but significant liabilities can raise funds at costs set solely on the quality of the cash flows by segregating them and issuing securities against them. Thus, a petroleum company with excellent cash flows but major environmental liabilities might be able to borrow funds itself at BBB rates (available to the firms with the lowest investment grade credit quality), but it could raise funds more cheaply at AAA rates (available to the firms with the highest investment grade credit quality) through securitization of the cash flows.[14]

The details of securitization vary by asset class, but residential mortgage securitizations generally involve the pooling of mortgage loans by a financial institution. The financial institution will then sell the loans to a special-purpose entity, typically a trust, which will have no assets other than the transferred assets. Through the sale, the mortgage loans are legally isolated from those of the financial institution and thus shielded from claims of, or against, the financial institution. The trust will pay for the mortgage loans by issuing securities, which the financial institution will then sell into the market. The debt service on the securities (as well as the trust's administrative costs) is covered by the collections on the mortgages. To the extent that the cash flows from the trust's assets are insufficient to make the periodic payments on the securities, the investors do not have recourse against the financial institution, absent specific contractual arrangement. Only the payments on the mortgages to the trust back the securities. Accordingly, the securities are known as "mortgage-backed securities" (MBS).[15]

What Ginnie Mae adds to a securitization is a layer of secondary government insurance. If a transaction meets Ginnie Mae's requirements, Ginnie Mae will guaranty the timely payment of principal and interest on the MBS in exchange for a guaranty fee from the financial institution. Ginnie Mae is just a governmental monoline MBS insurer.

What are called Ginnie Mae MBS are not, in fact, securitized by Ginnie Mae, but rather by private financial institutions, pursuant to Ginnie Mae guidelines. In a Ginnie Mae securitization, a private financial institution originates or acquires a pool of FHA-insured or VA-sponsored mortgages. The financial institution then issues MBS backed by a designated "cover pool" of mortgages. The cover pool is not necessarily a legally separate entity, but simply a bunch of assets held by the issuer that are earmarked for providing payments on the MBS.[16] Indeed, Ginnie Mae MBS are not true securitizations, but really a type of "covered bond." Thus, the payments on the mortgages in the cover pool are designated for payment of the MBS.[17]

Unlike most MBS, Ginnie Mae MBS include full recourse to the issuer. The financial institution that undertakes a Ginnie Mae securitization is responsible for making principal and interest payments to the MBS investors on any delinquent loans, as well as to "repurchase" from the cover pool any loans that go into foreclosure or are modified or fail to comply with representations and warranties made by the issuer.[18] The issuer can turn around and attempt to recover the funds from the FHA or VA, but that may take time. Only if the issuer is insolvent does the Ginnie Mae guaranty kick in.[19] Figure 3.2 shows the general structure of a Ginnie Mae securitization.

Thus, in a Ginnie Mae securitization, there are several layers of capital. First, there is the homeowner's monthly mortgage payments. Next, there is the collateral securing that mortgage, followed by FHA/VA insurance. Then there is the securitizing financial institution, which is liable for any losses that exceed the FHA/VA insurance. Only if the securitizing financial institution itself fails is Ginnie Mae's guaranty triggered. Because Ginnie Mae plays only a remote role of guarantor and standard setter, it is an incredibly small government agency: in 2018, it had only 154 employees (up from 59 in 2009).[20]

The critical feature of a Ginnie Mae MBS is the presence of the Ginnie Mae guaranty, which functionally standardizes the securities, at least in terms of their credit risk profile. While Ginnie Mae has hundreds of issuers,

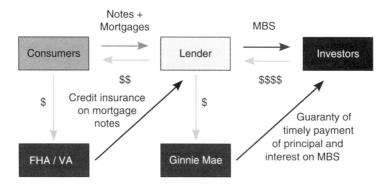

Figure 3.2. Ginnie Mae Securitization
Original creation by the authors.

their identity is irrelevant to investors because the investor assumes the credit risk of the US government.

It is important to see what a Ginnie Mae securitization adds to a loan that is already insured or guarantied by the FHA or VA. FHA insurance and VA guaranties do not promise *timely* payment; there can be a lag between the time of a default and the time an insurance payment is made. The benefit of the Ginnie Mae structure is that it guaranties MBS investors the *timely* payment of principal and interest on the bonds backed by the FHA-insured or VA-guarantied mortgages, whether by the homeowner, the financial institution that undertook the securitization, or Ginnie Mae itself. Thus, investors in Ginnie Mae MBS do not have to worry about disrupted payment streams because of mortgage defaults: the securitizing institution or Ginnie Mae will make up any shortfall on the mortgage payments and then look to recover on the mortgage insurance from FHA or VA. The result is a security with a completely reliable payment stream: credit and investment liquidity risks are eliminated for Ginnie Mae investors.

Ginnie Mae guaranteed its first securitization in 1970, in a securitization of $7.5 million in FHA-insured loans originated by Tower Mortgage.[21] Ginnie Mae's guaranty of timely payment transformed federally insured mortgages into highly liquid, federally insured securities. Ginnie Mae's provision of secondary market liquidity had the effect of lowering FHA borrowing rates by 60 to 80 basis points at a time when mortgage rates were 4–5 percent.[22] The market was willing to pay a substantial premium for the liquidity provided by bonds over insured whole loans.

Ginnie Mae was restricted to securitizing FHA/VA loans, but other parts of the mortgage market recognized the benefits of securitization and pushed for a securitization option for non-FHA/VA loans. Although Fannie Mae was authorized in 1968 to itself issue or guaranty MBS,[23] it did not do so until 1981, perhaps because leveraged financing of a portfolio, although riskier, was significantly more profitable than MBS.[24] Instead, the next advance in securitization required the creation of Freddie Mac, the second GSE.

The Creation of Freddie Mac

In 1969–1970, another market interest rate spike caused a further round of financial disintermediation. Still constrained by Reg Q, depositories were unable to offer competitive interest rates, and capital flowed out of them into rate-unconstrained investments. Moreover, as interest rates (and inflation) rose, home prices rose, and mortgages became less and less affordable.[25] Congress responded in 1970 with the Emergency Home Finance Act. The act authorized Fannie Mae to purchase conventional (non-FHA/VA) mortgages.[26]

The act also created another secondary market entity, the Federal Home Loan Mortgage Corporation, or Freddie Mac, which was similarly authorized to purchase conventional mortgages.[27] Freddie Mac began to purchase conventional mortgages in 1971, and Fannie began to do so in 1972.[28] In the early 1970s, FHA, Fannie, and Freddie also started to lower their down payment requirements to help support the housing market.[29]

The move to create a secondary market in conventional loans was an acknowledgment of the stresses of financial disintermediation on S&Ls. The FHLBs were concerned that they could not provide sufficient financing for the conventional mortgage market simply by rediscounting the S&Ls' loans.[30] Congress could have expanded Fannie Mae's mandate to include the conventional market, but Fannie Mae was viewed with suspicion by the S&Ls, which saw it as dominated by the interests of mortgage banks because of their FHA-insured business and unsympathetic to the concerns of S&Ls, which had traditionally avoided the FHA-insured market in which Fannie had operated.[31] The S&Ls, therefore, lobbied for their own secondary market organization under the aegis of the FHLB system, membership in which was, at the time, still limited to S&Ls.[32] Accordingly, Fannie Mae was given authority to deal in conventional mortgages, *and* Freddie Mac was created to do the same, but for S&Ls.

Thus, contrary to an oft-repeated claim, Freddie Mac was not created to generate competition for Fannie Mae, but rather to create a separate parallel market to serve a particular interest group. The story of Freddie Mac's creation was simply one of interest group politics, rather than of some compelling economic logic.

Freddie Mac was originally a subsidiary of the FHLB system. Freddie Mac was initially capitalized through a sale of nonvoting stock to the FHLBs, which were, in turn, owned by their member thrift institutions.[33] Freddie Mac was, therefore, not originally a publicly traded company, unlike post-1968 Fannie Mae. Instead, Freddie Mac was originally designed specifically to provide a secondary market for thrifts, enabling them to expand lending even when deposit growth slowed or declined.[34]

Although both Fannie and Freddie were authorized to issue MBS, as well as to hold loans in portfolio,[35] Freddie Mac originally operated quite differently from Fannie Mae. Through the 1970s, Fannie Mae held loans in portfolio, which it funded by issuing long-term bonds and short-term notes, but it did not undertake securitizations.

Freddie Mac, in contrast, was primarily as a securitization operation. Freddie Mac did not originally hold loans in portfolio, in order to avoid competing with the thrifts from which it bought mortgages (and which owned it indirectly). This difference meant that Fannie was exposed to both interest rate risk and credit risk, while Freddie only had credit risk.

Freddie Mac securitization operated differently from Ginnie Mae securitization. Whereas Ginnie Mae merely guarantied the MBS issued by qualified lenders, Freddie Mac would undertake the securitization itself. This meant that Freddie Mac would buy the mortgage loans from lenders. Freddie would then sell the mortgage loans to trusts it created and for which it served as trustee. The trusts would pay for the mortgage loans by issuing debt securities, repayment of which was backed by payment on the mortgages— hence, these were mortgage-backed securities. Freddie would then pay the lender either with the MBS (a "securities execution") or in cash (a "cash execution").

In a securities execution, as shown in Figure 3.3.a, the lender would then sell the securities to the public (or hold them itself), while in a cash execution, as shown in Figure 3.3.b, Freddie would sell the securities to the public (or hold them itself). In either case, Freddie Mac would guaranty timely payment of principal and interest on the MBS, such that Freddie Mac would hold all the credit risk on the mortgage loans, and the MBS investors would hold all the interest rate risk.

In a Freddie Mac securitization, the lender might continue its involvement in the securitization if it retained the servicing rights (selling on a "servicing retained" basis). Servicing rights are the rights to a servicing fee in exchange for day-to-day management of the loan, such as collecting payments and handling defaults. Alternatively, the lender might sell the loan on a "servicing released" basis, in which case Freddie Mac could sell the servicing rights separately to other servicers.

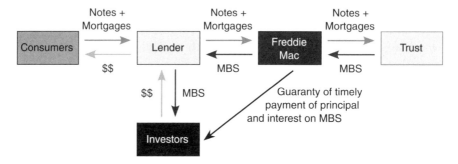

Figure 3.3.a. Freddie Mac Funding of Mortgages through Securitization (Securities Execution)

Original creation by the authors.

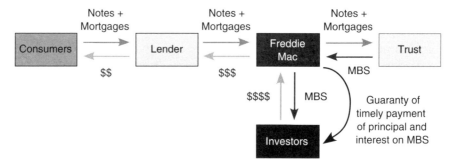

Figure 3.3.b. Freddie Mac Funding of Mortgages through Securitization (Cash Execution)

Original creation by the authors.

Freddie Mac created a secondary market for thrifts through the securitization of mortgages. Although Freddie Mac and Ginnie Mae securitizations were originally both guarantied pass-through MBS, there were significant differences. Ginnie Mae mortgages were securitizations of FHA/VA insured loans, while Freddie Mac securitized conventional mortgages.[36] Whereas Ginnie Mae merely guarantied that the MBS that were privately issued in accordance with Ginnie Mae guidelines, Freddie Mac would purchase the mortgages itself (but utilize third-party servicers, often the original lenders) and undertake the securitization itself. Ginnie Mae bears credit risk only through a secondary guaranty, such that it does not pay unless the issuer is insolvent. In contrast, Freddie Mac bears credit risk through a primary guaranty of timely payment of the principal and interest on the MBS, meaning that it covers all delinquent payments on its MBS. Thus, investors in Freddie Mac MBS assume the interest rate risk of a particular pool of securitized mortgages in which they invested as well as the overall credit risk of Freddie Mac, not of the mortgages. Finally, whereas the Ginnie Mae guaranty is formally backed by the full faith and credit of the US government, Freddie Mac's guaranty was not (and is not). Nor was it backed by the FHLB system and its members because Freddie Mac was a mere subsidiary of the FHLB system and limited liability law shielded the other assets of the FHLB system from claims against Freddie Mac.

As interest rates rose dramatically in 1974–1975 and 1979–1981, Fannie's long position on mortgage debt placed it under severe financial pressure.[37] Fannie had to finance itself at higher rates than the yield on the mortgages it held in portfolio.[38] Freddie Mac did not face this interest rate risk because it had no portfolio beyond what was in its securitization pipeline.

As a result of interest rate pressures, Fannie Mae began to engage in securitization in 1981.[39] In 1989 Freddie Mac was rechartered and privatized as part of a reform of the thrift industry and its regulation. Once Freddie Mac was privatized, the Fannie and Freddie models converged, with Fannie undertaking securitizations that are analogous to those of Freddie, and Freddie issuing corporate debt to finance mortgages that it held in portfolio. Still, it is important to recall that Fannie and Freddie began with different business models.[40]

The critical move presented by both Fannie and Freddie (the government-sponsored enterprises, or GSEs) was the division of credit risk from interest rate risk. Investors in the GSEs' MBS assumed interest rate risk on the securitized mortgages, but not credit risk on them. Instead, they assumed the GSEs' credit risk, which was implicitly backed by the federal government. Similarly, investors in GSE corporate debt were really investing in interest rate risk plus an implied government security.

Congress's goal in creating secondary market institutions that were authorized to deal in conventional mortgages was to create a marketable, standardized conventional mortgage instrument.[41] Thus, the standardization move that began in the government-owned or government-guaranteed mortgage market spread to the conventional mortgage market. Notably, however, while there was a standardization of mortgages, there was no standardization of MBS; it was in the interest of Fannie and Freddie to have noninterchangeable MBS, as product differentiation rationalized the existence of two separate entities, enabling some competition. Indeed, until the June 2019 implementation of the Uniform MBS structure, under regulatory directive, Fannie Mae and Freddie Mac MBS were not a good delivery for each other in the forward contract market, because they had different payment schedules, among other things.[42]

The creation of a robust secondary market for non-FHA/VA mortgages, under the then-privatized Fannie Mae and the eventually privatized Freddie Mac, appreciably loosened regulatory control over housing finance. The significance of this deregulation through privatization was not immediately apparent because numerous constraints on underwriting still existed in the mortgage market in the 1970s, but it set the stage for later developments in the 2000s, when market pressures and further deregulation loosened the remaining constraints on mortgage underwriting.

The privatization of Fannie Mae and Freddie Mac meant that their management would be subject to pressure from shareholders, who were not particularly concerned with the policy goals embodied in the GSEs. The privatized GSEs were subject to some command-and-control regulation. They were required to maintain minimum capital levels of 2.5 percent for on-balance-sheet obligations and .45 percent for off-balance-sheet obligations.[43] The GSEs' loan purchases were also subject to single exposure limitations (conforming loan limits) and LTV limitations absent mortgage insurance.[44] Generally, however, underwriting was left up to the GSEs, which chose to purchase only prime, conventional, conforming mortgages, and which were subject only to loose supervision by the Federal Home Loan Bank Board until 1992, and then by the Office of Federal Housing Enterprise Oversight (OFHEO) until 2008. The potential menu of loans that the GSEs could purchase was also impacted by what was possible in the loan origination market, so the GSEs were in effect also constrained by state and federal regulation of the primary market.

The Changing Face of the Mortgage Origination Market

The mortgage origination market changed significantly in the postwar years. While a range of secondary market institutions had been developed during the New Deal, they still played a relatively small role in the mortgage market prior to the 1980s. Most mortgages were still held either by their originators or by institutional lenders that worked through origination agents.[45] While secondary market institutions were able to provide liquidity and stability to the market, they were seldom used between the Depression and the late 1960s, except during a brief window in the late 1940s. As Figure 3.1 shows, the market share of Ginnie Mae, Fannie Mae, and Freddie Mac (collectively listed as Agency/Government Sponsored Enterprises Portfolios & MBS) was negligible until the late 1960s, and it was only in the 1980s that their market share soared from under 20 percent to 50 percent. The main effect of the GSEs prior to the 1980s was to provide assurance of liquidity—if the market needed it.

Even before the secondary market took off, other changes were occurring in the institutional makeup of the mortgage market. Noninstitutional lenders largely disappeared from the mortgage market in the postwar years.[46] While the market was becoming increasingly institutionalized prior to World War II, the FHLB's membership restrictions, the FHA's restriction on insurance endorsements to institutional lenders, and Fannie Mae's refusal to deal with noninstitutional parties drove the individual mortgage lender out of the market.

The makeup of institutional lenders also changed. While today one might think of "banks" as being the primary mortgage lenders, the term "bank" covers a broad range of financial institutions with varying business models and regulation. Most important for our purposes are the differences among commercial banks (whether state- or federally chartered), S&Ls and other savings institutions (collectively "thrifts"), and mortgage banks (also known as "mortgage companies" or "nonbanks"). Today the US financial landscape overall (and especially in consumer finance) is dominated by large commercial banks, but historically commercial banks were limited players in residential mortgage lending, not least because of legal limitations on their investment in home mortgages.[47] Instead, S&Ls and mortgage banks dominated the postwar mortgage origination market. (Refer back to Figure 3.1.)

S&Ls and mortgage banks had very different business models and market specializations. S&Ls were originally associations of savers in a single geographic area who banded their money together to invest in home purchase and home construction loans to each other.[48] The S&L business model, then, was to originate loans and retain them on their books, making a profit on the spread between what they paid their depositors for funds and what they earned on their mortgage investments.[49]

Mortgage banks, in contrast, largely emerged with the development of FHA/VA insurance/guaranties. They originated insured loans with the goal of selling them into the secondary market, either to Fannie Mae or to other institutional investors, like life insurance companies,[50] while retaining the servicing.[51] The mortgage banks were the original originate-to-distribute business model. Because the mortgage banks did not retain the credit risk on the mortgages they originated, they do not appear as a large part of the market in Figure 3.1, which reflects the levels of titular holders of mortgages at the time of reporting rather than flows of mortgages.

Given the mortgage banks' reliance on FHA/VA insurance to cover credit risk, they focused primarily on the FHA/VA market, while the S&Ls led the conventional mortgage market.[52] Thus, there was essentially a bifurcation of the origination side of the mortgage market, which mapped onto the secondary market side as well. The S&Ls originated conventional loans and obtained liquidity through the FHLBs. Because of interstate branch banking restrictions, their lending remained highly localized, leaving them exposed to local credit conditions. The mortgage banks, in contrast, originated FHA/VA loans and obtained liquidity through Fannie Mae, which tapped into national credit markets. Commercial banks and rapidly disappearing noninstitutional lenders rounded out the postwar origination market. (Refer back to Figure 3.1.)

The S&L Crisis

While securitization emerged in the 1970s, the mortgage market was still dominated by balance-sheet lending by S&Ls. As Figure 3.1, shows, from the late 1940s to the late 1970s, S&Ls reigned supreme in the US mortgage market. At their height, S&Ls held 55 percent of the residential mortgage loans outstanding. The first half of this period was one of relative stability in US housing finance markets and saw the massive suburbanization of the nation.[53]

The S&Ls, however, were unequipped to handle rising interest rates in the late 1960s and especially the 1970s. As rates rose with inflation, depositors sought rates of return that kept pace with inflation. Reg Q continued to restrict the interest rates that depositories could pay, and the advent of money market instruments[54] had resulted in a tremendous disintermediation from the depository system into the securities system.

Congress and federal regulators responded to this problem through deregulation of the S&Ls. Prior to the 1980s, the S&Ls were still subject to a battery of command-and-control regulations in addition to Reg Q. State-chartered S&Ls were subject to state regulations. The Home Owners Loan Act was interpreted as preempting state regulations for federal thrifts,[55] but the FHLBB had its own set of command-and-control regulations that limited the type of products S&Ls could originate.

In 1980, as part of the Depository Institutions Deregulation and Monetary Control Act (DIDMCA),[56] Congress revoked the Federal Reserve Board's authority to regulate the interest rate on nondemand deposits (with a six-year phaseout). Freed from Reg Q, the S&Ls began to offer ever-higher interest rates on deposits in order to retain their deposit base in the face of disintermediation. The S&Ls' assets, however, were long-term, fixed-rate mortgage loans. The result of paying higher interest rates on liabilities than those received on assets was the decapitalization of the S&Ls.

Congress attempted to address S&L decapitalization by enabling the S&Ls to invest in higher-yielding asset classes in addition to residential mortgages ("direct investment rules") and by enabling the S&Ls to engage in mortgage lending at higher interest rates. The direct investment rules allowed S&Ls to invest in assets with *potentially* higher yields than home mortgages, thereby offering the possible relief of their borrowing-return mismatch.[57] Also as part of DIDMCA, Congress abolished all interest rate ceilings set by state law on first-lien mortgage loans on residences and mobile homes, as well as limitations on points, broker and closing fees, and other closing costs.[58] FHA regulations had historically limited insurance eligibility to loans with an interest rates (exclusive of the insurance premium) below a cap that had varied between 4 and 5 percent.[59] This meant that the riskiest mortgages had a de facto national usury rate that was well below most states' usury caps. FHA's authority to restrict interest rates as an eligibility criteria was repealed in 1983, however.[60] The effect of the repeal, combined with DIDMCA, meant that there was no restriction on the rates of first-lien mortgages.[61]

Continuing the deregulation of the home mortgage market, Congress passed legislation in 1982 that preempted state laws prohibiting adjustable-rate mortgages, balloon payments and negative amortization.[62] The 1982 legislation further prohibited "due-on-sale" clauses in mortgages, which had prohibited second mortgages absent the first mortgagee's permission.[63] The FHLBB also rewrote its regulations for federal thrifts, allowing them to underwrite adjustable-rate mortgages.[64] These actions were all intended to revitalize the S&L industry by enabling S&Ls to lend more confidently in an environment of rapidly rising interest rates. Their effects reached further because the state regulation of interest rates, adjustable-rate mortgages, balloon payments, and negative amortization had the effect of limiting aggressive mortgage lending to riskier borrowers who could not handle the payments on a traditional 30-year fixed-rate, fully amortized mortgage. The preemption of state mortgage regulation ultimately paved the way for the nontraditional mortgage products that were the hallmark of the housing bubble in the 2000s.

In the short term, however, the deregulation of the S&Ls resulted in a different disaster, namely, the collapse of the S&L industry. In trying to fix one problem—the S&Ls' mismatch of asset and liability duration—Congress opened the door to another one—S&Ls chasing yield in markets in which they lacked experience. Freed of regulatory constraints, the decapitalized S&Ls doubled down on their bets and expanded into new and often ill-advised asset classes: commercial real estate, junk bonds, race horses, and so forth. As a result, many S&Ls found themselves insolvent and failed. The implosion of the S&L industry set the stage for the next chapter in American housing finance, the ascendancy of the GSEs.

CHAPTER FOUR

The Boom and the Bubble

THIS CHAPTER TELLS the story of how Fannie Mae and Freddie Mac came to dominate the US mortgage market in the wake of the S&L crisis and how so-called "private-label securitization"—securitization by Wall Street banks—emerged to briefly displace Fannie and Freddie and, in the process, fuel a housing bubble.

Although secondary market institutions had existed in the US mortgage market since the 1930s, they played a relatively small role until the 1980s. Instead, mortgages were still financed primarily through depository balance sheets. This was important because depositories were heavily regulated in terms of their safety and soundness. The collapse of the S&L industry in the 1980s resulted in agency securitization becoming the dominant financing channel for mortgages in the United States.

While Fannie and Freddie were private entities by the 1980s, they were still subject to the limitations of their special charters, which included constraints on their underwriting and a dedicated, if ineffectual, regulator. While there was no longer a strong regulatory hand on the secondary mortgage market, as there had been when Fannie was a governmental entity and FHA had a de facto usury cap, the nature of the Fannie/Freddie duopoly kept underwriting standards, and hence mortgage market risk, in check. Fannie and Freddie had little reason to stretch their underwriting standards because in a duopoly, there would be no long-term gains in market share from doing so; if Fannie lowered its underwriting standards,

Freddie could readily match it, and vice versa. The duopoly enabled a tacit agreement to avoid a destructive race to the bottom in underwriting standards to gain market share. While Fannie and Freddie were both subject to political pressure regarding underwriting, the pressure was in the form of targeted results—that is, the percentage of mortgages purchased for affordable housing, and so on—rather than in the form of specific underwriting directives. This enabled Fannie and Freddie to seek the safest ways of achieving their politically dictated targets, and it did not open the door to further declines in underwriting.

As long as Fannie and Freddie maintained their duopoly, there was a natural check on risk in the housing finance market, even though it was being done through duopolistic market power rather than command-and-control regulation. Fannie and Freddie lost their duopoly, however, in the years following the implosion of the Internet bubble in 2001. Low interest rates following the bubble's collapse produced the largest wave of refinancings ever seen. These refinancings were traditional 30-year fixed-rate mortgages (FRMs) funded through Fannie and Freddie. But they were followed by a marked shift in the housing market away from the 30-year fixed to nontraditional mortgage products, financed through private-label securitization. The rise of private-label securitization undid the Fannie-Freddie duopoly and set off a race to the bottom in underwriting standards as Wall Street banks sought to gain market share in the lucrative securitization market. This looser underwriting unleashed a glut of easy mortgage credit that allowed borrowers to bid up housing prices, setting off the bubble.

The ARM Experiment

In the previous chapter we saw how the S&Ls collapsed in the face of rising interest rates: the S&Ls had large books of long-term FRMs but flighty funding from demand deposits, which could be withdrawn on short notice. In order to retain their deposit bases, the S&Ls had to offer ever higher rates of interest, even above that generated on their assets. The result was that the they became decapitalized and pursued ever riskier investments in an attempt to earn their way back to solvency.

The primary lesson from the S&L crisis was that depositories were poorly suited for making long-term fixed-rate loans. Instead, they could either make adjustable-rate loans or sell their loans into the secondary market. While adjustable-rate loans had long been impossible to make given regulatory limits, that situation began to change. Regulatory restrictions on

ARMs were removed between 1979 and 1981,[1] and by 1982, ARMs accounted for 40 percent of all mortgage originations, a percentage that rose to 68 percent of mortgage originations by August 1984.[2] The market share for ARMs then fell as interest rates fell, but it again rose in 1987–1989, peaking at 69 percent of originations in 1987.[3] The proportion of ARMs as a share of outstanding mortgage debt rose as well, comprising just 9 percent of all residential debt at the end of 1983, but rising to 20 percent by 1985 and estimated at 25 percent in 1990.[4]

Notably, as soon as the regulatory carapace was lifted to permit ARMs, lenders started to advertise ARMs with "teaser rates"—lower initial fixed rates, followed by adjustment to an indexed rate.[5] While the interest rates on fully indexed ARMs were not significantly lower (on a non-option-adjusted basis) than FRMs, the spread between the teaser rates and FRMs made them very attractive to borrowers, both in the first ARM boom, in 1982–1983, and then in the second boom, in 1987–1989.[6] The ARM with a teaser rate was functionally a return to the pre-Depression bullet loan, as borrowers would seek to refinance on the expiration of the short teaser rate, much like the bullet loan borrower's need to constantly roll over or refinance the loan.

The immediate emergence of teaser-rate ARMs following deregulation suggests that when left to its own devices the market will produce some version of the bullet loan rather than the American mortgage. Indeed, outside the United States, adjustable-rate products, often with short-term fixed teaser periods, are the prevailing mortgage product.[7] At the same time, the fact that lenders needed to market ARMs with teaser rates indicates that American consumers have shown a strong taste for FRMs precisely because of their myriad benefits for household finances: a fixed, predictable monthly payment, forced savings, and protection against inflation and gentrification. These teaser rates are essentially a bet on whether enough consumers are sufficiently financially able and savvy to refinance into a fixed-rate mortgage when interest rates rise.

While many factors affect the market share of ARMs,[8] there is also a strong consumer taste for fixed-rate loans, around which they can budget.[9] This meant that there was always market demand for FRMs. Demand for FRMs plus the lessons of the S&L crisis fueled the rapid growth of the secondary market, which, in the 1980s consisted primarily of the government-sponsored enterprises (GSEs).[10]

Fixed-rate lending had previously prevailed worldwide, but inflationary pressures in the 1970s caused a shift to adjustable-rate lending. The United States started down that path in the 1980s, but reversed course due to the

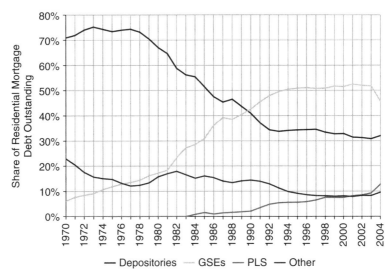

Figure 4.1. Residential Mortgage Market Share by Institution Type, 1970–2004

Data source: Bd. of Governors of the Fed. Reserve Sys., *Statistical Release Z.1, Financial Accounts of the United States*, tbl. L.218. "Depositories" consists of the sum of lines 11 through 14 (series FL763065105, FL753065103, FL743065103, and FL473065100). "GSEs" consists of the sum of lines 18 and 19 (series FL403065105 and FL413065105). "PLS" is line 20 (series FL673065105). "Other" consists of the difference between line 5 (series FL893065105) and the sum of Depositories, GSEs, and PLS.

rise of the GSEs, which assumed the interest rate risk that depositories were ill-equipped to handle. As Figure 4.1 shows, the market share of depository institutions fell from around 75 percent of the market in the late 1970s to around 33 percent of the market by the 1990s. Almost all the decline in the depositories' market share was mirrored by a gain in market share for the GSEs, which rose from around 15 percent to around 50 percent during this period.

The shift of interest rate risk to the GSEs relieved depositories of the need to engage in large-scale adjustable-rate lending. Instead, they could cater to the strong consumer taste for fixed-rate loans. The result was the heyday of the GSEs and a rebirth of the American Mortgage.

Fannie and Freddie Ascendant

As the S&Ls faded, the GSEs became the dominant player in the mortgage market. In 1980, the S&Ls were 49 percent of the mortgage market, while the GSEs were a mere 16 percent, but the S&Ls were rapidly losing market share while the GSEs were expanding.[11] The GSEs overtook the S&Ls in

1987, and by 1995, the situation was completely flipped: S&L market share was down to 16 percent and the GSEs had over 48 percent of the market.[12] Fannie and Freddie continued to dominate the mortgage market until 2003, when the market shifted to private-label securitization (PLS) with the onset of the bubble.[13]

The GSE ascendancy was a period of stability in the mortgage market that saw a substantial growth in homeownership. After stagnating in the 1980s and first half of the 1990s, homeownership began to rise again as the mortgage market moved to the GSEs. Overall homeownership was 64 percent in 1985, the year the GSEs became the dominant players in the mortgage market. It remained at that level until 1995, when it began a rise to a high of 69 percent in 2004, the year after the GSE's market share peaked.[14] The gains in homeownership were shared by white and black homeowners alike. White homeownership rates rose from 70 percent in 1995 to 76 percent in 2004,[15] while black homeownership rates rose from 42 percent in 1985 to 49 percent in 2004.[16] (Refer back to Figure 2.7.)

Multiple factors contributed to the increase in homeownership from the mid-1990s until the end of the GSE ascendancy. First, in 1993, HUD set Affordable Housing Goals for Fannie and Freddie, which encouraged the GSEs to seek out more low- to moderate-income and minority borrowers.[17] Second, Fannie and Freddie engaged in substantial outreach, particularly to minority communities. In this effort, Fannie and Freddie would sponsor job fairs and community events and partner with minority community development financial institutions. Finally, and most importantly, Fannie and Freddie each adopted automated underwriting technology (Desktop Underwriter and Loan Prospector, respectively) in 1995, and strongly encouraged its use by mortgage lenders who wished to sell them loans.[18]

Traditionally, each originator did its own underwriting pursuant to guidelines issued by Fannie and Freddie, but the originator had a lot of discretion in the process, which could set the stage for discrimination by loan originators. At the same time, originators tended to rely on "hard" factors of the three "Cs"—capacity (for example, debt-to-income ratios), collateral (for example, loan-to-value ratios), and credit (for example, credit scores).[19] Yet risk can be layered within these factors, and the interaction among the different variables that contribute to each factor can rapidly exceed human analytical capacity.[20] In particular, whether a certain combination of strengths in a borrower's loan application compensate against other weaknesses can be nearly impossible for an individual human underwriter to determine with statistical accuracy. Moreover, because traditional underwriting is dependent on humans' subjective judgment, it is susceptible to the biases of the underwriters, who are often able to directly observe the applicants and thus perceive their race or ethnicity.

Automated underwriting substituted a standardized computer algorithm for individual originators' disparate human underwriting methods. This early application of "Big Data" was able to draw on statistical analysis of past mortgage performance of enormous volumes of mortgage loans to analyze millions of possible risk combinations.[21] This enabled the use of compensating factors in underwriting that allowed Fannie and Freddie to qualify borrowers who would not have previously been able to get a loan.

Because the underwriting was automated, it removed both subjective human judgment and direct observation of the applicant's appearance, and thus reduced the likelihood of discrimination in the underwriting process. To be sure, the possibility of unintended discrimination through proxy variables remained, and to the extent that current wealth and income reflect past discrimination, a certain level of discrimination is inherently baked into the underwriting algorithms.

Automated underwriting also substantially lowered closing costs and sped up the underwriting process.[22] Lower closing costs are particularly important for promoting homeownership for lower-income households, as funds that would normally be spent on closing can instead be committed with significant leverage, to purchase prices. Likewise, a faster underwriting process reduces uncertainty from the mortgage-borrowing decision, enabling greater certainty and efficiency in the home sale market. In short, GSE automated underwriting was the original iteration of financial technology that enabled an expansion of the borrower base based on nontraditional underwriting factors.

Critically, the lending that Fannie and Freddie financed through their automated underwriting was primarily in the form of fully underwritten 30-year fixed-rate mortgages. While Fannie and Freddie were able to expand mortgage credit to traditionally underserved populations, they did so with a sustainable product, and not surprisingly, even though foreclosure rates increased, they remained low in absolute terms throughout the GSE ascendancy, despite the expansion of credit.[23] To be sure, there was a small amount of subprime lending concentrated in minority urban communities, but that was a separate phenomenon that was financed primarily by subprime finance companies and some early PLS, not by the GSEs.

No bubble resulted from the expansion of credit in the late 1990s, both because it was consistent with a shift in fundamentals enabled by new technology and because it was limited in volume. Some of these mortgages were refinanced into nontraditional products in the bubble years of the 2000s (often with cash out refinancings), but the key point is that Fannie and Freddie sustainably expanded mortgage credit, including to more marginal borrowers, in the second half of the 1990s.

The late 1990s expansion of credit was in no small part dependent on the secondary market's highly centralized structure. Automated underwriting required a substantial degree of standardization in the underwriting process, including in terms of data collection. This standardization and implementation of new technology would have been difficult to coordinate and fund but for the centralized GSE secondary market. The centralization of the secondary market gave Fannie and Freddie the market power necessary to facilitate the adoption of technological improvements that individual mortgage lenders might have otherwise resisted or at least taken longer to adopt. A more diffuse secondary market would have found it more difficult to push for the adoption of new technology and standards.

A major downside to this new technology was that the automated underwriting algorithms assumed housing prices would be unchanged by the expansion of credit that the technology enabled. In other words, the automated underwriting did not account for the endogeneity between credit terms and housing prices. Because the expansion of credit in the adoption period was limited, there was no major destabilizing impact on housing prices, and the credit box was widened to successfully expand homeownership. The successful expansion of credit in the late 1990s may have led some to believe that credit availability could be further expanded without adverse consequences, and as the scale of credit expansion increased during the bubble years through the PLS financing channel, the lack of recognition of the link between credit conditions and housing prices would come to haunt the housing market.

The Agency Securitization Market

Fannie and Freddie finance their mortgage purchases both through their corporate balance sheets and through securitization. Until the early 1990s, Fannie financed mortgages primarily through its balance sheet, whereas Freddie engaged primarily in securitization. Since the early 1990s, however, their business models converged, as did their once-distinct clienteles of mortgage banks and thrifts, respectively.

Fannie and Freddie balance-sheet financing involves funding mortgage purchases by issuing corporate debt, whose proceeds are used to purchase mortgages. This sort of balance-sheet funding posed the inverse duration risk to the S&Ls' balance-sheet funding. Whereas the S&Ls were funding long-term assets with short-term debt, the GSEs were historically issuing substantial amounts of noncallable debt, so the duration of their debt obligations could exceed that of the fully prepayable mortgages.[24] Therefore, the GSEs faced the risk that in a market with falling interest rates, the interest rate on their debt could exceed the rate they earned on their mortgage investments.

GSE securitization involves the GSE first purchasing mortgage loans from financial institutions sellers that have either originated the loans themselves or aggregated loans from smaller originators.[25] The GSE then transfers pools of these mortgages to legally separate, specially created trusts, which pay the GSE for the mortgages by issuing MBS.[26] The GSE guaranties the timely payment of principal and interest on the MBS to investors, just as Ginnie Mae does for Ginnie Mae MBS.[27] GSE MBS, together with Ginnie Mae MBS, are known as "Agency" MBS.

The defining feature of Agency MBS is that the credit risk on the securitized mortgages is held by Fannie, Freddie, or Ginnie, while investors assume the interest rate risk on the mortgages. This is not to say that there is no credit risk for investors in Agency MBS, but the credit risk they assume is primarily the credit risk of the GSEs (or of the U.S. government, for Ginnie Mae MBS), not that of the homeowners. Secondarily, however, for GSE MBS, investors also indirectly assume the credit risk on the mortgages because the GSEs' financial strength is heavily dependent upon the performance of the mortgages, but this risk is offset by the federal government's implicit guaranty of the GSEs.

The Financialization of Housing

The rise of securitization via the GSEs had a critical secondary effect: the financialization of housing, meaning that housing became a financial asset. A single mortgage loan, by itself, is a relatively illiquid investment. It is a concentrated risk exposure on a single borrower that is also exposed to interest rate risk and geographically and serially correlated asset prices movements. The single mortgage loan cannot be readily shorted, so there is no price discovery or market arbitrage.

Yet when mortgage loans are bundled together in securitizations, they become financial instruments that can be traded, arbitraged, and speculated on, by both longs and shorts. Securitization turned housing into a financial asset. The implicit US government guaranty of the GSEs added an imprimatur of safety to MBS as an asset class, as did the potential geographic diversification of the underlying mortgages, both of which protected investors from concentrated exposure to the regional housing markets. Not only did MBS become a major investment class themselves, but their apparent stability meant that they also began to be used as collateral by financial institutions and investors who were seeking to borrow funds. Housing debt became almost cash-like in its liquidity.

The financialization of housing was not limited to housing becoming a capital market asset. Housing also became monetizable for consumers, who were able to tap their home equity with cash-out refinancings and home equity lines of credit. Cash-out refinancings and home equity lines of credit make it possible for consumers to transform housing wealth into cash without having to sell the property, which would both impose substantial transaction costs and require the consumer to find alternative shelter. The ability to transform housing wealth into cash without selling the property makes housing a leveraged *financial* investment.

Indeed, housing became the *only* major leveraged investment class available to consumers. Consumers can purchase securities on margin—that is, on credit—but margin rules limit consumers' leverage to 50 percent,[28] meaning that they must pay at least 50 percent of the purchase price of the securities. Moreover, when securities' prices fall, the consumer may face a margin call—a requirement to pay more so as to limit the lender's exposure, so the consumer must have sufficient liquidity to meet the margin call. This risk of a margin call further limits consumers' effective leverage, by limiting their borrowing. Housing, in contrast, can readily be purchased with only 20 percent down, and frequently with much lower (or no) down payments. Additionally, a drop in home prices does not trigger a margin call.

If a consumer is looking to monetize housing most effectively, the best way to do so is to maximize leverage. Any increase in the property's value accretes to the consumer, who can cash it out, while a decrease in the property's value is only a loss to the consumer to the extent that he or she has paid money down or made subsequent mortgage payments. If the property value declines, the consumer can simply walk away from the property and allow the lender to foreclose. To be sure, the consumer is often liable for any deficiency resulting from the foreclosure, as most mortgage loans are formally recourse loans, but limitations on wage garnishment, the possibility of bankruptcy, and statutes of limitations make it hard for lenders to collect such unsecured deficiencies. Thus, the consumer effectively has a put option on the house, with the strike price comprising the down payment plus subsequent payments made.

With such a put option, the rational move for a consumer is to maximize leverage. Borrowers may choose to execute this option if the price of the home drops beneath the mortgage value. The upside of the invest-ment will be the consumer's, and the downside will be the lender's, but with downside externalities on neighboring properties and the community. A foreclosure will exert downward pressure on nearby housing prices, af-fecting municipal tax bases and possibly imposing direct costs on the mu-nicipal tax base if the foreclosed property becomes a public health or public safety problem. As it turns out, for reasons we will discuss later, in the event of price declines, borrowers do not typically exercise this option, yet the option exists.

Another financial option imbedded in the American Mortgage is the refi option, because when interest rates fall, borrowers can refinance at lower rates without a penalty. This is an option that borrowers generally do pursue. Moreover, with mortgage rates tied to global interest rates, any substantial change in interest rates impacts housing markets because they are inte-grated with financial markets. Indeed, investors in mortgage securities de-mand a globally determined yield on the securities they purchase to compen-sate for the risks that they perceive, and that yield will, in turn, determine the interest rates on mortgage loans. The market-clearing yield can change minute by minute. Such changes in yield, and hence mortgage rates, impact housing costs for new borrowers with FRMs and all borrowers with ARMs, with feedback effects on the overall economy through the changing costs of homeownership to households.

The financialization of housing for both investors and consumers did not happen immediately following the entry of the GSEs into the market. It was a process that took time, but it fundamentally transformed the nature of housing, tying it to financial markets, such that it was both exposed to shocks in financial markets and could provide the shock to those markets both directly and through the consumer spending channel. The full impact of these changes would not be felt until the de facto regulation of securiti-zation became undone. As long as lending standards were set by the GSEs and FHA/VA, as opposed to markets, and rates moved in parallel with Treasuries, the volatility of mortgage rates and terms was limited.

GSEs as Market Setters

Because of the GSEs' dominance in the secondary market, the terms on which Fannie and Freddie were willing to purchase mortgages set the terms for much of the primary mortgage market. Fannie and Freddie's under-writing standards for loan purchases were de facto underwriting standards for mortgage origination. Thus, Fannie and Freddie generally mandated the use of their standardized mortgage documentation for loans that were to be eligible for purchase.[29] They also refused to purchase loans with credit scores of under 660 on the same terms as those with higher scores.[30] The 660 credit score became the de facto subprime cutoff (although 620 later emerged as a standard, and later still, in the aftermath of the financial crisis, 700 has become the new normal). Similarly, Fannie and Freddie's refusal in 2004 to purchase mortgages with binding mandatory arbitration clauses meant that these clauses remained generally absent in mortgages, even as they proliferated in other consumer financial products.[31]

Nor was Fannie and Freddie's market-setting role limited to underwriting standards per se. It also extended to the embrace of automated underwriting models and the use of credit scores in mortgage underwriting, just as the valuation methods pioneered by HOLC and FHA had, decades earlier, become the market standard.

During the 1990s and early 2000s, Fannie and Freddie generally maintained underwriting standards for the mortgages they were willing to purchase. Because the GSEs bore the credit risk on the mortgages, they were incentivized to insist on careful underwriting.[32] Moreover, because of their effective duopoly, they had little incentive to lower underwriting standards to gain market share. Any move made by one could be quickly matched by the other, resulting greater risk without any gain in market share. Accordingly, competition between Fannie and Freddie was less on price than on service to financial institutions from which they bought loans.

The duopoly status, as much as anything, held mortgage credit risk in check during the GSEs' ascendancy. There were only two noteworthy statutory restrictions on Fannie and Freddie's underwriting: (1) the conforming loan limit, which restricted the size of the mortgage loans that the GSEs could purchase, and (2) the requirement of private mortgage insurance (or recourse to the seller) for mortgages with loan to value ratios (LTVs) of over 80 percent.[33] Fannie and Freddie were never subject to statutory restrictions on borrower credit quality or other underwriting features.

The conforming loan limit and LTV limit both had an effect of limiting the formation of bubbles. Because the conforming loan limit was likely to lag behind any rapid housing price appreciation, it meant that housing markets could only overheat by a significant degree if there was a financing channel available beside the GSEs. Likewise, the LTV limit meant that if borrowers wanted to bid up housing prices by incurring greater leverage, they would have to pay private mortgage insurance premia, which would increase the cost of borrowing and thus reduce the ability to bid up prices. Again, this limit only mattered if the GSEs were the only financing channel.

Although Fannie and Freddie were not statutorily required to have other underwriting criteria, their duopoly status enabled them to maintain such criteria as a prudential matter, and they generally refused to purchase loans from borrowers with poor credit quality or loans that were not fully amortized or had teaser rates.

While there were few formal requirements for Fannie and Freddie underwriting standards, their own prudential limitations on underwriting shaped the market. GSE "regulation" through underwriting standards were not the only limitation on the terms they obtained in the mortgage market. GSE underwriting was layered on top of other federal or state mortgage regulation. The federal Home Owners Equity Protection Act (HOEPA) of 1994 created a number of protections for borrowers of certain high-cost mortgages.[34] Additionally, although many state regulations had been preempted in the early 1980s by the federal Depository Institutions Deregulation and Monetary Control Act of 1980 and the Alternative Mortgage Transaction Parity Act of 1982, states still had some ability to regulate mortgage lenders, and some enacted their own mini-HOEPA anti-predatory lending statutes. As long as these direct regulations of the mortgage market were in place, Fannie and Freddie could be assured of a certain minimum quality of any mortgages they purchased. Further regulatory changes in the 1990s and 2000s, however, undermined what was left of the state mortgage regulation structure on which Fannie and Freddie's underwriting standards piggybacked, and left the mortgage market vulnerable to a disruption of the GSE duopoly that prevented competition on underwriting standards.

Deregulation via Preemption

Between 1996 and 2007, federal banking regulators pursued a single-minded campaign of deregulation via preemption, unraveling both state consumer protection laws and state attempts to enforce federal laws.[35] This campaign included both preemption via regulation (arguably exceeding the federal agencies' statutory authority) and via litigation. The litigation culminated in the Supreme Court's 2007 ruling in *Watters v. Wachovia*, which upheld the Office of the Comptroller of the Currency's preemption of Michigan's attempt to regulate a subprime lender that was an unregulated operating subsidiary of a national bank.[36]

At the same time that federal banking regulators were blocking states from regulating mortgage lending, the federal regulators refused to enforce the powers they had. Federal banking regulators brought only a handful of enforcement actions under their power to prosecute "unfair and deceptive acts and practices" during the entire period from 1990 until 2006, and almost never on issues involving mortgages.[37] Even when Congress directed regulators to take action, they did not. In 1994, in response to concerns about predatory lending (which was then a more limited problem), Congress passed HOEPA, which prohibited certain predatory lending practices for certain "high-cost" refinancing loans.[38] The act regulated balloon payments, negative amortization, postdefault interest rates, prepayment penalties, due-on-demand clauses, lending without regard to the borrower's ability to repay, and payments to home improvement contractors.[39] It also required special additional Truth in Lending disclosures and counseling for borrowers and imposed assignee liability that trumped state holder-in-due-course status, which would otherwise protect good faith purchasers of mortgages from most liability,[40] enabling (among other things) rescission of loans made in violation of Truth in Lending Act requirements.[41] HOEPA also directed the Federal Reserve Board to prohibit unfair or deceptive mortgage loans or refinancings that are "abusive" or not in the interest of the borrower.[42]

HOEPA's narrow scope limited its effectiveness because lenders could avoid its application by pricing loans just under the act's rate triggers. Moreover, the Federal Reserve, under Alan Greenspan's chairmanship, engaged in a studious policy of inaction or "nonfeasance," refusing to engage in a HOEPA rulemaking despite repeated requests from consumer groups and in derogation of its statutory duty.[43] While many states, however, passed their own mini-HOEPA statutes,[44] these statutes were nullified by federal regulators' preemption campaign.

The preemption campaign of the 1990s and 2000s was materially different from previous federal preemption efforts. In the 1930s and 1940s, the federal government had pushed preemption under the Home Owners Loan Act (HOLA) in order to enable FHA-insured lending. FHA-insured lending, however, came with national standards that substituted for preempted state regulations. The goal of HOLA preemption was the standardization, rather than the gutting, of regulation.

In contrast, the preemption campaign of the 1990s and 2000s was not coupled with substitute federal regulation. Its goal was simply to unshackle federally regulated depositories from any regulation. As a result, a regulatory vacuum replaced disparate state regulation. The preemption campaign of the 1990s and 2000s followed on the heels of the significant statutory deregulation of mortgage lending by Congress in the early 1980s, which was part of an attempt to save the S&L industry by enabling it to originate nontraditional mortgage products that would have less of a mismatch between asset and liability duration.[45] The remaining state regulation was undercut through federal preemption and refusal to implement the HOEPA or otherwise limit aggressive mortgage lending.[46] The result, by the early 2000s, was a multi-trillion-dollar national mortgage market with little remaining regulation. At the same time, financial institution leverage was increasing generally and being amplified through the growth of credit derivatives markets, which eroded the financial system's ability to withstand a shock.

Structural Pressures on the GSEs

Even as state and federal regulation of the mortgage market was undermined, the GSEs held the line on underwriting into the early 2000s. To understand why, it is important to recognize that the GSEs had little reason to loosen their underwriting criteria. Until the early 2000s, the GSEs' only real competition for market share was each other. The GSEs competed, but primarily on service to their sellers, not on underwriting, which would have been mutually cannibalistic. Thus, as long as GSE securitization dominated the mortgage market, credit risk was kept in check, and there was not much of a market for nonprime, nonconforming, conventional loans.

While Fannie and Freddie helped to maintain a stable mortgage market in the 1990s, they were far from perfect institutions. Their private ownership structure meant that they faced shareholder pressure to expand their business and increase returns, even when competition was not necessarily ideal for market stability. In a normal private business, shareholders must balance their desire to see business expansion with the risk of business failure. If a business is too aggressive in its expansion, it may fail. The quasi-governmental nature of the GSEs warped the traditional shareholder calculus. Fannie and Freddie were (rightly) understood as implicitly guarantied by the federal government.[47] As a result, shareholders were less concerned about the possibility of failure.[48] At the same time, the GSEs' creditors—such as the purchasers of their corporate debt and guaranteed MBS—were willing to tolerate greater levels of credit risk because of the implicit government guaranty. Accordingly, investors were not as worried about the quality of the GSE underwriting and did not demand detailed information about the default risk on the mortgages; what investors cared about was information that could help them anticipate prepayment speeds so they could gauge the MBS' convexity risk—the risk of losses resulting from adverse changes in MBS' market price relative to their yield.[49] This information was fairly easy to obtain, particularly on standardized mortgage products, and modeling and pricing the interest rate risk was a far simpler task than modeling the credit risk. As a result, the usual measure of market discipline on GSE credit risk was weaker for the GSEs than it would have been for private firms.

Fannie and Freddie also faced bipartisan political pressure to increase homeownership. Both the Clinton and George W. Bush administrations made increased homeownership a cornerstone of the domestic policy in the ideal of an ownership society, and Fannie and Freddie found their statutory Affordable Housing Goals repeatedly increased. These affordable housing goals were targets for the percentage of the GSE business that would qualify as "affordable housing." The push for expanding homeownership put pressure on the GSEs to loosen their underwriting standards. It remains unclear how much this political pressure actually changed their behavior, however. While many of the GSEs' critics have harped on the politicization of the GSEs (as discussed in Chapter 8), the evidence does not indicate that affordable homeownership policies had a significant effect on the GSE's underwriting.[50]

Emergence of the Private Secondary Market: Private-Label Securitization

Although the GSEs dominated the post-S&L crisis mortgage market, competition began to emerge in the form of a completely private, largely unregulated secondary mortgage market. This new market was the private-label securitization (PLS) market, in which Wall Street investment banks sponsored (organized) the securitization transactions.

As with GSE securitization, PLS involved the pooling of thousands of mortgage loans that were then sold to specially created trusts that would issue MBS to pay for the mortgage loans. Unlike the GSEs, however, the PLS sponsors did not guaranty the timely payment of interest and principal on the PLS. PLS investors, therefore, assumed both credit risk and interest rate risk on the MBS, in contrast to GSE MBS, for which investors assumed only interest rate risk. (See Figure 4.2.)

Significantly, whereas the GSEs would purchase only loans that conformed to their underwriting guidelines, there were no such general guidelines for the investment banks that served as PLS sponsors.[51] The only constraint was whether a buyer could profitably be found. Thus, PLS created a market for both nonprime and nonconforming conventional loans.[52]

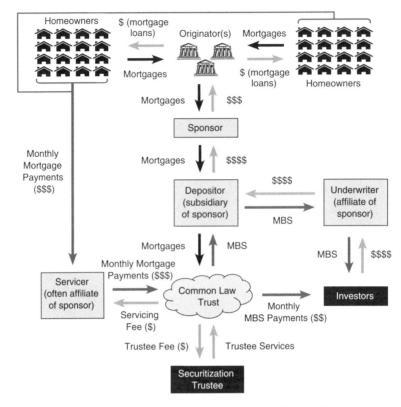

Figure 4.2. Funding of Mortgages through Private-Label Securitization

Data source: Adam J. Levitin, *Business Bankruptcy: Financial Restructuring and Modern Commercial Markets* 124 (2nd ed. 2018).

Some securitizations, such as many Ginnie, Fannie, and Freddie MBS offerings, are pass-throughs, in which the payments on the mortgages are simply passed through, on a pro rata basis to the MBS holders (minus administrative expenses). Thus, in a pass-through structure, a pool of thirty-year mortgages that have a weighted average 5.00 percent coupon might support thirty-year securities, all of which would have a 4.75 percent coupon (with 0.25 percent of the mortgage coupon paying for the administration, or "servicing," of the securitized loans). Any credit losses and prepayments would be shared pro rata among the MBS investors. This means that an investor holding 10 percent of this pass-through MBS issuance would receive 10 percent of the monthly principal and interest payments collected on the underlying mortgages, net administrative expenses.

Other securitizations, including most PLS, are "structured securities," meaning that they are produced through a transaction design method known as "structured financing." Structured financing refers to transactions that purposefully produce a tiered allocation of risks and rewards among investors. This is achieved through the use of senior-subordinate structures known as "tranching" or slicing, because the risks are divvied up into "tranches" or slices, with the subordinated tranches holding more risk than the senior tranches, but correspondingly higher returns. Credit risk and interest rate (prepayment) risk are often tranched separately in a PLS transaction.

The variety of risk/return profiles that tranching produces enables structured securitizations to cater to particular risk appetites and thereby maximize on investor demand. Thus, in a structured securitization, the pool of 30-year mortgages with a weighted average coupon of 5.00 percent from the previous example might now support a variety of securities with 3-year, 10-year, 20-year, and 30-year durations, and interest rates ranging from 4.00 to 6.00 percent. Credit losses might be allocated first to the 3-year securities, which might also receive all prepayments until paid off. The point here is not about the specifics, but rather that the design of the structured securities is flexible and can be tailored to specific investor tastes.

The easiest way to understand structured financing is by analogy to a grade point average. If a student has a B grade point average, that could indicate that he or she got straight Bs. However, it could also indicate that the student had a mix of As and Cs, or even some A+s to counterbalance an F, and so on.

Structured securities work the same way. A nonstructured MBS, such as a Freddie Mac pass-through, allocates risk and reward on a pro rated basis to all investors. This is equivalent to the student who has gotten straight Bs. Every investor in the pass-through gets a security with the same risk/reward profile as every other investor.

The structured security, in contrast, would take that B average but break it down into a bunch of As and Cs or A+s and an F (each one being a technically separate security). Some investors would have very safe securities (the A+s and the As), while others would have less safe ones (equivalent to the Cs and Fs). Thus, a structured security, such as almost all PLS, is deliberately designed to produce an uneven allocation of risk and reward to investors. Some investors take on less risk and less reward and some take on more of both.

To give a very simple illustration, imagine a pool of three mortgages that all have a B credit rating. A pass-through security based on these mortgages would also, presumably, have a B credit rating. But let's now imagine that the pass-through security is split into three securities, which are then given a senior-subordinate payment structure, so that all payments first go to the senior security, then to the mezzanine, and then to the junior security. This sort of senior-subordinate credit risk tranching is the hallmark of PLS. It means that in any particular distribution period, some securities were paid first out of the collections on the mortgages. This senior-subordinate structure is sometimes referred to as the "cashflow waterfall" because the cash collected on the mortgages is poured in at the top, where it flows to the senior securities first and only then, after they have received their full payment for that distribution period, trickles down to more junior securities.

In our example, this senior-subordinate structuring might result in the senior security getting an A rating, the mezzanine getting a B rating, and the junior getting a C rating. Thus, A-rated securities can be created out of a set of B mortgages, but it is only possible with a byproduct of C or F securities with concentrated credit risk. This is the alchemy of structured financing. Financial lead can be turned into gold, but only with a radioactive byproduct. Structured financing can be used to generate seemingly indefinite quantities of investment-grade, and even AAA-rated, securities. It does not do so by eliminating risk, but rather by shifting it to a set of noninvestment-grade securities that feature highly concentrated risk.

PLS emerged slowly. The first deal was done in 1977,[53] but market share remained small until the mid-1990s. The shape of the early PLS market reflected the fact that the initial investors in PLS were familiar with interest rate risk on mortgages, from GSE MBS, but not with credit risk. Thus, the PLS market initially developed products with a low credit risk, particularly jumbo mortgages—loans that were larger than the GSEs' conforming loan limit. Jumbos were essentially prime, conventional mortgages for larger amounts than conforming loans. Although PLS investors did face credit risk on jumbos, it was low. In part this was because only high-quality jumbos were securitized because credit-rating agencies initially insisted that jumbo securitizations follow GSE underwriting guidelines (other than conforming loan limits) in order to be rated.[54] Loss rates on jumbos between 1992 and 2006 were less than 0.5 percent.[55]

Credit risk for jumbos was mitigated on both the loan level, through high down payments (low LTVs) and private mortgage insurance, and at the MBS level, through credit enhancements, particularly credit risk "tranching." Jumbo PLS settled on a largely standardized form—the "six-pack" structure, in which six subordinated tranches supported a senior, AAA-rated tranche that comprised well over 90 percent of the MBS by dollar amount.[56]

Moreover, jumbo PLS became sufficiently standardized to be priced based on Agency MBS, which trade in a forward contract market known as the To-Be-Announced (TBA) market. This is a market in which MBS are sold even before they are actually issued because it is sufficiently easy to find an MBS that meets the sale delivery requirements.[57] The TBA market facilitates interest rate hedging and also makes it possible for consumers to get rate-locks on mortgage offers. A forward market in MBS is only possible when there is a liquid secondary market for the mortgages with sufficient mortgage standardization. The importance of the TBA market to the smooth functioning of the mortgage market generally is a topic we return to in detail in Chapters 11 and 12.

The success of PLS products depended heavily on the ability to achieve high-investment-grade ratings for most securities because fixed-income investor demand is highest for high-investment-grade products.[58] For jumbos, it was relatively easy to achieve AAA ratings because of the solid underlying collateral.[59] Over time, however, the PLS market began to expand beyond prime jumbos, encouraged in part by the work of the Resolution Trust Corporation (RTC), a receiver for failed S&Ls, in securitizing nonperforming, nonconforming mortgages—mortgages that were originally prime, but were in default when the RTC securitized them.[60] Starting in the early 1990s, PLS products backed by nonprime mortgages (now referred to as "subprime" mortgages, but at the time referred to as "B&C" mortgages) began to appear. We have not been able to definitively identify the first nonprime PLS deal, but it is clear that nonprime mortgages were being securitized into PLS products by 1993.[61]

For the securitization of nonprime mortgages, greater credit enhancements and structural creativity were necessary to obtain the credit ratings that made the securities sufficiently marketable. For example, the mean number of tranches in nonprime PLS products in 2003 was approximately ten, compared with seven for jumbo six-packs. By 2007, the mean number of tranches for PLS products had increased to over fourteen.[62] Other types of internal and external credit enhancements were also much more common in nonprime PLS products: overcollateralization,[63] excess spread,[64] shifting interest,[65] reserve accounts,[66] and pool and bond insurance.[67]

Nonprime PLS thus inevitably involved more complex and heterogeneous deal structures to compensate for the weaker quality of the underlying assets.[68] The growing heterogeneity frustrated comparative and market-level analysis, especially as the available data were limited and not loan level. Prior to 2006, securities law did not require any specific disclosures for PLS products, only the general requirement of disclosure of material terms in offering materials for those that were publicly offered. Beginning in 2006, the Securities and Exchange Commission (SEC) began to require pool-level disclosures about the underlying mortgages—that is, the disclosure of aggregate characteristics of the loans—but did not specify exactly which characteristics had to be disclosed or the precise manner of the disclosure.[69] Investor visibility into PLS was limited and inconsistent.

A Tale of Two Booms

Nonprime PLS products remained a small share of the mortgage-finance market from their origins in 1977 through the 1990s. As of 2003, nonprime first-lien loans were only 10 percent of all mortgage originations and subprime/Alt-A PLS products were only 10 percent of all MBS issuance.[70] Nonprime PLS products did not take off until 2003, at which point they grew rapidly until the bursting of the housing bubble. (See Figures 4.3 and 4.4.) The inflection point came with the introduction and spiraling growth of nonprime mortgages in 2003 and 2004, as PLS products jumped from being 22 percent of MBS issued by dollar volume in 2003 to 46 percent in 2004. (See Figures 4.3 and 4.4.) By 2006, almost half of all mortgage originations were nontraditional products, and private-label securitization had grown to 56 percent of the securitization market.[71]

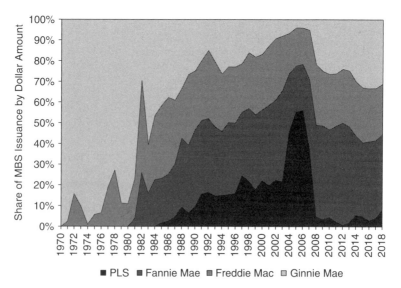

Figure 4.3. Share of MBS Issuance by Securitization Type, 1970–2018

Data source: Inside Mortgage Finance, *2019 Mortgage Market Statistical Annual.*

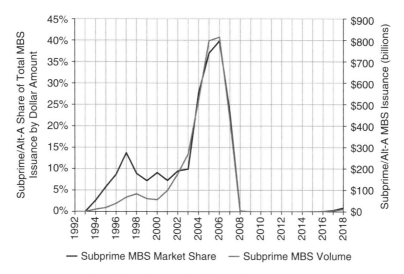

Figure 4.4. Annual Market Share and Volume of Subprime/Alt-A MBS Issuance, 1992–2018

Data source: Inside Mortgage Finance, *2019 Mortgage Market Statistical Annual.*

The nonprime-mortgage market (and nonprime-PLS market) boomed as a consequence of the tapering off of a preceding prime refinancing boom. From 2001 to 2003, historically low interest rates brought on an orgy of refinancing. In 2003, mortgage originations peaked, with 72 percent of originations (by dollar volume) as refinancings.[72] Virtually all the refinancing activity from 2001 to 2003 was in prime FRMs.[73] (See Figure 4.5.) The prime refinancing boom meant that mortgage originators and securitizers had a few years of increased earnings.

By 2003, however, long-term interest rates had started to rise (short-term rates moved up starting in 2004), and the refinancing boom ended. This meant that the mortgage industry was hard-pressed to maintain its 2001–2003 earnings levels.[74] The solution post-2003 was to find more product to move in order to maintain origination volumes and hence earnings. Because the prime borrowing pool was exhausted, it was necessary to loosen underwriting standards and look more to marginal borrowers to support origination volume levels. This meant a growth in subprime and alt-A (limited documentation) mortgages, as well as in second mortgages (home equity loans).[75] (See Figures 4.6 and 4.7.) As a result, combined loan-to-value (CLTV) ratios increased and borrowers' income was less well documented, if at all. (See Figure 4.8.)

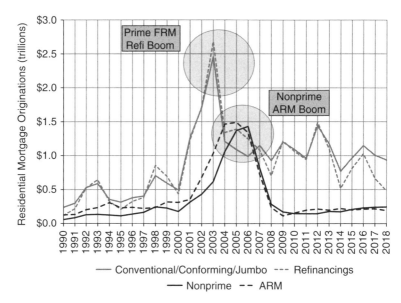

Figure 4.5. A Tale of Two Booms: Residential Mortgage Originations by Type, 1990–2018

Data source: Inside Mortgage Finance, *2019 Mortgage Market Statistical Annual.*

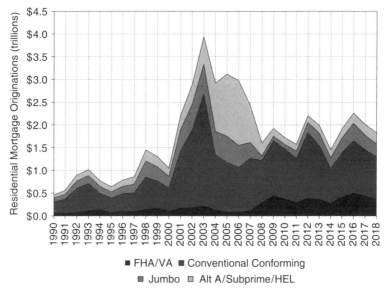

Figure 4.6. Residential Mortgage Originations by Mortgage Type, 1990–2018

Data source: Inside Mortgage Finance, *2019 Mortgage Market Statistical Annual.*

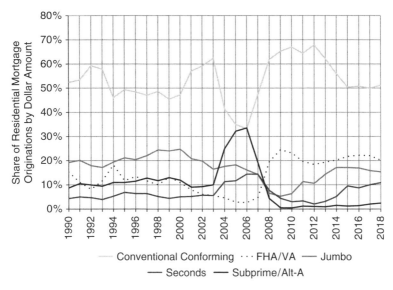

Figure 4.7. Share of Residential Mortgage Originations by Mortgage Type, 1990–2018

Data source: Inside Mortgage Finance, *2019 Mortgage Market Statistical Annual.*

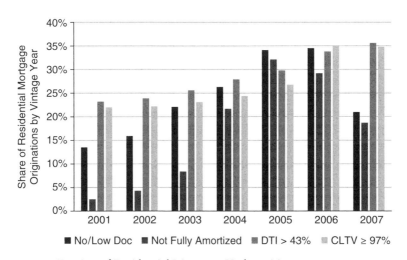

Figure 4.8. Erosion of Residential Mortgage Underwriting, 2001–2007

Data source: Morris A. Davis *et al.*, "A Quarter Century of Mortgage Risk," FHFA Staff Working Paper No. 19-02, Oct. 2019, data supplement, *at* https://www.fhfa.gov/PolicyProgramsResearch/Research/PaperDocuments/wp1902-data -supplement-october-2019.xlsx.

Fueling the PLS Boom: The Rise of
Nontraditional Mortgages

The decline in underwriting standards after 2003 was also reflected in a shift in mortgage products.[76] Nontraditional mortgage products are generally structured for initial affordability; the costs are back-loaded, either with balloon payments or increasing interest rates. Table 4.1 illustrates the relative initial affordability of various mortgage products. It shows that adjustable-rate mortgage (ARM) products, particularly nontraditional ARMs with balloon payments due to limited or extended amortization, can drastically reduce initial monthly payments for borrowers.

During this same time in 2004 and 2005, the yield curve—the relationship between interest rates and loan maturities—was flattening. When the yield curve is upward sloping—meaning that the cost of long-term borrowing is greater than the cost of short-term borrowing, as reflected by initial rates—borrowers rationally choose ARMs because it costs more to borrow with an FRM. In 2000, the yield curve was flat but shifted to an upward slope from 2001 to 2003. But then the yield curve began to flatten out in 2004 and 2005 and became flat in 2006 and 2007.

Prior to 2005, borrowers had shifted from ARMs to FRMs at every point in recent history when yield curves flattened in order to lock in lower long-term rates.[77] Despite the flat yield curve during the peak of the housing bubble, however, borrowers increasingly chose ARMs. The explanation for the shift to ARMs cannot be found in the cost charged over the full term

Table 4.1. Relative Affordability of Mortgage Products

Mortgage Product	Initial Monthly Payment	Payment as Percentage of Fixed-Rate-Mortgage (FRM) Payment
FRM	$1,079.19	100.0%
ARM	$903.50	83.7%
Extended-Amortization ARM	$799.98	74.1%
Interest-Only ARM	$663.00	61.4%
Negative-Amortization ARM	$150.00	13.9%
Payment-Option ARM	<$150.00	<13.9%

Source: Ben S. Bernanke, chairman, Fed. Reserve Sys., Speech at the Annual Meeting of the American Economic Association: Monetary Policy and the Housing Bubble (Jan. 3, 2010), at fig. 7, *available at* http://www.federalreserve.gov/newsevents/speech/bernanke20100103a .htm. Note: The figures we present assume a prime borrower with a $180,000 mortgage securing a $225,000 property (20 percent down), 6 percent APR FRM, and 4.42 percent APR.

of the mortgage; rationally, borrowers considering the full-term cost would have gravitated to FRMs. Instead, the explanation lies in the relatively low initial payments of the ARMs.

This means that there were two possible, nonexclusive "supply-side" reasons for the expansion of ARM market share, that is, the expansion of lending due to changes in lender behavior. First, ARM share growth could be explained by the fact that ARMs were affordability products, into which financial institutions were able to underwrite weaker borrowers. And second, ARM market-share growth could be explained by a drop in the price of the implicit put option on nonrecourse mortgages. The implicit put option refers to homeowners' ability to walk away from a nonrecourse (or functionally nonrecourse) mortgage without personal liability by surrendering the house. If the cost of the put option—which is included in the cost of mortgage finance—was becoming cheaper relative to renting, it would mean that consumers were more willing to speculate on rising housing prices with nonrecourse mortgages.[78] Thus, cheaper mortgage credit made it easier to gamble on housing.

There is reason to believe that both explanations are correct. The phenomenon of house flipping—treating houses as pure (or primarily) investments rather than mixed investment and consumption assets—became pronounced during the bubble. A cheaper put option due to underpriced mortgages would have encouraged this sort of investment.

There is also reason to believe that the growth in ARMs reflected their role as an affordability product that enabled market expansion, both in terms of the number of borrowers and the size of loans. The annual price of housing finance has two main components: a cost of funds and a risk premium. The cost of funds is a function of long-term interest rates, whereas the risk premium is a function of underwriting (including product type). A decline in either component reduces the cost of housing finance and thus allows borrowers to borrow more and bid up home prices.[79] The deterioration of underwriting standards and the shift in mortgage products had the same effect as falling interest rates: all these factors reduced the initial cost of mortgage credit, thereby increasing the quantity of mortgage credit that was consumed, and putting upward pressure on home prices.[80]

Much of the growth in mortgages was in nontraditional products[81] such as interest-only mortgages;[82] payment-option mortgages;[83] forty-year, extended-amortization balloon mortgages;[84] and hybrid ARMs.[85] (See Figure 4.9. Also refer back to Figure 4.8.) Borrowers were generally approved based on their ability to pay the initial below-market teaser rate rather than their ability to pay for the product through its full term. Moreover, borrowers were approved more frequently at higher debt-to-income

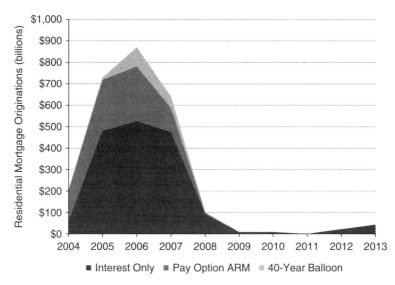

Figure 4.9. Growth of Nontraditional Mortgage Products, 2004–2013

Data source: Inside Mortgage Finance, *2014 Mortgage Market Statistical Annual.*

ratios.[86] (Refer back to Figure 4.8.) Each of these factors increased risk, and these risk factors were frequently layered and cumulative.

Freed of its New Deal regulations, the U.S. mortgage market quickly reverted to Depression-era "bullet" loans, shifting interest rate and refinancing risk back to borrowers.[87] Nonamortizing loans, and even negatively amortizing loans, proliferated in the private-label market, as did loans like so-called 2/28s and 3/27s—nominally 30-year loans with short-term fixed-rate teaser periods of two or three years before resetting to much higher adjustable rates. These mortgages were designed to be refinanced upon the expiration of the teaser period, just like bullet loans, and they carried the risk that the borrower would not be able to refinance either because of a change in the borrower's finances, a decline in the value of the property, or a market freeze. Because these new bullet loans were at high LTVs, only a small decline in property values was necessary to inhibit refinancing. As noted above, the teaser rate bullet loans had briefly reappeared before in the 1980s with the initial emergence of ARMs.[88]

The expanded share of these products was a sure sign of an increasingly risky mortgage market, as they were not products underwritten for long-term success, only for immediate-term affordability. Yet for lenders, nontraditional mortgages were gifts that kept giving. The back-loaded cost structure of these mortgages created an incentive for borrowers to refinance when monthly payments increased, thereby generating future refinancing origination business. The exotic products that marked the housing bubble were just the reincarnation of pre–New Deal bullet loans—nonamortizing products designed to be refinanced frequently.

Nontraditional mortgage products also fueled their own proliferation as part of a homebuyers' arms race. The expansion of the borrower base and borrower capacity because of loosened underwriting standards also increased demand for housing supply and drove real-estate prices upwards. As housing prices rose, nontraditional affordability products became increasingly attractive to borrowers who saw their purchasing power diminish. Thus, nontraditional mortgage products generated additional origination business. The growth of nontraditional products suggests the shift to ARMs was driven by their use as initial affordability for market expansion.

While the lower initial monthly payments on nontraditional mortgage products enabled borrowers to bid up home prices, the increase in home prices did not translate into an increase in home equity for many homeowners. This is because the boom in home prices was also accompanied by substantial home equity extraction. As borrowers refinanced their mortgages, they maintained their LTVs, meaning they borrowed more money against their higher home price, cashing out the equity they had built up. Whereas nontraditional mortgage products expanded homeownership in the short run, cash-out refinancings had no effect on homeownership, only on the risk in the housing finance system.

The growth in cash-out refinancings was substantial. From 2003 through 2007 over \$1.1 trillion of home equity was cashed out by borrowers, a sum equal to 22 percent of the \$5 trillion increase in aggregate home equity from 2002–2006 (we are assuming refinancings lag home price increases).[89] Given that a substantial portion of aggregate home equity (well over half) is held by unmortgaged households, the equity extraction accounted for a major share of the equity gains of mortgaged households. As Figure 4.10 shows, the total amount cashed out as a percentage of the total unpaid balance on the mortgages that were refinanced soared from 5 to 10 percent to over 30 percent during the bubble.

The effect of depleting home equity was to leave borrowers more vulnerable in the event of price declines, for if a borrower ends up with no equity, it is difficult to sell the home. Thus, not only did nontraditional mortgage products add to the increased risk in the mortgage market by enabling prices to be bid up unsustainably, so too did the home equity extraction that followed the price increases, as there was now more aggregate debt without a corresponding increase in home equity.

Private-label securitization was the dominant funding mechanism for nontraditional mortgages.[90] PLS made the expansion in the nontraditional

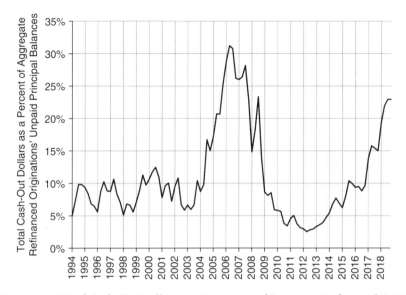

Figure 4.10. Total Cash-Out Dollars as a Percentage of Aggregate Refinanced Originations' Unpaid Principal Balances for Freddie Mac Originations, 1994–2018

Data source: Freddie Mac, "Quarterly Refinance Statistics," *at* http://www.freddiemac.com/fmac-resources/research/docs/q3_refinance_2019.xls.

mortgage market possible, and nontraditional mortgages made the expansion of the PLS market possible. Without PLS, most nontraditional mortgages would not have been originated because banks would simply have been unwilling to carry the risks from nontraditional mortgages on their balance sheets. Similarly, without nontraditional mortgages, PLS would have remained a market of under $300 billion in issuance per year, rather than one that grew to nearly $1.2 trillion. Indeed, as Figure 4.11 shows, PLS share of MBS issuance closely tracks the share of nontraditional mortgage product origination. The GSEs' economies of scale and implicit government guaranty gave them operating efficiencies that PLS could not match for traditional, conventional conforming loans; but for the growth of nontraditional mortgages, the only market left for PLS would have been in financing conventional jumbo mortgages.[91]

Ultimately, the expansion of PLS and nontraditional mortgages was its own undoing. PLS based on nontraditional mortgages enabled more mortgage credit, which bid up housing prices, and those increased housing prices then became part of the underwriting that enabled the further expansion of mortgage credit. During the bubble, however, housing price appreciation depended on the continued expansion of the borrower base, much like a pyramid scheme. Yet not all consumers were looking to purchase homes,

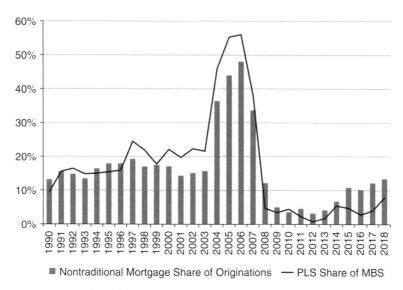

Figure 4.11. Residential Mortgage Market Share of Nontraditional Mortgage Products and Private-Label Securitization, 1990–2018

Data source: Inside Mortgage Finance, *2019 Mortgage Market Statistical Annual.*

and the increase in house prices eventually priced out other potential homeowners, even with loosened (or fraudulent) underwriting standards.[92] The inability to keep expanding the borrower base made price increases unsustainable. Without home price appreciation, homeowners could not refinance their way out of highly leveraged, nontraditional mortgages when payment shocks—large increases in monthly mortgage payments upon the expiration of teaser interest rates—occurred. Moreover, without the continued expected price appreciation, prices did not simply level off, but actually collapsed because part of the high prices was due to the expected future increase in prices.[93] The recognition that this was the case may also have played a part in the bubble's collapse because mortgage credit tightened, becoming a self-fulfilling prophecy. The result was a cycle of declining housing prices and rising foreclosures: the bubble had burst.

CHAPTER FIVE

The Bubble Bursts

THE STORY WE have told thus far is one of the rise and fall of the American Mortgage—the 30-year fixed. The American Mortgage and the institutions that support it emerged in the New Deal and postwar period in reaction to the collapse of pre–New Deal housing market and its bullet loan products. During the Great American Housing Bubble, however, the American Mortgage was displaced by nontraditional mortgage products that harkened back to pre-Depression bullet loans—interest-only and adjustable-rate products designed to be frequently refinanced. The shift to more initially affordable nontraditional mortgages was part of a market share race to the bottom. The shift enabled buyers to bid up home prices, but with products that were inherently unstable because of payment shock risk built into the product should refinancing be impossible because of a decline in the borrower's credit quality, a decline in home prices, or a market freeze.

This chapter tells the story of the bursting of the bubble and the regulatory reaction, thus bringing us up to the present day. Our interest here is not in the financial crisis of 2008 writ large. The story of how the financial crisis unfolded in fall 2008 as the housing bubble burst is an important story, but it is not really a housing story. It is also a story that has been ably related in numerous other works. Accordingly, we do not aim to tell the full story of the 2008 financial crisis here. Instead, we summarize the crisis *as seen from the housing market's perspective*. This means that we will not concern ourselves here with the crisis's spread into broader financial markets except to the extent that it, in turn, affected the housing finance market.

Early Signs of the Crisis: Collapse
of Warehouse Lending

Residential mortgage securitizations involve the pooling of hundreds or thousands of mortgages into an investment vehicle. It can take a while for a securitization sponsor to assemble such a pool of mortgages, which means there is a lag between when a mortgage is originated and when it is securitized. That lag—termed "pipeline" delay—can be days or months. During that lag the originator needs to finance the mortgage: the originator laid out cash to make the loan and needs to replenish its cash stock to make more loans. In order to finance the mortgage, the originator must either sell the loan borrow against it. Some originators would simply sell to third parties that would ultimately securitize the loans, but those third parties faced the same need as the originators for financing the loan. Borrowing against loans that are being held for securitization is known as "warehouse financing." Warehouse financing typically consists of lines of credit secured by the mortgages.

Warehouse lenders must themselves find financing. Many warehouse lines of credit come from banks. Banks use their deposit funding bases to finance the revolving warehouse credit. While the deposits are often demand liabilities, they are sticky to the extent that they are FDIC insured, so there is not a tremendous danger of a mismatch in asset and liability durations with the warehouse line. Even if the securitization pipeline time lengthened, banks would be unlikely to find their depositors demanding their funds back. Still, banks are wary of credit risk, and warehouse lines of credit come with various types of debt covenants, a violation of which entitles the lender to cut off the line of credit and demand immediate repayment of the outstanding balance.

Among those covenants are cross-default clauses providing that among the events of default on the loan is a default on the borrower's line of credit from *another* warehouse lender. Cross-default clauses make warehouse lending one of the most fragile parts of the securitization pipeline; if one warehouse lender gets skittish and declares a covenant default, it can pull the plug on its loans, and cross-default clauses will result in other lenders to the same borrower doing the same, resulting in the collapse of the securitization program, and leaving originators without a source of funding for new originations.

Exacerbating the flightiness of warehouse lending are the 2005 amendments to the Bankruptcy Code. Warehouse lending was traditionally structured as secured lines of credit. But the Bankruptcy Abuse Prevention and Consumer Protection Act of 2005 changed the bankruptcy and bank insolvency treatment of mortgage repo agreements, giving them better treatment than secured lines of credit. As a result, warehouse lending shifted from secured lines of credit to mortgage repos.

A mortgage repo agreement is comprised of the sale and repurchase agreements for the financed mortgages. The borrower (the repo seller) sells the mortgages to the lender (the repo buyer) and agrees to repurchase those mortgages at a future date for a price that is higher than the original sale price. The repo transaction is equivalent to a secured loan, with the difference between the sale prices being the finance charge and the mortgages that are sold serving as the collateral; if the repo seller is unable to meet its repurchase obligation, the repo buyer can sell the mortgages to a third party and apply the proceeds against the repurchase obligation.

A key feature of bankruptcy law (and bank insolvency law) is that following a bankruptcy filing, a federal injunction known as the "automatic stay" stops most collection activity by creditors outside the bankruptcy process. The stay has the effect of channeling all collection activity into the bankruptcy proceeding and preventing creditors from engaging in a race to grab the debtor's limited assets.

The 2005 bankruptcy amendments exempted mortgage repos from the automatic stay.[1] This meant that a mortgage repo lender could liquidate the mortgage collateral posted by the originator repo borrower as soon as the originator filed for bankruptcy. In contrast, a traditional secured line of credit would still be subject to the automatic stay, meaning that the lender could not liquidate the collateral without the leave of the bankruptcy court and would have no right to receive periodic payments on the line of credit in the interim. Moreover, if the lender were undersecured, meaning that the collateral value was less than the loan amount, the lender would not accrue any interest on the debt during the bankruptcy.

The change in bankruptcy law encouraged warehouse lenders to shift the form of their loans to mortgage repo agreements (which were seen as safer than secured lines of credit) and thereby encouraged them to lend more liberally because they believed that their bankruptcy risk was reduced, as they could immediately liquidate the mortgages posted as collateral by the originator in the event of that party's bankruptcy. Even if the repo lender were undersecured, it could still reinvest the liquidation proceeds and receive interest on them immediately, while also avoiding the uncertainty of the bankruptcy.

The result was greater and cheaper warehouse credit availability, which facilitated private-label securitization. At the same time, however, the shift to repo financing made warehouse lending flightier because warehouse lenders would not be locked into existing repos by the automatic stay. Indeed, the exemption from the stay strengthened the incentive for lenders to use their cross-default clauses to flee a troubled borrower. Thus, even while they were intended to protect lenders, the 2005 bankruptcy amendments made the US financial system more fragile.

Warehouse lending was the canary in the coalmine for the US mortgage market. The earliest signs of trouble emerged in 2006. In the first two quarters of 2006, there was a substantial uptick in the number of early payment defaults—defaults within the first few months of the loan—particularly on subprime loans. Whereas only 0.84 percent of subprime loans were in foreclosure within their first six months since origination in the first quarter of 2005, by the second quarter of 2006, the rate of early payment defaults had risen to 2.59 percent.[2] A rise in early payment defaults is a red flag for fraud by either the borrower or originator because a properly underwritten mortgage should not default in the first few months absent extreme life events of death, divorce, dismissal, or disability. The rate of such events tends to be relatively steady in the market, so a sharp uptick without a major rise in unemployment is suspicious.

The rise in early payment defaults was not visible market-wide in real time; it took some time for information to be collected, disseminated, and analyzed. Yet by fall 2006, the increase in early payment defaults was known.[3] The initial consequence of these early payment defaults was that subprime lenders were forced to repurchase loans that they had sold. This shifted the losses to the lenders, which were also forced to reserve more funds for future repurchases. The losses and reserving constrained the liquidity of these subprime lenders, but the real hit was to come later in the fall, when warehouse lenders began to cut off their lines of credit. On November 15, 2006, JPMorgan Chase, the distribution agent for subprime lender Ownit Mortgage Solutions' "wet" line of credit, which financed loans before they were made, declared an event of default.[4] The precise basis for the event of default is not public, but warehouse lines generally had covenants against excessive early payment defaults.[5] Other lenders exercised their cross-default clauses and subsequently made margin calls on Ownit, leaving it with no liquidity and no choice but to file for bankruptcy.[6]

The failure of Ownit and two other subprime lenders, Sebring Capital Partners LP and Harbourton Mortgage Investment Corporation, in December 2006, spooked the warehouse lending market. Wet lenders significantly lowered their advance rates on funds to subprime lenders, meaning that the subprime originators had to post additional collateral as security for funds.[7] When the originators could not, their lines were shut down and they were out of business. Thus, other subprime lenders started to fail in early 2007. Merrill Lynch seems to have been particularly aggressive in making margin calls based on early payment defaults, both with Ownit and with Mortgage Lenders Network and ResMae.[8]

In January 2007, months after subprime lenders had started to fail, Moody's credit rating agency came out with a detailed report on these defaults that removed any doubt about the rising problems in subprime.[9] Subprime and other nontraditional lending fell sharply in 2007 (see Figure 7.5 in Chapter 7), and by the end of 2007, almost all subprime lending had ceased.[10] Thus, in 2006, "expanded credit" lending (subprime and Alt-A loans) plus home equity loans (mainly second-lien loans) had peaked at nearly 50 percent of originations by dollar amount.[11] By 2008, "expanded credit" accounted for only 4 percent of lending, with home equity loans comprising another 8 percent.[12] This contraction resulted in over $1 trillion of annual funding for mortgages leaving the market. (See Figure 5.1.)

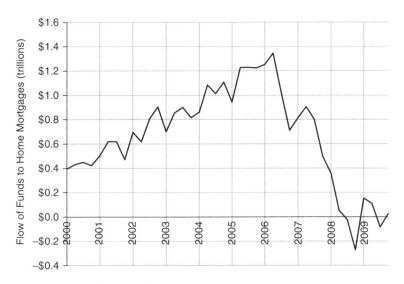

Figure 5.1. Flow of Funds to Home Mortgages, 2000–2009

Data source: Bd. of Governors of the Fed. Reserve Sys., *Statistical Release Z.1, Financial Accounts of the United States,* tbl. F.218, line 1 (series FA893065105).

The Crisis Spreads

The crisis spread from the housing market to financial markets more broadly for a simple reason: MBS were frequently used as collateral for all sorts of financing deals between financial institutions, particular the repo and securities lending markets. When the value of that collateral became uncertain or ratings were downgraded, lenders made margin calls demanding the posting of additional collateral. The valuation uncertainty of mortgage-related securities put the solvency of many highly leveraged financial institutions in question, such that counterparties refused to deal with them. And to the extent that financial institutions were creditors of firms with large mortgage market exposure, their own solvency became questionable because it was unclear what and when they could recover from their own debtors.

A key link in the transmission chain involved the structured investment vehicles (SIVs) and asset-backed commercial paper (ABCP) conduits. SIVs and ABCP conduits were investment structures that financed themselves by issuing medium-term notes and commercial paper, respectively. While some SIVs and ABCP conduits engaged in a simple duration arbitrage—financing longer-term assets with shorter-term liabilities—others were used as warehouse financing channels by securitization sponsors. Many securitization sponsors supplemented warehouse lines of credit from unaffiliated lenders with in-house financing from an affiliated SIV or ABCP conduit. SIVs and ABCP were often supported with market-value swaps that would cover any decline in collateral value between purchase and securitization. These market-value swap providers could place margin calls, just like warehouse lenders, if the value of the mortgage-related collateral declined.

As 2007 went on, SIVs found themselves unable to roll over their debt because of concerns about their mortgage market exposure and thus were forced to go into wind-down, further constraining the flow of credit to the mortgage market and depressing house prices. The slow run on mortgages became a self-fulfilling prophecy as the credit contraction pushed down home prices. As home prices fell, mortgage defaults rose and credit-rating agencies downgraded PLS, starting with a massive downgrade of 431 subprime PLS in July 2007.[13] This drove a reinforcing cycle of price declines and credit contraction. The downgrades triggered margin calls, constraining liquidity throughout the highly leveraged financial system. The great contraction had begun, and the result was a market freeze in fall 2008.

Critically, the trigger for the crisis was not the actual realization of losses on home mortgages themselves. As Figure 5.2 shows, most loss recognition on mortgages occurred *after* the crisis broke in fall 2008. From 2007

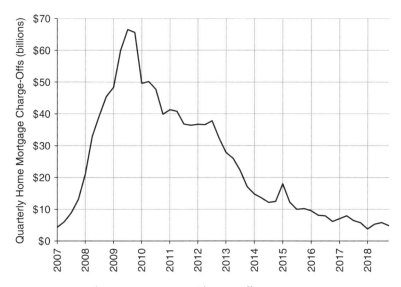

Figure 5.2. Quarterly Home Mortgage Charge-Offs, 2007–2018

Data source: Bd. of Governors of the Fed. Reserve Sys., *Statistical Release Z.1, Financial Accounts of the United States*, tbl. F.218, line 23 (series FV893065153).

through the third quarter of 2008, only $125 billion of losses had been recognized on home mortgages—just 11 percent of the total losses on mortgages eventually recognized between 2007 and 2016, the last year with elevated mortgage charge-offs.

Instead, the trigger for the crisis was the market's recognition of the *coming* losses on home mortgages and the uncertainty about both the precise size of the losses and their allocation. It was clear by fall 2008 that there were going to be losses on home mortgages, but it was not yet clear just how massive those losses would be. More importantly, perhaps, it was not clear where those losses lay. Financial institutions could not be sure of the extent of their counterparties' exposure to the mortgage market, either directly (through mortgage holdings), derivatively (through holdings of MBS), or indirectly (as counterparties to other parties with direct or derivative exposure).

The uncertainty about the extent of counterparty exposure to mortgages meant that firms could not be sure if their counterparties were impaired or would be money good on obligations, and this risk could not be adequately priced. Moreover, the use of collateral could not assuage concerns regarding counterparty risk because PLS, a favored form of collateral, were of questionable value, as were all institutional obligations. The uncertainty about the extent and distribution of losses prevented the market from clearing. The result was the market freeze that forced substantial intervention by the federal government to instill confidence in firms that their counterparties would be able to meet their payment obligations. And of course, this market freeze then redounded to push down housing prices, thus becoming a self-fulfilling prophecy by exacerbating losses on mortgages and thus on PLS.

GSE Conservatorship and Federal Interventions to Support the Market

Among the firms with substantial exposure to the mortgage market were, of course, Fannie Mae and Freddie Mac. Fannie and Freddie's exposure was not simply through the loans they held in portfolio or the securitizations they guarantied, but also through their investments in PLS. Fannie and Freddie had large holdings of PLS, and valuation adjustments prompted by ratings downgrades on these PLS eroded the GSEs' capital, even as they began to see losses on their own mortgage holdings and guaranties rise.

Even as warning signs appeared for the GSEs, they were encouraged to expand their mortgage purchase activity to serve as a type of buyer of last resort to support the housing market, since serving as a market stabilizer is part of their mission. At the same time, since 1992, the GSEs had been required to maintain equity capital equal to 2.5 percent of their on-balance-sheet exposures and 0.45 percent of their off-balance-sheet exposures (including guaranties on MBS).[14] Additionally, in 2006, in response to an accounting scandal and the finding that the GSEs were not sufficiently capitalized, the Office of Federal Housing Enterprise Oversight (OFHEO), the GSEs' regulator from 1992 to 2008, had required the GSEs to have a 30 percent capital surplus and placed restrictions on the growth of the GSEs' retained mortgage portfolios. OFHEO lifted the portfolio caps and reduced the 30 percent surplus requirement in March 2008, hoping that this would enable the GSEs to expand their activity to stabilize the falling housing market.

As late as summer 2008, just before the financial crisis fully erupted, Congress was also encouraging the GSEs and FHA to expand their activity to support the housing market. Congress's first response to the declining housing market was the Housing and Economic Recovery Act of 2008 (HERA), passed at the end of July 2008. HERA raised conforming loan limits substantially for "high-cost" areas, from $417,00 to $729,000.[15] This enabled Fannie and Freddie to support previously jumbo loan markets in areas where housing prices had been bid up during the bubble.

HERA also authorized the Hope for Homeowners program for FHA to insure up to $300 billion of thirty-year fixed-rate refinancing loans for up to 90 percent of newly appraised value for distressed borrowers.[16] The refinancing, however, required existing mortgagees to accept the proceeds of the insured loan as payment in full. In other words, for the borrower to get the refinancing, existing lenders had to agree to a write-down to 90 percent LTV calculated using the prices in the current, declining market. Moreover, if the property were sold in the first five years after the refinancing, the government would be entitled to up to half the appreciation. This refinancing program was projected to help 400,000 homeowners, but it was a complete bust—only 2,342 applications were received before the program was terminated in September 2011, and only 655 loans were refinanced.[17] Hope for Homeowners was not the first unsuccessful government refinancing program. In August 2007, FHA announced a new program called FHASecure, which was designed to refinance conventional mortgages with recent rate resets into FHA mortgages. The program had little success, however, and refinanced only 4,130 delinquent mortgages before it was terminated at the end of 2008.[18] Current borrowers were also eligible, but it is impossible to determine how many were able to refinance only because of the program.

HERA's most significant contribution, however, was to reform the regulation of the GSEs by creating a new regulator, the Federal Housing Finance Agency (FHFA), to replace the OFHEO.[19] OFHEO was an office within HUD, whose Director could be removed at will by the President. OFHEO was also funded via congressional appropriations. In contrast, FHFA is an independent agency whose director serves a five-year term (longer than a presidential administration) and can only be removed for cause. Moreover, FHFA is not funded through congressional appropriations, but instead through fees it charges the GSEs. This means that FHFA is much more insulated from political pressure from either the White House or Congress than was OFHEO. FHFA was also given stronger tools for putting the GSEs into conservatorship if their financial situation sufficiently deteriorated.

On September 6, 2008, FHFA placed both Fannie Mae and Freddie Mac (but not the Federal Home Loan Banks) into conservatorship. OFHEO had found both GSEs to be adequately capitalized as of June 30, 2008, with several billion dollars of capital above the statutory minimums, but the GSEs' capital situation rapidly deteriorated over the summer, and they had found themselves unable to raise capital or issue debt, according to some reports. The conservatorship meant that FHFA assumed overall management of the GSEs, which continued to operate. The FHFA has not attempted to manage the day-to-day operations of the GSEs, but has instead reconstituted the GSEs' boards of directors and charged them with running these enterprises, subject to FHFA review and approval of certain critical matters.

The GSEs were able to remain in conservatorship rather than being taken into receivership (and liquidated) only because of financial commitments from the Treasury Department known as Senior Preferred Stock Purchase Agreements. Upon the commencement of the conservatorships, the Treasury Department gave each GSE a $100 billion commitment to be drawn upon to the extent the GSE's liabilities exceeded its assets.[20] In exchange for the commitment, the GSEs each gave the Treasury $1 billion in nonvoting senior preferred stock accruing 10 percent annual dividends,[21] and warrants to purchase up to 79.9 percent of the common stock in the GSEs at a nominal price.[22] (An 80 percent or higher stake would have resulted in the GSEs coming onto the federal government's balance sheet.)

As part of the Senior Preferred Stock Purchase Agreements, Treasury also gained significant veto rights over GSE activities, including the termination of the conservatorship.[23] This meant that the continuation of the GSEs' conservatorship was no longer simply a decision for the FHFA, an independent agency, but also one for Treasury, a political agency under direct presidential control.

Additionally, the initial version of the Senior Preferred Stock Purchase Agreements required the GSEs to reduce their portfolios of mortgages and MBS by 10 percent per year until each reached $250 billion, roughly a two-thirds reduction in the size of both GSEs' portfolios from their 2008 10-K valuations.[24] The GSEs would still be able to guaranty any number of mortgages up to the conforming loan limits, but would be limited in their capacity to invest in mortgages or MBS.

Treasury and the GSEs have since amended the terms of the Senior Preferred Stock Purchase Agreements several times. Most significantly, an August 2012 amendment eliminated the 10 percent dividend on the senior preferred stock. The amendments instead entitled Treasury to sweep the GSEs' quarterly net worth based on a formula that generally meant that all profits would be swept into Treasury.[25] The change from a fixed dividend to a profit sweep occurred at a time when the GSEs had returned to profitability. The profit sweep ensured that the GSEs would not be able to pay dividends to their other shareholders (including by drawing on the Treasury line of credit), and instead that all profits would go to Treasury. It also prevented the GSEs from recapitalizing themselves through retained earnings. Additionally, the 2012 amendment accelerated the reduction of the GSEs' portfolios from 10 percent annually to 15 percent annually, so that by 2018 the portfolios were supposed to each be reduced to $250 billion.[26]

The August 2012 amendment was a de facto nationalization of the GSEs. From 2012 to 2019, The Department of the Treasury retained all the upside of each GSE's performance over the $6 billion in combined capital reserves and formally hold all the downside risk beyond that reserve up to $100 billion. For all purposes, though, there is an unlimited commitment from Treasury, given how critical the GSEs remain to the national economy. Treasury also maintains substantial control over major GSE actions through the covenants in the Senior Preferred Stock Purchase Agreements. The arrangement is one in which the GSEs remain formally private companies, albeit in a never-ending conservatorship, and are functionally nationalized. The fact that the GSEs retain control of their day-to-day operations is solely by the grace of the FHFA.

This de facto nationalization has been loosened in degree, but not in kind. In 2017, the Senior Preferred Stock Purchase Agreements were again amended, with Treasury agreeing to allow each GSE to retain a $3 billion capital reserve,[27] enough to allow the GSEs from having to make an embarrassing draw on the Treasury line of credit on account of limited losses. Then, in 2019, as a first step to recapitalizing the GSEs, Treasury permitted Fannie Mae to retain capital up to $25 billion and Freddie Mac to retain capital up to $20 billion, before any profit sweeps.[28]

While the 2019 amendments allow Fannie and Freddie to retain substantial capital, they are still a far cry from complete recapitalization. To wit, in 2018, the FHFA proposed new capital requirements for Fannie and Freddie. Had the proposed rule been in effect on September 30, 2017, the GSEs would have been required to have core capital (equity value plus retained earnings) of at least $103.5 billion under one proposed alternative and $139.5 billion under another.[29]

The 2019 amendments enable the GSEs to build up a substantial first-loss capital barrier ahead of any losses the Treasury may incur. But without the 2019 (and 2017) amendments, all GSE profits would have been swept into Treasury, so any GSE losses would have simply been offset against these profits. The current arrangement enables the future privatization of GSE profits accumulated during conservatorship, even while Treasury remains formally committed during the conservatorship for up to $100 billion for each GSE and functionally committed to an unlimited amount, for which it is not being compensated. In other words, the 2017 and 2019 amendments enable a future privatization of GSE gains, while losses remain socialized.

Beyond the virtually unlimited support for the GSEs through Treasury's Preferred Stock Purchase Agreements, Congress and the Federal Reserve also acted to prop up the housing finance market through a number of programs designed to provide liquidity to effectively insolvent financial institutions, which could then recognize losses over time as they returned to solvency by retaining their earnings. Some of these programs involved the Federal Reserve buying large amounts of MBS, essentially taking the bad assets off the books of financial institutions and parking them on the balance sheet of "bad banks" created by the Fed (the Maiden Lane LLCs). The Fed also undertook measures that lowered interest rates to near zero, while Treasury undertook initiatives to subsidize modifications and refinancings of underwater mortgages.

The immediate effect of these interventions was an environment with very low interest rates, but also highly constrained credit. Lenders' own cost of funds was quite low, but many originators were out of business, and those that remained were chary of lending to any but low-risk borrowers with high FICO scores (a common type of credit score) and low LTVs. Additionally, put-backs (contractually required repurchases by originators of mortgages that fail to conform to specifications) and threats of put-backs from the GSEs and Ginnie Mae chilled the market. Even when the market stabilized, the contraction in lending continued to put downward pressure on home prices.

Market Clearing through Foreclosures

Governmental market stabilization programs were primarily targeted at propping up financial institutions by providing liquidity and capital support. Relatively little was done to stabilize the market on the consumer side, even as delinquency and foreclosure rates soared. (See Figure 5.3.)

The bailout legislation of September 2008, which was dubbed the Emergency Economic Stabilization Act, called for funds to be used to help homeowners, but it did not specify how, leaving the decision in the hands of Treasury.[30] In February 2009, the Barack Obama administration announced a pair of new consumer-assistance programs, the Home Affordable Modification Program (HAMP) and the Home Affordable Refinancing Program (HARP). HAMP was a program that paid bounties to mortgage servicers for modifying loans in accordance with Treasury guidelines, while HARP was a program that allowed underwater homeowners whose loans were owned or guaranteed by the GSEs to refinance their mortgages into lower-rate mortgages without acquiring PMI.

The main goals of HAMP and HARP were to keep consumers current in their mortgages. This was not simply for consumers' sake, but also because

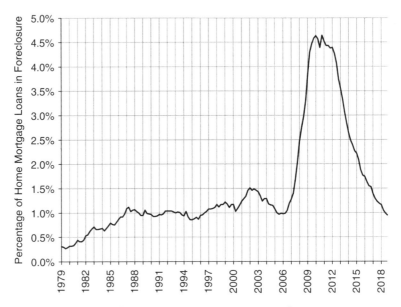

Figure 5.3. Percentage of Home Mortgage Loans in Foreclosure, 1979–2018
Data source: Mortgage Bankers Association, "National Delinquency Survey."

doing so enabled financial institutions to avoid recognizing losses and helped to support home prices by reducing the inventory of homes coming on the market through foreclosure sales.

Generally, HAMP loan modification consisted of term extensions and temporary interest rate reductions. Principal reduction was uncommon, particularly in the early years of the program. The rate reductions and term extensions had the effect of reducing monthly payments, which addressed problems of unaffordability, but the program's lack of aggressive principal reduction meant that it never squarely addressed the problem of underwater mortgages. Indeed, many modifications capitalized delinquent interest and fees, thereby increasing loan balances, which undercut the effect of rate reductions.[31] When a homeowner has an underwater mortgage, he or she has a reduced incentive to make the mortgage payments; if the payments are at all a stretch, the homeowner may well rationally decide to walk away from the home because he or she is not building any equity in the property and is also not losing any equity value in the foreclosure. Moreover, US debt collection laws make it difficult for creditors to collect any deficiencies owed on the mortgage.

Nationwide, aggregate home mortgage debt exceeded aggregate home equity starting in 2007 and continuing until 2012. (See Figure 5.4.) The aggregate figures do not tell the whole story, of course, as home equity and

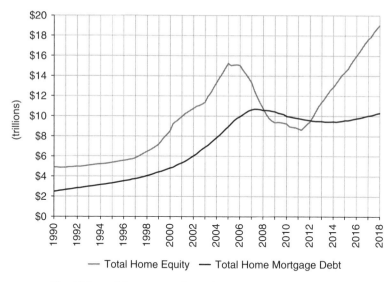

Figure 5.4. Total Home Mortgage Debt and Equity, 1990–2018

Data source: Bd. of Governors of the Fed. Reserve Sys., *Statistical Release Z.1, Financial Accounts of the United States*, tbl. L.218 and tbl. B.101. Total Home Equity is tbl. B.101, line 4 (series LM155035015), multiplied by the quotient of tbl. L.218, line 1 (series FL893065105), over tbl. L.218, line 2 (series FL153165105), in order to reflect home purchases through corporate entities. Total Home Mortgage Debt is tbl. L.218, line 1 (series FL893065105).

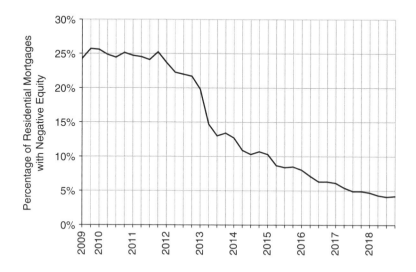

Figure 5.5. Percentage of Mortgages with Negative Equity, 2009–2018

Data source: FirstAmerican CoreLogic.

mortgage debt are not evenly distributed. At the height of the crisis, nearly 12 million mortgages—a quarter of all mortgages or around 10 percent of all properties—were underwater. (See Figure 5.5.) Another 2.5 million mortgages—3 percent of all mortgages—had "near-negative equity," meaning that they had so little positive equity that the properties could not be sold without a loss after accounting for sale expenses. Underwater and near-underwater properties were heavily concentrated in a handful of "bubble" states: Nevada, Florida, Arizona, Georgia, and Michigan in particular. At one point over 72 percent of mortgages in Nevada were underwater.[32]

The goal of HAMP, however, was never to clear the housing market by reducing mortgage principal to housing prices, which would have enabled underwater borrowers to sell their homes. Instead, the program's goal was to buy time for the market to rebound such that housing prices would catch up with mortgage debt (which would be lowered by additional payments) and bring borrowers back into positive equity.[33]

The main tool for addressing negative equity was not HAMP, but rather HARP, a program (extended until December 2018) that allowed for the re-financing of loans that were underwater but performing. HARP thereby helped underwater homeowners take advantage of the lower-rate environment that obtained post-2008, thereby lowering monthly payments. HARP refinancings also often extended the loan's term, which lowered monthly payments further. HARP refinancings, however, did not reduce borrowers' principal, and in fact increased it if they financed their closing costs. Still, by lowering monthly payments, HARP lowered borrower default rates. Because the program only applied to loans owned or guaranteed by the GSEs, however, it was of no assistance to borrowers with loans securitized into PLS, which is precisely where the most troubled loans were.

Some 2.5 million borrowers began trial modifications under HAMP, and 1.7 million borrowers moved on to permanent loan modifications before the program closed at the end of 2016.[34] As of the end of 2017, 650,000 borrowers had flunked out of their permanent modifications and 200,000 had paid off their loans, leaving 875,000 modifications that were still active.[35] Borrowers who did not qualify for HAMP often received some other sort of modification, but many still ultimately lost their house, whether through a negotiated exit (a deed in lieu of foreclosure or a short sale) or a foreclosure. Additionally, over 3.4 million loans were refinanced via HARP through 2018,[36] but not all HARP refinancings were of underwater mortgages.

In comparison with the 1.7 million permanent HAMP modifications commenced from 2008 to 2016, there were over 7.2 million foreclosures completed between 2008 and 2016 (not to mention another 600,000 in

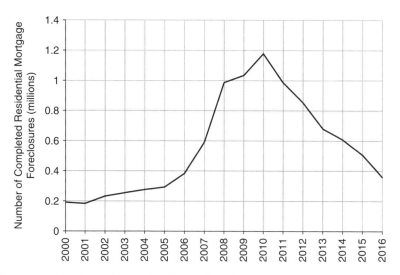

Figure 5.6. Number of Completed Residential Mortgage Foreclosures by Year, 2000–2016

Data source: CoreLogic, *United States Residential Foreclosure Crisis: Ten Years Later*, 4–5 (Mar. 2017), https://www.corelogic.com/research/foreclosure-report/national-foreclosure-report-10-year.pdf.

2007). (See Figure 5.6.) When HAMP's numbers are viewed against the total number of foreclosures, it would appear to be an abject failure: at best, HAMP will help 1 million homeowners keep their homes long term, and likely it will help far fewer. When seen in this way, HAMP had roughly a one in nine success rate. From the perspective of consumers desperate to hang on to their family homes, HAMP stacks up poorly.

From a macroeconomic perspective, however, HAMP is more complicated. While it did not prevent most foreclosures, it did delay several million foreclosures, which relieved downward pressure on the housing market from the flood of foreclosure properties. The delay also enabled financial institutions to recognize losses over a longer period of time, which allowed them to recapitalize themselves through retained earnings.

Despite the intervention of HAMP, the primary form by which the housing market "cleared" was through foreclosure. When housing prices fall, a mortgaged homeowner's debt obligation is not reduced correspondingly; on the contrary, the debt amount is fixed. If the home price falls below the amount owed on the mortgage, the homeowner is underwater, and cannot sell the house at market rates without the consent of the lender because all mortgages contain "due on sale" clauses that require payment of the mortgage when the property is sold. While it is possible for a lender to approve a "short sale" of the property, that is a sale for less than the amount owed, lenders are traditionally wary of short sales, lest the buyer be in collusion with the seller, and mortgage servicers have often not wanted to trouble themselves with dealing with them. Thus, with a quarter of mortgaged properties underwater, the housing market was not clearing—willing buyers and willing sellers could not do transactions at market prices because of the presence of mortgages that exceeded the value of the homes.

The housing market eventually cleared, but it did so through foreclosures, which are a particularly poor clearing mechanism because foreclosure sales are not true arm's-length sales. The precise mechanism for foreclosure sales varies by state (and even by county), but the basics hold true throughout: sales are not advertised the way a private sale would be advertised, potential buyers have no right to enter to inspect the property before bidding, and properties are sold "as is." As a result, foreclosure sale prices are typically at far below the price that would obtain in an arm's-length private sale. Because they lack the ability to inspect the property, foreclosure sale bidders must discount the price to account for the possibility that the home is in poor condition. Buyers may not know the home's layout, whether the fixtures have been stripped, whether it is up to code, and so on. In perhaps the most extreme case, a foreclosure sale buyer in New Jersey paid $2.6 million for a property, only to discover that the house was uninhabitable due to an infestation of at least 142 cats, both living and dead, including in the walls.[37] While this particular unfortunate buyer was able to reverse the sale, that is the exception in foreclosure sales. Stripped fixtures or piping or other damage not observable from inspection of the outside of the property are not usually grounds for reversing a sale.

The rule of caveat emptor depresses prices in foreclosure sales as does the general stigma of foreclosed properties. Moreover, the bidding is house by house, so transaction costs are higher, and the lender's ability to credit bid against the debt chills third-party bidding. The frequent result in foreclosure sales is that the foreclosing lender wins the bid and is then able to inspect the house (although this may first require an eviction action if the former homeowner has not vacated the property), after which the lender resells the property in a private sale. The market only clears with the second, private sale out of real estate owned (REO) properties. Even so, properties sold by lenders generally bring in lower prices than properties sold by owners. In part this is because lenders are incentivized to sell fast in order to avoid the costs of carrying the house (for which they receive no consumption value, unlike a natural person owner). Lower sale prices may also be due to the fact that unoccupied houses tend to sell for less, perhaps because prospective buyers have trouble picturing themselves living in the unoccupied houses.

The negative price effects of residential foreclosure are not limited to the property in foreclosure. Foreclosure sale properties, in turn, depress the price of nearby properties.[38] In part this is because properties that are in foreclosure may not be adequately maintained; a house with an unmowed lawn affects the neighboring house prices adversely. It is also in part, however, because foreclosure sales compete with regular sales and thereby push down prices. A flood of foreclosed properties has the fire-sale effect of depressing the whole market. On top of everything, there is a limited institutional bandwidth for foreclosures in states that conduct foreclosure sales judicially, but delayed foreclosure can result in a serious depreciation of property value as well as a public nuisance.[39] Indeed, residential foreclosures have tremendous spillover costs and tax municipal resources,[40] and they can even create public health problems.[41] All of this meant that the housing market overcorrected in many places, as the clearing price was not an arm's-length sale price, but rather a foreclosure sale price.

Yet it was ultimately left to the foreclosure process to clear the housing market. The main legislative proposal for fixing the market was a proposal to loosen bankruptcy laws to enable consumers to use bankruptcy proceedings to reduce their mortgage debt to the current market value of the property, as could be done with nearly all other types of secured debt. This "cramdown" proposal would have cleared the market to judicial valuations of property—the norm in bankruptcy—and without the social dislocations and other spillover effects of foreclosures.

The argument against cramdown was that underwater borrowers would opportunistically default to get access to a principal reduction in bankruptcy when they could, in fact, continue to make payments. In fact, almost 75 percent of underwater homeowners continued to pay their mortgages (perhaps in the expectation that prices would rise, thus making ruthless default nonoptimal). This meant that lenders did not have to mark to market defaulting mortgages—that is, write them down to their actual value on their balance sheets—at a time when the solvency of the banking system in its entirety was in question. If the loans were marked to market, the decapitalization of lenders would have been apparent to all and lenders would have been required to raise more capital (basically equity). The cramdown proposal was passed by the House but failed to get a final vote in the Senate in the face of the quiet opposition of the Obama Treasury Department, which worried that it would destabilize financial institutions' balance sheets.[42]

The inadequate and often inept government and market response to the foreclosure crisis exacerbated the already serious consequences of the collapse of the housing market. As bad as the parallel commercial real estate crisis was (see Chapter 8 and especially Figure 8.1), it did not decapitalize

American households or lead to a downward spiral of housing prices because the tenants in commercial properties continued to occupy the properties and pay rents even if the landlord was in foreclosure. Residential foreclosure, by comparison, is an incredibly inefficient process that generates tremendous deadweight loss, but the regulatory response concentrated on protecting bank balance sheets from immediate loss recognition, rather than preventing households and communities from the ravages of foreclosure.

In light of this outcome, it's worth considering the final "bill" for the housing bubble, which amounted to over $1 trillion in losses on home mortgages. (See Figure 5.7.) Nearly 8 million homeowners lost their properties in foreclosure, a potentially traumatic event with far-reaching consequences: families having to relocate, kids having to change schools, dreams lost. Investors saw their assets disappear as home prices plunged, and municipal tax bases were eroded. The collateral damage from the collapse of the housing bubble is immeasurable in dollar amounts, but there is no understating the havoc it wreaked on the United States and on the global economy.

The losses from the collapse of the housing market were not distributed equally in the mortgage market. Just over half the losses were in the PLS market, with almost another quarter involving depositories. (See Figure 5.8.) The GSEs were but 14 percent of the losses, and even counting most of the mortgage insurance losses as being insurance on GSE loans, the GSEs,

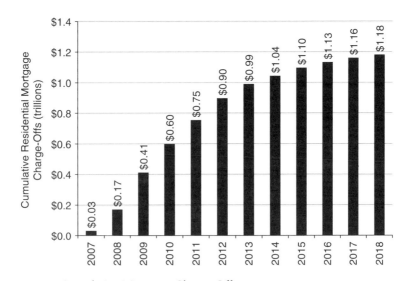

Figure 5.7. Cumulative Mortgage Charge-Offs, 2007–2018

Data source: Bd. of Governors of the Fed. Reserve Sys., *Statistical Release Z.1, Financial Accounts of the United States*, tbl. F.218, line 23 (series FV893065153).

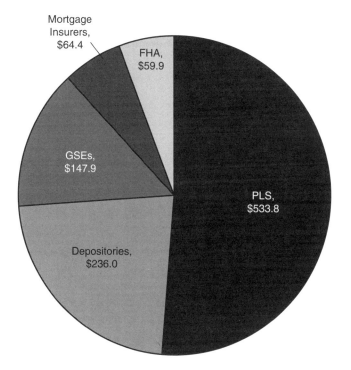

Figure 5.8. Distribution of Mortgage Losses, 2006–2014

Data source: Mark Zandi *et al.*, "Who Bears the Risk in Risk Transfers?" *Moody's Analytics*, Aug. 2017, at 3, *available at* https://www.economy.com/mark-zandi/documents/2017-08-02-who-bears-the-risk.pdf.

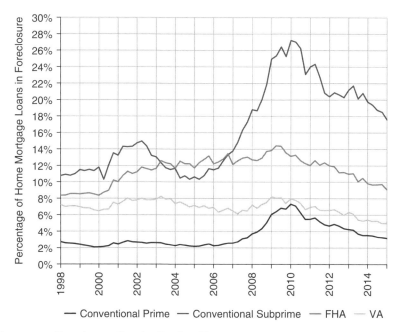

Figure 5.9. Foreclosure Rate by Product Type, 1998–2015

Data source: Mortgage Bankers Association, "National Delinquency Survey."

mortgage insurers, and FHA collectively accounted for only a quarter of the losses, despite Agency MBS never being less than 63 percent of outstanding MBS.[43]

Similarly, Figure 5.9 shows the foreclosure rate by product class, with subprime conventional loans, which were the product funded primarily through PLS, having a substantially higher foreclosure rate than all other types of loans.[44] Moreover, the rise in subprime foreclosures is discernible even in late 2006, and then spiking in 2007–2008, whereas prime foreclosures do not start moving upward until around 2007, and had their largest rise in 2008–2009. This lag is consistent with the possibility that subprime foreclosures drove price declines, which then put pressure on prime homeowners, setting up half of the double trigger of default: negative equity and income disruption.

More than anything else, these foreclosure rate and loss figures tell the story of the bubble—that it was a private-label securitization affair first and foremost. Thus, it is to the rise of private-label securitization that we must turn to ferret out the origins of the housing bubble.

CHAPTER SIX

Timing the Bubble

THE PRECEDING CHAPTERS of this book have presented an extended narrative history of housing finance in the United States leading up to the collapse of the housing finance market in 2008. This chapter and subsequent ones turn to a more explicitly analytical consideration of the housing bubble that burst in 2008. This chapter begins with an examination of the timing of the bubble, which is critical for evaluating the competing causal explanations of the bubble to which we then turn. Subsequent chapters address whether the bubble was a supply- or demand-side phenomenon, consider various theories of the bubble, and present our argument about what caused it.

In order to determine the timing of the bubble, we have to begin at a more fundamental point, namely what is a bubble?[1] A bubble is known by its bursting: a bubble is marked by a rise and then subsequent collapse in an asset price. Not all rises in asset prices, however, are bubbles. Instead, we can distinguish between asset price increases that are driven by changes in fundamental values—the consumption value of an asset or the interest rates used to value assets—and those that are not. In our view, a bubble exists when asset prices deviate materially upward from fundamental values, such that prices are based solely on irrational expectations of future values.[2]

When, then, did asset prices begin to depart from fundamentals in the US housing market? Identifying the beginning of the bubble is particularly important to identifying its causes; any explanation of the bubble must be able to explain the bubble's timing. To the extent that an explanation points to a cause that does not align with the timing, such an explanation is not credible.

There is little consensus among commentators as to when the bubble began, and surprisingly little direct discussion of the issue in the literature, given how critical the timing question is to evaluating causal explanations. This much is clear: on a nominal basis, national housing prices marched upward from 1997–2006, but there was substantial local variation in when the upward price movement began.[3] Thus, some commentators place the start of the bubble in 1997, when the period of unabated appreciation began,[4] and others place the start of the bubble in 2001–2002, when the Federal Reserve lowered short-term interest rates significantly.[5]

We believe the bubble began substantially later—only in 2004 (or possibly 2003). There was an increase in nominal home prices starting in 1997, but a movement in nominal home prices alone does not necessarily indicate a bubble. To get a true sense of the bubble, we need to examine inflation-adjusted housing prices (presented in Figure 6.1) rather than the nominal housing prices that are typically reported by housing price indices (see also Figure 6.2). Figure 6.1 shows that while housing prices moved upward from 1997 until 2007, inflation-adjusted housing prices did not pass their previous peak level until 2000. The increase in housing prices from 1997 to

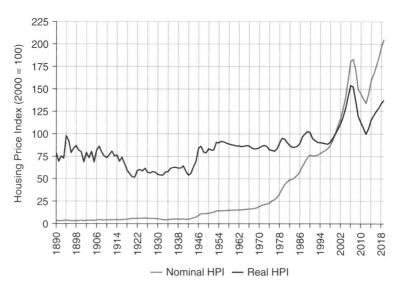

Figure 6.1. US Nominal and Inflation-Adjusted Housing Price Indexes, 1890–2019

Data source: Robert J. Shiller, *irrationalexuberance.com*.

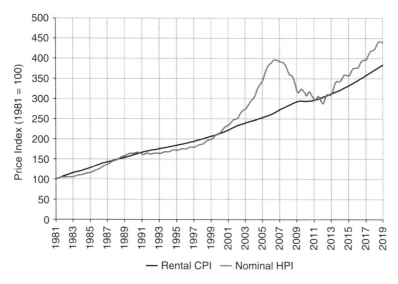

Figure 6.2. Nominal US Housing Price Index and Rental Consumer Price Index, 1981–2019

Data source: *S&P/Case-Shiller Housing Price Index (HPI)*; Bureau of Labor Statistics, *Rent of Primary Residence (Rental CPI)*.

2000 was within the regular historic range of inflation-adjusted housing price fluctuations, indicating that they were not necessarily part of a bubble.

Housing prices also kept pace with rental prices during the period from 1997 to 2000, as Figure 6.2 shows.[6] The rate of appreciation of both housing and rental costs remained basically identical, as they had since at least 1981, when the Bureau of Labor Statistics began to compile a rental price index. This indicates that into 2000, housing prices did not stray from their fundamental values.

Starting in 2000, however, housing prices began to appreciate at a much faster rate than rental prices, as Figure 6.2 shows. This divergence in rates of appreciation does not necessarily indicate the existence of a bubble. Instead, the years 2001–2003 were marked by historically low interest rates. Low interest rates explain the faster increase in housing prices than rental prices from 2001 to 2003 because they made home purchases relatively cheaper. With fully amortized fixed-rate mortgages—the overwhelming bulk of the mortgage market prior to 2004—the cost of financing a home purchase is heavily dependent on interest rates.[7] With low mortgage interest rates during this period, the cost of homeownership fell relative to the cost of renting. Indeed, this is consistent with the finding by real estate economists Fernando Ferreira and Joseph Gyourko that the upward rise of housing prices in local markets was driven first by conventional mortgage financing, with nontraditional mortgages substituting later.[8] Accordingly, it follows that housing prices would rise faster than rental prices. Indeed, real estate economists Charles Himmelberg, Chris Mayer, and Todd Sinai have argued that the increase in housing prices through 2004 was not a bubble, but in fact reflected fundamentals, as shown by the imputed annual rental cost of owning a house.[9] The housing price increase that accompanied the refinancing boom in 2001–2003 does not appear to have been a bubble, but was instead driven by fundamentals.[10]

From 2004 onward, however, real estate fundamentals did not support any further price increases. Interest rates rose, thereby reducing the attractiveness of homeownership relative to renting, yet price increases still occurred. This is a strong indication that although there was housing price appreciation from the mid-1990s, there was not a bubble until 2004.[11] As discussed in the next chapter, this timing does not appear to be coincidental. Instead, it fits neatly with the change in the financing channel, which shifted from semi-regulated GSE securitization of prime, fixed-rate mortgages to unregulated private-label securitization of nontraditional adjustable-rate mortgages.

What we see, then, is that only the last few years of the decade-long appreciation in home prices that started in the 1990s were actually a bubble. The rest of the appreciation is explained by fundamentals. The bubble only lasted from 2004 until 2006. Home prices started to fall in mid-2006, although the bottom did not fully fall out until 2008. In other words, the bubble itself was a very short period.

Timing the bubble not only provides an important tool for evaluating causal explanations, it also points to the limitations on market discipline in preventing bubbles. It did not take very long for a massively destructive housing bubble to form. Given how quickly a bubble can form, it is very hard for the market or regulators to identify a bubble before it is too late. Housing price and mortgage performance data do not percolate into the market in real time. Instead, they are generally delayed by months, and even when data does reach the market, it may take several months for there to be enough data for trends to become apparent and to be able to discount the possibility that a single data point is an outlier. This means that by the time the market recognizes that a bubble is forming, it is too late: the bubble is already there. Market discipline depends on *real-time* information and an investment vehicle for acting on that information effectively. In the absence of a system with real-time information, market discipline cannot prevent bubbles. This problem is one to which we will return in Chapter 10 when considering information failures during the bubble, and Chapter 12, when considering how to reform the housing finance system.

CHAPTER SEVEN

Demand or Supply?

IN THE PREVIOUS chapter we established that the bubble was a very brief affair, from roughly 2004 to 2006. The growth in real home prices in the 2001–2003 period can be explained by changes in fundamentals, but the meteoric growth in 2004–2006 cannot.

But it is not enough merely to identify a bubble. The real question is: what caused the bubble? There is no shortage of theories about what caused the housing bubble, and these different theories point to very different policy responses, ranging from stricter regulation to deregulation.

All theories of the bubble can be categorized in two groups: demand-side theories and supply-side theories. The demand-side theories argue that the bubble was spurred by consumer demand for housing, either because of a secular increase in consumer demand or because of naturally increasing demand running into constraints in housing supply or because irrational exuberance takes over previously rational decisions to buy. In all cases, consumer demand for housing translated into consumer demand for housing finance. Most consumers buy homes on credit, and consumers used more and more credit to bid up housing price, as they anticipated ever higher home prices.

In contrast, supply-side theories see the bubble as driven by a glut of cheap mortgage financing that enabled previously credit-constrained consumers to bid up housing prices. In both demand-side and supply-side theories, then, it is mortgage borrowing that drives the housing bubble. Indeed, as Figure 7.1

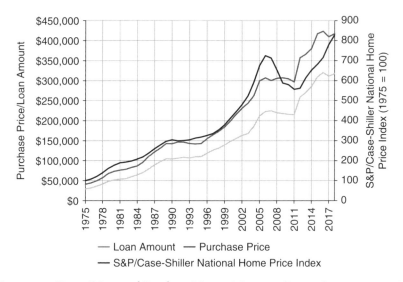

Figure 7.1. Home Prices and Purchase Money Mortgage Borrowing, 1975–2018

Data source: FHFA, *Monthly Interest Rate Survey*, tbl. 9; *S&P/Case-Shiller National Home Price Index* (monthly June index values, 1975 = 100).

shows, first-lien purchase-money mortgage borrowing rose in sync with home price increases, as purchase prices and loan amounts went up in lock step.[1] This should hardly be surprising, as most home purchases are made on credit, and with home prices rising faster than incomes, credit was needed to make up the difference. The question is whether that increase in credit was a response to demand growth or whether easier credit was the factor that unleashed existing, but credit-constrained demand to bid up home prices.

Whether the bubble was a demand- or supply-side phenomenon matters for two reasons. First, in thinking about how to prevent future bubbles, it is necessary to understand the cause of this one. If the bubble was supply-driven, it is possible to prevent future bubbles through regulation of the financial sector. In contrast, demand-driven bubbles may be more difficult to prevent, particularly if they are based on human psychology.

Second, the different theories of the bubble predict different impacts on mortgage finance pricing and availability, and therefore enable us to test them. In particular, a demand-side theory posits a rightward shift of the demand curve, meaning an increase in the price of mortgage finance and an increase in the quantity provided. (See Figure 7.2.)

A supply-side theory, in contrast, posits a rightward shift of the supply curve, which would mean a decrease in mortgage pricing and an increase in mortgage quantity. (See Figure 7.3.)

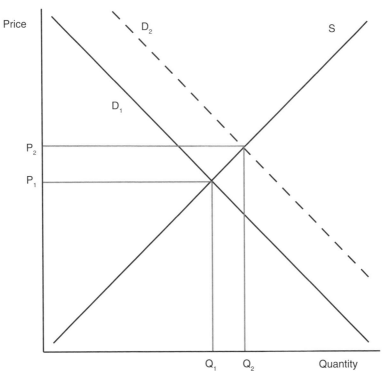

Figure 7.2. Demand-Side Theory: A Rightward Shift in Housing Finance Demand Curve

Original creation by the authors.

We can empirically test which scenario—a shift of the demand curve or of the supply curve—fits with the movements of price and quantity in the mortgage market. It is possible, of course, that there was a shift in *both* the demand and supply curves. Observations of price and quantity movement only tell us which shift predominated; they do not disprove that a lesser shift could have occurred in the other curve.

The evidence concerning both the quantity and the price of mortgage lending points to the bubble being predominantly a supply-side phenomenon.

Mortgage Quantity

Data on mortgage lending volume has not always been readily available, much less in real time and for the entire market. Even today, the FHFA's Mortgage Interest Rate Survey, which claims to be "the nation's most

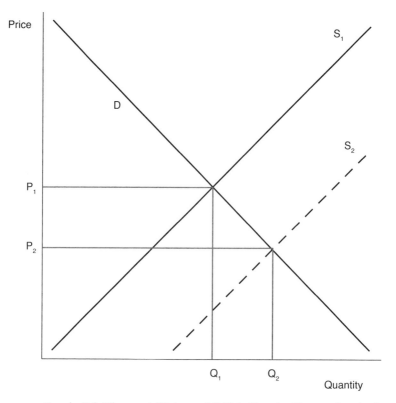

Figure 7.3. Supply-Side Theory: A Rightward Shift in Housing Finance Supply Curve
Original creation by the authors.

comprehensive source of information on conventional mortgage rates and terms," excludes refinancings, nonamortizing loans and junior lien loans, which were a substantial share of the market during the bubble years.[2]

Overall mortgage lending volume (including refinancings) peaked in 2003, but it was at historically elevated levels throughout the 2002–2007 period. (See Figure 7.4.) As noted, however, there was a marked shift in mortgage *products* during the bubble. Nontraditional mortgages, such as interest-only and balloon mortgages, proliferated, as did underwriting based on stated income and assets (otherwise known as "liar" loans). Moreover, the bubble years were marked by an increase in so-called subprime mortgages made to borrowers with poor credit quality as measured by credit scores. Prior to the bubble years, these borrowers were often credit constrained; there were a limited number of lenders who were willing to treat with them, and these lenders charged a premium because of the risk posed by these borrowers.

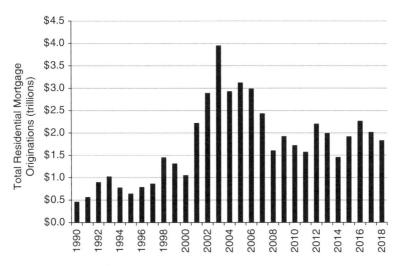

Figure 7.4. Residential Mortgage Originations, 1990–2018

Data source: Inside Mortgage Finance, *2019 Mortgage Market Statistical Annual.*

Figure 7.5 shows that nontraditional mortgage lending (subprime and alt-A) grew from 2000 to 2005 and fell only slightly in 2006 before declining steeply in 2007, once home prices were already falling. Home equity loans—both second-lien loans and first-lien non-purchase money, non-refinance loans for extracting equity from homes already owned free and clear—also increased sharply during this period but lagged behind the growth of nontraditional mortgages by about a year. Figure 7.6 shows that not only did the dollar volume of these loans increase, so too did their combined market share, which reached hitting nearly 50 percent of all lending in 2006.

We also show, in Table 7.1, that these years saw an increase in private-label securitization, which funded much of the nontraditional and subprime lending and grew its share of total origination from 13 percent in 2000 to nearly 40 percent in 2006. Notably, Figure 7.7 shows that while there was a surge in PLS backed by nonprime or subprime mortgages, there was no growth during the bubble years in the PLS backed by prime jumbo mortgages. The PLS boom was entirely linked to nontraditional mortgages.

Such an increase in the volume of subprime and nontraditional mortgage lending during the bubble years of 2004–2006 is itself consistent with both demand-side and supply-side theories. It is consistent with a growth in demand for the cheapest possible mortgage credit founded on expectations of ever-higher home prices, but it is also consistent with an easing of supply

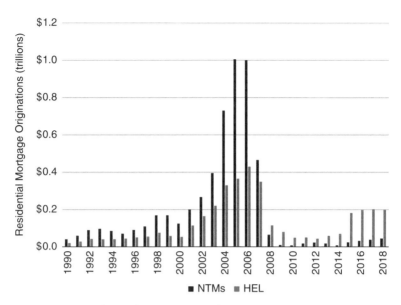

Figure 7.5. Nontraditional Mortgage and Home Equity Loan Originations, 1990–2018

Data source: Inside Mortgage Finance, *2019 Mortgage Market Statistical Annual*.

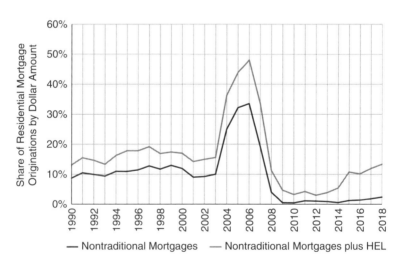

Figure 7.6. Market Share of Nontraditional Mortgage Originations, 1990–2018

Data source: Inside Mortgage Finance, *2019 Mortgage Market Statistical Annual*.

Table 7.1. Volume of Subprime Mortgage Originations, 2000–2008

Year	2000	2001	2002	2003	2004	2005	2006	2007	2008
Total Originations ($ billions)	1,048	2,215	2,885	3,945	2,920	3,120	2,980	2,430	1,485
Total Mortgages Securitized ($ billions)	615	1,355	1,857	2,716	1,882	2,156	2,045	1,864	1,264
% of Originations Securitized	59%	61%	64%	69%	64%	69%	69%	77%	85%
PLS Issuance ($ billions)	136	267	413	586	864	1,191	1,145	707	58
PLS Issuance as % of Total Originations	13%	12%	14%	15%	30%	38%	38%	29%	4%
GSE MBS Issuance as % of Total Originations	46%	49%	50%	54%	35%	31%	30%	48%	81%

Source: Inside Mortgage Finance, *2019 Mortgage Market Statistical Annual.*

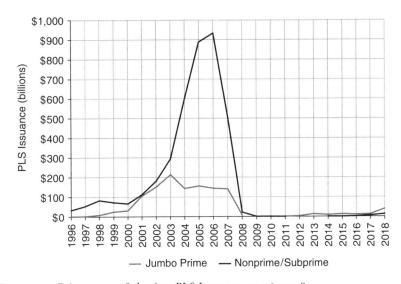

Figure 7.7. Prime versus Subprime PLS Issuance, 1996–2018

Data source: Securities Industry and Financial Markets Association (SIFMA), *U.S. Non-Agency Commercial and Residential Real Estate Securities (CMBS and RMBS) Issuance.*

constraints. Thus, it is to mortgage pricing that we must turn to resolve the question of whether the bubble was primarily a demand-side or supply-side phenomenon.

Mortgage Pricing and Risk during the Bubble

The risk of subprime mortgages *increased* noticeably during the bubble years in several dimensions, while the spreads on these mortgages over maturity-matched Treasuries *decreased*. Thus, risk-adjusted pricing on these mortgages *fell* even as the volume of mortgage lending *increased*. The increase in quantity, accompanied by a decrease in the price of risk, indicates that the bubble was primarily a supply-side phenomenon.

Specifically, looking back before the bubble to 2001, we see the average loan size in subprime securitizations grew substantially, from around $96,000 in 2001 to almost $200,000 in 2007.[3] The growth of loan sizes is hardly surprising. Loan sizes and housing prices were in an upward spiral: as we saw in Figure 7.1, larger loans allowed borrowers to bid up home prices, and higher home prices necessitated more borrowing. Indeed, for the period 2001–2007 there is a 96 percent correlation between the average loan size and housing prices. (See Figure 7.8.) As housing prices peaked in 2006, it is

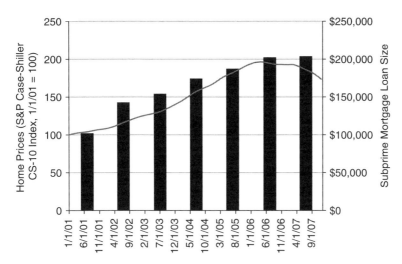

Figure 7.8. Correlation between Subprime Loan Size and Housing Prices, 2001–2007

Data source: Levitin-Wachter Subprime PLS Database (average subprime mortgage amount; annual July 1 dates used); *S&P Case-Shiller CS-10 Index* (housing prices) (January 1, 2001 = 100).

not surprising that loan size plateaued in 2007, especially as the volume of subprime originations fell by over two-thirds.[4] Again, however, recall that house price increases alone are not necessarily a bubble.

While loan sizes increased substantially from 2001 to 2007, LTVs remained basically static, only rising from 79 to 81 percent. The fact that LTVs remained constant on first liens meant that loan sizes were keeping pace with property valuations, which in turn meant that the security of the loans was based on the maintenance of home prices. This was a particularly risky gamble in a market in which home prices are both serially and geographically correlated such that one lender's bad lending can have spillover effects on the value of another lender's collateral.

Credit scores in subprime PLS also remained largely static, rising about 10–15 points from 2001–2002 to 2004–2007. One should not read much into this rise for two reasons. First, credit scores under 650 are definitional for subprime PLS; and second, it is unclear whether weighted-average credit scores rising from 613 to 625 is in any way significant in terms of credit quality. In any event, one would expect to see some increase in credit scores in the face of a booming economy, as credit scores are most heavily influenced by borrowers' recent payment history. In a strong economy, one would expect borrowers' payment history to improve overall.

Declared owner occupancy levels remained stable throughout the 2001–2007 period, in the low 90 percent range. The percentage of fully documented loans dropped noticeably, however, starting in 2004. In the 2001–2003 period, over 70 percent of loans were fully documented, and during the 2004–2007 period, the percentage of fully documented loans fell to around 60 percent.

Interest-only periods were rare for subprime loans prior to 2004. Starting in 2004, however, a substantial portion of loans—ultimately over 15 percent—began to have such periods.[5] The appearance of interest-only products in 2004–2007 is notable for two reasons.

First, the increase in interest-only loans is a sign of lenders seeking to expand the borrower base by decreasing monthly payments on loans, which enables them to buy more. The beneficiaries of lower payments are not necessarily first-time home buyers or even low- to moderate-income households, but include existing home buyers seeking to upgrade and property investors.[6] The interest-only periods that were offered were typically between one and five years, and they had the effect of decreasing the monthly payment amount due on the loan.

Second, loans with interest-only periods are similar to those with teaser rates: there will be a payment shock when the interest-only or teaser period ends. If the loan is underwritten based on the interest-only payment or the teaser rate, the borrower will be unlikely to be able to afford the full payment rate and will default. Thus, interest-only loans, like loans with teaser rates, are dependent on the borrower being able to refinance before the expiry of the interest-only period. Many of these loans had prepayment penalties, however, which disincentivized refinancings. The increase in interest-only loans thus marked a sharp increase in the riskiness of subprime mortgage loans.

A similar (and related) story appears with the incidence of balloon loans, including thirty-year loans with forty- or fifty-year amortizations and fifteen-year loans with thirty-year amortizations. The balloon payment structure has the effect of decreasing monthly payments prior to the balloon coming due and is, in a sense, an affordability product. As with interest-only loans, the maturity of the balloon payment presents the risk of a payment shock, and thus a default if the loan has not been refinanced. Balloon loans were relatively uncommon prior to 2006, when they shot up to nearly 29 percent of lending volume, and by 2007 they were nearly 37 percent of lending volume. Beyond interest-only and balloon payments, payment-option ARMs, which gave borrowers an option of negative amortization, also proliferated.

Another measure of risk in PLS—the frequency of second liens being included in the collateral backing these products—also increased starting in

2004, rising from around 2 percent in the 2001–2003 period to as high as 9 percent in 2006. Second liens have a higher risk of loss on default than first liens because of their subordinate lien position, so an increase in the volume of second-lien loans in securitizations is a mark of an increase of risk in those securitizations.

Simultaneously, lending volume moved away from FRMs to ARMs, further increasing the credit risk on the loans because of the risk of rate shock. By 2006, ARMs accounted for 70 percent of the number and 80 percent of the dollar volume of loans in private-label securitizations,[7] and nearly half of overall originations by dollar volume.[8]

What we see, then, is that by several measures—loan size, full-documentation percentage, interest-only percentage, balloon loan percentage, second-lien percentage, and ARM percentage—the loans securitized into subprime PLS grew markedly riskier from 2004 to 2007. (Table 7.2 provides a summary.) These risks were not offset by changes in LTV (which actually increased) or in credit scores (which saw only a modest increase). Indeed, because these risk factors were often layered in the same loan, the total measure of risk increased more than any single factor reflects.

The increase in risk in subprime PLS between 2001 and 2007 is not itself indicative of a supply- or demand-side bubble. This determination depends on whether that risk was being priced in the market. One would expect that riskier mortgages would bear greater spreads over a risk-free rate (such as a maturity-matched Treasury security). Or, alternatively, one would expect the volume of lending to shrink as risk rose.

Neither of those things happened, however. Instead, spreads on the mortgages in subprime PLS *decreased* during the 2001–2006 period (rising only slightly in 2007), and volume increased substantially. (Refer back to Figure 7.7.) Figure 7.9 shows the spread between the weighted-average in-

Table 7.2. Subprime Mortgage Loan Risk Characteristics

Deal Year	Loan Size	LTV	Credit Score	Owner Occupied %	Full Doc %	IO%	Balloon %	Second Lien %
2001	$96,209	79.6	613	90.7	75.7	0.5	10.1	1.5
2002	$137,145	79.8	612	93.8	71.2	0.1	3.6	2.1
2003	$148,128	79.1	621	93.0	72.4	0.7	2.1	1.9
2004	$168,925	82.0	626	92.0	65.4	7.6	2.0	4.1
2005	$181,015	81.1	628	91.7	60.4	17.4	4.9	6.2
2006	$195,625	81.0	628	92.0	58.5	16.4	28.6	8.9
2007	$197,467	81.3	625	92.5	59.7	15.5	36.8	3.5

Source: Levitin-Wachter Subprime PLS Database. Other than average loan-size data, data are weighted averages with weighting by dollar volume of PLS group within securitizations.

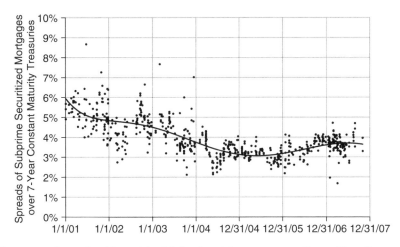

Figure 7.9. Spreads of Securitized Subprime Mortgages over Seven-Year Constant Maturity Treasuries, 2001–2007

Data source: Levitin-Wachter Subprime PLS Database; Bd. of Governors of the Fed. Reserve Sys., *7-Year Treasury Constant Maturity Rate [DGS7]*, retrieved from FRED, Federal Reserve Bank of St. Louis, *at* https://fred.stlouisfed.org/series/DGS7.

terest rate of the mortgages that were securitized in subprime PLS over seven-year constant-maturity Treasuries.[9] Figure 7.9 includes a polynomial trend line that facilitates the identification of the movement of spreads. What it shows is that spreads were in the range of 5–6 percent in 2001 and fell to around 3 percent in 2004–2005. The spreads rose slightly in 2006 to between 3 and 4 percent, but still remained at much lower levels than in the 2001–2003 period. Thus, during the bubble years of 2004–2006, there were significantly compressed spreads on subprime mortgages.

The decrease in mortgage spreads indicates a decrease in the aggregate spreads on PLS themselves. This is because the coupon on PLS is necessarily the weighted-average mortgage rate minus certain expenses (servicer and trustee fees). These expenses are standardized at around 50 basis points (0.5 percent) in a subprime PLS without monoline insurance.

The weighted-average coupon on all the tranches in a PLS deal is a function of the weighted-average rate of the underlying mortgages. While some PLS tranches sold with an original issuance discount, mortgage spreads are still a strong measure of the weighted-average risk premiums provided to investors.

Observable mortgage characteristics became increasingly risky as the housing bubble expanded from 2004 to 2006, as indicated by the shift in products to balloon and interest-only mortgages, the decline in full documentation of borrowers' incomes, the greater share of ARMs, the increased number of second mortgages in the deals, steady FICOs despite a booming economy, and the fact that LTVs remaining steady despite a sharp increase in property valuations. The growth in mortgage risk necessarily meant a growth in risk on PLS. Yet what we see from the data is that the spread on the mortgages, and thus on the PLS themselves, *decreased*. Risk premia declined at the very time that observable risk was increasing.

Even when risk premia increased slightly in 2006–2007, as housing prices peaked and began to decline, the premia were hardly commensurate with the increase in observable risk characteristics, because it did not return to pre-2004 levels prior to the financial crisis in 2008, despite the observable risk characteristics being substantially elevated above pre-2004 levels. In other words, on a risk-adjusted basis, we see an even sharper decline in the price of mortgage financing. Mortgage financing was becoming *cheaper* during the bubble, even as the volume of mortgages and PLS *increased*.[10]

A decrease in pricing combined with an increase in quantity is consistent with an outward (rightward) shift of the housing finance supply curve. In other words, there was a glut of mortgage financing during the bubble; the bubble was predominantly a supply-side phenomenon. There might have been an increase in demand for the incentive to borrow increases as the cost of borrowing declines. But even with an increase in the demand for housing finance, there was a greater increase in housing finance supply. Indeed, investors' demand for subprime PLS was outstripping the supply of mortgages.[11] As the following chapters explicate, this observation is critical for understanding the cause of the housing bubble, because it forces us to ask why the market failed to respond to the growing risk.

CHAPTER EIGHT

Theories of the Bubble

IN THE PREVIOUS chapter, we saw that theories of the housing bubble fall into two general categories: demand-side theories and supply-side theories. The demand-side theories see the bubble as driven by an increase in consumer demand for housing finance. Alternatively, supply-side theories see the bubble as driven by a glut of mortgage financing. What caused the shift in demand or supply is a matter of considerable debate among theorists.

In this chapter we test these various theories of the bubble against the facts, particularly what we have seen about when the bubble occurred (Chapter 6) and the movement in the pricing and volume of mortgage lending (Chapter 7). It is important to recognize that theories about the *housing bubble* are distinct from theories about the *financial crisis* that followed. There is general agreement that the collapse of the housing bubble was the catalyst for the financial crisis, but the literature on why the financial system was so vulnerable to a shock from a collapse in housing prices is distinct from the question of why a bubble formed in the housing market. Our focus here is solely on theories about what caused the housing bubble itself.

What we see is that all of the existing theories of the bubble are, at worst, unsupported and, at best, incomplete. While the evidence supports a supply-side theory, the question remains as to why the supply of mortgage finance expanded at the time and to the degree that it did. The existing supply-side theories that focus variously on monetary policy, inelastic housing supply, and government policy are insufficient in their explanatory power. Although we believe that all these factors contributed in some way, none of them alone, or even in combination, however, can provide a sufficient explanation for why the bubble emerged when and how it did. Instead, as we explain in the following chapters, the driving force behind the bubble was a supply-side change in the pricing and availability of mortgage credit caused by the shift in the primary financing channel from the GSEs to PLS. However, this proximate cause raises the deeper question (also addressed in following chapters) of why markets failed to move against the mispricing and oversupply of credit and resulting rises in housing prices.

We proceed in this chapter by first reviewing demand-side theories of the bubble, before turning to supply-side theories. We lay out our own theory in detail in the following chapters.

Demand-Side Theories

Mass Psychology, Irrational Exuberance, and Flippers

Among the dominant explanations of the housing bubble to date have been demand-side explanations. For example, Nobel Prize–winning economist Robert Shiller has argued that the bubble was driven by consumers' irrational exuberance and belief that real estate prices would continue to appreciate, stoking the demand for housing finance.[1]

We do not question the existence of irrational consumer expectations and behavior. There was undoubtedly a great deal of irrational or misguided consumer behavior in real estate investment, and Shiller has ably explored the psychology of bubbles. Consumers' price expectations are generally set by projecting forward past price movements. If the appreciation is due to a loosening of constraints on supply or demand, they do not expect a discontinuity to that loosening and may thus continue to consume based on an expectation of continued price increases.

But consumer psychology is an incomplete explanation of the bubble. However exuberant consumers were to buy housing, they could not do so absent readily available financing. What we saw in Chapter 7 is that lenders more than met consumer demand, increasing the supply of mortgage financing and dropping its price even as risk increased. Shiller's demand-side theory cannot explain this movement in pricing and quantity of mortgage lending.[2]

Housing Supply Constraints

Another demand-side quasi-hypothesis for the housing bubble emphasizes the geographic variation in the housing bubble. This theory, which was presented by economists Edward Glaeser, Joseph Gyourko, and Albert Saiz,[3] notes that there was considerable regional and local variance. Some regions and states, such as Texas, did not experience a bubble, while others experienced bubbles of greater or lesser size.

Glaeser, Gyourko, and Saiz explain the variation in house price outcomes based in part on variations in the elasticity of housing supply, that is its propensity to expand to meet demand. If housing supply is inelastic, then housing prices will increase with population growth and income growth just as a matter of fundamentals. The elasticity of housing supply depends in part on local regulations affecting land use and construction costs. One would expect, then, for housing prices to grow faster in regions with more population and income growth along with more constrained housing supply.

Glaeser, Gyourko, and Saiz do not explicitly present housing supply constraints as the explanation for the bubble, although others do.[4] Instead, they present supply inelasticity as affecting variations in how the bubble played out regionally. They argue that supply inelastic regions are more likely to experience greater price volatility and bubbles and that the extent of the bubble was determined to some degree by the inelasticity of housing supply.[5]

We agree that supply inelasticity affected regional variations in the bubble, but it does not explain the bubble generally. Housing supply constraints undoubtedly caused some regional variation in the bubble—in regions with abundant housing options and responsive supply, borrowers would be unlikely to bid up housing prices, even if offered underpriced mortgage finance—but we find the housing supply constraint an incomplete explanation insofar as it does not explain why the bubble occurred when it did, why there was a collapse, and why mortgage pricing and volume moved as documented in the previous chapter.

Supply-Side Theories

Government Fair Lending and Affordable Housing Policy

Several politically conservative commentators have pointed to federal fair lending and affordable housing policies as being critical in inflating the housing bubble by encouraging financial institutions to lend improvidently to low- or moderate-income (and impliedly minority) consumers.[6] In particular, these commentators focus on the Community Reinvestment Act of 1977 (the CRA) and the GSEs' Affordable Housing Goals.

This narrative of the crisis, which we call the "Government Made Me Do It" theory of the bubble, emphasizes the adverse, unintended consequences of government interference in the market. The Government Made Me Do It narrative also comes with an obvious policy prescription of ending government intervention in housing markets.

COMMUNITY REINVESTMENT ACT

The least sophisticated versions of the Government Made Me Do It theory focus on the CRA. The CRA was passed in 1977 in response to the discriminatory lending practice known as "redlining"—the practice of lenders refusing to offer financial services in minority or low-income neighborhoods.

The CRA "encourages federally insured banks and thrifts to meet the credit needs of the entire communities that they serve, including low- and moderate-income areas, consistent with safe and sound banking practices."[7] Critically, the CRA applies only to banks and thrifts, and does not apply to nonbank lenders. Moreover, even for banks and thrifts, the CRA does not require them to make loans. Rather, covered financial institutions are evaluated by regulators on how well they serve the needs of low- to moderate-income (LTMI) borrowers in their CRA geographic assessment area. The evaluations are used as a factor in determining whether to approve the institutions' mergers with and acquisitions of other depository institutions, as well as whether to approve the expansion of bank holding companies into other types of financial activities.[8] Regulators' CRA evaluation methods have remained constant since 1995.[9]

The consensus in the scholarly literature is that the CRA did not directly contribute to the bubble.[10] Institutions that were subject to the CRA made a disproportionately small share of subprime mortgage loans—that is, loans made to borrowers with subprime credit scores.[11] Indeed, it bears emphasis that LTMI borrowers are not the same thing as subprime borrowers. Subprime status is a function of credit scores, but credit scores are a poor proxy for income.[12]

Moreover, relatively few subprime loans even qualified for CRA credit either because they were made outside CRA assessment areas or were made to higher-income borrowers.[13] Census tracts served disproportionately by CRA-covered lenders had less risky loans and lower delinquency rates than those served disproportionately by non-CRA lenders.[14] Similarly, there is no evidence of a change in riskiness of loans or loan performance at the discontinuity threshold for CRA eligibility.[15] It is possible that depositories were driven to purchase a greater volume of loans originated by independent mortgage companies in order to gain CRA credit, but sufficient data do not exist on this point.

Ultimately, though, blaming the housing bubble on the CRA suffers from three fundamental logical flaws. First, the residential housing bubble was mirrored almost exactly by a commercial real estate bubble.[16] (See Figure 8.1, below.) While there is some interlinkage between residential and commercial real estate prices, the commercial real estate bubble cannot be attributed to the residential bubble. As the CRA does not apply to commercial real estate lending, it cannot explain the existence of the commercial real estate bubble. Yet the synchronous growth and collapse of the residential and commercial real estate bubbles cannot be coincidental.

Second, there were also contemporaneous, and in some cases even more severe, residential real estate bubbles in Denmark, Ireland, Iceland, the Netherlands, Spain, and the United Kingdom.[17] (See Figure 8.2.) It is hard to explain these parallel foreign bubbles as the product of the domestic CRA.

Third, the timing of the bubble vitiates the CRA explanation. The CRA substantially predates the bubble, so it is difficult to attribute housing price rises in 2004–2006 to a 1977 statute with a regulatory implementation that was last revised in 1995.[18] While one would expect some time lag before

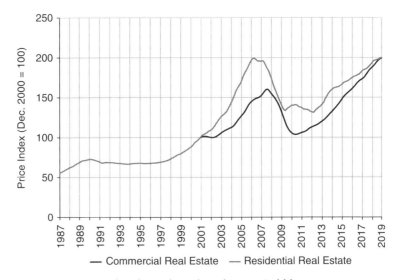

Figure 8.1. Commercial and Residential Real Estate Bubbles, 1987–2018

Data source: *S&P/Case-Shiller Housing Price Index CS-10* (residential price index); *Moody's/RCA Commercial Property Price Index-National All Properties* (commercial price index).

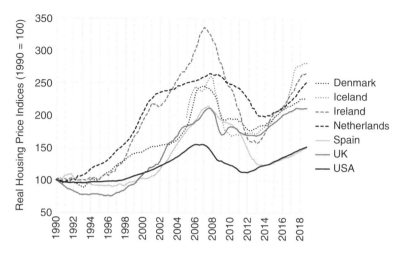

Figure 8.2. Real Housing Price Indices, Select Bubble Countries, 1990–2018
Data source: Organisation for Economic Co-operation and Development (OECD).

seeing the result of the CRA, the time lag is far too long to make the connection plausible. The case that the CRA drove banks to improvident lending is not tenable.[19]

GSE AFFORDABLE HOUSING GOALS

The more sophisticated versions of the Government Made Me Do It theory focus on the GSEs' Affordable Housing Goals. The GSEs have been subject to regulatory Affordable Housing Goals since 1993.[20] These goals, set by the Department of Housing and Urban Development, are designed "to facilitate credit access and homeownership among lower-income and minority households."[21] If a GSE fails to meet the Affordable Housing Goals and does not present and pursue an acceptable remedial plan, monetary penalties and injunctive relief are available to its regulator.[22]

The Goals consist of three general measures: an LTMI Goal, a Special Affordable Goal, and an Underserved Areas Goal, as well as subgoals for special affordable multifamily and home purchase (as opposed to refinancing).[23] The Goals are measured as the ratio of qualifying mortgages financed to total mortgages financed. High-priced "HOEPA" mortgages are disqualified from counting toward Affordable Housing Goals,[24] as are mortgages for second residences, and "mortgages with unacceptable terms," which are defined as including those with excessive fees, prepayment penalties, credit life insurance, or that did not adequately consider the borrower's ability to pay.[25] Starting in 1995, the GSEs were able to get Affordable Housing Goal credit for purchases of MBS, including PLS.[26]

Although the Affordable Housing Goals are often cast as being about channeling credit to the poor, this is not quite accurate. The LTMI Goal does not distinguish between low and moderate income, and moderate income is defined as anything up to the median income level in an area.[27] That hardly includes only the poor, and indeed, the truly poor typically cannot amass enough funds for a down payment on even a modest property.

Likewise, the Special Affordable Housing Goal is limited to low-income households—those with income of no more than 80 percent of the area's median income—and with requirements that certain multifamily units be affordable by "very low-income" or "especially low-income" households. The Special Affordable Housing Goal anticipates that it will be met primarily with multifamily housing—not the source of the residential real estate bubble—as each unit in a multifamily dwelling is counted separately.[28] Double counting is permitted for the Goals,[29] and the Special Affordable Goal has never been more than two-fifths of the LTMI Goal, so most of the LTMI Goal could have been met with median or near-median income households—hardly an inherently uncreditworthy population.

The GSE Affordable Housing Goals were increased in 1997, 2001, and 2005. The GSEs generally met the Goals and were never penalized for failing to do so.[30] In order to meet the Goals, the GSEs increased their proportion of loans made to target populations[31] and expanded their underwriting criteria to enable the purchase of riskier loans.[32] Yet GSE loans substantially outperformed non-GSE loans in terms of default rates when the bubble burst.

Moreover, there is little evidence that the GSE Affordable Housing Goals increased the total amount of credit available to underserved communities.[33] One possible explanation of this is that GSE activity crowded out the FHA for lending to underserved borrowers. Thus, economists Xudong An and Raphael Bostic argue that the GSEs' affordable lending merely substituted for FHA affordable lending.[34]

The GSEs' investment portfolios also count for Affordable Housing Goals.[35] The GSEs are limited to investing in mortgage related assets, but that enables them to purchase their own MBS, other Agency MBS, and PLS, and they were major buyers of PLS. If the underlying mortgages in an MBS would count for Affordable Housing Goal credit, the MBS can also count toward the affordable housing goal credit.

The GSEs may have invested in PLS simply because of attractive yields, but there is also the possibility that they did so because of the Affordable Housing Goals. The GSEs' purchases of PLS undoubtedly contributed to the bubble by adding to demand for PLS. But it is notable that the amount of subprime PLS in the GSEs' portfolios, as well as their portfolios' absolute share of the subprime PLS market, decreased after 2004, as PLS yield spreads declined.[36] This means that other investors were more than substituting for the GSEs' demand for PLS, such that even if the GSEs were still contributing to the bubble through PLS purchases, they were not driving it.[37]

Indeed, the GSEs' contribution to total mortgage market funding (through MBS and their balance sheets) dropped sharply after 2003, even as PLS issuance grew. The GSEs' total mortgage funding increased in 2006, but they substantially ramped up their activity only in 2007, *after* housing prices had peaked and the subprime lending market had collapsed. (See Figure 8.3.) In other words, the GSEs came to the party late, after housing prices had already peaked, but they were left holding the bag.

Ultimately, the evidence connecting the GSE Affordable Housing Goals to the bubble is weak. There is no evidence of a change in riskiness of loans or loan performance at the discontinuity threshold for GSE Affordable Housing Goal eligibility.[38] Thus, a 2012 study by economists from the Federal Reserve Bank of St. Louis used a regression discontinuity analysis and found that there is "no evidence that lenders increased subprime originations or altered loan pricing around the discrete eligibility cutoffs for the Government Sponsored Enterprises' (GSEs) Affordable Housing Goals or the Community Reinvestment Act."[39] While the study found "evidence that the GSEs bought significant quantities of subprime securities, [the] results

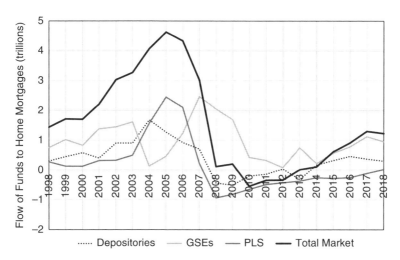

Figure 8.3. Flow of Funds to Home Mortgages, 1998–2018

Data source: Bd. of Governors of the Fed. Reserve Sys., *Statistical Release Z.1, Financial Accounts of the United States*, tbl. F.218. "Depositories" consists of banks and credit unions and is the sum of lines 11–14 (series FA763065105, FA 753065103, FA743065103, and FA473065100). "GSEs" consists of GSE balance sheets plus Ginnie Mae and GSE MBS and is the sum of lines 18 and 19 (series FA403065105 and FA413065105). "PLS" is line 20 (series FA673065105).

indicate that these purchases were not directly related to affordable housing mandates."[40]

Moreover, as with the CRA-based version of the Government Made Me Do It theory, the Affordable Housing Goals version has no answer for the parallel commercial real estate bubble or foreign residential real estate bubbles.

EXPLAINING GSE BEHAVIOR DURING THE BUBBLE

The evidence does not support the Government Made Me Do It theory of the bubble insofar as it points that finger at federal affordable housing policies. Moreover, any attempt to pin the bubble on the GSEs faces an insurmountable obstacle regarding timing—the GSEs' contribution came primarily *after* housing prices had peaked.

The evidence does not, however, entirely absolve Fannie and Freddie from any role in the bubble. The GSEs certainly contributed to the housing bubble, most critically as major purchasers of PLS, and we do not question that there was an easing of their lending standards during the bubble years, although the precise details remain unknown. Moreover, the GSEs did contribute in a critical, if indirect, way to the bubble through the automated underwriting they pioneered in the mid-1990s.

Automated underwriting was heralded as a way to increase access to affordable loans, and it did in fact result in an expansion of affordable credit. As discussed in Chapter 4, automated underwriting freed mortgage lending from the rigid formula of the three C's—capacity, collateral, and credit—and encouraged the use of "compensating factors" in loan decisions that enabled an expansion of credit.

The GSEs' automated underwriting failed to recognize that default rates were dependent on housing prices remaining at fundamentally sound levels. While this was fine in the 1990s, it did not serve in the bubble years. Yet when the bubble emerged, none of this was yet understood. Instead, from the vantage point of 2004, GSE-automated underwriting appeared to be a transformative success that encouraged further attempts to expand credit through compensating factors. The mortgages financed through PLS did not use automated underwriting; every investment bank had different underwriting guidelines (and often more than one set) for its products. Whether these guidelines bore any relation to a predictive default model is unclear, and post-bubble litigation has indicated that many loans failed to even comply with these guidelines. Nonetheless, it is notable these guidelines also authorized the extensive use of compensating factors, which was a legacy of GSE automated underwriting. For example, one Countrywide PLS prospectus noted that

> On a case by case basis, Countrywide Home Loans may determine that, based upon compensating factors, a prospective borrower not strictly qualifying under its applicable underwriting risk category guidelines warrants an underwriting exception. It is expected that a significant number of the mortgage loans will have been originated based on such underwriting exceptions.[41]

This sort of disclosure was typical. The market was willing to accept the extensive use of compensating factors in the underwriting of nontraditional mortgages in PLS because it had been acclimated to the use of such compensating factors through GSE automated underwriting. The GSEs' development of automated underwriting helped pave the way for the bubble by its implicit assumption that the default model would remain stable as house prices endogenously increased with lending expansion, but it was far from the cause of the bubble.

Monetary Policy and the Global Supply of Credit

FAILURE TO FOLLOW THE TAYLOR RULE

A totally different theory of the bubble has been expounded by macroeconomist John B. Taylor, the inventor of the eponymous Taylor Rule for setting monetary policy.[42] Taylor has argued that the housing bubble was the inevitable consequence of mishandled monetary policy.[43] Taylor's contention is that after the Internet bubble burst in 2000, the Federal Reserve held interest rates too low for too long. Low rates produced artificially cheap mortgage credit, which led to excessive demand for mortgages. Because mortgages are the largest form of leverage for consumers, housing was the asset class where a bubble was most likely to form. Because consumers were able to incur greater leverage for lower cost, their purchasing power increased, and therefore housing prices were bid up.[44] Although Taylor does not invoke the commercial real estate market or parallel international housing bubbles, we would expect his theory to have similar applicability, unlike the Government Made Me Do It theory or any of the demand-side theories. Taylor's counterfactual regressions suggest that housing prices would have been far less inflated if the Fed had adhered more closely to the Taylor Rule in the wake of the 2000 stock market crash and the 9/11 attacks.

Monetary policy played a role in the housing bubble, but it is an incomplete explanation for several reasons. First, short-term interest rates only have a weak effect on housing prices in a market predominated by fixed-rate mortgages.[45] The Federal Funds rate—the rate that the Fed controls—is a short-term rate, which differs from the long-term rate that is charged on mortgages.[46] Thus, previous declines in the Federal Funds rate have not produced housing bubbles. For example, between late 1990 and 1993, the effective Federal Funds rate fell from around 8 percent to 3 percent, a similar sized drop to that between late 2000 and 2003, when the rate declined from around 6 percent to 1 percent. Yet no housing bubble ensued in the early 1990s. Likewise, the timing of the bubble does not track with interest rates. The bubble continued to grow even once the Fed started to raise rates in 2005.[47] (See Figure 8.4.)

Second, while long-term interest rates do have an effect on housing prices, the decline in long-term rates was insufficient to explain the entirety of the bubble.[48] Nor does a monetary policy explanation explain why underwriting standards deteriorated or the product mix changed. Monetary policy might have made mortgage credit cheap, but declines in underwriting standards and shifts to initial affordability products made it even cheaper.

Finally, monetary policy does not explain the occurrence of mortgage bubbles in some countries outside the United States, but not in others. Adherence to, or divergence from, the Taylor Rule seems to have had little impact on which developed countries experienced bubbles and which did not.[49] Countries like Canada, with very similar monetary policy to the United States, did not have bubbles.[50] Countries like Spain and Ireland that saw a decrease in lending controls similar to the United States also had significant bubbles, but such bubbles emerged only after a steep drop in interest rates.[51]

Monetary policy helps explain the refinancing boom that occurred in 2001–2003 and why housing price appreciation exceeded rental cost appreciation during that period. But it comes up short in explaining the rest of the housing bubble.

BERNANKE'S GLOBAL SAVINGS GLUT THEORY

A related macroeconomic explanation comes from Federal Reserve chairman Ben Bernanke and is endorsed by one of the dissents from the report of the Financial Crisis Inquiry Commission.[52] Bernanke has argued that an increase in the savings rate in many emerging market countries had led to a "global savings glut."[53] These foreign emerging market countries, particularly China, were running massive current account surpluses and lacked sufficiently appealing domestic investment opportunities. As a result, savings flowed

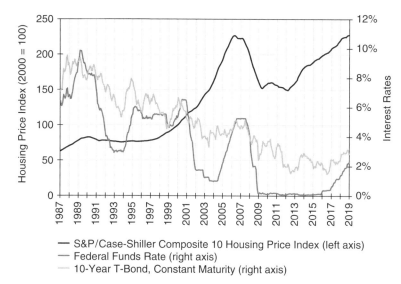

Figure 8.4. Housing Prices (Nominal) and Interest Rates, 1987–2018

Data source: S&P Dow Jones Indices LLC, *S&P/Case-Shiller 10-City Composite Home Price Index* [SPCS10RSA], retrieved from FRED, Federal Reserve Bank of St. Louis, *at* https://fred.stlouisfed.org/series/SPCS10RSA (housing price index); Bd. of Governors of the Fed. Reserve Sys., *Effective Federal Funds Rate* [FEDFUNDS], retrieved from FRED, Federal Reserve Bank of St. Louis, *at* https://fred.stlouisfed.org/series/FEDFUNDS (Fed. Funds Rate); Bd. of Governors of the Fed. Reserve Sys., *10-Year Treasury Constant Maturity Rate* [GS10], retrieved from FRED, Federal Reserve Bank of St. Louis, *at* https://fred.stlouisfed.org/series/GS10 (T-Bond rate).

to the United States for investment, which held down long-term interest rates, thereby contributing to the housing bubble.[54]

Bernanke argues that these foreign capital inflows were invested not only in US Treasury and Agency securities (including GSE MBS), but also in AAA-rated PLS and commercial mortgage-backed securities (CMBS).[55] Bernanke also notes that other advanced economies—Europe and Japan—showed a similar appetite for "safe U.S. assets," despite running roughly balanced current accounts.[56]

For investors seeking AAA-rated assets, there were few options other than sovereign, Agency, and structured products. As Lloyd Blankfein, CEO of Goldman Sachs, noted, "In January 2008, there were 12 triple A-rated companies in the world. At the same time, there were 64,000 structured finance instruments . . . rated triple A."[57] (See Figure 8.5.) Those AAA-rated structured finance instruments were mainly PLS based on US mortgages. Those AAA-rated PLS were where substantial foreign investment landed, for as Bernanke argues, "investors were willing to reach for some additional yield by purchasing AAA-rated MBS rather than Agency debt (or sovereign bonds at home)."[58]

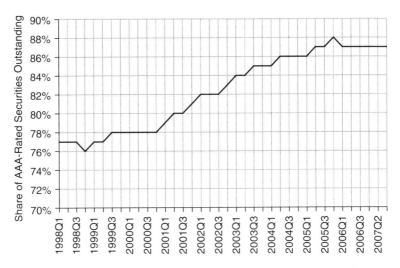

Figure 8.5. PLS, CMBS, and ABS Share of Non-Sovereign AAA-Rated Securities Outstanding, 1998–2007

Data source: Ben S. Bernanke *et al.*, *International Capital Flows and the Returns to Safe Assets in the United States, 2003–2007*, Feb. 2011, *at* http://www.federalreserve.gov/pubs/ifdp/2011/1014/ifdp1014.htm.

Bernanke's global savings glut explains an expansion in credit in the United States. But Bernanke's explanation overlooks a crucial detail: the only way that dodgy subprime mortgages could be converted into AAA-rated bonds was through structured finance. Structured finance does not eliminate risk; it merely concentrates it, and it did so in the junior tranches in PLS deals.

The creation of AAA-rated PLS necessitated the creation of non-investment-grade PLS. The by-product of structuring a securitization of subprime mortgages so that some tranches are AAA-rated is a bunch of lower-rated tranches. The alchemy of securitization can turn financial lead into gold, but it also leaves behind a radioactive residue of some securities with highly concentrated risk. This is a pivotal insight that many commentators fail to understand.

While the vast majority of the PLS—nearly 90 percent by dollar amount—were AAA-rated, securitization deal economics were simply not workable unless there were also buyers for the lower-rated pieces at reasonable yields. The strength of the demand for AAA-rated PLS is irrelevant unless there is sufficient demand for the lower grade tranches that are necessary for creating the investment-grade PLS. Without demand for *both* the AAA-tranches and the lower-rated tranches, securitization transactions will not be undertaken.

The catalyst, then, for the oversupply of underpriced mortgage credit was the demand for the *lower-grade* PLS. Absent this demand, PLS would not have been economically viable, and the global savings glut would have had to find a home in other asset classes. Accordingly, Bernanke's Global Savings Glut story is incomplete because it does not explain the demand for the lower-grade PLS necessary for generating the AAA-rated PLS.

The problems with the Global Savings Glut theory do not end there. Neither the Bernanke explanation, nor the Taylor explanation for that matter, explains why lenders mispriced mortgage credit risk. Being flush with cash does not have to translate into mispricing of risk. Nor does either theory explain why there was a compression of default risk premia for PLS, but not for corporate securities. The cost of credit is always the risk-free rate— which is set by the Fed for short-term rates—*plus* a risk premium. Even if the risk-free rate was historically low, the risk premium should not have changed. Why would yield spreads (the risk premium) drop even when risk was rising? Finally, neither Bernanke nor Taylor explains the concomitant explosion of this form of credit relative to GDP rather than that of corporate debt, which stayed in relative fixed proportion to output.[59] Global savings flows, just like monetary policy, is an incomplete story.

The Market Relaxation of Underwriting Standards

A number of studies, most notably the work of economists Atif Mian and Amir Sufi, present what might be called a latent supply-side theory that emphasizes easier credit, in response to a growing need for credit.[60] Mian and Sufi point to growing income inequality in the decade prior to the expansion of credit and then argue that the credit expansion was a response through the easing of lending terms for LTMI borrowers. Hence, they argue that there was a relaxation of credit terms, through securitization, particularly for lower-income, subprime borrowers, that was critical in inflating the bubble.

We call this a latent supply-side theory because it does not explain why such a relaxation of credit terms resulted in an asset price bubble, much less one with systemic implications. Moreover, the bubble was not merely a low-income phenomenon. Indeed, there was little change during the bubble period in the cross-sectional distribution of either debt or housing wealth.[61]

A contrasting theory has been championed by economists Christopher Foote, Lara Loewenstein, and Paul Willen, who argue that the bubble emerged from an easing of mortgage supply constraints but that this easing was endogenous—that is, it occurred in response to home price increases—and was not the cause of the bubble, but rather a response.[62] Their endogenous easing theory is similar to one put forth by finance theorists, that a relaxation of supply constraints occurred due to an (un-specified) technological innovation that then enabled an easing of bor-rowing constraints, which in itself led to lower risk premia because the economy became *less* risky.[63] Neither theory comports with the evidence on the price of risk, which declined as risk increased. The economy obvi-ously became *riskier* as housing prices departed from fundamentals and as underwriting deteriorated.

A number of other studies have pointed to securitization as being crit-ical to the relaxation of credit terms.[64] Some of these studies emphasize the principal-agent problem inherent in securitization.[65] These studies, how-ever, do not attempt to provide complete explanations of the housing bubble, but instead test more focused propositions about whether securiti-zation facilitated laxer lending standards. Accordingly, they do not explain the timing of the bubble and do not integrate the institutional changes in the mortgage market. These studies also do not explain *why* securitization led to laxer lending standards or why normal market discipline failed.

It is also important to emphasize that even though PLS were the vehicle through which the credit supply expanded in the United States, they are not the only way to arrive at a credit-fueled bubble. Internationally, par-allel housing price bubbles occurred in countries such as Ireland, where se-curitization provided little of the financing,[66] or Spain, where securitiza-tion took the form of covered bonds that remained a secured obligation of the bank. (Refer back to Figure 8.2.) Moral hazard in securitization might have contributed to the US housing bubble, but it lacks broader explana-tory power about why the US housing bubble emerged when it did and re-garding the emergence of housing bubbles generally.

The existing explanations of the bubble are either inconsistent with the evidence or incomplete. In the next chapter we present our own supply-side theory. Our theory connects the relaxation of underwriting standards to the change in mortgage products and the mortgage market's institutional shift from the GSE securitization duopoly to unregulated private-label se-curitization. It explains why this shift in products and securitization chan-nels resulted in the underpriced credit that fueled the bubble and why the bubble was broad-based across the credit spectrum.

CHAPTER NINE

The Wall Street
Securitization Bubble

IN THE PREVIOUS chapter we explored various theories of the bubble and found them either incomplete or inconsistent with the evidence. We now present our theory of the bubble.

The bubble was caused by the underpricing of mortgage credit due the shift in mortgage financing from quasi-regulated GSE securitization to un-regulated private-label securitization by private investment banks. This shift occurred starting around 2003 and was facilitated by the emergence of collateralized debt obligations (CDOs), a new class of investment vehicles. CDOs provided the investment for the riskiest pieces of PLS, without which the much-sought-after AAA-pieces of PLS could not be created. This meant that credit risk in the mortgage market was concentrated on CDOs, but CDO, as we shall see, were incentivized to underprice risk.

The expansion and underpricing of the housing finance supply through PLS enabled and encouraged borrowers to bid up home prices by making credit cheaper and more available. This credit expansion fueled a bubble, not only in residential real estate, but also in commercial real estate, where CDOs played a parallel role in the underpricing of risk by private-label commercial mortgage-backed securities (CMBS).[1] (Refer back to Figure 8.1.) The expansion of mortgage credit (through different financing channels) had the same effect on home prices in some European countries, such as Iceland, Ireland, Spain, and the United Kingdom, where credit expansions resulted in housing bubbles. (Refer back to Figure 8.2).

The expansion of underpriced housing finance incentivized investors to buy and flip homes cheaply and enabled borrowers who were previously constrained—meaning borrowers who had previously faced limits on their ability to obtain mortgage credit and thus on their home purchase capacity—to buy more housing. Importantly, constrained home buyers are not just low-income borrowers. Any potential buyers who optimally would buy more of a house, given the absence of financing constraints, are also enabled by the easing of lending limits. Given the upward pressure placed on home prices across the income spectrum from the expansion of the mortgage supply to previously constrained borrowers, previously unconstrained borrowers also had to borrow more in order to remain competitive in the home purchase market.

The expansion of mortgage credit collided with an inelastic housing supply, with the result that home prices were bid up. Home construction does not take place overnight, and even as home building expanded, it still lagged behind demand in the wake of the credit expansion. Thus, there were more bidders willing to pay more for the same limited supply of housing, resulting in home prices rising rapidly.

But because the higher home prices depended on mispriced credit and on underwriting that would predictably raise default rates, once the momentum in demand growth and price rises ended, the price increase was unsustainable. In other words, home prices were bid up beyond fundamentals, and when the credit supply then ultimately faltered because of the unsustainable nature of the mortgage products it was financing and the exhaustion of the borrower pool, a collapse in home prices was inevitable.

Thus, the shift in the financing channel from GSE securitization to PLS produced an underpricing of risk that was the proximate cause of the bubble. The GSEs' duopoly had kept risk in check, in part because the GSEs internalized the risk of inflated housing prices from overly easy credit because they were the market and in part because the GSEs' competition with each other, such as it was, was primarily not price competition, but rather competition in service provision to lenders that sold mortgages to them.[2] PLS, in contrast, lacked such structural constraints on risk. Once PLS broke the GSE duopoly, however, then the GSEs, as private, shareholder-controlled firms, were compelled to take part in the race to the bottom in underwriting standards in order to retain market share. Yet as we showed in the previous chapter, the GSEs were late arrivals; they stepped up their financing of housing only after home prices had peaked.

This chapter details this explanation of the bubble with a particular emphasis on why the shift in financing to PLS resulted in an underpricing of risk. Our explanation necessitates a deeper question, however, about the broader efficiency of markets. Why did the market not move against the increasing underpricing of risk in the PLS and the resulting overpricing of housing? In a world of perfect markets, investors would have spotted the underpricing of risk and priced against it, returning the housing finance, and thus the home price market, to its original equilibrium.

That, of course, did not happen. Instead, there was a market failure. We believe that the market failure is the inability of investors to short housing. Housing markets are incomplete, given that there is no instrument to sell housing short. While unsustainable debt propelled prices upward, there was no countervailing downward pressure from short investors to stop the bubble. The rise in housing prices, which was untethered to fundamentals, was not countered by short selling, as would be the case for any other asset. It was not countered because that would have required both adequate information about the mispricing of housing and an investment vehicle for going short, but neither existed, as we explain in the next chapter.

The Securitization Daisy Chain

Now that we have previewed our theory of the bubble, let's take stock of what we have seen thus far, as it provides the building blocks for our theory of the bubble.

- First, we saw in Chapter 7 that the bubble was a supply-side phenomenon: the supply of mortgage financing increased even as the price fell, indicating that the supply curve for mortgage finance moved rightward. Thus, the bubble was the product of an oversupply of underpriced mortgage financing.
- Second, we had previously seen, in Chapter 6, that the housing bubble was a relatively brief phenomenon, lasting from around 2003 or 2004 until 2006.
- Third, Chapter 4 demonstrated that the 2003–2006 period corresponded with a sharp shift in mortgage products from the traditional 30-year fixed to a variety of risky, nontraditional mortgage products that harkened back to the bullet loans of the Great Depression, in that they relied on borrowers being able to refinance the loan rather than pay it off according to its terms.
- And fourth, Chapter 4 also showed that the 2003–2006 period corresponded with a dramatic shift in the mortgage-financing channel from regulated GSE securitization to unregulated PLS.

Together, these four observations point to the explosive growth of PLS as the prime factor in the housing bubble. The housing bubble was fueled by nontraditional mortgages. Nontraditional mortgages and relaxed underwriting standards that relied heavily on questionable "compensating factors" enabled the expansion of the borrower pool, which pressured previously unconstrained borrowers to borrow up to their constraints in order to remain competitive in the home purchase market. Nontraditional mortgages also enabled all borrowers to bid up prices higher than they could with traditional 30-year FRMs because of lower (initial) monthly payment structures. The expanded supply of mortgage credit collided with the inelastic housing supply, resulting in a boom in housing prices.

The expanded supply of nontraditional mortgages needed to be financed, and the financing came from PLS, not GSE securitization. The shift from GSE securitization to PLS as the dominant financing channel in the US mortgage market was essential for the formation of the bubble. But for the funding from PLS, there would not have been the growth in nontraditional mortgages or expansion of the borrower base. No PLS, no bubble.

What explains the explosive growth of PLS between 2003 and 2006? In the previous chapter we saw former Federal Reserve chairman Ben Bernanke's attempt at an explanation, namely, that there was a global savings glut that meant investors had an excess of funds they were seeking to park in "safe assets." Because there is a limited supply of traditional safe assets, such as US Treasury securities, GSE securities, and AAA-rated corporate securities, investors instead turned to manufactured safe assets, namely, AAA-rated structured securities, and PLS were the largest structured securities market.

As we have seen, however, Bernanke's explanation was incomplete. While Bernanke explains the demand for AAA-rated PLS, he does not address the demand for PLS's lower-grade by-product securities. It is not possible to create AAA-rated PLS without generating a lower, often noninvestment-grade by-product. For alt-A and Jumbo PLS deals, over 90 percent of bonds would have been rated AAA at issuance, while for subprime PLS transactions, the figure is closer to 75 percent.[3] Most of the non-AAA bonds would be investment grade (at least BBB), yet there was always a tail of noninvestment grade (junk) bonds produced by a PLS. For the economics of a securitization transaction to work, however, there must be a market for *both* the AAA-rated PLS and the lower-grade PLS. Unless someone is willing to purchase the lower-grade tranches, the deal will not be made, even if there is robust demand for the AAA-rated tranches.

Understanding the demand for the lower grade tranches of PLS is particularly key to understanding the bubble because the credit risk of the entire housing finance system was concentrated on the holders of those lower grade PLS tranches. Who were these investors, and why did they underprice the risk on mortgages so badly?

The A-Piece and the B-Piece

PLS have been around since the late 1970s, and there was always a need to place the lower grade junior tranches of PLS. A small market existed for these tranches, among a number of investment funds that specialized in buying subordinated debt—the lower-grade tranches.[4] These subordinated-debt investors tended to be quite circumspect about credit risk precisely because they were the most exposed to it by virtue of their subordination.[5] These subordinated-debt investors were also quite focused on interest rate risk because the prepayment speeds on the senior tranches affected the credit risk on the junior tranches; to the extent that a loan was refinanced, it meant that no loss would be incurred on that loan.

The senior tranches of PLS were known as the A-piece, while the junior (credit-subordinated) tranches were called the B-piece. Because there was a much more limited market for the B-piece than the A-piece, the B-piece was traditionally sold first, prior to the sale of the A-piece. Once the pricing on the B-piece had been worked out, then the A-piece could be priced. Because of their relative market power, B-piece buyers were historically able to obtain substantial loan-level information about the proposed mortgage pools underlying the securities prior to the sale of the B-piece. B-piece buyers also had the ability to have individual properties that they did not want removed from the pool.

B-piece investors' risk tolerance should have provided a limit on the expansion of PLS: as the junior tranches of PLS became riskier, investors would have demanded a higher yield or simply would not have bought them. In order to support the higher yields on PLS, the underlying mortgages would have had to have higher interest rates or the PLS would have to have been issued at a discount from par.[6] Higher interest rates on the mortgages would have pushed down home prices, while deeper discounts from par would have reduced the funding available for mortgages, again pushing down home prices. Either way, if the market had worked efficiently, the end result should have been for real estate prices to return to an equilibrium. Subordinated-debt B-piece buyers should thus have provided a natural limitation on risk and restored correct asset prices according to the fundamental theorem of asset pricing, which teaches that if an asset is overvalued, then investors will be against it, resulting in the asset's price falling.[7] Yet this is not what happened during the bubble years. Why did

B-piece investors—those most exposed to credit risk on US mortgages—fail to properly price for risk?

The Change in the B-Piece Market

The B-piece market failed to constrain the expansion of risk in PLS because of a change in the B-piece market place. Prior to the bubble, there had been only a limited number of B-piece buyers. These traditional B-piece buyers had expertise in evaluating credit risk, but they were displaced in the 2002–2004 period by new entrants in the B-piece market. These new entrants were a type of investment fund, which is known as structured-finance collateralized debt obligations (CDOs).[8]

CDOs outbid traditional B-piece buyers for the junior tranches of PLS by CDOs, meaning that the CDOs were willing to purchase the junior tranches at a lower yield.[9] The CDOs expanded the B-piece market, which eroded buyers' market power, even as the CDOs lacked traditional B-piece buyers' expertise in evaluating credit risk. Moreover, CDO managers were incentivized with compensation structures that encouraged the purchase of B-pieces irrespective of risk on the underlying mortgages.[10] Thus, from 1997 to 2007, CDOs were the buyers of around 80 percent of all BBB-rated subprime PLS bonds.[11] Given that the overwhelming majority of CDOs were issued from 2004 to 2007,[12] we can safely say that well over 90 percent of BBB-rated subprime PLS bonds issued during this period were purchased by CDOs.

Because the CDOs were willing to accept a lower yield for the B-pieces, the yield that had to be generated by the securitized mortgages did not increase even as the riskiness of the mortgages did. Thus, because of the growth of the B-piece market due to the CDOs, interest rates on mortgages did not rise even as the mortgages became substantially riskier, both on an individualized basis and, given the correlated effects of home prices on each other, on a market-wide basis.[13] The expansion of the B-piece market through CDOs undermined a key limitation on the riskiness of securitized mortgages.

The institutional change in the B-piece market structure was an essential ingredient for the PLS boom that financed the Great American Housing Bubble. CDOs were *the* main source of demand for the lower grade PLS tranches.[14] Structured-finance CDOs were virtually nonexistent before 2000 and only took off in 2004, rapidly peaking in 2006.[15] (See Figure 9.1.) From 2004 to 2007 there some $3.9 trillion of PLS were issued. Of that, roughly $3.5 trillion (92 percent) was AAA-rated at issuance. That meant that some $300 billion of non-AAA-rated PLS were issued, most of which went into

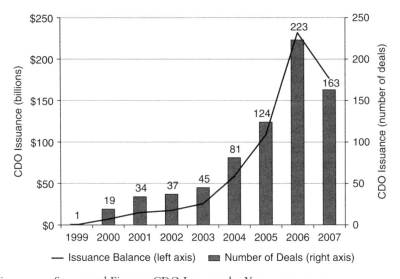

Figure 9.1. Structured Finance CDO Issuance by Year, 1999–2007

Data source: Larry Cordell *et al.*, "Collateral Damage: Sizing and Assessing the Subprime CDO Crisis," Fed. Reserve Bank of Phila. working paper no. 11-30, at 31, tbl. 2 (Aug. 2011).

structured-finance CDOs. CDOs accounted for over two-thirds of the demand for non-AAA-rated PLS.[16]

By 2005, most of the lower-rated subprime PLS were being resecuritized into CDOs,[17] and structured-finance products accounted for over half of global CDO assets between 2004 and 2007.[18] Without CDOs there was almost no demand for the B-piece of PLS, and without demand for the B-piece, it was impossible to sell the A-piece.

In other words, the massive shift in the financing channel from regulated GSE securitization to unregulated PLS that drove the bubble could not have occurred without CDOs. Without CDO demand for the B-piece, the PLS market would have remained a small, niche market, no matter the size of the global savings glut demand for the A-piece. The CDOs were not the only factor in the housing bubble. Nonetheless, but for the entry of CDOs into the B-piece market, the Great American Housing Bubble would not have occurred.

The same story is true for the parallel commercial real estate bubble. CDOs outbid the traditional B-piece buyers in CMBS, which witnessed a subsequent underpricing of risk, which enabled commercial real estate prices to be bid up in those urban markets financed by CMBS.[19] (Refer back to Figure 8.1.)

What's a CDO?

Recognizing the shift in the financing channel and expansion of mortgage credit that fueled the bubble was possible only due to the emergence of CDOs raises a further question: why were CDOs buying the non-AAA-rated tranches of PLS (and CMBS)?

To answer this question, it is necessary to understand in some technical detail what a CDO is. A CDO is a type of closed-ended investment fund. The CDO will be created by an equity "sponsor," typically an affiliate of a major securitization sponsor. In other words, a CDO will generally be created by a large investment bank. The CDO will raise funds from investors by selling securities, which are confusingly known themselves as CDOs. For the sake of clarity, we will refer to the securities as "CDO securities." The CDO (entity) will then use those funds to purchase a pool of assets that comply with certain investor guidelines. Many CDOs are actively managed, and even those that are not have reinvestment criteria, so the assets held by the CDO may change over time, even though there is no new investment in the CDO itself.

CDOs differ from other types of closed-end investment funds in two key ways. First, investments in the CDO are tranched in a senior-subordinate structure, and second, CDOs invest mainly in other structured securities. A CDO is a structured securitization of structured securities. For example, a CDO would purchase a set of PLS and then issue its own tranched securities. The CDO securities would be backed largely by the B-pieces of PLS, which would, in turn be backed by nontraditional mortgages.

The effect of tranching on CDO securities is the same as with PLS: when a CDO (entity) purchases a set of PLS B-pieces and resecuritizes them, it produces a set of AAA-rated CDO securities and also a CDO B-piece securities by-product. Those CDO B-piece securities would themselves be resecuritized into what's known as a CDO^2, an investment fund whose assets are CDO securities or a CDO of CDOs. The process could in theory be repeated infinitely with CDO^3s, etc. Notably, most CDO^2s were not purely resecuritizations of CDO tranches, but also included some PLS tranches, making the labeling messy. Figure 9.2 illustrates this process.

The theoretical result is an endless daisy chain of resecuritization that expands demand for the B-piece in PLS. Given how short-lived the bubble was, however, the CDO daisy chain did not go through very many iterations before it collapsed; there were only a handful of deals that included resecuritizations of CDO^2 tranches. Nonetheless, the CDO market both enabled the creation of many more AAA-rated securities to satisfy demand from the global savings glut and also provided a home for PLS's unwelcome B-piece by-product.

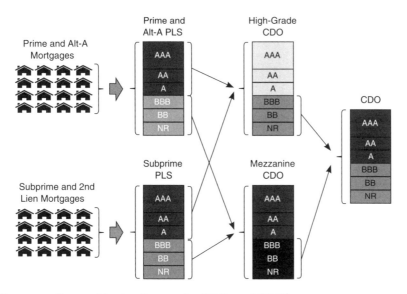

Figure 9.2. Resecuritization Process for CDOs and CDO²s

Data source: Larry Cordell *et al.*, "Collateral Damage: Sizing and Assessing the Subprime CDO Crisis," Fed. Reserve Bank of Phila. working paper no. 11-30, at 44, fig. 1 (Aug. 2011).

Amplification of Implicit Leverage via CDOs

Most CDOs were based on junior tranches of PLS, so even though the majority of the CDO securities would be investment grade, they had a much higher degree of implicit leverage than investment-grade PLS. A rise in defaults on the underlying mortgages would hit the investment-grade CDO securities before it hit the investment-grade PLS.

To see how, imagine a securitization of $100 million in mortgages, which generates $100 million in face amount of PLS. The PLS are structured so that all credit losses on the mortgages first flow to the B-piece, which is the junior 10 percent of the securities. Only after that $10 million B-piece is exhausted do losses then flow, on a pro-rated basis, to the A-piece.

Now suppose that ten of those $10 million B-pieces are then resecuritized into a $100 million CDO, which is again tranched so that all the losses first flow to the junior-most tranches of the CDO, again a 10 percent ($10 million) B-piece. If there are losses of 0.5 percent on all of the mortgage pools (that is $5 million total losses on the $1 billion of mortgages), there will be no effect on any of the A-piece investors in the PLS. Each of the ten PLS B-pieces, however, will have a 5 percent loss ($500,000 out of $10 million). There will not be any losses on the CDO securities A-piece, but there will be 50 percent losses for the B-piece investors in the CDO securities ($5 million out of $10 million).

Now imagine that the losses on the mortgages are 3 percent ($30 million out of $1 billion). Each of the ten PLS B-pieces will suffer losses of 30 percent ($3 million out of $10 million), but there will still be no losses for the PLS A-piece investors. For the CDO, however, the $30 million in aggregate losses will wipe out the entire $10 million B-piece, and the A-piece will incur $20 million in losses, a 22 percent loss rate. Thus, even the investment-grade securities in the CDOs had a much higher degree of implicit leverage. A CDO² will, of course, only amplify this degree of leverage. The point is that a CDO's junior tranches are substantially riskier than the junior tranches of the underlying PLS.

Why Did CDOs Buy B-Pieces?

Why did CDOs outbid traditional, savvy subordinated-debt investors for the junior tranches of PLS? Why weren't the CDOs just as savvy? The answer lies in the warped incentive structures of CDO managers, such that the displacement of traditional B-piece buyers by CDOs meant a severe loss in attention to credit risk.

CDOs are actively managed investment vehicles, meaning that the specific securities in which a CDO invests are determined by its manager, rather than being preset according to contract with the CDO investors (although investors do contract to place limitations on the CDO's investments). CDO managers have been derided as not so sharp, little more than "two guys and a Bloomberg terminal in New Jersey."[20]

We are not in a position to evaluate the acuity of CDO managers' investment acumen without the benefit of hindsight, other than to note that few CDO managers were, by background, mortgage credit risk specialists. Yet the problem with CDO managers may not have been their lack of sophistication as much as their incentives.

SOURCE OF CDO MANAGER BUSINESS

As the PLS market took off, the banks that securitized loans found themselves constrained by the limited demand for increasingly risky B-pieces. CDOs provided the answer. CDOs have been around since 1987. From their origins they were used as a device to create artificial demand for risky securities, rather than for any positive economic purpose.[21]

While CDOs were an exceedingly small market prior to 2002, often involving resecuritization of assets other than PLS, they were a transactional solution to the organic demand limitation banks faced with PLS. By creating CDOs, the banks generated artificial demand for the B-pieces and thereby allowed much greater transaction volume in PLS overall, not to mention fees for the banks that arranged and sold the transactions.

CDO managers got their business in the first instance from the investment bank that arranges the CDO. While it was necessary for the managers to inspire sufficient confidence to get investors to buy into the CDO, the managers were not chosen by the investors in the CDO's securities but by the CDO's arranger, which meant that CDO managers who wanted to get future business needed to keep the arranger happy. Indeed, CDO managers appear to have been willing to purchase bad securities—or at least not ask too many questions—in order to attract future deal flow from CDO arrangers.[22]

Some CDO arrangers were banks that were fully or partially integrated through the whole mortgage chain, from origination to securitization and servicing. Vertically integrated firms had an informational advantage over investors, because they could obtain servicing data about loan performance in real time, unlike investors. This meant, among other things, that they could observe warning signs of credit losses like early payment defaults and identify which PLS tranches were lemons.

Given that banking institutions were looking for a place to park the B-pieces from their PLS deals, there was a strong pressure on CDO managers to buy B-pieces.[23] The result was that CDOs were used by investment bank arrangers to offload their PLS B-piece lemons, as evidenced by higher losses on the CDOs arranged by vertically integrated banks (which had an informational advantage and could better identify lemons) than on those arranged by nonintegrated banks.[24]

CDO MANAGER COMPENSATION

CDO appetite for B-pieces was further whetted by CDO manager compensation structures that created a host of misaligned incentives that discouraged managers from using careful diligence with investment risks, while also encouraging investment, particularly in PLS and PLS-based derivatives (that is, selling CDS protection on PLS). The details of CDO manager compensation structures are discussed in Appendix C. These incorrectly structured incentives, combined with the CDO managers' need to please CDO arrangers to get a future deal flow, meant that CDO managers had little reason to carefully diligence with the securities they were purchasing and even had incentives to purchase particularly risky securities.

But Who Was Buying the CDOs?

CDOs themselves needed buyers. Again, the AAA-rated senior tranches of CDOs were relatively easy to sell, but the junior positions posed a challenge, and unless the junior tranches could be sold, the economics of resecuritization would not work. There were always some quantum of unsophisticated investors who could be stuffed with some of the B-pieces of the CDOs. To the extent that they did not exhaust the supply, the CDO B-pieces could be placed by simply extending the daisy chain and placing them into a CDO^2 or, more commonly, into another CDO alongside PLS B-pieces. The result, with each round of resecuritization, was an ever-more-toxic by-product of concentrated credit risk.

At the same time, however, the dollar volume of invesment necessary to support this inverted risk pyramid decreased with each round of securitization. The resecuritization process created a massive amount of implicit leverage, which had the effect of amplifying losses. It also meant that deals could get done with very little in the way of investment in whatever the ultimate B-pieces were.

Thus, over the 2004–2007 period, it took only $28 billion of CDO^2 to support some $557 billion of CDOs, which in turn supported $3.9 trillion of PLS.[25] In other words, a mere $28 billion of CDO^2 supported a multi-trillion-dollar PLS market that in turn funded the nontraditional mortgages that enabled housing prices to be bid up beyond fundamentals. But for this relatively small amount of investment in CDO^2s, the bubble would not have happened. In other words, it took only a very small amount of dumb or conflicted money in CDOs to build an enormous pyramid of leverage in the housing market.

In theory, the resecuritization daisy chain is endless, but in practice, it did not have very many iterations. There were some 318 structured-finance CDOs from 2004 to 2007, but only 48 of those were CDO^2s or beyond, meaning that at least half of their collateral consisted of tranches of other CDOs.[26] The extreme concentration of risk in these vehicles made them simply too hard to sell. The inability to extend the daisy chain by further iterations did not really matter, however, because the housing bubble was so short-lived; the bubble collapsed even before the daisy chain was exhausted. While the bubble existed, the CDOs financed the B-piece of the PLS, and with the B-piece sold, it was easy to then find buyers for the AAA-rated A-piece.

The result was, in the short term, an enormous amount of underpriced mortgage finance that enabled buyers of homes, both homeowners and property investors, to bid up home prices—as long as the borrower pool continued to grow at a sufficient rate. When growth of this pool slowed, the bubble could not be sustained, and the fuse for the financial crisis was lit.

The Mortgage Arms Race

CDO underpricing of B-piece risk enabled the sale of PLS, which in turn provided the financing for nontraditional mortgages. These nontraditional mortgages had lower initial monthly payments because they were often not fully amortized or had initial teaser rate periods (such as 2/28s and 3/27s). These lower payments enabled borrowers to borrow more, based on the affordability of the initial payments, with the assumption that the loan would be refinanced before payments increased. Similarly, these nontraditional mortgages were often made at higher LTVs than traditional underwriting allowed, which enabled borrowers to borrow more, and they were frequently coupled with a second mortgage that increased leverage further. These second mortgages were often piggybacks designed to enable the borrower to borrow at a high CLTV without private mortgage insurance, which meant that the borrower could borrow more because funds could be used for monthly mortgage payments instead for PMI premiums. The underwriting on the nontraditional mortgages was also laxer. DTI ratios were higher than on traditionally underwritten mortgages, meaning that the borrower was permitted to take out a larger loan than otherwise. And nontraditional mortgages were often not fully documented, meaning that the lender would rely on borrower representations of income and assets, which were frequently inflated.

The effect of all of this was to expand the demand for housing through increased credit availability to borrowers who were previously constrained in their borrowing ability by their credit quality. In particular, the shift in mortgage products to nontraditional mortgages financed by PLS expanded credit availability to two distinct groups of credit-constrained borrowers. First, it enabled homeownership for borrowers who had previously been shut out of the housing market, which had the effect of driving up home-ownership rates. These were generally low- to moderate-income (LTMI) borrowers. Second, nontraditional mortgages increased credit availability for constrained borrowers who were already homeowners but wanted to purchase more home. These borrowers were not generally LTMI borrowers but were instead in the middle or upper part of the income distribution, as they were already homeowners.

The expansion of the mortgage supply enabled previously constrained households from across the income spectrum to bid more for homes. Because the housing supply cannot expand in real time to keep up with an expansion of the mortgage supply, these higher bids put competitive pressure in the home purchase market on previously unconstrained households, which responded by borrowing up to their constraints in order to keep up, both because their demand for housing is not perfectly elastic and because the cost of credit was falling during the bubble period. In addition, the expansion of underpriced credit increased the incentives for property investors to borrow more because the default put option imbedded in functionally non-recourse mortgages was underpriced.

Thus, an initial expansion of mortgage credit to constrained borrowers set off an "arms race" among all borrowers for housing debt.[27] Consumer price expectations likely contributed to this arms race, but they were not necessary for it. Even if home price expectations remained unchanged, the competitive pressure of an arms race would have resulted in an increase in housing prices beyond fundamentals, as they did in some markets where rates of change in prices did not increase but remained far above fundamentals nonetheless, such as in the lower Midwest.

Mr. CDO in the Market with a PLS

At this point, we have the simple answer to the whodunit about the Great American Housing Bubble. The bubble was a supply-side phenomenon fueled by underpriced mortgage credit. The underpriced mortgage credit was provided in the form of nontraditional mortgages, which were financed primarily by PLS, and which were only possible in volume because of CDO demand for the B-piece.

Thus, in a reductionist sense, we can point the finger squarely at Wall Street for the bubble. The bubble was not the result of government policies supporting fair lending and affordable housing, but rather the result of a shift in mortgage financing from quasi-regulated securitization by the GSE duopoly to unregulated securitization by Wall Street. This shift was facilitated by a quarter-century of incremental financial market deregulation and the advent of automated underwriting, but the ultimate cause of the bubble was a shift in the financing channel that resulted in credit risk moving from control by the Fannie/Freddie duopoly to the private-label market that lacked the ability, incentive, or regulation to restrain it.

Our explanation of the bubble represents a third position between opposing economist camps. Their scholarly debate is over both who were the borrowers and also over the role of credit, with the "credit supply view" opposed to the "passive credit view." Atif Mian and Amir Sufi, the chief proponents of the credit supply view argue that it is lower-income borrowing, financed by subprime credit that drove the bubble. The credit supply view correctly identifies the expansion of credit unrelated to fundamentals, but it errs in identifying the expansion of credit as being concentrated on LTMI subprime borrowers and neighborhoods.[28] Instead, as the proponents of the passive credit view have shown, there was a broad-based expansion of credit across the spectrum.[29]

It does not follow, however, that the expansion of credit merely followed the increase in pricing without a causal role,[30] or that the upward march of home prices was predicated on a change in consumers' price expectations,[31] as various proponents of the passive credit view have argued. Our arms race theory explains a mechanism whereby an expansion of credit to constrained borrowers would force unconstrained borrowers to borrow up to their constraints without any growth in demand. Indeed, the bubble was clearly driven by the expansion of the credit supply, given that the price of mortgage credit decreased even while risk increased during the bubble period. (See Chapter 7.) Demand might well have increased because of irrational exuberance about future house price appreciation, but the movement in mortgage pricing indicates that supply expansion outpaced any growth in demand. The evidence is for the bubble being driven by a credit expansion to all borrowers, including property investors.

Indeed, the prominence of property investors, or "flippers," in the bubble is a strong indication of both the credit-fueled nature of the bubble and of that credit expanding across the spectrum, including to higher-income borrowers, because property investors tend to be in the higher income brackets. Investor properties accounted for a substantial portion of mortgage activity in bubble states during the boom,[32] as well as in defaults during the bust.[33] The availability and price of mortgage credit is the key to the flipper business model because flippers capture all the upside of home price appreciation with limited investment of their own, yet bear little of the risk of depreciation. Because of the effectively non-recourse nature of most US mortgages, flippers can exercise their "default put option" if property values fall. Moreover, flippers can exercise the put option for a lower "strike price" than an owner-occupant because they do not have relocation expenses.

Without cheap leverage, the returns on flipping a property are not likely to be competitive with other investment options. Because property investors have unlimited demand for property purchases, a growth in flipping activity indicates an expansion of the credit supply. A rise in house flipping is the inevitable response to a loosening of mortgage credit standards and a decreased price of the default put option. The increase in house flipping during the bubble is further evidence of the bubble being a supply-side explanation, but the increase was caused by an across-the-board expansion of credit, not merely an expansion of credit to LTMI subprime borrowers, even if it was initially so limited.

Explaining the GSEs' Behavior during the Bubble

This is our explanation of what caused the housing bubble. But there are still some unanswered questions that need to be addressed. First among them is the role of the GSEs in the bubble. In the previous chapter we explained that the GSEs could not be held responsible for the bubble: although they loosened their underwriting standards, they ramped up their lending after home prices had already peaked. Nonetheless, it is necessary to explain why the GSEs would have relaxed their underwriting standards during the bubble years.

The GSEs' behavior appears to be a competitive response to PLS. As long as the securitization field consisted predominantly of the GSEs and Ginnie Mae, there was no race to the bottom in underwriting standards. There was always the potential for a rate war between Fannie and Freddie, but it never materialized; the regulated duopoly was stable in this regard. Instead, Fannie and Freddie preferred to compete on other, non-price dimensions, such as customer service to the financial institutions from which they purchased loans and the payment terms of their MBS.

The growth of PLS, however, changed things. In 2003, the GSEs had issued 70 percent of all MBS. That figure had fallen to 47 percent in 2004, and to 41 percent by 2005, while PLS rose from 22 percent in 2003 to 55 percent in 2005. PLS rapidly displaced the GSEs as the dominate financing channel in the US mortgage market. (See Figure 9.3.)

Prior to the growth of PLS, the GSEs had held firm on their underwriting standards. The loss of market share forced the GSEs to relax their underwriting standards to compete with PLS in order to please their private shareholders. In contrast, the wholly public FHA/Ginnie Mae maintained underwriting standards and ceded market share.

The GSEs' situation relative to PLS resembles the classic insurance regulation problem of a rate war for market share that results in all participants becoming insufficiently capitalized because they fail to charge adequate premiums for the risk they assume. The GSEs' guaranty business is nothing more than a bond insurance operation. Indeed, the GSEs competed for a while with monoline bond insurers to insure certain PLS, such as with the Freddie Mac T-series.[34] Yet the GSEs were not regulated in the same way

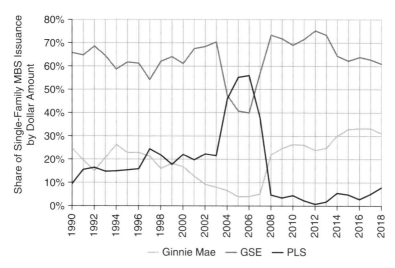

Figure 9.3. Share of Single-Family MBS Issuance, 1990–2018
Data source: Inside Mortgage Finance, *2019 Mortgage Market Statistical Annual.*

as insurers. Insurance regulators not only require mandatory reserving, but generally must approve the insurers' rate schedules. The approval of rate schedules is done with an eye to prevent insurers from underpricing risk in order to gain market share because it can ultimately result in undercapitalized insurers. The GSEs, however, were free to set their guaranty fees as they wished and to be highly leveraged, dividending out the income from their guaranty business to shareholders rather than holding it in reserve against losses.

What's more, a key concern in the insurance business is the possibility of correlated losses. Insurance works quite well as a business when losses are uncorrelated, say, with title insurance. A blot on one homeowner's title is unlikely to have any connection with a blot on other homeowners' titles, so losses will occur as one-offs, which are easy for an insurer to reserve against. But when risks are correlated, there is the possibility of unexpected catastrophic and simultaneous losses, against which it is difficult to reserve. For example, Hurricane Andrew devastated the Florida home insurance industry because insurers did not have clear hurricane damage exclusions for wind and water damage. This meant that Florida home insurers faced massive correlated losses all at once, and many of them ended up insolvent and unable to cover claims.

Housing prices—and thus losses, given default—are both geographically and serially correlated. This makes insuring mortgage bonds a particularly risky endeavor. Moreover, housing prices are not simply correlated, but the causation is mutual, rather than from common external shocks, such as with a hurricane. This means that there is a built-in set of systemic externalities with housing, yet by definition, no one prices in these externalities.

With loosened underwriting standards, the GSEs ended up partially replicating the PLS market,[35] and they paid dearly for it.[36] The GSEs were collateral damage in a rate war ignited by the growth of private-label securitization. Under pressure from shareholders to protect their market share, the GSEs were caught up in a race to the bottom against PLS, and as late entrants to the race, the GSEs found themselves stepping up their lending in 2007 at precisely the time when the market was collapsing.

That the GSEs got into a rate war was a failure of regulation. Congress imposed relatively few statutory restrictions on what the GSEs could do. The only material statutory restrictions on GSE underwriting were the conforming loan limit and requirement of private mortgage insurance for high-LTV loans, but that could be circumvented through piggyback loans. Congress also tasked a feckless regulator, the Office of Federal Housing Enterprise Oversight (OFHEO), with supervision of the GSEs. The GSEs routinely flouted the implied charter restrictions on their activities without regulatory consequence, investing in tobacco stock and even (in the case of Fannie Mae) guarantying a CDO of PLS in September 2007.[37] Part of the reason why the GSEs were able to do this was that they excelled in mobilizing domestic political constituencies against any attempt by OFHEO to exert tighter regulation.

At the same time, the deregulation of the financial markets that had begun in the 1980s ensured that there were few restraints on other pieces of the mortgage market. As we have seen, Congress preempted a number of state mortgage regulations in the 1980s and federal banking regulators pushed in the 2000s to preempt state attempts to supervise bank-affiliated mortgage lenders. The only thing, then, that held the GSEs in check was their duopoly market power, which encouraged each to act as if it were a monopolist, which meant internalization of the risk in the entire market.[38] Duopoly kept the market in check—until the duopoly faltered with the rise of PLS.[39]

While the GSEs' behavior may be explained as the result of being drawn into a rate for market share, other questions still remain. Turn back, for a second, to Bernanke's AAA-investors, who were also necessary as part of the equation. Why did the A-piece investors view their investments as in fact being safe? And why didn't the smart money recognize the problems with the CDOs and move against them? Why was there such widespread mispricing of risk? Why didn't the market catch on to the problem? The next chapter takes up these questions.

CHAPTER TEN

The Key Market Failure

IN THE PREVIOUS chapters we explained how PLS fueled the US housing bubble, how PLS were enabled on scale only through CDOs, and that CDOs failed to price risk because of a set of serious incentive problems. While this might suffice for a whodunnit mystery, it still leaves a key question unanswered: why did the market fail to price against the bubble?

We both believe in the power of markets, so the market's failure presents a conundrum. The fundamental theorem of asset pricing teaches that if an asset is overvalued, then investors will move against it, resulting in the asset's price falling.[1] That's what's supposed to happen when markets work properly. So, why didn't investors recognize PLS as overvalued and bet against them? If the market had moved against PLS, it would have raised the yields necessary to sell PLS and thus raised the price of mortgage credit, which would have stifled the bubble before it could grow to devastating size. Similarly, if CDOs were underpricing PLS because of bad managerial incentives, why didn't the market price against the CDOs? Put another way, did some sort of fundamental market failure occur?

Our answer is yes. The fundamental market failure that drove the housing bubble was the inability to short housing. In order to short housing, an investor requires two things. The first is information. That is, the investor must be able to tell that housing is overpriced. The second is an investment vehicle that allows for the expression of short pressure. That is, the investor must be able to act in the market against the overvalued housing.

As it happened, neither condition was readily met in regard to the US housing market. Investors were unable to recognize the existence of a housing bubble in anything close to real time. When investors did catch on to the overpricing, they faced a faced a problem because housing cannot be easily shorted. The method that investors used to short the housing market actually increased system-wide leverage and exacerbated the effects of the collapse of the bubble and turned it into a full-blown financial crisis. The market's inability to observe risk pricing in real time and self-correct through short selling was the fundamental market failure that produced the bubble.

An explanation based on the underlying inability to short the housing market is an explanation that does not depend on the particulars of the financing channel. The US bubble was a PLS phenomenon, but other housing bubbles have occurred without the involvement of securitization. Our theory applies with equal force to credit-fueled housing bubbles outside the United States. It posits a simple proposition: markets cannot price correctly, absent sufficient information about risk and a vehicle to arbitrage mispricing. The information needed in the mortgage market is particularly complicated given the correlated nature of home prices, but at core it boils down to a risk-adjusted compression in mortgage spreads, a measure known as the Pavlov-Wachter indicator.[2] When the Pavlov-Wachter indicator is observable, markets will price to prevent bubbles.[3] When it is not, markets remain vulnerable. As we show in this chapter, investors were unable to observe market-wide risk metrics in real time, and, indeed, remain unable to do so today.

Information Failures in the Mortgage Market

The first step in preventing a bubble is identifying in real time that one is forming. How does one know that there is a bubble forming? We have defined a bubble as occurring when asset prices rise above those predicted by fundamental values. This means that a bubble is identifiable if one can predict asset valuations based on fundamentals.

In the case of a national housing market this is not a simple task. While some fundamentals, such as risk-free interest rates, are national in nature, others, such as population growth, secular growth in demand for homeownership among households, land use restrictions, and construction are local in nature. One cannot look simply to an expansion of credit as a sign of a bubble; a growth in credit might simply reflect a deepening of the market.

There is, however, one detectable signal of bubbles in the housing market—mortgage rates decreasing relative to Treasuries or to deposit rates despite increasing risk. A compression in credit spreads on mortgages—the Pavlov-Wachter indicator—is the mark of a housing bubble. It explains housing price increases that cannot be explained by fundamentals, and it predicts subsequent price crashes because, unlike changes in fundamentals, a credit spread compression while risk increases is not a sustainable equilibrium.[4]

To determine a credit spread compression, however, it is necessary to consider the value of two options embedded in US mortgages. The first option is what we call the "default put option," which is the option for a borrower to walk away from a mortgage debt. This means that on default, a borrower can chose to surrender the property with few additional consequences; the debt is either not owed or is functionally not collectible. For owner occupants default is generally a function of a "double trigger": lack of home equity plus a disruption to income, such as death, disability, divorce, or dismissal from a job. Thus, the default put option becomes attractive with negative equity plus an income shock. For property investors, negative equity alone (a single trigger) may suffice.

The second option is what we call the "leverage call option," which is the option for a borrower to further encumber a property with junior mortgages, irrespective of the senior mortgagee's consent or even knowledge.

These two options interface: the value of the default put option rises with greater leverage. The more indebted a mortgage borrower is, the more likely the borrower will have negative equity (half of the double trigger for owner occupants or the single trigger for property investors) and the more debt that can be avoided through the exercise of the put option. Thus, greater mortgage indebtedness increases the value of the put option. That greater mortgage leverage depends in part on the exercise of the leverage call option, because one way for a borrower to increase leverage is through junior mortgages. The following sections consider why investors failed to accurately price for these options.

Failure to Price the Default Put Option

THE DEFAULT PUT OPTION

Mortgage loans are formally either recourse loans or nonrecourse loans. On a nonrecourse loan, the borrower is not liable for the debt beyond the foreclosure value of the collateral property—the borrower's liability is restricted to the loss of the collateral. In contrast, on a recourse loan, the borrower remains liable for any deficiency that might be owed on the loan beyond the foreclosure value of the collateral property.

Borrowers on nonrecourse mortgage loans have an imbedded put option: the borrower can, by defaulting, put or "sell" the asset to the lender for the outstanding balance on the loan.[5] If the loan is nonrecourse, the borrower can then simply walk away from the debt to the extent it exceeds the value of the property. The borrower merely defaults on the loan and allows the lender to foreclose and the default put option is exercised.

The default option has a strike price that consists of (1) the loss of any equity the borrower has in the property, (2) the loss of the possibility of future equity appreciation, (3) damage to the borrower's credit score, and (4) the costs of relocating. If the value of the property declines below the amount of the mortgage debt, then the first element of the strike price is satisfied, and if the property value declines sufficiently, then the second element of the strike price will be satisfied as well. If the borrower has equity in the property, he or she will not exercise the put option, but will instead just sell the property and use the sale proceeds to repay the loan.[6] The borrower's credit score will be damaged if he or she defaults, but federal limitations on credit reporting mean that a foreclosure only stays on a credit report for a maximum of seven years.[7] Moreover, the foreclosure is unlikely to substantially affect a credit score after just a few years, and in any case, it is difficult for borrowers to determine the exact cost of a lowered credit score, so they are likely to discount this part of the strike price.

When a property is underwater, the most important part of the strike price is the borrower's cost of relocating. This is not merely the pecuniary transaction costs of moving, but the disruption to the borrower's life—schooling, employment, and other relationships may be tied up in the location of one's home. Thus, for resident borrowers, the exercise of the default option often requires a double trigger of both negative equity and a loss of income that makes the debt service on the property too burdensome. If the borrower is not the resident of the property, however—that is, the borrower is an investor—then this part of the strike price is also readily satisfied. Property flippers have a lower strike price on the default put option than do owner-occupants, and flippers represented a disproportionately high share of defaults during the bust.[8]

Most mortgage loans in the United States loans are formally recourse loans. *Functionally*, however, virtually all US mortgage loans are nonrecourse because of the difficulty in collecting unsecured debt. First, debtors may simply lack the assets to repay the deficiency on a mortgage; blood cannot be squeezed from a stone. Second, state property exemption laws make it difficult to recover large debt obligations like most mortgage deficiencies from a debtor's current assets. Third, federal and state limitations on wage garnishment make it extremely difficult to compel repayment of unsecured debts from future income.[9] Even with maximum wage garnishment, repayment might take years. Fourth, a determined debtor can readily evade most collection attempts. And fifth, if the debtor files for bankruptcy, unsecured debts, such as mortgage deficiencies, can be discharged. Indeed, the threat of filing for bankruptcy may chill more aggressive collection efforts.

While there are costs to borrowers from avoiding debt repayment, these costs may be unavoidable if the borrower cannot repay or may still be deemed worthwhile by the borrower. Moreover, these costs are generally indirect and nonpecuniary, such as a damaged credit score. All of this means that US mortgage lending is, for all practical purposes, nonrecourse, so US mortgage borrowers have a default put option.

THE PAVLOV-WACHTER INDICATOR

The embedded default put option is priced into the credit spread on the mortgage. The value of the put option is part of the spread between duration-matched mortgage rates and deposit or Treasury rates.[10] If priced correctly, the imbedded put option should have no impact on housing prices.[11] If it is underpriced, however, then the underpricing should be incorporated by efficient markets into housing prices, as it means that credit is underpriced, so that housing is relatively cheaper for borrowers.[12] Underpricing of the put option leads to housing prices that are inflated above their fundamental level.[13]

There are two reasons why credit spreads on mortgage loans over duration-matched deposits or Treasuries fall. First, the spread may compress because of a decline in the expected future volatility of housing prices, which reduces the put option's value to nondiversified homeowners.[14] A decrease in the credit spread for this reason is rational and does not impact housing prices.

Second, lenders may simply underprice the default risk. In such a situation, housing prices will increase because rational borrowers take advantage of the underpriced nonrecourse lending even if they are fully diversified.[15] Again, flippers are more likely to take advantage of the underpriced put option because they are diversified and less personally attached to a property. Indeed, flippers did contribute substantially to the growth of borrowing during the bubble.[16]

The differential response of housing prices to a decline in credit spreads under these two reasons enables the identification of a signal of default risk underpricing. If credit spread compression is not correlated with housing prices, then the credit spread compression may very well be rational as outlined in the first reason above. However, if the credit spread compression is correlated with housing prices, then the compression is likely due to underpricing, with all of its consequences as discussed below.

A compression of credit spreads on mortgages—the Pavlov-Wachter indicator—is the telltale sign of a bubble. The Pavlov-Wachter indicator distinguishes between rational changes in the lending spread based on fundamentals and those based on an underpricing of the put option. The presence of the Pavlov-Wachter indicator signals an unsustainable price rise and therefore a coming market crash, and the greater the compression of spreads, the larger the extent of the crash will be. Thus, identifying a compression of credit spreads on mortgages is the key to identifying the formation of a housing price bubble.

The Pavlov-Wachter indicator can be applied to PLS as well. With a pass-through security, a compression of credit spreads on the mortgages will translate directly to a compression of credit spreads on the PLS. With structured securities, the analysis of the credit spreads is more complicated, but the weighted average credit spread on the different structured securities in a PLS should be equivalent to that of a pass-through with the same underlying mortgages, as structuring allocates risk but does not reduce aggregate risk.

While re-creating the weighted average credit spread on a structured security is complicated, it can be simulated simply by looking at the credit spread on the underlying mortgages because the credit spread on the PLS will be derivative of the credit spread on the mortgages, because the cash flows to the PLS are simply the cashflows on the mortgages minus servicing and other administrative expenses. This is exactly what we calculated in Chapter 7—we used the credit spreads on mortgages in PLS to test for the presence of the Pavlov-Wachter indicator of compressed credit spreads.[17]

WHY THE US MORTGAGE MARKET FAILED TO PRICE
THE DEFAULT PUT OPTION

A compression of credit spreads on mortgages is not always readily detectible, at least in real time. If mortgage products are constant and homogeneous in the market, then the compression in credit spreads should be readily detectible. Because all other risk characteristics of the mortgages are held constant, any underpricing of risk will appear in credit spreads. But if mortgages are heterogenous or if there is a change in mortgage products, then it becomes much more difficult to detect a compression in credit spreads, because those spreads must be evaluated on a risk-adjusted basis in a heterogeneous market. When mortgages are not homogeneous, risk can seep in in many different forms, not simply in terms of the interest rate charged, but in terms of the interest rate relative to the other idiosyncratic risk features of the particular mortgage.

For example, consider what is involved in comparing the credit spread on a fully documented thirty-year fixed-rate, fully amortized purchase-money mortgage, made at a 95 percent loan-to-value (LTV) ratio to a borrower with a 720 FICO score with that on a 2/28 ARM limited documentation refinancing with an initial below-market teaser rate, made at 90 percent LTV to a borrower with a 780 FICO score. To have an apples-to-apples comparison of the credit spreads, one has to be able to adjust for each of the different characteristics of the loans and their various interactions, and that requires having complete information about the loans and then knowing how to adjust credit spreads based on that information. In other words, identification of credit spread compression in heterogenous and shifting markets is substantially more difficult—if not impossible—than in a relative homogeneous market.

Thus, in Chapter 7 we demonstrated that there was a material decrease in the risk premium on mortgages during the bubble. But we were only able to do so well after the fact and only after laborious hand-collection of data, which, while we believe is broadly representative, is not a random market sampling.

The US housing bubble was marked by the extraordinary growth of two types of interrelated, complex, heterogeneous, and novel products: nontraditional mortgages and PLS. These products shrouded mortgage credit spreads because credit spreads must be examined on a risk-adjusted basis and these products introduced a bewildering array of risks that needed to be accounted for if one were to attempt to calculate their movement.

When markets work, costs and risks are signaled through prices, which allows for efficient resource allocation. In markets in which information flows are shrouded or blocked, prices do not reflect costs, and risks and resources are allocated inefficiently. Complexity, heterogeneity, and novelty shroud information and thereby make it more difficult to evaluate investments. Complexity overwhelms the computational capacity of the human brain and even standard pricing models, while heterogeneity defeats cross-product comparisons, an inductive method upon which much of our pricing behavior relies.[18] Novelty frustrates attempts to predict future performance based on past performance. Therefore, as complexity, heterogeneity, and novelty increase, mispricing becomes increasingly likely.

PLS are unusually complex and heterogeneous products. First, the underlying mortgages in a PLS tend to be complex and heterogeneous. Whereas a traditional GSE securitization consisted of a pool of thirty-year (or perhaps fifteen-year) FRMs with little variation in interest rates or underwriting criteria, a PLS would be based on a pool of mortgages with tremendous variation in loan structure and underwriting. Some loans would be fully amortizing, and some would not (balloon loans). Some loans would have interest-only periods, and others would not. Some loans would be thirty-year loans, while others would be twenty- or fifteen-year. Some loans would be adjustable-rate, and others would be fixed-rate. The ARMs would be of varying structures: 5/1s, 7/1s, 2/28s, 3/27s, and so on. Some loans would be underwritten based on full documentation, and others, on various lesser degrees of documentation of income and assets. Some of the loans would be first liens, and others would be junior liens. Thus, any particular PLS would be supported by a unique pool of collateral.

The complexity and heterogeneity of PLS does not stop with the underlying mortgage collateral, however. Every PLS deal has its own particular waterfalls for allocating credit and interest rate risk and its own set of credit enhancements—tranching, overcollateralization, excess spread, shifting interest, reserve accounts, pool insurance, and bond insurance—resulting in a unique payment structure. Thus, PLS involved complexity and heterogeneity at both the collateral level and at the securities level.

While it is common to talk about categories of PLS, such as "subprime PLS," the truth is that there are substantial differences among subprime deals. A subprime PLS might have an average or weighted average FICO score beneath 620—but there is a material difference between a 618 pool and a 580 pool. Likewise, even for two deals with the same average FICO score, the distribution of FICO scores within the pools backing the PLS might be substantially different. Additionally, one "subprime" deal might be all ARM, another might be all FRM, and yet another might be a mix. The percentage of fully documented loans or of owner-occupied properties might vary, and so on. Thus, shorthand categories such as "subprime" are of limited usefulness.

PLS were not only complex and heterogeneous, but also novel. Whereas the long track record of 30-year fixed-rate mortgages makes their performance relatively predictable, nontraditional mortgages had little performance history, so investors had a limited basis for predicting their future performance, much less what would happen in a housing market with correlated asset prices as nontraditional mortgages became common products.

This, in turn, made it difficult to predict the performance of PLS based on nontraditional mortgages, particularly as the PLS themselves involved novel structures. The PLS of 2006 looked substantially different from the PLS of 2000 or of 1990.

Complexity and novelty shrouded the risks inherent in PLS, and that, in turn, made it difficult to observe the compression of risk-adjusted credit spreads. If investors in 2005 or 2006 had wanted to undertake a technical analysis the credit risk on a PLS deal, it would have required three things that did not exist. First, it would have required loan-level data on all the loans in the deal. Second, it would have required data about the loans being made in other deals. Third, it would have required a performance track record on which to build an analytical model, including the impact of the lending on the volatility of the underlying collateral and its impact on housing prices. None of these existed during the bubble.

Loan-level data were not available on PLS deals. Historically B-piece buyers were able to get a "loan tape" before buying and exercise "kick-out" rights to exclude particularly risky mortgages from deals, but this practice ceased with the entry of CDOs to the market, as the CDO managers were not interested in the detailed credit risk analysis.

The SEC only started requiring disclosures for PLS offerings in 2006 under Regulation AB. Reg AB's disclosure requirements only applied to registered securities, so some offerings were not covered (although most were). Moreover, it did not apply to offerings that were of primarily synthetic securities. But even for covered offerings, the SEC did not mandate any particular disclosure, only that of "material" information. The SEC strongly suggested that this material information would include certain types of aggregate, pool-level information, but did not specify the format in which such information was to be presented or exactly what information needed to be included. Disclosure of various types of aggregate loan pool information was already commonly included in pre-2006 prospectus supplements, but even after 2006 it was not standardized, either in terms of what types of loan characteristics were disclosed or how they were disclosed (for example, weighted averages or also deciles, often distributions, or maximums or minimums). The data that were disclosed were often disclosed on paper and in nonstandardized formats, making it harder for investors to collect and compare.

Critically, the data disclosed during the bubble years in PLS offerings never had loan-level information in advance, and even post-issuance data disclosures, were often plagued with missing data.[19] This meant that it was difficult to know if the disclosed weighted averages were in fact typical of the loans in the pool or merely reflected an average of very good and very bad loans. Additionally, the disclosure even of aggregate information was done in prospectus supplements, which were generally made available only at the time deals were actually being sold. As a result, investors had almost no time to analyze the specifics of deals in the original issuance market.

Even if investors had had loan-level data on deals in advance that alone would not have been enough. Housing is unique among assets in that prices are geographically and serially correlated. It is not enough to know what one deal looks like in isolation; to understand whether collateral values (and hence LTVs) have been inflated based on easy credit, it is necessary to be able to see the entire market. That sort of market-wide, bird's-eye view was simply not available to anyone during the bubble years, much less in real time.

Even with real time, loan-level data for the entire market, investors would still have needed the analytical capacity to handle it. To analyze such a vast dataset, however, would require a performance track record, and no such record existed for nontraditional mortgages.

At best, investors could guestimate the effects of rising levels of nontraditional mortgage characteristics on future loan performance. It does not take a financial maven to recognize that many no-document, high-LTV, interest-only loans are likely to result in substantial defaults, but determining just how substantial is another matter, much less determining what would be losses-given-default, which depends in turn on the overall state of the housing market.

The novelty and complexity of nontraditional mortgages and PLS created information opacity that precluded accurate credit analysis. Risks were changing along too many dimensions, all of which needed to be interacted with each other on each loan, and then with the mix of other products in the market to determine what was happening with risk-adjusted credit spreads. Accordingly, it was impossible for anyone to observe the Pavlov-Wachter indicator in the US mortgage market in real time.

Moreover, the heterogeneity of PLS meant that there was not a liquid secondary market in PLS because one PLS, even from a different tranche in the same securitization, was not good delivery for another PLS. As a result, no market-pricing mechanism existed for PLS, many of which did not trade.[20] Thus, investors failed to properly price for risk because they did not perceive the full extent of the risk involved. The housing bubble was fueled by mispriced mortgage finance, and the mispricing occurred because of information failures. At the core of the housing bubble was an information failure: investors lacked adequate information about the risks on nontraditional mortgages and PLS as well as the ability to gauge risk market-wide.

Failure to Price the Leverage Call Option

THE LEVERAGE CALL OPTION

The pricing of the default put option depends on the option's strike price. All else being equal, the default option should cost more when the strike price is lower, as it is more likely to be exercised, and thus more valuable to the borrower. One reason why the default option was underpriced in the US housing market was because of a second and often overlooked option embedded in all US mortgages, something we term the "leverage option."[21] The leverage option is the borrower's option to further leverage the same collateral property with a junior mortgage. It can be thought of as a type of "call" option with which the borrower can obtain further leverage.

The leverage option is an unintended by-product of an obscure federal statutory provision from the Garn–St. Germain Depository Institutions Act of 1982. The Garn–St. Germain Act prohibits lenders from exercising, in certain circumstances, "due-on-sale" clauses that let them call a loan, demanding immediate repayment in full. Among the circumstances in which a lender is prohibited from calling a loan is the creation of a junior lien on the property.[22] The Garn–St. Germain Act thus prohibits mortgage lenders in the United States from preventing borrowers from subsequently increasing the total leverage on a collateral property by adding a junior mortgage. Indeed, the mortgage lender might not even know of the existence of the junior mortgage,[23] and in any case cannot adjust its loan's pricing subsequently in reaction to the increase in leverage.[24]

The leverage option is important because it changes the strike price for the default put option. For the default put option to be in the money, the property must be underwater: the borrower must have negative equity, accounting for costs of sale. While owner-occupants usually require a "double trigger" of an impairment of income, investors are more likely to simply require a "single trigger" of negative equity: there is no sense carrying a mortgage on an underwater investment property unless one expects large future appreciation. The likelihood of negative equity increases with the total leverage on a property—more leverage, and less equity. The leverage option gives the borrower the possibility of increasing the leverage on the property and thus reducing equity and therefore reducing the strike price for the default put option.

The leverage option matters not simply because it lowers the strike price for the put option on a particular mortgage made by a lender, but also because it lowers the strike price for the put option on *other* mortgages, including those made by other lenders. The leverage option lowers the strike price for the put option on *all* mortgages. The leverage option enabled the aggregate level of leverage in the housing market to rise, and because of the geographic and serial correlation of housing prices, it became, through appraisals and LTV-based lending limits, a self-reinforcing financial accelerant that increased real leverage on all mortgages and, by lowering the strike price of the default put option, exacerbated the underpricing and overextension of mortgage credit.

IMPACT OF THE LEVERAGE CALL OPTION

Figure 10.1 shows the impact of the leverage option in the US housing market during the bubble. While LTVs remained static, CLTVs rose.[25] Figure 10.1 shows that combined-loan-to-value (CLTV) ratios rose dramatically from 2003 to 2007, even though LTV ratios remained within historical ranges. In other words, borrowers became significantly more leveraged during the housing bubble, and the increased leverage was from junior liens, not senior liens.

The contribution of second liens to the US housing bubble has not previously been fully appreciated by market participants or the scholarly literature. But as Figure 10.2 indicates, the increase in CLTV ratios at purchase closely tracked the increase in housing prices. This increase was attributable in large part to second-lien lending because mean first-lien LTV

Figure 10.1. LTV and CTLV Ratios, 1995–2011

Data source: "FHFA Monthly Interest Rate Survey: All Homes." tbl.9 (2015) (LTV data); Andrew Davidson *et al.*, "Mortgage Default Option Mispricing and Procyclicality," in *Homeownership Built to Last*, at 207, 290 (Eric S. Belsky *et al.*, eds., 2014) (CLTV data).

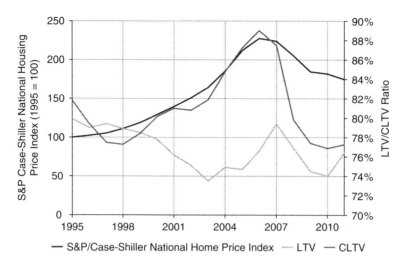

Figure 10.2. LTV Ratio, CLTV Ratio, and Home Prices, 1995–2011

Data source: "FHFA Monthly Interest Rate Survey: All Homes," tbl. 9 (2015) (LTV data); Andrew Davidson *et al.*, "Mortgage Default Option Mispricing and Procyclicality," in *Homeownership Built to Last*, at 207, 290 (Eric S. Belsky *et al.*, eds., 2014) (CLTV data); *S&P/Case-Shiller National Home Price Index* (1979 = 100) (HPI data).

ratios did not grow nearly enough during the bubble to account for the increase and in fact remained within their historical range.

The increase of mortgage market leverage through second liens not only led to an underpricing of the default put option, it also directly contributed to subsequent defaults by making the exercise of the put option more affordable.[26] Thus, studies have found that the presence of a junior lien increases default risk on the first lien.[27] Indeed, the growth in second-lien lending in general,[28] and of piggyback lending in particular,[29] is associated with higher subsequent default rates. Second-lien lending played a large and underappreciated role in the housing bubble in the United States.

WHY LENDERS FAILED TO PRICE THE LEVERAGE CALL OPTION

Lenders failed to price the leverage call option for two reasons. First, they could not observe its exercise in many cases, and thus did not know how prevalent its exercise was market-wide. And second, even had they been able to observe its exercise, the Garn–St. Germain Act and competitive pressures limited their ability to price adversely to the leverage option.

Because the leverage option is exercised after a first mortgage loan is made and because its exercise does not require notification of the existing lenders, first mortgage lenders did not know just how leveraged their borrowers were, much less the aggregate level of leverage in the home mortgage market. Lenders lacked real-time access to market-wide data on junior liens, so they could not determine how leveraged the market was becoming.[30] The data we present in Figure 10.1 were not available to most market participants during the bubble. No one—neither market participants nor regulators—had a market-wide view of total mortgage leverage.[31]

To be sure, during the housing bubble there was anecdotal information available about loosened credit standards and an expansion of mortgage credit, including through second-lien lending. But lenders did not know exactly how much additional mortgage credit was in the economy, nor did they know whether the additional leverage was sustainable, much less for how long.

Even today, there is still no complete source for market-wide CLTV data, including in commercial databases.[32] CLTV ratios remain largely untrackable and unmonitorable because there is no duty for lenders to report junior-lien lending on any source that matches the junior lien with any senior liens. The junior lien will be filed (typically on paper) in the local county recording office, where it can be matched with any senior liens, but turning such data into a commercially useable electronic database would involve a tremendous effort.

Not only was a market-wide picture unavailable during the bubble, but first-lien lenders were often unaware of the CLTV picture for their own collateral properties.[33] In some circumstances, the first-lien lender would know of a simultaneous piggyback second mortgage, but not all piggybacks were known to first-lien lenders, and subsequent seconds (so-called "silent seconds") were by definition unknown to first-lien lenders. Thus, a first-lien lender could believe it was lending at 80 percent LTV (and CLTV), but within days or months hence, the CLTV could have soared to 100 percent without the first-lien lender being aware.

Historically, borrowers did not exercise the leverage option very frequently so lenders were unlikely to price for it at all. But during the housing bubble this changed: junior mortgages became much more common, both as a way of avoiding having to pay for private mortgage insurance (which does not reduce home equity) and simply to facilitate greater borrowing in order to be competitive in bidding in a market with rising prices. Because the lender cannot control the exercise of the leverage option, they must price for it (if at all) ex ante, without knowing whether any particular borrower is likely to exercise the option. This means that lenders will price it at the average expected cost of the option. If that pricing is based on the past, less frequent use of the option, it will be inherently underpriced.

Even if lenders had had better information about the growth of leverage market-wide, competitive pressures would have pushed down the pricing of the option to that of the lender that priced it the lowest. Any individual lender that responded to increased market leverage by tightening credit would lose market share in the short term for an uncertain long-term benefit. Publicly traded firms, be they lenders or secondary market institutions, could not afford to tighten credit without losing market share and having their stock prices suffer.[34] Thus, the market is likely to underprice the leverage option, and that, in turn, means that the default put option will be underpriced.

Even when first-lien lenders knew of piggybacks, they often had no reason to care. Under the Garn-St. Germain Act, first-lien lenders are legally prohibited from calling a loan if a borrower increases CLTV by means of junior liens.[35] Thus, knowledge of specific cases of increased CLTV was not actionable by first-lien lenders other than to adjust pricing for future mortgages, which would do little to rectify the problem for existing loans.[36] By the time lenders adjust, it might be too late to avoid a junior-lien-fueled bubble.

Moreover, first-lien mortgages that had a piggyback mortgage were likely to be sold to Fannie Mae and Freddie Mac, so the first-lien mortgage loans' performance was not a concern of the first-lien lender. The reason for a borrower doing a piggyback second-lien mortgage rather than just having a first-lien mortgage for a larger amount (and higher LTV ratio) is that Fannie Mae and Freddie Mac are statutorily forbidden from purchasing mortgages with LTV ratios above 80 percent unless there is private mortgage insurance (PMI) on the loan.[37] PMI premia add to the cost of borrowing for higher LTV ratio loans. Thus, a borrower who wanted to borrow above 80 percent LTV ratio without paying for PMI would get a first-lien loan for 80 percent LTV ratio and a piggyback second-lien loan for the additional amount. In such cases, the first-lien lender would have no reason to care about the CLTV ratios because the loan would be sold to Fannie Mae or Freddie Mac, which lacked the ability to identify and price against loans with piggyback seconds.[38]

The inability of lenders to discern whether the leverage option had been exercised is a second information failure, and their inability to take actions to either prevent its exercise or to reprice following its exercise are an example of an incomplete market due to a statutory restriction on contract.

The leverage option exacerbated the underpricing of the default put option, such that risk-adjusted mortgage credit spreads actually compressed more than was observable simply through first-lien LTV data. The leverage option thus further masked the presence of the Pavlov-Wachter indicator and created an information failure that prevented the market from pricing adversely to housing once prices rose beyond the level warranted by fundamentals.

Institutional Information Failures: Credit Ratings

While information failures set the scene for an oversupply of underpriced housing finance, there were institutional checks that should, in theory, have ameliorated this information failure. One was the B-piece market. Prior to the entry of CDOs into the B-piece market, it served as an important check upon the total credit risk in the PLS market. The A-piece buyers were able to piggyback on the diligence of the B-piece buyers. But, as we have seen, once the CDOs outbid the traditional B-piece buyers that market discipline disappeared.

A-piece buyers had another source of information, however: credit ratings. Credit ratings should have been an initial constraint on default risk in PLS. According to Bernanke's global savings glut theory, the market was awash with funds from investors seeking safe assets. These investors were not experts in credit risk analysis, and instead looked to rating agencies to serve as information proxies regarding credit risk. Credit-rating agencies rate individual securities, such as distinct PLS tranches. The rating is an indication of either default risk or loss risk, depending on the agency. There are three major credit-rating agencies, and most PLS were rated by at least one, if not two, agencies.

Approximately 90 percent of PLS initially bore AAA ratings, meaning that the risk of default or loss was negligible.[39] Investors in the AAA-rated securities market do not appear to have been informationally sensitive.[40] A study by economist Manuel Adelino found that investors in AAA-rated PLS did not demand higher yields for what turned out to be riskier deals.[41] In other words, AAA-rated PLS investors were not themselves capable of sorting between deals and determining which ones were riskier within the AAA rating. Instead, these investors were simply purchasing the rating as a proxy for the existence of virtually no credit risk. Rating agencies thus played a critical informational intermediary role for the PLS market.

As it turned out, however, the rating agencies were woefully inadequate informational proxies; many AAA-rated PLS were subsequently downgraded.[42] Several factors contributed to the failure of the rating agencies in the PLS market. Many commentators have pointed to the rating agencies' lack of liability for misrating and lack of financial stake in any particular rating, beyond its long-term reputational effect.[43] While these factors surely contributed to the ratings problem, they are not unique to PLS.

PLS ratings, however, differ from those of corporate bonds, because corporate bonds are largely homogeneous products for which the ratings agencies have time-tested models going back over a century.[44] PLS, however, lacked multicycle experience and are heterogeneous products: no two deals are alike. The underlying collateral, borrower strength, and credit enhancements vary across deals. The novelty, heterogeneity, and complexity of structured-finance products made ratings much more speculative. Even as specialists in credit risk analysis, the rating agencies faced the same informational obstacles as individual investors.

The rating agencies also played a different role in structured-finance ratings than in corporate-bond ratings. The rating agencies were not merely objective commentators on structured-finance products. They were also intimately involved in the structuring of individual deals as part of an "iterative and interactive" process about how the issuer may attain the desired rating.[45]

This iterative and interactive rating process exists in structured finance because structured-finance ratings are model-driven rather than empirically driven. The ratings agencies' models, however, turned out to be deeply flawed. These models had never been tested in a period of sustained economic volatility or stress.[46] For CDOs, rating agencies' models assumed that diversification across different PLS pools would lower risk, without evidence of increased geographical diversification.[47] Moreover, the models failed to account for correlated housing prices or for price correlations between PLS and exogenous macroeconomic conditions (rather than enterprise-specific conditions).[48] The connections in particular between home prices and defaults and availability of credit were not made, and the models did not account for the possibility of a national housing-price decline.[49] The ratings agencies did not analyze the underlying collateral of the PLS to identify the probability of default or price fluctuation.[50] A basic assumption of the ratings agencies was that housing prices would remain constant, as they represented in their disclosures. This assumption is implicit in the use of appraised values of collateral, which are based on comparable properties.

Finally, the ratings agencies, like other participants in the market, were heavily dependent on fees from structured finance. Structured-finance ratings commanded premium prices, and the growth in the PLS market meant fees on more deals. Structured financing's share of rating agency revenue rose steeply during the bubble. By 2007, structured products like PLS accounted for 40 percent of the rating agencies' total revenue and over 50 percent of their ratings revenue.[51] The rating agencies' dependence on structured financing ratings as a revenue source incentivized them to provide issuers with the sought-after ratings lest they lose business to other rating agencies and kill the goose that was laying golden eggs.

The ratings agencies' problems went beyond flawed models and misaligned incentives, however. PLS heterogeneity and complexity also enabled issuers to shop for ratings in a way that was not possible for corporate bonds. As economists Vasiliki Skreta and Laura Veldkamp have argued, increased complexity in products makes ratings more variable between agencies, and this encourages issuers to shop for the most favorable rating.[52] Given the iterative and interactive nature of structured-finance ratings, such shopping was easy to do.

The ratings agencies were beset by a variety of problems that made them ineffective informational proxies for investors. While there were serious incentive problems for rating agencies, their involvement in the structuring of structured financial products and the inadequacy of their structured-finance ratings models were key. Even if incentive alignment had been better, the rating agencies still would likely have failed in their PLS ratings. The informational problems with PLS affected ratings agencies as well as investors.

Going Short

Information failures plagued the housing market, but they did not prevent all investors from recognizing the problems in the market. Some investors recognized that housing was overpriced. We cannot precisely pinpoint when investors started to recognize that there was a bubble, but it does not appear that any did so until around the end of 2004 or beginning of 2005.[53]

Once the smart money identified the bubble, some of the prescient investors simply pulled back from the market, but others actively sought to invest based on their insight. These were "short" investors in that they expected a drop in housing prices and hence in PLS values. The problem these short investors faced was that it is not possible to short housing through traditional means. The means they found for shorting the housing market actually *exacerbated* the bubble, which turned out to be exactly what they wanted, as it maximized their returns. Thus, while most investors failed to see the bubble forming, those who did had every incentive to make it worse in the short-term.

The standard way to short an asset is to sell it without owning it and then purchase it in time to meet the delivery obligation on the sale. The short seller's hope is that the asset price will decline between the time it enters into the sale contract and the time of the delivery obligation. For example, a short investor sells an asset for $100, with delivery due in three days. The short investor is hoping that the asset's market price will fall below $100 in the next three days. If it does—let's imagine it goes down to $97—the short investor will buy the asset for $97 and then deliver it to its buyer, keeping the $3 difference in sale prices.

Another way to short is through a put option: one can buy a put option allowing the sale of an asset at a particular price. If an investor buys a put option with a strike price of $100, then the investor will exercise the option if the asset price falls below $100, as the investor will go and buy the asset at the lower price (say $97) and then exercise the option to sell it for $100, keeping again the $3 difference in sale prices.

Real estate is different. It is a fundamentally incomplete market because of the unique nature of different properties, none of which are good delivery for each other. Blackacre cannot be tendered as delivery in a contract for Greenacre, nor even one tract in Levittown for another. This means that it is impossible to sell real estate short.[54] Because every parcel of real estate is unique, the short seller cannot meet its delivery obligation.[55] To short the Empire State Building, one would have to sell the building without actually owning it, and then manage to buy it at a lower price in time to deliver it to the buyer at the closing of the first sale! Likewise, a put option on the Empire State Building is not very helpful if one cannot first purchase the building. Shorting only works in liquid markets, and liquidity requires standardized assets that are good delivery for each other.

Real estate markets (but not individual properties) can be shorted indirectly, by shorting the stock of homebuilders or real estate investment trusts (REITs) or the like, but these regional stocks are imperfectly correlated with national housing markets with limited trading volume, and thus insufficient for shorting the whole of the housing market.

Another option for shorting real estate is to short PLS. PLS are themselves a type of real estate derivative, so they can, in theory be shorted directly,[56] but doing so is unattractive because they are insufficiently liquid; the short seller may not be able to find the particular PLS to purchase that meets its delivery obligation.

Credit-Default Swaps

It is possible, however, to short real estate markets indirectly, and more efficiently, through credit-default swaps (CDS). The problem is that doing so, given the way in which CDS markets were structured, increased the counterparty risk.

A CDS is a form of credit insurance[57] in which one party (the protection buyer) agrees to pay regular premia to its counterparty (the protection seller) until and unless a defined credit event occurs on a reference asset (here, a PLS).[58] Upon the occurrence of a credit event, the payment flow reverses, and the protection seller pays the protection buyer the agreed-upon level of insurance coverage. Thus, the protection buyer is short and the protection seller is long on the reference asset, *without either having to own the reference asset*. A CDS is generally written on a particular bond, meaning that a single CDS is written on a single PLS tranche, not on an entire PLS deal.[59]

Although CDS are a derivative instrument that need not involve any actual owner of a PLS security in the swap contract, CDS pricing was inherently linked to PLS yields. Every CDS needs to have both a short party (the protection buyer) and a long party (the protection seller). In other words, it is impossible to go short via a CDS unless another party is willing to take a matching long position.

Moreover, CDS protection sellers faced a serious correlation risk problem. CDS protection sellers they were exposed to numerous PLS, either directly or derivatively through the CDS. These PLS were based on similar mortgages, such that a downturn in the US mortgage market would mean drop in value or credit rating on the PLS and the triggering of the CDS based on them.

The CDS market did not account for this correlation risk. There was no reserving for correlation risk, such as is required in insurance markets. This was, in part because states did not regulate CDS as insurance.[60] No federal law expressly prohibited them from doing so prior to the Dodd-Frank Wall Street Reform and Consumer Protection Act of 2010.[61] Federal law merely prohibited states from regulating CDS under gaming and bucket shop laws.[62] But because CDS are formally "swaps," they were treated like any other OTC derivative. That meant that under the Commodity Futures Modernization Act of 2000, CDS were not subject to the Commodity Exchange Act's requirements of exchange trading and clearing.[63] As a result, there were no federal capital adequacy requirements or even reporting and disclosure requirements or bars on fraud and manipulation and excessive speculation for CDS. CDS operated in a regulatory vacuum in which no regulator could impose reserving requirements on protection sellers, which would have translated into higher CDS protection premia.

CDS protection sellers—the insurers of credit risks—had no incentive themselves to price for correlation risk. Any protection seller that priced for correlation risk would be at a serious competitive disadvantage and lose short-term market share. Moreover, the benefit of pricing for correlation risk inures, not to the protection seller, but to its counterparties: in the event of large, correlated losses, the CDS protection seller would be insolvent and unable to fulfill all of its obligations on the CDS. Thus, pricing for correlation risk would benefit the protection seller's creditors, but the loss in market share from higher pricing would have an immediate and definite negative impact on the protection seller's shareholders, with only a remote possibility of a future benefit of solvency that would be enjoyed only when protection buyers had been paid. Therefore, there was no shareholder demand for protection sellers to price for correlation risk.

Even if CDS protection sellers had wanted to price for correlation risk, however, they would have been hard-pressed to do so because of the lack of aggregate, real-time market information on the PLS market. Likewise, protection buyers could not know that they were buying insurance from firms that were inadequately reserving because they lacked the ability not just to see the entire market-wide exposure, but even the total book of CDS protection sold by any particular protection seller. The lack of aggregate, real-time, market-wide information on both PLS and on the CDS market made it impossible for anyone to price for correlation risk. As a result, CDS protection was inherently underpriced. Because of the arbitrage between CDS and PLS, this meant that there was less short-pressure on PLS.

Synthetic CDOs

Despite the oversupply of mortgage credit, the housing finance market could not produce a sufficient volume of mortgage notes for PLS to meet investor demand.

The solution to this shortage of PLS was to produce "synthetic CDOs" (or, more typically, hybrid, cash-synthetic CDOs) whose assets consisted of credit-default swaps rather than PLS B-pieces. Synthetic CDOs sold credit default protection, meaning that they were long on the reference assets, namely PLS or other CDOs' securities. The synthetic collateral in CDOs consisted primarily CDS on lower-rated tranches of subprime PLS.[64] The amount and share of synthetic collateral in CDOs grew explosively, jumping from $6 billion in 2004 to nearly $96 billion in 2006, when it accounted for over 40 percent of CDO collateral.[65] (See Figure 10.3.)

The growth in synthetic collateral indicates a massive growth in short positions on PLS because the synthetic longs (CDOs serving as CDS protection sellers) could not exist without synthetic shorts (CDS protection buyers). The betting against the mortgage market was particularly focused on the performance of subprime PLS that were originally rated BBB.[66] For every $1 of BBB-rated subprime PLS, there was $1.82 betting against it. But this also means, by definition that there were also $1.82 dollars of synthetic long positions, amplifying the size of the total long positions to $2.82, so that the total long to short ratio was 155 percent.

Synthetic CDOs were also used as part of a "long-short" strategy to pump up the market temporarily in order to increase the returns on short

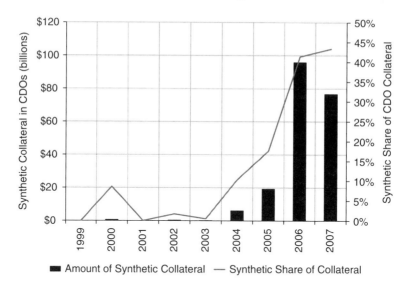

Figure 10.3. Growth of Synthetic CDO Collateral, 1999–2007

Data source: Larry Cordell *et al.*, "Collateral Damage: Sizing and Assessing the Subprime CDO Crisis," Fed. Reserve Bank of Phila. working paper no. 11–30, at 33, tbl. 4 (Aug. 2011).

positions. Some short investors, such as John Paulson in Goldman Sachs' infamous Abacus 2007-AC1 CDO deal, simply shorted the market by taking out naked CDS positions on PLS via a swap with a CDO.[67] Other shorts, such as the Magnetar hedge fund, devised a more sophisticated long-short strategy.[68] These investors purchased long positions in the equity tranches of CDOs, which they used to influence the CDOs to purchase particularly bad PLS, while at the same time the investors used the high coupons on these junior tranches to fund much larger short positions on the mezzanine tranches of the CDOs using CDS.[69] These investors thus took a junior long position in order to go short on a larger mezzanine position.

As explained earlier in the previous chapter, the CDO market meant that every dollar of investment in the equity tranche of a CDO was effectively leveraged into a much greater supply of mortgage finance.[70] As financial commentator Yves Smith describes it, "Every dollar in mezz ABS CDO equity that funded cash bonds created 533 dollars of subprime demand."[71] Thus, it is estimated that Magnetar's investment in the equity tranches of CDOs alone was responsible for between 35 and 60 percent of the subprime PLS issued in 2006, all based on an investment of perhaps $30 billion in equity positions in CDOs.[72] By purchasing the "equity" layer of CDOs, it made possible the existence of the CDO, including all the senior positions— which Magnetar then shorted.[73] The relatively small (if vociferous) demand for junior CDO tranches to fund short positions made huge PLS issuance possible and thus fueled the underpriced supply of mortgage credit.

The ABX Indices

It was possible, starting in 2006, for investors to go short on the mortgages derivatively by taking a position on the ABX, a series of indices that track the pricing of CDS written on PLS.[74] CDS pricing in the dealer market had been opaque, and because CDS involved counterparty risk, they were bespoke and seldom traded. The ABX was supposed to provide a transparent measure of pricing of risk on PLS than the dealer market, as well as a more liquid, tradable asset in which investors could express both long and short positions. In other words, the ABX was designed to complete the incomplete housing market both addressing informational problems and simultaneously creating an investment vehicle to act on that information. Yet even if it had worked perfectly, the ABX would have been reflecting not just the risk on PLS, but also the counterparty risk in the CDS market.

The ABX failed to deliver on its promise. In its first year, 2006, there was no significant movement of the ABX, despite the growing risk apparent in house price declines in mid-2006 and the rise in early defaults. That is, the cost of insurance against defaults was static, even as risk, including counterparty risk, was increasing. The obvious reason for the lack of movement in the ABX was the continued sale of CDS protection on PLS at prices unrelated to risk.

On July 10, 2007, the rating agencies announced the first mass downgrade of subprime PLS. The ABX indices began a dramatic descent, and CDS spreads soared, as the entire market could see the risk rising, not just the smart money, and the synthetic CDO market—and demand for long positions on CDS collapsed.[75] The ABX indices ended up being reactive, rather than predictive.

An information failure enabled the inflation of the housing bubble, and once investors did catch on, the incomplete nature of the housing finance market meant that their attempts to go short on PLS *increased* counterparty risk through the growing CDS market making the entire market more leveraged and fragile. This is the fundamental market failure underlying the Great American Housing Bubble. We now turn to the question of what has been done to remedy this market failure since the bubble burst.

CHAPTER ELEVEN

Postcrisis Reforms and Developments

A FTER THE CRISIS, Congress undertook several key regulatory reforms affecting the housing finance market.[1] These reforms were mainly of the primary market, not the secondary market. At the same time, however, market changes occurred in the secondary market, not as the result of explicit regulation, but because of regulatory pressure from the Federal Housing Finance Agency on the GSEs to derisk themselves while in conservatorship.

This chapter details these postcrisis changes in order to set the stage for our discussion of what work remains in housing finance reform. While we believe that there are still significant reforms needed, we think it is important to emphasize just how much reform has happened postcrisis. The housing finance market is substantially different in 2019 than it was in 2007. Most obviously, new PLS issuance has decreased; the market is dominated by Fannie, Freddie, and Ginnie. But there is also a dramatically different cast of regulators, most notably the Federal Housing Finance Agency and the Consumer Financial Protection Bureau, and much stronger mortgage lending regulations. Additionally, the GSEs have considerably reduced their portfolios, developed a common securitization platform with a uniform security, undertaken a massive synthetic credit risk transfer program, and moved to more explicit risk-based pricing for their mortgage purchases.

The net effect of all of this is to substantially derisk the mortgage market. Yet the current situation, while improved, is still jury-rigged, as Fannie and

Freddie continue to be in government conservatorship, and much of the derisking has happened outside of the rubric of formal regulation.

Regulatory Reform

Abolition of OFHEO and Establishment of FHFA

Reforms of the housing finance market actually began even before the financial crisis fully arrived. In June 2008, Congress passed the Housing and Economic Recovery Act, which abolished the Office of Federal Housing Enterprise Oversight (OFHEO) and replaced it with a new regulator, the Federal Housing Finance Agency (FHFA).

FHFA received a greater set of regulatory powers than OFHEO had had. These include the authority to impose prudential standards, including capital standards on the GSEs, obtain any data requested from the GSEs, undertake supervisory examinations of the GSEs, and require the GSEs to undertake remedial actions. OFHEO had been funded through the annual congressional appropriation process, which meant that it was acutely vulnerable to political pressure; FHFA in contrast is funded directly by the GSEs, which politically insulates the agency. And most importantly, perhaps, FHFA was granted authority to serve as conservator or receiver for the GSEs, a tool that turned out to be promptly used. Thus, just as the crisis was breaking, Congress acted to ensure that there would be a stronger regulator for the secondary housing market going forward.

The Consumer Financial Protection Bureau and the Qualified Mortgage Rule

The major vehicle for formal postcrisis regulatory reform was the Dodd-Frank Wall Street Reform and Consumer Protection Act of 2010 and the regulations enacted thereunder. Dodd-Frank did two critical things for the primary mortgage market. First, it created a new dedicated consumer protection regulator, the Consumer Financial Protection Bureau (CFPB), a well-funded, nonconflicted regulator with authority over the entire mortgage market.[2] Prior to the CFPB, authority over the mortgage market had been splintered among regulators: the Board of Governors of the Federal Reserve had rulemaking authority under the Truth in Lending Act, the Department of Housing and Urban Development had rulemaking authority under the Real Estate Settlement Procedures Act, and states had additional legislative authority, although it was often challenged on the grounds of federal preemption. At the same time, enforcement authority was scattered among federal and state agencies: the Federal Reserve Board, the Office of the Comptroller of the Currency, the FDIC, the National Credit Union Administration, the Federal Trade Commission, HUD, and various state bank supervisors and attorneys general all had authority over parts of the market.

This situation was problematic because prudential bank regulators are concerned, first and foremost, about bank solvency, which requires profitability, and more aggressive lending practices are often profitable in the short-run. Thus, there was a mission conflict for bank regulators between bank solvency and consumer protection and systemic stability. The division of regulatory authority also enabled regulatory arbitrage, as financial institutions, such as Countrywide Financial, switched charters, and hence regulators, in order to gain more favorable regulation.[3] The creation of the CFPB ended the internal mission conflict and regulatory arbitrage problems by creating a single, dedicated regulator for the entire mortgage market.

The Dodd-Frank Act's other major reform was a set of substantive rules about mortgage lending. Most significantly, Dodd-Frank prohibited lenders from making mortgage loans without regard to the borrower's ability to repay.[4] Specifically, creditors are now required to make a "reasonable and good faith determination based on verified and documented information that, at the time the loan is consummated, the consumer has a reasonable ability to repay the loan, according to its terms, and all applicable taxes, insurance (including mortgage guarantee insurance), and assessments."[5]

Ability-to-repay must be calculated based on a payment schedule that fully amortizes the loan over its term and, for adjustable rate mortgages, uses the fully-indexed rate, rather than a teaser rate.[6]

The adoption of an ability-to-repay requirement is itself a remarkable testament to the transformation of lending markets. Traditionally lenders were assumed to lend only to borrowers who could repay based on their own self-interest because the lender would be stuck with the loss from a defaulted loan. But in the private-label mortgage-backed securities market, lenders routinely ignored the need for ability-to-repay documentation. Hence, Congress mandated the consideration of a factor that self-interested lenders traditionally considered as a matter of course.

The penalty for violating the ability-to-repay requirement is fairly mild. It is simply a violation of the Truth in Lending Act, which gives individual borrowers a remedy of actual damages plus statutory damages of between $400 and $4,000 and reasonable attorneys' fees. Damages in class actions are capped at the lesser of paltry $1 million or 1 percent of the defendant's net worth.[7] There is a three-year statute of limitations for bringing actions for an ability-to-repay violation,[8] but borrowers can raise an ability-to-repay violation in a foreclosure and offset any damages against their liability on the mortgage without regard to the statute of limitations.[9] In other words, a violation of the ability-to-repay requirement is not likely to result in ruinous damages because the individual damages are quite limited and the class actions damages are so limited as to effectively preclude class litigation absent other class-wide claims.

Consumers are unlikely to raise ability-to-repay issues except in the case of foreclosure (where they cannot bring a class action), and most foreclosures do not result in litigation. The ability-to-repay requirement simply does not have much bite in terms of private liability. Instead, the real force behind the ability-to-repay requirement is the threat of regulatory enforcement by the CFPB (for banks with over $10 billion in total assets and all nonbanks) or various federal bank regulators (for banks with up to $10 billion in total assets).

There is a statutory safe harbor from the ability-to-repay requirement for "qualified mortgages" (QM). QM status allows a lender to benefit from a presumption of compliance with the ability-to-repay requirement. For most loans, this is an irrebuttable presumption,[10] but for "higher-priced" QMs (priced at 150 basis points over Prime for first liens mortgages and 350 basis points over Prime for junior liens), the presumption is rebuttable.[11]

To be a QM mortgage, a mortgage must have regular periodic payments that are substantially equal (other than changes due to an ARM rate reset), a term of no more than thirty years, limited points and fees (with the cap varying by loan size), and no negative amortization, balloon payments, or deferred principal. Additionally, the loan must either be eligible for purchase by the GSEs (the "GSE patch") or FHA/VA insurance or it must be underwritten to the maximum interest rate in the first five years of the loan, have verified income or assets, and have a back-end debt-to-income ratio of no more than 43 percent. Obviously jumbo loans are not eligible to satisfy these criteria through the GSE patch. A 2018 law also created an exception (the "portfolio patch") for the debt-to-income ratio for mortgages held in portfolio by small financial institutions ($10 billion or less in total consolidated assets).[12]

The QM Rule went into effect in January 2014. The effect of the QM Rule on mortgage origination seems limited; after the excesses of the bubble, most lenders had already abandoned exotic loan products and returned to solid underwriting fundamentals, including verification of ability to repay. The biggest effect of the QM rule seems to have been on portfolio lending above 43 percent of the debt-to-income (DTI) ratio. That lending dropped off sharply[13] but is likely to rebound somewhat because of the 2018 legislative portfolio patch. Because of the GSE patch, the QM rule seems to have had little effect on the prevalence of mortgages with DTI ratios over 43 percent.[14] The GSE patch is currently set to expire in January 2021. It is unclear whether it will be temporally extended or modified in terms of substance, such as by raising the general DTI ratio allowed, but the consequences could be significant for the housing market.[15]

Otherwise, the QM rule seems to have had little effect on the market—interest-only loans and prepayment penalties had largely disappeared before QM went into effect, the ARM rate continues to track interest rate movements, and small loans' prevalence (potentially affected by the points and fees cap) seems unaffected.[16] The importance of the QM rule, then, is less in terms of forcing a change on the market than in ensuring that the market does not slide back into the nontraditional mortgage products and risky underwriting that marked the bubble years.

Perhaps the most important point about the QM rule is that it has encouraged lenders to make QM mortgages and, in many cases, this means loans that qualify for purchase by Fannie or Freddie. In other words, the QM rule channels conforming mortgage lending into GSE-eligible loans. While there is non-QM lending occurring, the GSE patch has essentially codified the GSEs' dominance of the mortgage market.

Ability-to-repay is not the only regulation that the Dodd-Frank Act placed on the mortgage market. Among other things, Dodd-Frank prohibited prepayment penalties on non-QM loans,[17] required independent appraisals,[18] mandated appraisals for higher-cost non-QM mortgages,[19] and imposed limitations on lender payment of incentives to mortgage brokers for steering consumers into higher-cost loans.[20]

Taken all together, the Dodd-Frank reforms of the mortgage market have had the effect of substantially standardizing mortgage products: thirty-year maximum term, full amortization, no prepayment penalties, fully underwritten, full documentation. DTI has also been standardized to some degree with the 43 percent QM cap for non-GSE/FHA/VA loans. Formally, there is still room for nonstandard products. But the regulatory design heavily favors standardized products, such that nonstandard products may remain the exception rather than the rule. In many ways, the QM is a return to the sound principles of the American Mortgage that emerged after the Great Depression.

The Dodd-Frank reforms did not, however, standardize all mortgage features: whether mortgages are adjustable or fixed rate, the term under thirty years, and most critically LTV ratios, as discussed next.

The Qualified Residential Mortgage Rule and the Failure to Regulate LTV Ratios

The QM rule does not address loan-to-value ratios (LTVs), which was viewed as solely an investor protection, not a consumer protection.[21] The Dodd-Frank Act attempted to address LTV ratios through a separate requirement of risk retention for securitizations.[22] The theory behind this requirement was that if mortgage securitizers had to retain some of the risk on their own products, it would reduce moral hazard. The risk retention requirement has an exception for "qualified residential mortgages" (QRMs), as defined by a consortium of federal financial regulators. While federal financial regulators originally proposed an 80 percent LTV limit for QRMs, the final regulation defines QRM as equivalent to QM, so postcrisis there is still no federal regulation of LTVs.[23] The closest thing to LTV regulation is a new statutory mandate of appraisal independence.[24] This will presumably result in more accurate LTVs, but there is nothing currently limiting LTVs of 100 percent or more. The leverage call option continues to exist for US consumers, and so does the default put option because US mortgages remain functionally or formally nonrecourse. The effect is to impede identification of credit spread compressions that signal a bubble.

Regulation X and Mortgage Servicing Reform

The CFPB also undertook a major overhaul of mortgage servicing regulations. The mortgage servicing system essentially collapsed as delinquencies soared in 2007. Servicing involves two dissimilar lines of business. The servicing of performing loans is largely ministerial work: sending out billing statements and processing payments.[25] Because it requires little discretion, it can be heavily automated, and because it does not require a cadre of highly trained personnel, it is susceptible to economies of scale.[26] In contrast, the servicing of nonperforming loans requires substantial discretion and skilled personnel if there is to be any attempt at loss mitigation rather than simply proceeding to foreclosure.[27]

The mortgage servicing industry was built to deal with performing loans. The low foreclosure rate during the bubble years meant that servicers had not invested in the capacity to handle a large volume of nonperforming loans in a competent fashion. For example, many servicers still used fax machines to receive documents from borrowers, rather than online portals, virtually ensuring lost documentation. The result was bungled servicing that increased losses for investors and resulted in more foreclosures than should otherwise have happened. Moreover, servicers' incompetence and corner-cutting in terms of maintaining appropriate paperwork meant that some homeowners lost their homes without appropriate legal process and were charged inappropriate fees (which often translated into a transfer of foreclosure proceeds from investors to servicers).[28] For example, Wells Fargo was sanctioned by a federal bankruptcy judge for charging collateral inspection fees on a property that was literally underwater and in an evacuation zone in New Orleans following a hurricane.[29] As servicing outrages gained media attention, state attorneys general and federal regulators brought enforcement actions that resulted in 2012 in a $25 billion settlement with the five largest mortgage servicers.

In 2013, the CFPB announced new servicing regulations (effective January 2014) that prohibit servicers from commencing a foreclosure until a loan is at least 120 days delinquent, mandate early intervention and continuity of contact with borrowers, and establish a particular loss mitigation eligibility evaluation procedure and appeals process if the servicer offers any sort of loss mitigation options.[30] No loss mitigation is required, however. The servicing rules also limit servicers' ability to profit off of force placing insurance on delinquent mortgaged properties with affiliates at above-market rates.[31]

While the servicing regulations provide much needed protection for consumers, they do add to the cost of servicing delinquent loans. Servicing fees are essentially a piece of the interest paid on a mortgage: 12 to 50 basis points, depending on the type of mortgage. Servicers have never previously properly priced for the servicing of delinquent loans because these loans were very much the exception historically. The CFPB's servicing rules require minimum servicing standards for delinquent loans and reduce servicer opportunities to profit off of distressed borrowers, and this may have the effect of making lenders with servicing affiliates chary of extending credit to more marginal borrowers who are more likely to default.

Regulation AB II Disclosures

In December 2004, well before the financial crisis, the SEC finalized Regulation AB, the major securities regulation specifically of private-label asset-backed securities. In its original form, which went into effect at the start of 2006, Reg AB's key provisions for our purposes were two sets of disclosure requirements.

First, Reg AB required pool-level disclosures about the securitized assets. Such disclosure is potentially useful for investors if it is sufficiently standardized, but it is substantially less useful than loan-level disclosures because pool-level information discloses only averages and potentially maximums and minimums for different risk characteristics. It does not disclose the distribution of any particular risk characteristic, much less the layering of risk characteristics. For example, a pool might have a weighted average FICO score of 680, but that could be based on 1,000 loans all with 680 FICOs or 500 loans with 740 FICOs and 500 loans with 620 FICOs. Those are materially different pools, but the difference would not be apparent from the original Reg AB disclosures. Likewise, one could not tell from the original Reg AB disclosures how FICO scores mapped onto LTVs in a pool—were low FICOs compensated for with low LTVs on the same loans or not?

Even more problematically, the original version of Reg AB did not specify the particular terms that had to be disclosed. Instead, it only required that the "material terms" of the assets be disclosed, as well as the underwriting criteria, the identify of any originator of over 10 percent of assets, the selection criteria for the asset pool, and the cut-off date for establishing the asset pool.[32] As a result, disclosures on PLS were nonstandardized in both content and form. Not all securitizers disclosed the same types of information, and when they did, they often varied in how they presented it. For example, some might present LTV ratios, and others CLTV ratios. For those presenting LTV ratios, some might simply disclose an average LTV, while others might also list the minimum and maximums, and yet others might also disclose a distribution by LTV decile. The flawed nature of Reg AB's pool-level disclosure requirements meant that it was impossible for investors to determine the concentration of risk in particular securitizations, much less to undertake a systematic comparison of deals or track the whole market.

Reg AB also required disclosure of "static pool" information—information about the performance of the securitizer's previous securitizations in terms of delinquencies, losses, and prepayments, for up to five years by vintage.[33] While static pool information made sense for corporate bonds, it had the potential to be misleading for PLS given serially correlated housing prices and loan performance. Static pool information released in 2006 would have shown the presumably strong performance of loans from 2001 to 2005, when the bubble was forming. This information would have conveyed exactly the wrong signal to an investor considering buying PLS products in 2006.

Beyond these limitations in the nature of the disclosures required, the effectiveness of Reg AB was also seriously hampered by the scope of its coverage. Reg AB applied only to registered debt securities. This meant that private placements of PLS products or CDOs (that is, offerings only to qualified institutional buyers) were not covered. Given that most of the market for PLS are institutional investors, it was easy for securitizers to avoid Reg AB by relying on the private-placement exception to securities registration. Reg AB also excluded primarily synthetic securitizations, such as many CDOs, from its coverage. As a result, Reg AB simply did not cover substantial parts of the market. In any case, Reg AB only went into effect in 2006, by which time it was too late for it to have much effect.

In 2010, the SEC proposed a substantial revision to Reg AB, known as Reg AB II. The revision was finally adopted in August 2014. Among the changes are a requirement that issuers of asset-backed securities, including

PLS, provide standardized loan-level information in the prospectus and on-going reports. In particular, Reg AB II requires standardized asset-level disclosures, including 272 separate items for residential mortgage securitizations.[34] While many of the disclosure items are only applicable to certain types of mortgages—ARMs, for example, require more disclosures than FRMs, and many disclosure items deal with loan modifications or private mortgage insurance (PMI) coverage—the list is nearly exhaustive. These loan-level disclosures must be provided to the SEC in XML format,[35] so they are readily downloaded and useable by investors. In the past, data would have had to have been laborious gathered by hand (as we did for the data presented in Chapter 7) because of nonstandard formatting of disclosures in prospectus supplements.

Reg AB II also includes a provision designed to ensure that investors have adequate time to analyze securitization deals prior to investing. It does so by mandating a delay between disclosure of the terms of the deals and sale. Securities offered to the general public must be registered with the SEC, which entails making various disclosures about the security as part of a registration statement and potentially SEC staff review.

Certain securities, however, are eligible for "shelf registration," which means that they can be registered with the SEC in advance by including as part of the registration statement a "base prospectus" that gives general information about the type of securities to be offered, the issuer's business and risk factors, as well as a generic form of prospectus supplement that will be used to provide specific information about securities offered. When market conditions for a securities issuance are favorable, the issuer can then take the securities down "off the shelf" and quickly sell them without subsequent SEC staff review, using a "prospectus supplement" that contains more specific information about the particular securities being offered.

Asset-backed securities have been able to use shelf registration since 1992,[36] and for PLS issuers, shelf registration allows the sale of multiple securitization deals all covered by an initial prospectus that generally describes the securitization structure. Prior to Reg AB II, the prospectus supplement merely had to be provided to buyers at the time of sale and to the SEC two business days later. This meant that investors had almost no time to analyze the specific collateral underlying any particular PLS deal when it was offered; they could only see the prospectus supplement that contained deal-level disclosures around the time they committed to buy.

Reg AB II mandates disclosure of the prospectus supplement at least three business days before the first sale and also requires a 48-hour delay on pricing after any material change.[37] This delay gives investors a chance to digest the information on the underlying collateral in the prospectus supplement.

The mandate of loan-level disclosures in XML format and advance disclosure was a move in the right direction, but it changed the problem from being one of too little information to one of too much. It is difficult to readily model the behavior of 272 separate variables, even with substantial computing power. The only way to make analysis more readily feasible is to simplify mortgage loans through standardization, so that there are fewer dimensions on which they may vary. Reg AB did impose standardization of certain reporting on mortgages, such as delinquency intervals, but much of this was already largely standardized in the mortgage industry, not least because of widely used servicing platform technology. Reg AB II could have gone much further in promoting standardization on the PLS level, much as the QM rule did on the mortgage level.

Moreover, it is not sufficient simply to consider the characteristics of a single loan or pool of loans, but it is also necessary to understand what is going on market-wide. If LTVs are increasing market-wide, for example, then there may be an inherently inflated LTV on any particular loan because the LTV on that loan is based on comparables, but those comparables might not be based on sound fundamentals. Reg AB II does not enable market-wide analysis because it applies only to offerings of registered securities. This means that all private placements remain exempt, and the PLS market, such as it is, has now shifted almost entirely to private placements; not a single registered PLS was issued between 2014 and the end of 2019.[38] Likewise, synthetic deals remain exempt, and Fannie Mae, Freddie Mac, and Ginnie Mae MBS are all also exempt from registration.[39] Thus, while Reg AB II is an improvement on the original Reg AB, it still has a long way to go to cure information problems in the mortgage market.

Despite the shortcomings of its improved disclosure regime, Reg AB II still includes an important set of investor protections that may help set market standards. A major frustration for PLS investors postcrisis was to discover that it was extremely difficult to enforce the representations and warranties made about the securitized assets by the transaction sponsor. All securitizations come with a set of representations and warranties about the securitized assets—that's how investors have confidence about what they are invested in. Without representations and warranties, investors would be buying a black box of unknown contents and would have no idea how to price for the risks they would assume from this mystery security. If there is a violation of the representations and warranties, the sponsor (or its subsidiary depositor) is generally supposed to repurchase the loan from the securitization pool, meaning that any losses on the loan would shift to the sponsor.

The responsibility for enforcing representations and warranties rests, in the first instance, on the mortgage servicer, through what is called the "put-back" process. The servicer, however, typically has little incentive to pursue representation and warranty violations. The servicer is not compensated additionally for doing so, and the servicer is often an affiliate of the sponsor, so a put-back would be against its interests. Additionally, the sponsor will often fight put-back requests, and there is no mechanism in securitization deals for resolving disputes; the expectation was that there would not be put-backs except in rare instances, when they would be readily resolved in good faith.

Postcrisis, investors found that they had little ability to compel servicers to act and that sponsors would regularly fight put-back requests. As Bank of America CEO Brian Moynihan stated, his bank would fight put-backs "hand-to-hand."[40] The investors cannot themselves direct the servicer to bring put-back actions; only the securitization trustee can. Securitization trustees, however, also have little incentive to act. Trustees may themselves have liability in certain instances because they are responsible for ensuring that proper documentation for the mortgage loans was received by the trust. Trustees do not want their performance in this regard investigated. Moreover, trustees get their business flow from sponsors, not investors, and often are the "backup" servicer, meaning that if they have to fire the servicer, the trustee is stuck with the hassle and cost of servicing the loans. Trustees are also broadly exculpated other than for their specifically required duties, so they are generally not inclined to act unless they receive direction and indemnification from investors. Additionally, securitization deals all have "no action" clauses that prohibit individual investors from bringing suit themselves against the servicer in most instances; instead, in order to direct the trustee, investors must reach a certain threshold of holdings, typically 25 percent of a series, and post satisfactory indemnity to the trustee. Investors, however, had no ready way of ascertaining each other's identities and communicating, making it difficult to achieve the 25 percent threshold. While investors managed to overcome these problems in some instances and forced trustees to act, the difficulties they experienced in enforcing representations and warranties is a substantial concern that made investors shy of purchasing PLS products again.

Reg AB II attempts to address this by making shelf registration eligibility contingent upon a securitization transaction having four terms.[41] First, the securitization must have a certification by the CEO of the depositor (the entity that transfers the loans to the securitization entity) that the prospectus information is correct and that the deal should be able to generate the cash flows to pay all of the securities in full. The certification provision puts more teeth into the representations and warranties; a violation of representations and warranties is now a securities law violation directly enforceable by investors, not merely a contractual violation with remedies limited to put-backs.

Second, the transaction must provide that if defaults hit a specified level, an investor vote is triggered upon the request of no more than 5 percent of the total interest in the pool. If that vote is affirmative, there will be an independent investigation of possible representation and warranty violations on at least all loans that are more than sixty days delinquent. Based on the findings of the investigation, the trustee must then decide whether to pursue put-backs, and the trustee must provide investors with a summary of any report provided to investors. This process removes the put-back decision from the hands of the servicer, although it still allows the trustee substantial control over the scope of the review and the process by which votes are solicited. Third, the transaction must allow the party bringing the put-back request to seek arbitration or mediation at its option if the dispute is not resolved within 180 days. That means that put-back requests no longer assume good faith informal resolution but contain a relatively cost-effective resolution mechanism. And finally, trustees are required to disclose all investor requests to communicate with each other, which facilitates surmounting collective action thresholds.

Reg AB II was overall an important reform of the PLS market. But it occurred when the PLS market was virtually dead. Should PLS ever revive, Reg AB II will take on new importance in channeling information to the market. Even so, there is a question whether Reg AB II would be sufficient to bring back a robust PLS market in residential mortgages. Investors recognize that they are at risk not only of bad underwriting in a particular security, which they can diligence and address contractually, but for the spillover risk of bad underwriting in the market overall, which they cannot diligence or protect themselves from contractually.

Today, however, Reg AB II has little importance because the mortgage market is dominated by the GSEs and Ginnie Mae. Indeed, there have been no registered PLS issuances since 2014,[42] so Reg AB II is a regulation with no current application. The lack of registered issuances is less a matter of Reg AB II than of a general move away from PLS; there has been only very limited unregistered PLS issuance postcrisis. Instead, credit risk investment in the US secondary mortgage market has migrated from PLS to the GSEs' synthetic credit risk transfers, discussed in the next section. Reg AB II is a state-of-the-art weapon—but only for the last war.

Market Developments

Winding Down of the GSE Portfolios

Four important market developments have occurred since the financial crisis. First, the GSEs have been winding down their portfolios. When the GSEs hold mortgages or MBS in their investment portfolios, they are assuming interest rate risk. Indeed, the major concern many expressed about the GSEs prior to the bubble was not credit risk, but interest rate risk.

The Senior Preferred Stock Purchase Agreements were amended in 2012 to require the GSEs to reduce their portfolios of mortgages and MBS by 10 percent per year until they reached $250 billion,[43] roughly a two-thirds reduction in the size of both GSEs' portfolios from their 2008 10-K valuations. The GSEs are still allowed to guarantee any number of conforming mortgages, but are now restricted in their capacity to invest in mortgages or MBS, as long as the Senior Preferred Stock Purchase Agreements are in place. The result of the portfolio winddown is that the GSEs bear much less interest rate risk, and the interest rate risk in mortgages that the GSEs insure is entirely borne and priced competitively by the private sector.

Common Securitization Platform

The second major market change is that Fannie Mae and Freddie Mac have developed, per FHFA regulation, a Uniform MBS that is designed such that Fannie Mae Uniform MBS are good delivery for Freddie Mac Uniform MBS in the forward contract market known as the To-Be-Announced (TBA) market.[44] Fannie Mae, Freddie Mac, and Ginnie Mae MBS all trade in the TBA markets. In these markets, parties contract for sale of an MBS to be delivered on a future date, but the parties do not designate the specific security to be delivered. Instead, the contracts specify only the issuer/guarantor (Fannie, Freddie, or Ginnie), the maturity, the coupon rate, the face value, the price, and the settlement date.[45] The actual security to be delivered is "to be announced" 48 hours before the settlement date.[46] The market works because of an assumption of homogeneity among each issuer/guarantor's MBS.[47]

The TBA market, which dates from the 1970s, is the second-most liquid market in the world, surpassed only by US Treasuries, although historically the TBA market was not one market, but three separate markets.[48] The TBA market provides both consumers and lenders with valuable services. For consumers, the TBA market ensures their ability to get preclosing rate-locks. Consumers want to know their cost of financing before they bid on properties because the terms on which consumers can obtain financing affect consumers' bidding capacity. This means that consumers generally want to get financing terms well before the loan actually closes, which is when the property sale closes. The problem is that market conditions can change during the window between the lender offering financing terms and the closing. If the lender makes the consumer a firm offer of financing at a fixed rate, the lender is then exposed to market swings during the window between agreeing to the financing and the closing. In particular, the lender might find itself with a below-market loan that it can only sell at a discount. Yet lenders often offer preclosing rate-locks on fixed-rate loans for thirty to ninety days.

Lenders are able to offer these rate-locks because they can hedge out their rate risk through the TBA market. For example, if a lender agrees to a loan at 6 percent APR, the lender could hedge its risk by selling a forward contract for Fannie Mae MBS with a 6 percent yield. If interest rates rise to 8 percent prior to the closing, the lender will be stuck with a below-market loan, but the lender will also be getting paid a market rate to deliver an MBS with an equivalently below-market coupon, offsetting the loss on the loan.[49] While other hedges are theoretically possible, rate movements in the TBA market are most likely to track those in the mortgage market, compared with, say Treasury futures, and no market exists in mortgage futures.[50]

For lenders, the TBA market provides an important source of financing through a mechanism known as the "dollar roll."[51] A dollar roll is a combination of two simultaneous and offsetting TBA trades with different settlement dates. For example, a lender might sell a Fannie Mae MBS for settlement on June 1 and buy one with the same terms for settlement on September 1. The effect is equivalent to obtaining a three-month loan, with the interest rate being based on the differential in transaction prices. The dollar roll transaction functions much like an MBS repo, but the two legs of the transaction—the sale and purchase—do not need to be with the same counterparty nor does the same security need to be used for both legs of the transaction, only sufficiently similar ones.

Historically, Fannie Mae MBS, Freddie Mac Participation Certificates (PCs, the name of the Freddie Mac MBS product) and Ginnie Mae MBS were not good delivery for each other in the To-Be-Announced forward contract market. The Fannie, Freddie, and Ginnie products differed from each other in terms of format and content of disclosures, in terms of payment schedules, and in terms of the guarantor entity. As a result, there were separate TBA markets for Fannie Mae MBS, Freddie Mac PCs, and Ginnie Mae MBS. By virtue of being the smallest issuer, Freddie Mac's PCs would normally suffer from a liquidity discount (and possibly also a discount from a perceived weaker guarantee). Freddie Mac therefore had to subsidize its securitizations to offset that discount.

In 2014, however, the FHFA, as conservator of Fannie and Freddie, announced a goal of developing a uniform MBS for both GSEs that would be good delivery for each other in the TBA market. By making Fannie Mae MBS and Freddie Mac PCs good delivery for each other in the TBA market, there would cease to be separate Fannie and Freddie TBA markets. Instead, there would be a larger and more liquid joint market. That liquidity would enable Freddie to stop subsidizing its PCs, which after the capital support agreements were in place came at the expense of Treasury by reducing the profits available to sweep.

The solution, implemented in June 2019 per regulation,[52] was the development of the Uniform MBS. Uniform MBS are issued separately by both Fannie and Freddie through a new Common Securitization Platform owned by Common Securitization Solutions, LLC, a joint venture of Fannie Mae and Freddie Mac. The Uniform MBS is structured like Fannie Mae MBS (with a fifty-five-day investor payment delay), but with Freddie Mac-style disclosures. Fannie and Freddie are obligated by regulation to keep the terms of their securities substantially aligned in terms of prepayment speeds.[53]

The guarantees on Fannie Mae Uniform MBS continue to be obligations solely of Fannie Mae, and those the guarantees on Freddie Mac Uniform MBS continue to be obligations of solely Freddie Mac, but Fannie and Freddie Uniform MBS will be good delivery for each other in the TBA market. The fact that Fannie Mae MBS and Freddie Mac PCs are good delivery for each other despite different guarantors is a strong indication of the implicit government guarantee of Fannie and Freddie and increasing convergence of the enterprises, who are now required by regulation to have substantial standardization of their MBS' prepayment speeds (which includes foreclosure rates because foreclosures are a type of prepayment) and therefore, by implication, standardization of their underwriting. Ginnie Mae MBS continue to trade in a separate TBA market and are not part of the Uniform MBS project.

GSE Credit Risk Transfers

The third major market development is the adoption at FHFA insistence of credit risk transfer programs by both Fannie Mae and Freddie Mac.[54] From 2013 through 2018, the GSEs cumulatively transferred over $91 billion of credit risk on $2.7 trillion of mortgages.[55] While this is only around a 3 percent transfer of credit risk, most of the risk transferred is either first-loss or junior mezzanine loss, so much of the GSEs' expected credit risk exposure has been transferred. For 2019, FHFA required that the GSEs transfer a meaningful portion of credit risk on at least 90 percent of the unpaid principal balance of newly acquired single-family mortgages.[56]

These credit risk transfers have occurred through a range of transactions: loan-level mortgage insurance, pool-level mortgage reinsurance, lender risk-sharing agreements, and the issuance of subordinated, non-guaranteed MBS,[57] but the vast majority of the credit risk transfers ($66 billion on $2.2 trillion in mortgages through 2018) have been so-called "synthetic" credit risk transfers through derivatives.[58] These synthetic credit risk transfer transactions, which premiered in 2013, involve the sale of credit-linked notes (CLNs), the payment of which is based on the performance of the mortgages in a Fannie or Freddie MBS.

The great innovation of GSE securitization was to separate interest rate risk and credit risk. The MBS investors assumed the interest rate risk, while the GSEs retained the credit risk through their guarantee of timely payment of principal and interest on the MBS. The synthetic credit risk transfers are the next logical step in this progression—there is no need for the credit risk to rest entirely with the GSEs; instead, they can sell it to third parties separately from the interest rate risk. Indeed, this is what the GSEs have been doing in various forms for some time. The GSEs have long had PMI coverage on many mortgages, which is a form of credit risk transfer, and they also have programs for seller/servicers to retain a portion of the credit risk, for the sale of participation interests in MBS pools, and for credit reinsurance. The net effect of the synthetic credit risk transfers is that the GSE MBS investors assume all of the interest rate risk, and the GSE CLN investors assume a portion of the credit risk on the GSEs' mortgage pools.

The form of the synthetic credit risk transfers has changed over time, but in the post-2018 form, Fannie or Freddie enters into a credit-default swap with a bankruptcy-remote trust it has created, in which the trust sells credit-default protection to the GSE on a specified pool of mortgages.[59] As long as the mortgages perform, the GSE will make periodic protection payments to the trust, while if a defined credit event occurs, the trust will pay the GSE up to the specified level of coverage. The trust thus assumes the credit risk on the mortgages. The trust is itself capitalized by selling notes that are obligations of the trust, not the GSE, to investors. The trust then invests the proceeds from the notes in highly liquid, safe assets (for example, Treasuries) that can be used to pay the GSE if there is ever a credit event. This form of CLNs is effectively a securitization of a credit-default swap, such that the real protection sellers—the ultimate holders of the credit risk on the mortgages—are the investors in the CLNs. Figure 11.1 illustrates this transaction structure.

Notably, the GSEs do not transfer all of the credit risk on the reference pool for the CDS. While the precise structure has varied by transaction, a

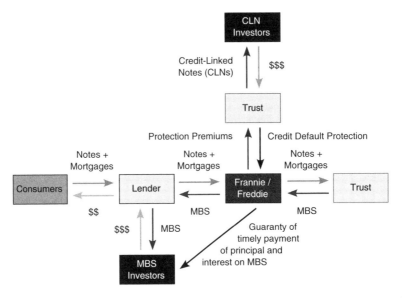

Figure 11.1. Fannie/Freddie Funding of Mortgages through Securitization with Back-End Credit Risk Transfers

Original creation by the authors.

common structure is for the transaction's GSE sponsor to retain the first-loss position of 0.5 percent of the reference pool (much like an insurance deductible), as well as the senior 97 percent of the pool. The GSE would sell only a second-loss mezzanine slice of 2.5 percent of the pool to investors, but also retain at least 5 percent of all mezzanine tranches, for a total risk transfer of 2.375 percent of the credit risk on the reference pool.

While 2.375 percent of the credit risk may sound small, it is most of the first 3 percent of losses on the pool, a level that exceeds expected losses in most market situations. Figure 11.2 illustrates this division of credit risk. The idea is that the GSE will bear normal operating risk, the CLN investors will bear the risk of a serious market downturn, and the GSE (and thus effectively the federal government) will bear the tail risk of a market catastrophe.

In synthetic credit risk transfers, the GSE shifts part of the credit risk on the referenced mortgage pool to the CLN investors. The CLN investors are effectively guarantors of the mortgages. Critically, however, the mortgages themselves are never transferred in this process; they remain the property of the GSEs and in the possession of their regular servicers.

The synthetic credit risk transfer programs have substantially derisked the Fannie and Freddie. In so doing, they have also fundamentally changed the housing finance market. Prior to the GSEs' synthetic credit risk transfers,

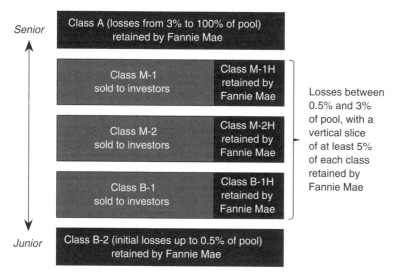

Figure 11.2. Fannie Mae Connecticut Avenue Securities Credit-Linked Notes Structure

Original creation by the authors.

investors in GSE securities assumed no credit risk; investors that wanted credit risk on mortgages had to purchase PLS products. Now, investors can assume credit risk on mortgages synthetically through the CLNs. This new product presents a substantial competitive challenge for the return of PLS on any scale. At the same, time, however, it has shifted the locus of the problems associated with mortgage credit risk from the PLS market to the CLN market.

Investors had difficulty properly pricing for credit risk on PLS because PLS are opaque, heterogeneous products. If investors are to properly price credit risk, they need information about the loans. This can be accomplished either by substantial loan-level disclosure, of which Reg AB II is an excessive model, or through standardization of loan products.

The GSEs have been disclosing substantial loan-level and pool-level information for the reference pools for their CLNs including the first three digits of collateral properties' ZIP codes. Yet this is all voluntary disclosure because Reg AB and Reg AB II do not apply to the GSEs (or to synthetic securitizations generally). Moreover, the procedural protections for investors created by Reg AB II, particularly the time between disclosure and sale, do not exist for the CLNs, and investors do not have the ability to meaningfully diligence 100,000 plus loans in the underlying reference pools before having to make a decision to purchase.

The GSE CLNs do, however, offer potentially substantial standardization. First, they shift only credit risk, not credit risk and interest rate risk, to investors, so they have inherently simpler cashflow waterfalls and less informational complexity. Second, all of the mortgages in the pools are, to date, thirty-year fixed-rate conventional loans, originated and underwritten pursuant to the GSEs' standards.

Yet there are signs of increasing heterogeneity in the credit-linked note programs. First, unlike the Uniform MBS, there are no uniform CLNs; a Fannie Mae Connecticut Avenue Securities (CAS) note is not good deliver for a Freddie Mac Structured Agency Credit Risk (STACR) note. Moreover, within each program, there are already several types of credit risk transfers. For example, within the STACR program, there are securities with payments based on actual loss and those based on a fixed severity, those referencing mortgages with low LTVs (≤80 percent) and those referencing mortgages with high LTVs (greater than 80 percent), and those based on HARP and Relief Refi collateral. Likewise, Freddie Mac has a nonsynthetic credit risk transfer MBS (STACR Secured Participation Interests) that competes with its STACR CLNs.

Heterogeneity also looms for the mortgages in the reference pools. To date the reference pools have been large and highly diversified geographically, containing only conventional thirty-year fixed-rate loans underwritten to the GSEs' standards, albeit of different vintages. Yet one could readily imagine there being deals based on fifteen-year fixed-rate loans or various flavors of ARMs. Likewise, geographic diversity need hardly be maintained; one might imagine California-only deals in the future.

The synthetic credit risk transfer market could reduce, but not eliminate, the informational problems that were so rank for PLS. There is little guarantee, however, that this will remain the case in the synthetic credit risk transfer market under the current housing finance system, and it is a major point of concern for any reform proposal, as we discuss in the following chapter. In particular, maintaining standardization of the CLN market is critical for ensuring that it works as a mechanism for revealing the level of risk in the mortgage market. The CLN market will only operate as an efficient risk-pricing market if it is a liquid market, such that it can sustain a futures market. Liquidity in the CLN market depends on standardization of the CLNs. To the extent that there is either a lack of standardization in the referenced mortgage pools, other than by origination vintage, or a lack of standardization in the structure of the CLN themselves, they will not be liquid instruments.

Indeed, the CLN market does not currently look to be particularly liquid; there are some 205 unique investors in Freddie Mac STACR CLNs, but most of them are in the senior tranches; the most junior tranches have had only thirty-six unique investors total, with most deals having a little over a dozen.[60] The small size of the primary market suggests that there is not yet a robust secondary market in the CLNs.

Additionally, it is possible that various derivative products will develop around the GSEs' CLN. While a futures market in CLNs would be a positive development for completing the market, other derivative products could be more problematic. In particular, nothing prevents the issuance of CLNs by other entities that reference the same GSE pools. That is, Fannie Mae could issue $1 billion of notes referencing a particular pool, and Morgan Stanley could arrange for the issuance of another similar pool, enabling parties to go both long and short on the mortgages, just as existed with the market for CDS on PLS products. This opens the door to various arbitrage strategies and the risk of market manipulation through the derivative market. GSE CLN transactions are exposing new parties to mortgage credit risk, and the implications are not yet apparent.

The Growth of Risk-Based Pricing

The fourth key postcrisis market development has been the expansion of risk-based pricing. Prior to 2008, the GSEs did not engage in risk-based pricing. The GSEs would charge a guarantee fee ("g-fee") to lenders that sold loans to the GSEs in the form of a discount on the purchase price. The g-fee is intended to cover the GSEs' (1) expected credit losses, (2) cost of capital, and (3) administrative expenses and overhead. The g-fee was, with few exceptions, the same for all loans of each product type (30-year fixed, 15-year fixed, 5/1 ARM, etc.), expressed as a number of basis points on the loan. The same was true for FHA and VA insurance premia; they did not differ by LTV or by credit score, for example. In contrast, PMI has long had a degree of risk-based pricing with different premia schedules for lower credit score borrowers.

While FHA and VA continue to have one-size-fits-all pricing, the GSEs have adopted risk-based pricing in two forms. First, in November 2007, Fannie and then Freddie adopted loan-level pricing adjustments (LLPAs), effective as of March 2008.[61] The LLPAs are additional fees over and above the g-fee charged by the GSEs in the form of discounts from what they will pay to purchase mortgages. The LLPAs have changed subsequently in conservatorship at the FHFA's directive, but as they currently stand, they act as surcharges based on a range of loan characteristics: credit score, LTV, CLTV, product features, ARMs, residency status, multiunit properties, manufactured housing, cash-out refis, high balances, and limited mortgage insurance. The pricing adjustments are cumulative, such that a borrower with a low credit score and a high LTV and an ARM would pay three separate loan-level pricing adjustments. PMI coverage is not taken into account as a factor reducing the borrower's risk for any LLPAs unless the PMI coverage exceeds the minimum coverage requirement amount.[62]

The LLPAs are charged to the financial institutions that sell loans to the GSEs and not directly to consumers. Lenders may pass these along in the form of higher rates to consumers, although there is no requirement that lenders pass through the fees or that they pass on a particular LLPA to a particular consumer. In other words, lenders are free to have cross-subsidies among consumers, but competitive pressures mean that this is unlikely to happen, for if a lender wanted its less-risky consumers to subsidize its riskier ones, the less risky consumers would presumably go to another lender that did not impose the cross-subsidization. As a result, the LLPAs are likely to be passed through to consumers.

Second, in addition to the LLPAs, the GSEs both also adopted an "Adverse Market Delivery Charge" or "Market Condition Delivery Fee."[63] These charges were originally a flat 25 basis point charge applied to all mortgages after March 2008, but FHFA ordered it to be lifted for all states except those with particularly high foreclosure costs.[64] This had the effect of creating geographically distinguished pricing by state, with higher fees charged for loans in riskier states. These fees were discontinued by the FHFA entirely in April 2015, effective as of September 2015.[65]

Notably, although the GSEs themselves have adopted risk-based pricing, it has not yet manifested itself in the pricing of their credit risk transfer transactions. These transactions have generally been priced based on the aggregate risk in large mortgage pools of 30-year fixeds, rather than on individual loan characteristics or on the risk in pools that have been segmented into fine-grained risk-buckets. Whether this will remain the case in the future, however, is questionable, as there is substantial market pressure for risk-segmented pools and risk-based pricing. Already, one level of segmentation has appeared: high-LTV loans are pooled separately from low LTV loans for the credit risk transfer transactions. Further risk-segmentation may appear, and indeed there is likely to be market pressure for finer-grained risk segmentation.

While the GSEs moved to an explicitly risk-based pricing formula with the LLPAs, PMI companies doubled down on risk-based pricing. Most of the PMI market is dominated by a half-dozen insurers, and their rate schedules are virtually identical, because they do not generally compete for the consumer's business, but instead compete for the lender's business. PMI is often paid by the borrower, but with the lender as the loss-payee. Accordingly, consumers do not particularly care which company provides their PMI given that their premia are identical. Instead, the PMI firms get their business by ceding reinsurance to captive reinsurance affiliates of lenders, a practice of questionable legality.[66]

Prior to the financial crisis, PMI pricing was risk-based, depending on LTV, credit score, and a number of factors such as cash-out refi, investor property, second home, multiunit dwelling, or manufactured housing. Over time, however, PMI pricing has become ever more finely risk-based, with eight credit score bands now standard, up from four previously.[67] Moreover, PMI rates now include additional adjustment factors, such as high debt-to-income ratios.[68] Thus, the movement across the whole market is to increasingly risk-based pricing.

The effect of risk-based pricing has varied by consumer. Some consumers have seen a decrease in their borrowing costs, while others have seen an increase. The total effect can add substantially to the cost of a mortgage. For example, in summer 2019, a borrower with a credit score of 679 and an 85 percent LTV with a regular thirty-year fixed-rate purchase-money loan with minimum PMI coverage would be paying an additional 437 basis points (4.37 percent annual interest) in LLPAs and PMI premia.[69] This could nearly double the cost of borrowing for many borrowers. The result is that the riskiest borrowers end up with FHA loans, the credit risk of which is entirely born by taxpayers.

While mortgages may have become comparatively more affordable for consumers perceived as lower-risk, higher-risk consumers may be getting priced out of the market entirely by risk-based pricing, resulting in a smaller conventional market and contributing to the decline in homeownership rates. Nonetheless, there still is substantial cross-subsidization of loans to first-time borrowers with less than pristine credit by the GSEs.[70] Without such cross-subsidies, rates for such borrowers could be several hundred basis points higher even in normal times, with multiples of such increases occurring in times of market stress.

Where Things Stand Today

Taking stock of where things stand today—as of fall 2019—the good news is that the housing market has stabilized. Foreclosure rates are no longer at their historic elevated levels, and negative equity has substantially disappeared in most markets. As of the second quarter of 2019, only 3.8 percent of mortgaged properties—roughly 2 million homes—had negative equity.[71] Housing prices are marching upwards again in some markets but are largely in sync with rents, although some geographically constrained urban markets are seeing substantial price increases. The parallel movement of prices and rents provides reassurance that there is another bubble forming. Nonetheless, the tightness of the overall housing market revealed by these rent and price rises is constraining homeownership to post–World War II historic lows, with the greatest impact on first-time borrowers, as we discuss next.

The mortgage product mix has shifted away from the exotic, nontraditional mortgages that marked the bubble years to the American mortgage: as of July 2019, nearly 90 percent of all mortgages loans were 30-year fixeds.[72]

While this is good news, a closer look shows that the housing finance market remains unhealthy in important ways. First, the market is now substantially a government market. As of 2018, the GSEs accounted for 46 percent of first-lien originations, with FHA/VA loans accounting for another 23 percent.[73] In other words, 70 percent of the mortgage market is, as of the writing of this book, a government market. Yet today's GSEs are substantially different from the precrisis GSEs. Their investment portfolios are shrinking in accordance with the Senior Preferred Stock Purchase Agreement, and they have transferred a substantial share of their expected credit risk to the private market.

In 2018, portfolio lending accounted for another 30 percent of first-lien originations, with PLS financing only 1.8 percent of first-lien originations.[74] PLS remains moribund postcrisis. Regulation has made some of the products that PLS financed difficult or impossible to originate, and PLS has trouble competing with the GSEs on conventional conforming loans given the efficiency advantages of the GESs' economies of scale. Moreover, postcrisis litigation about the underwriting quality of PLS has left investors without any confidence that the trustee and servicer structures in PLS are sufficient to protect their interests, and solving that problem will make PLS administration costlier and thus reduce returns to PLS investors. On top of these problems, PLS now have to compete against GSE credit risk transfer transactions for investment from investors seeking to take on mortgage credit risk.

Second, while the market today is a government market, it stands on shaky ground. Not only is there the overarching and continuing uncertainty about GSE reform, but there is also litigation brought by the GSEs' preferred shareholders seeking to recover the dividends that were diverted to Treasury under the capital support agreements, and the question of how long Treasury is willing to support the GSEs, especially if they are forced to draw down on their line of credit from Treasury.[75]

FHA has its problems too; as FHA lending has ballooned, so too has Ginnie Mae securitization, but Ginnie Mae lacks the capacity to adequately oversee its myriad seller-servicers at current volumes, so Ginnie Mae faces substantial operational risk.[76] In particular, there has been a marked shift from bank to nonbank origination. Overall, nonbanks are now originating over 50 percent of mortgages. The shift has been particularly stark for Ginnie Mae. As of September 2019, 92 percent of Ginnie Mae originations were through nonbanks, and even the GSEs were getting over half of their originations from nonbanks.[77] Nonbanks have also increased their share of the servicing market and concentrated the servicing among fewer entities. The nonbanks lack capital and are subject to runs on the lines of credit (from banks) that they need to do business. If nonbanks' servicing costs increase due to heightened defaults, banks could call their lines of credit, causing a liquidity crisis for the nonbanks and knock-on effects to mortgage and housing markets. Without credit from the nonbank sector, lending will be curtailed and prices will fall. Illiquidity would have consequences for the insolvency of these thinly capitalized entities. The risks to these entities also pose potential systemic risk to the economy under stress conditions. As of now, there is no monitoring or oversight of this potentially systemic risk.[78]

Third, first-time homebuyers frequently have little real equity in their homes. The old standard 20 percent down payment no longer holds in the postcrisis market. Instead, borrowers are frequently buying homes with small down payments such that they barely have positive equity after sale expenses. In 2016, 60 percent of first-time homebuyers made a down payment of 6 percent or less.[79] FHA has long offered 3 percent down payments, but low down payments have expanded into the conventional market as well.

Lower down payments help expand the homebuyer market and buoy up prices, but any market downturn will leave such borrowers with negative equity. The back-loaded structure of typical level payment amortization schedules means that these borrowers will accrue little home equity during the first several years of their loans. For example, a $282,000 thirty-year, 4.5 percent, fixed-rate loan on a $300,000 property will result in the accrual of about $25,000 in equity over five years—often the tenure in a property— if property prices remain steady. It only takes a small decline in property values to wipe out this equity. Borrowers might gladly be willing to assume this leveraged gamble, particularly given the obstacles to lender recourse, but it means that ability-to-repay, rather than LTVs is now the bulwark of lender protection, and ability-to-repay is always subject to the five "Ds"— death, disability, dismissal, delivery, and divorce. The importance of ability-to-repay makes the fate of the GSE patch to the QM Rule particularly fraught.

Fourth, the "credit box"—the terms on which consumers can obtain credit—is much more constrained than prior to 2008. Pre-2008 underwriting is hardly a baseline for normal market conditions, but the QM rule has constrained underwriting to some degree, as have loan servicing reforms and a heightened awareness of put-back risk. But the credit box is tighter than it was in 2000, which was a period of low default rates.[80] What this all means is that some creditworthy, but riskier borrowers are finding it difficult to obtain credit, even with risk-based pricing, and risk-based pricing has been pricing other consumers out of the market, even in a low-rate environment. The result is that the overall homeownership rate in 2019 is 2.4 percent lower than the rate in 2000, a decline that can be attributed entirely to the tightening of credit standards beyond the levels of 2000.[81]

Fifth, low interest rates have resulted in most mortgaged homeowners with positive equity obtaining very low-cost fixed-rate financing. If rates rise appreciably, these homeowners will be locked into their homes; if they seek to move, they will be able to afford less house because of higher financing costs, which may discourage moving and distort labor markets. Importantly for stability, any sudden rise in mortgage rates will have the potential of dissuading new buyers. A sudden rise in to the interest rates could cause major disruption to housing markets.

All this means that housing markets are stable—for now—but there are real questions about their long-term stability. Addressing their stability will require a reform of the housing finance system, a politically fraught issue that is taken up in the next chapter.

While the housing market has stabilized, the social reverberations of the housing crash may still be shaping American society and politics. Housing is among the most widely held financial assets; for many middle-class households, home equity is the main asset. The decline in housing prices raised real fears for some households about their continued position in the middle class, and this in turn had effects on the political system: the Tea Party and even Trumpism have their roots in part in the socioeconomic fear created by the collapse of the housing market.

It was the middle class, not the poor, who bore the immediate cost of the bursting of the bubble. The poor were never homeowners, so they had no home equity to lose. Instead, they suffered collaterally, such as through job loss in the recession and through evictions when their landlords were foreclosed on. The bubble directly hit middle-class households, and this jolt was radicalizing for some who feared falling out of the middle class. Thus, one study finds "remarkably higher Tea Party activity in 'housing bubble' states such as Nevada, Florida, Arizona, and California."[82] The study did not find any correlation between Tea Party activity and high un-employment rates, but it did find that Tea Party activity was highly corre-lated with foreclosure rates.[83]

Likewise, another study found that there were larger proportions of un-derwater homeowners in "counties where support for the Republican Party increased from 2012 to 2016, compared with where the Democratic Party gained or maintained a foothold in 2016."[84] Conversely, the study found that counties with strong housing markets—low and decreasing negative equity rates—tended to result in Democratic gains between 2012 and 2016.[85] The study found that negative equity rates actually increased in 2015–2016 in over a third of the counties that had voted for Barack Obama in 2012 but for Donald Trump in 2016.[86] The divergence in actual and per-ceived fortunes continues, as those who do not own in prosperous metro-politan areas with job growth are faced with higher hurdles to ever own first homes and get on the homeownership wealth building ladder.

The bursting of the bubble did not harm only the home-owning middle class, however. It also harmed Millennials, who were just reaching the age to enter the homeownership market. Millennials already faced an obstacle to homeownership that previous generations did not—student loan debt, which limited their ability to save and to service mortgage debt. The post-bubble higher standards for mortgage underwriting, which were tougher than they were in prebubble years, combined with the GSEs' loan-level pricing adjustments to make homeownership less attainable for first-time homebuyers, particularly those with less-than-stellar credit. The retrench-ment of underwriting standards postcrisis impedes homeownership for Mil-lennials on the margin—where it counts.

Political Failure of GSE Reform

The unfinished state of affairs in housing finance begs the question of why we have not seen comprehensive reform. The answer seems to lie in the politics of housing finance. Five factors contribute to the lack of reform: (1) an ideological divide about the organization and regulation of markets, (2) the fact that housing finance markets are basically working, (3) the de-velopment of synthetic credit risk transfers by the GSEs, (4) unresolved litigation brought by GSE shareholders, and (5) the lack of any clear po-litical benefit from reforming a critical but obscure market.

The GSEs are ground zero in a deep ideological chasm about the organ-ization of markets. For some conservatives, the GSEs are an offensive gov-ernmental interference in private markets, readily abused by politicians who seek a short-term political gain by goosing the credit channel: give people subsidized mortgages, and they'll buy homes and be happy voters. These conservatives see the GSEs as squeezing out private capital because of an unfair advantage through an implicit guarantee, and as ultimately inflating housing prices nationwide and distorting the allocation of resources in the economy in favor of housing. This is a long-standing critique of the GSEs, but it also dovetails with the Government Made Me Do It theory of the bubble propounded by long-time GSE critics such as Peter Wallison.

For the purposes of housing finance reform, it doesn't matter that the Government Made Me Do It theory utterly lacks evidentiary support. Instead, what matters is that it is believed by many on the political right and has particular support among Republicans in the House of Representatives. If one believes that the GSEs were the root of the financial crisis, rather than collateral damage from the disaster created by the private-label securitization market, then the road to reform points to an elimination of the GSEs and the privatization of all credit risk in housing finance. Such a privatization of credit risk also conveniently comports with a "free-market," antiregulatory worldview that brooks no compromise on government involvement in markets.

It is hard to square such a position with a view of the crisis as driven by the excesses of the private market, rather than by the GSEs, or with an understanding that housing finance markets have benefited from some form of government involvement, in particular a government backstop for catastrophic risk. This ideological divide has meant that the legislative reform proposals that have advanced by Republicans in the House and by a more moderate bipartisan group in the Senate have been miles apart from each other, with no obvious reconciliation possible.

Housing finance reform is also the victim of the success of the bailouts in 2008–2009. Despite the painful bursting of the housing bubble and millions of foreclosures, the housing finance market has stabilized. Mortgages are widely available and at historically low interest rates (ignoring LLPAs and PMI adjustments) because of the Federal Reserve's monetary policy interventions to boost markets. While most of housing finance is now running through government-guaranteed markets, this is of little concern to most voters. What matters is that cheap mortgage financing is available to many borrowers, and those borrowers who are having trouble accessing the market lack political heft. Put another way, if markets are working well enough, why tamper with them? Indeed, while the Treasury Department produced a plan for housing finance reform in September 2019,[87] numerous key issues remain unresolved in the plan, such that the main takeaway is that no major changes are likely to be made to the system in the near future.

Indeed, perhaps the most significant change has been a September 2019 increase in the amount of capital the GSEs are allowed to retain under the Preferred Stock Purchase Agreements—now a total of $45 billion[88]—but this is still nowhere close to the capital the GSEs will require under FHFA's proposed capital requirements for the GSEs.[89]

Postcrisis market developments have also taken away some of the impetus for regulatory reform. In particular, Fannie Mae and Freddie Mac synthetic credit risk transfers have resulted in a substantial shift of credit risk from public to private capital.

Another factor impeding reform is the presence of ongoing litigation brought by GSE preferred shareholders. These shareholders allege that they were wrongfully deprived of their property rights in the conservatorship because as a condition of providing capital support to Fannie Mae and Freddie Mac, the Treasury Department insisted on a sweep of all GSE profits into the Treasury (through the 2012 amendment of the Preferred Stock Purchase Agreements), rather than allowing dividends to be paid to shareholders. The litigation complicates attempts to reform the GSEs without legislative action because any unilateral changes by Treasury and FHFA could prejudice the shareholders in the litigation and would therefore likely be opposed by the Department of Justice.

Further complicating reform attempts is that there is no real political upside to either party or to any individual politician from championing reform (of any type) of secondary markets in housing finance. Secondary markets are by definition not consumer-interfacing markets, so the workings of these markets are not well understood by voters. Fannie Mae is as likely to be thought of as the candy brand Fannie May as a secondary mortgage market institution. Few Americans are actually able to explain what the GSEs do, other than that they have something with mortgages and that they were somehow associated with the financial crisis. In such circumstances, there is little political upside to a politician claiming the glory of having reformed the (functioning if unsettled) secondary housing finance market. In a world in which politicians have limited political capital, few want to spend their chits on a legislative project that is complicated, politically costly, and unlikely to return much if any political benefit.[90]

The combination of these factors explains why the GSEs have continued in a decade-long conservatorship with no end in sight. Nevertheless, proposals for housing finance reform continue to proliferate, and that is what we turn to in the next and final chapter, where we present our own reform proposal.

CHAPTER TWELVE

Principles for Reform

W HAT SHOULD THE housing finance market look like going forward? In this chapter, we turn to the vexing question of how to reform the housing finance system. Any reform proposal will have to run
a daunting political gauntlet; we do not attempt to navigate a political
path to reform here. Instead, our focus is on what an optimal reform should
look like.

In this chapter we lay out what we believe should be the guiding principles for any housing finance reform: stability and affordability. From these
twin objectives of stability and affordability, a number of system design details follow. After laying out these objectives and their design implications,
we then turn to an evaluation of the major existing proposals under these
metrics. We find that they generally fall short. In the next and final chapter,
we present our vision for a reformed American housing finance system.

Stability and Affordability: A Virtuous Cycle

Stability begets affordability, and affordability begets stability. The unique
nature of housing as an asset class means that stability and affordability
are positively linked. Affordable housing products do not come at the expense of stability, but rather bolster stability, which in turn has affordability
benefits.[1] In contrast, a volatile housing finance system will bear a volatility

premium that erodes affordability, while an unaffordable housing finance system will be riskier, less liquid, and less stable.

All homebuyers benefit from stability, which minimizes housing price volatility and enables homeowners to build wealth over the long run. Home-buyers benefit from stability in the mortgage market directly because mortgage rates inevitably reflect past risk. Even today's low mortgage rates include a volatility premium as a result of the financial crisis. Avoiding such crises by constructing a stable mortgage system will reduce mortgage rates and allow for lower-cost, more-affordable mortgages over the long run. Above all, then, a housing financing system should be a source of stability rather than instability, and such stability is tied to affordability.

The virtuous cycle of stability and affordability should be the lodestar for housing finance reform because a housing finance system that delivers stable and affordable mortgages maximizes the tremendous positive social benefits of homeownership. Housing is critical to American families and to American society and the economy in general. Having a stable and at the same time affordable housing finance system is necessary to support continuous access to housing for consumers, to protect household wealth, to protect the financial system, and to promote the commonwealth and civic engagement.

An Affordable Housing Finance System Is Necessary for the Stability of the Housing Finance System

The more affordable housing finance is, the wider and deeper the home-ownership market. By affordable, we mean *long-term affordability*, not products that have initial affordability and then need to be refinanced. It is important not to view affordable finance housing as simple a matter of the cost of shelter. Homeownership, as we have seen, is more than shelter. It is also a hedge against gentrification and inflation. An apples-to-apples comparison of the benefits consumers obtain from housing is not simply the cost of renting versus the cost of homeownership, but must adjust for all the benefits of homeownership as a financial asset, and most critically its role as a hedge.

The homeowner is able to remain anchored in a community even in the face of gentrification and inflation. This encourages him or her to be more civically involved in maintaining and improving the community. The renter, in contrast, risks having to move at the end of every (short) rental contract if rents have gone up, and is subject to the very real risk of eviction. Viewed this way, homeownership is, dollar for dollar, cheaper than renting. Accordingly, affordable housing means, in our view, the readily accessible option of affordable homeownership, not merely low-cost rentals. Because of the cost of housing relative to incomes, affordable homeownership involves affordable mortgage financing that allows borrowers to telescope their future lifetime earnings power into present consumption.

Affordability in housing starts with affordable mortgage finance, but ultimately it begets stable communities because residents are not priced out of their neighborhoods and because they are not forced out of their homes through foreclosure. As we discussed in the Introduction, such stability has enormous positive social benefits in terms of crime reduction, educational achievement, health, and civic engagement, property reinvestment, and community stability.

To the extent that mortgages are sustainably affordable, borrowers are less likely to exercise their default put option even if prices decline. If a housing finance system generates truly affordable mortgage products, it can have the beneficial effect of crowding out and substituting for destabilizing faux-affordable products.

A Stable Housing Finance System Is Necessary to Protect Financial Markets from Unpriceable Risk

Home prices are critical to the state of the financial economy, and a stable housing finance system is also necessary to protect the economy more broadly. A major development in housing finance since the New Deal is the financialization of housing. Today housing is not simply shelter, but also a financial asset, whose pricing moves with global financial markets. Moreover, just as homeowners cannot readily hedge against the risks of a volatile housing finance system, so too is it difficult for financial institutions because of the incomplete and yet correlated nature of housing and housing finance markets. As we showed in Chapter 10, housing markets are incomplete because it is impossible to short housing directly.

Nor can lenders properly price the housing market's risk in aggregate. It is possible to price an individual mortgage loan in isolation, but that does not account for geographic and serial correlation of the home prices. When a lender makes a mortgage loan, the lender compensates for the risk *it bears* with a higher rate. But that higher rate only captures the internalized risk; it does not capture the externalized risk of a default, such as the effect on neighboring properties from a foreclosure. Nor does the lender capture the externalized risk of a bubble due to upward pressure on property values from the excessive loosening of demand constraints. Any nonsustainable loosening of lending constraints will allow prices to be bid up, which will inflate comparables and thus further loosen lending constraints, creating a boom cycle.[2]

Eventually the limit of the easing of constraints will be reached. At that point, rather than there being a new equilibrium reflecting the changed fundamentals, there will instead be a collapse because prices will have extended above what is supportable based on expectations of a continued easing of lending constraints. These price expectations will surpass fundamentals because price expectations are generally future projections based on the past and do not include the discontinuity of constraint easing. Without the ability to sell homes short, compensating downward pressure that prevents bubbles is absent.

The resulting bust is particularly damaging because the economic instability induced by a housing market collapse is not self-limiting. As prices decline, housing finance seizes up, and prices decline further, leading to foreclosures and further price declines. The downward spiral implicates the financial sector, as the value of the large asset class of MBS and derivatives referencing MBS becomes uncertain, and thus the solvency of firms with large exposures to the mortgage market becomes uncertain, and ultimately the solvency of those firms' counterparties becomes uncertain as well, and so on.

If easy finance allows property prices to be bid up, existing lenders are affected because they have priced their loans based on the market conditions at the time they loaned rather than on the subsequent eased credit terms that may increase their risk, either directly, in the case of subsequent junior mortgages on their collateral properties, or indirectly because of the increased systemic instability created by increased leverage. Subsequent lenders are also affected by a loosening of finance supply constraints, because they cannot accurately price to fundamentals absent information on how much of the demand is a function of easier credit. That information does not exist in real time. Given that not all lenders will estimate the risk of inflated prices the same, competition will push down the market-clearing risk premium to the lowest estimate. This means that smart money will lose to dumb money (which underestimates risk) in the short term. Even smart lenders may have to continue to dance as long as the music plays and hope that they can stuff the risk of bad loans to someone else.

At the point of collapse it becomes necessary to protect the public fisc. Limiting this risk means having a stable housing finance system. Stability is necessary to reduce the moral hazard of a government guarantee, whether implicit or explicit. When private markets fail, the government will have to pick up the tab, just as it will if it explicitly backs a housing finance system. A government-supported housing finance system should include stability and long-run affordability by design.

A Stable Housing Finance System Is Necessary to
Maximize the Positive Benefits of Homeownership

A stable housing finance system is also necessary to capture the systemic benefits of homeownership. Housing is also home. It is the home base for the family, which is the geographic lynchpin of most Americans' lives and what ties us to our communities. Homeownership promotes community stability in a way renting does not because long-term rental contracts are rare due to landlords' inability to distinguish prospectively between good and risky tenants. Homeownership and the community stability it promotes have positive spillover effects on society, ranging from appreciation in the value of neighboring properties to improved health and education outcomes and increased civic participation. These benefits are hard to quantify but of tremendous value. They are maximized with a stable housing finance system because only a stable housing finance system can produce the continuous financing availability necessary to avoid clusters and spikes in foreclosures.

While a borrower's *financial* downside on a mortgage may be capped at the amount borrowed (or even less if the loan is non-recourse), there are other financial costs from a mortgage default and foreclosure, such as relocation expenses, as well as significant nonfinancial costs from losing a home, such as disruption to children's education.

There are also important negative spillovers from foreclosures. Foreclosures depress neighboring property values and erode local tax bases, and vacant properties can impose costs on local communities in terms of public safety and health. This all means that from both a homeowner perspective and a social perspective, stability in home prices is prized.

A stable housing finance system is necessary to protect and preserve the benefits to households and communities from homeownership. Because of the connections between homeownership and financing and the geographic and serial correlation of housing prices, a volatile housing finance system will lead to extreme booms and busts, against which households cannot adequately insure.

For all of these reasons, we believe that the single most critical lesson to learn from the Great American Housing Bubble is the importance of stability in a housing finance system. Stability should be prioritized over all other goals when designing a housing finance system. Housing is simply too important to households, to the financial sector, and to the state of the economy writ large. From this stability-first principle, and the recognition that stability begets affordability and vice-versa, several design implications follow.

Design Implications from Affordability and Stability

From the twin objectives of stability and affordability, a number of detailed design points follow.

Competition for Mortgage Credit Risk Must Be Restricted to Competition for Market-Wide Risk

The first implication of a stability-first approach is the necessity of restricting competition that results in underpriced credit risk in mortgage markets. Specifically, competition for credit risk needs to be limited to being competition for market-wide risk, rather than competition for risk in particular fragments of the national market, and the pricing of credit risk needs to be delinked from an immediate impact on prospective mortgage pricing.

Mortgage lending involves two types of risk: interest rate risk and credit risk. Historically, interest rate risk was a major concern in US housing finance. Interest rate risk plagued the housing finance system in the 1970s and 1980s, led to the S&L crisis, and threatened Fannie Mae in the 1980s (before Fannie undertook securitizations) and Freddie Mac (because of noncallable corporate debt) in 2003.

Today, however, because of securitization we are not particularly concerned about interest rate risk. While we implicate private-label securitization in the housing bubble, our book should not be read as a condemnation of securitization generally. It is important to recognize that securitization has been an incredibly valuable development for housing finance. Securitization enables the vast resources of global capital markets to fund US homeownership. Securitization also enables geographic diversification through the pooling of loans, the matching of demand to supply across the nation, and the insurance against regional economic shocks. And securitization capably handles the allocation of interest rate risk by transferring it to capital markets investors.

The shifting of interest rate risk away from depositories is what enables the continued vitality of the consumer-friendly long-term, fixed-rate mortgage. Capital market investors are well suited for handling interest rate risk, in contrast to depository institutions, and have a variety of means of hedging against it if they so choose.

Credit risk is another story. The key unresolved design issue for achieving a stable housing finance system is the allocation of credit risk. Stability requires the restriction of competition for credit risk on mortgages.

LIMIT UNDERWRITING RACES TO THE BOTTOM

Competition is often taken as an unalloyed positive that produces efficient outcomes. This is a naïve view of competition. Competition is desirable in some circumstances, but not in others. In particular, competition creates pressure for short-term gains, even at the expense of long-term stability. For example, price competition is undesirable in insurance markets because insurers will be tempted to lower their prices to gain market share at the expense of adequate reserving for future losses. For this reason, many insurance markets feature explicit rate regulation to prevent underpricing.

A similar problem exists in insuring against housing finance credit risk. To the extent competition is allowed for credit risk on mortgages, there will be a temptation for parties to gain market share by underpricing risk. This could be done either with lower rates or with looser underwriting criteria. Indeed, this is exactly what happened during the Great American Housing Bubble: PLS gained market share by loosening underwriting standards. Under shareholder pressure, Fannie and Freddie belatedly sought to catch up and maintain market share by loosening their own standards. Only Ginnie Mae, which was not answerable to shareholders, did not play the game. As a result, Ginnie Mae lost considerable market share. (Refer back to Figure 4.3.)

The underpricing of risk is destabilizing to the financial system writ large in an age when housing is financialized through securitization. The problem is exacerbated by the fact that the geographic and serial correlations of housing prices produce systemic externalities that are never priced in the first place. Underpricing of risk does not merely affect the individual lender or guarantor's portfolio; it affects the entire market. Prevention of underpricing of credit risk by mortgage guarantors or insurers that are not capitalized for the long run to preserve financial stability over the cycle is a necessary public good.[3]

Historically, the desire to produce competition has never motivated the structure of the US housing finance system. The existence of (originally) twelve Federal Home Loan Banks was because of the regional nature of the market, not because of a desire for competition. Indeed, their joint liability meant that they were never fully competitors. Similarly, Freddie Mac was not created so that there would be competition with Fannie Mae, as is often wrongly believed, but simply as a result of the politics of the division within the mortgage industry between S&Ls and mortgage banks, with each group wanting its own captive GSE.[4]

Ensure Funding across the Cycle

Privately owned market entities that are designed to compete for market share through discretionary setting of standards inevitably make markets unstable over the cycle. The short-termist tendency of competition also makes markets flighty. Flighty markets are bad because they are, by definition, the opposite of financial stability—they are boom and bust markets. Competition makes markets flighty because it encourages lending intermediaries to cut back on reserves, ease standards, and seek out cheaper, riskier shorter-term funding. Competitive firms see their own risk, but may not see or care about systemic risk as they engage in a race for market share, the race to the bottom that causes market instability.

In good economic times, the buildup of risk will not be noticed because the provision of cheaper, more available credit raises housing prices and will suppress the level of defaults. Competition for market share will drive excessive leverage and risky lending with no consequences at first since higher house prices will hide the poor underwriting of the loans, and despite risky loans, defaults will fall as housing prices rise. Nonetheless, at the sign of trouble, financial markets will pull back on their provision of credit. Without the resources to stay in the market for the long run, and facing market declines, firms will withdraw lending, furthering the downward spiral. The result will be lending cycles, procyclical behavior in general, and in severe cycles, systemic risk.

Preserve the National Market

Restricting competition for credit risk is not simply a matter of maintaining underwriting standards, however. It is also necessary to preserve a national market and to ensure the availability of funding across the economic cycle for regions which otherwise would be forced into their own booms and busts.

Competition fragments markets. A housing finance market with full competition on pricing has different rates across the credit score spectrum and by loan product feature, including geography. Geographic segmentation might be by state, but could be done with a much finer geographic scope, such as by metropolitan area, or even by ZIP code, census tract, or neighborhood. This is hardly speculative: the GSEs had geographically differentiated rates by state under their Adverse Market Delivery Charge from 2007 to 2013, which penalized borrowers in states with longer foreclosure timelines (namely, with better consumer protections).

Fragmented markets can further instability. Fragmented markets will price adversely to the specific conditions of the local market. Homeowners have a voice in some of those conditions—state or local government finances, for example—but not in others, such as the boom or bust of a regional industry, the failure of a large local employer, or natural disasters. In geographically segmented markets, the collapse of the oil industry in west Texas, the decline of the Maine lobster fishery, the bankruptcy of General Motors, an earthquake in California, or a hurricane in Florida will result in a subsequent jump in interest rates or tightening of underwriting criteria in those markets, which would turn into a self-fulfilling prophesy of downward home prices.

Fragmented markets were the story of pre–New Deal housing finance. Before the New Deal there were regional and local markets with substantially different credit terms, and these regional markets were much less stable than a national market. Geographically segmented housing finance markets will amplify local economic conditions; a national market smooths out local economic booms and busts.

PRESERVE PRODUCT STANDARDIZATION AT THE MORTGAGE LEVEL AND THE MBS LEVEL

Competition for credit risk in housing finance markets is likely to reduce product standardization at both the origination level and the secondary markets level. Competitors are incentivized to eschew standardization because standardization leads to commoditization and thinner profit margins. Furthermore, to the extent that products are not standardized, it is easy for sellers to pack in complexity that has the effect of obfuscating product costs and risks.

Thus, to the extent there is competition for credit risk, it could readily result in a move away from standardized loan products like the 30-year fixed, to bespoke, nontraditional products and, ultimately, even to nonstandardized loan documentation. This is precisely what we saw during the housing bubble. Competition for credit risk emerged in the form of the PLS market, a nonstandardized secondary market product based on nonstandardized, nontraditional mortgage products.

Product standardization is desirable because it has benefits in terms of systemic stability, investor protection, consumer protection, and affordability. Pricing of risk is only possible if risk can be identified. This is true for risk in pools of mortgages and also for systemic risk. Bubbles can only be prevented if they can be identified, and the only way to identify a housing bubble is when a compression in mortgage credit spreads accompanies a rise in housing prices that cannot otherwise be explained by fundamentals.

The presence of compressed mortgage credit spreads with credit risk increases (the Pavlov-Wachter indicator) is the tell-tale sign of a bubble. This is because borrowers—particularly home flippers—will rationally borrow to bid up housing prices whenever they can, given the default put option that exists because almost all US mortgages are effectively nonrecourse. The default put option creates a heads-I-win-tails-you-lose gamble for the mortgaged homebuyer, and a compression in credit spreads reduces the cost of purchasing that option, thereby increasing its prevalence.

The Pavlov-Wachter indicator cannot be identified in real time, however, unless there is a high degree of product standardization in the mortgage market or the secondary market. This is because mortgage credit spreads and MBS spreads must be analyzed on a risk-adjusted basis that accounts for shifts not just in interest rates, but in other product terms.

For example, a 5 percent interest rate on a thirty-year FRM at an 80 percent LTV ratio is not readily comparable to a 6 percent interest rate on a 2/28 ARM at a 95 percent LTV ratio. If the market shifts from the former product to the latter while Treasury rates are constant, has there been a compression in credit spreads? To make such a determination, we would need to come up with a risk-adjusted interest rate.

Given the large number of dimensions on which mortgage loans vary—credit scores, LTVs, amortization schedules, maturities, occupancy, documentation, and so on—arriving at a risk-adjusted interest rate is difficult, especially because the analysis must account for the interactions between these different risk factors. The greater the degree of product heterogeneity, the harder the analysis becomes. To the extent that there is standardization in the market around particular products, there is greater homogeneity and easier analysis of spread compression. Product diversity obfuscates risk and frustrates efficient pricing.

The same holds true in the MBS market: GSE and Ginnie Mae MBS all had a fundamental homogeneity of credit risk because they were guaranteed by the GSEs and by Ginnie Mae, respectively. Implicit recourse to the US government for the GSEs, further homogenized credit risk among the GSEs and Ginnie.

In contrast, PLS were heterogeneous in terms of their allocation of credit risk. They varied in terms of the number of tranches, the structure of cash flow waterfalls, and the presence of various credit enhancements, such as overcollateralization, excess spread, and bond insurance. This meant that the spreads on one set of PLS were not comparable with those on another, absent a complex risk adjustment calculation. Nor did the spreads on PLS compensate for the risk. As we have shown, the smart money in the market eventually caught on to the existence of a bubble—but only a year to two after it had formed, in part because the increasing heterogeneity of the market due to the rise of nontraditional mortgage products financed through PLS. For there to be any chance of regulators or the market generally identifying bubbles early enough before they have inflated, it is necessary to have a reasonably standardized market.

Product standardization also benefits consumers. It does so in three ways. First, it reduces transaction costs for lenders, which should result in consumer savings in a competitive origination market. Second, it facilitates price comparisons for consumers. Bespoke products are harder for consumers to compare on an apples-to-apples price basis and thus lessen competitive pressures on price. Third, and most importantly, it enables the existence of the To-Be-Announced (TBA) market, which both provides financing for lenders through the dollar roll and enables borrowers to lock in rates on fixed-rate mortgages as much as ninety days prior to closing. Preservation of the TBA market should be an important goal for housing finance reform, and that will require product standardization, particularly at the secondary market level, which will in turn require limitations on competition.

THE APPROPRIATE PLACE FOR CREDIT RISK COMPETITION

A limitation on competition for credit risk means, among other things, a limitation on the privatization of risk. Our skepticism of risk privatization as a goal in and of itself derives from four insights. First, we do not believe that all risk in the housing finance system can ever be truly privatized. Housing is simply too important of an asset socially and economically for government to turn its back in a systemic crisis, and that means that it is key to have a system designed so as to prevent systemic crises. This points to the need to layer on private-risk capital to create a buffer against the socialization of losses, but at the end of the day, government inevitably holds the uninsurable catastrophic tail risk in the housing market.

Second, the incomplete and imperfect nature of housing finance markets means that the more fragmented the pricing of national credit risk, the more unstable markets will become. In particular, as discussed further below, fragmented privatized markets will demand risk-based pricing, but risk-based pricing becomes a self-fulfilling prophecy of collapse in a market where asset prices are serially and geographically correlated and tied to credit prices. Indeed, because markets will recognize in a downturn that risk is market-wide, privatized markets will run and cause the catastrophe that well designed markets can prevent.

Moreover, if private capital, without uniform standards, bore the credit risk on mortgages directly, such as through competing guarantees of timely payment of principal and interest on MBS, the TBA market would cease to exist. The MBS guaranteed by party X would not be good delivery for those guaranteed by party Y because guarantors X and Y have inherently different credit risk profiles. Indeed, historically there were separate TBA markets for Fannie MBS and Freddie MBS. With multiple competing guarantors, the TBA market's liquidity would suffer for all flavors of MBS, to the point that a TBA market would not be sustainable for the least liquid guarantors, which would render them uncompetitive.

In addition, to the extent one cares about affordability of housing, privatized risk is problematic because privatized risk will ultimately price many households out of homeownership. This is both because markets with privatized risk are less stable and therefore riskier markets, which imparts an additional risk premium to all mortgages, and because privatized markets will insist on risk-based pricing, which will impose additional costs on riskier households, fragmenting the pool. In other words, complete privatization of risk is fundamentally incompatible with stability and affordability.

Again, this is not to say that credit risk cannot be privatized, but that market design matters. Also, the problems that follow even from national competition for credit risk hinge on the assumption that the terms that are obtained in the secondary market for credit risk will be transmitted continuously into the terms of prospective mortgages. If mortgage rates and terms are delinked from the procyclical terms on which investors will assume credit risk in secondary markets, then the problems that follow from competition disappear. In other words, if credit risk can be sold to the private market after the fact of lending, competition for that risk will not have a deleterious effect on the system. We address whether this is possible, as part of our proposal for a reformed housing finance system.

A Housing Finance System Must Ensure the Widespread Availability of the 30-Year Fixed

The standardization of housing finance products, on both the loan level and MBS level, facilitates analysis of compression of credit spreads, the tell-tale sign of a bubble. But what should the standardized product, or products, be?

We do not argue that there is a one-size-fits-all mortgage product. Different products are better suited for some consumers than for others. But there is one product that is generally well suited for consumers, which matches consumer tastes, and which serves the goal of financial stability. This is the thirty-year fixed-rate mortgage, the American Mortgage.

The 30-year fixed is the crowning achievement of the New Deal's myriad reforms of the housing market and their postwar development. The 30-year fixed was the cornerstone for postwar American economic stability, and its abandonment as the dominant market product in favor of the modern reincarnation of the 1920s bullet loans was what led to the housing bubble and the subsequent financial crisis.

The 30-year fixed is particular well-suited for most consumers because it is long-term, fixed-rate, fully amortized, and freely prepayable. The long term and free-prepayment ability give the homeowner substantial optionality regarding length of housing tenure. The homeowner can pay off the mortgage if she or he moves or keep it while staying in the house without having to refinance or pay off the loan. The fixed rate creates household economic stability because it means that the household can budget around what is typically its largest monthly expense. The fixed rate shields households from interest rate risk, which consumers are otherwise ill-prepared to address. The long term also keeps down monthly payments, which gives households' economic flexibility and increases housing affordability. And the full amortization means that households are constantly building equity and avoid bullet payments. Not surprisingly, US consumers have shown a strong taste for long-term FRMs, particularly the 30-year fixed.

The thirty-year term of the American Mortgage is not imbued with a totemistic quality. Instead, it happens to roughly coincide with the remaining working lifetime of individuals who form households around age thirty. Age thirty is slightly over the median age of marriage and of first child birth in the United States. A household that is formed at age thirty and acquires a home in the next few years then has roughly thirty years of expected income before retirement. A thirty-year mortgage lets that household telescope all thirty-years of future earning power into current purchasing power. Terms longer than thirty years are likely to take many households past retirement age (which is of course true with older households), while terms under thirty years do not let households capture the entirety of their future expected earnings power. The critical feature, however, is the long term, not the precise thirty years.

The stability-first principle means ensuring the widespread availability of the 30-year fixed. If it is widely available, it will generally be chosen by consumers. The 30-year fixed, however, is not a product that the market produces on its own. It is not available in almost any other country. Long-term, fixed-rate, fully prepayable mortgages can be found only in the United States and Denmark. The private market will readily revert to either adjustable-rate or short-term loans in order to manage interest rates for the lender.

The emergence of the 30-year fixed in the United States was the result of substantial government intervention and innovation. While other countries have comparable homeownership rates to that of the United States without having long-term FRMs, these countries provide a range of other support to their mortgage markets. In Canada, for example, the government has historically directly insured much of the mortgage market. The 30-year fixed has been substituted for other types of government support of the mortgage market. All else being equal, homeownership based on the 30-year fixed is fundamentally more secure.

The widespread availability of the 30-year fixed requires a securitization market, and also a TBA market. It also requires a market that does not have granular risk-based pricing and that discourages bullet products, such as balloon mortgages with back-loaded payment structures. It is imperative that a housing finance system continue to offer these features in order to ensure the widespread availability of the American Mortgage and its substantial consumer and systemic benefits.

The Leverage Call Option Must Be Unembedded

One reason that housing is so sensitive to credit-fueled bubbles is the existence of the default put option. The default put option makes an investment in housing something close to a heads-I-win-tails-you-lose investment. If housing prices go up, the investor makes money, while if prices fall, the investor exercises the put option by defaulting and "selling" the housing back to the lender through foreclosure. The cost of exercising the put option is the loss of any home equity and any future appreciation, a damaged credit score, and the costs of relocation.

The "leverage call option"—the ability of homeowners to increase their leverage through a junior mortgage without the consent of the senior mortgagee—reduces the strike price for the default put option in that if the borrower is more leveraged, there is less home equity for the borrower to lose and a lower likelihood of future appreciation accruing to the borrower. The leverage call option is not just a problem for lenders on their own loans, but its existence on *other* lenders' loans has the effect of inflating leverage—and hence prices—market-wide through the serially correlated nature of housing prices. The leverage call option is a financial accelerant that exacerbates any underpricing of mortgage credit.

The leverage call option is an idiosyncratic and unintended feature of the American mortgage market. It exists solely because of a statutory provision in the Garn–St. Germain Depository Institutions Act of 1982 that prohibits lenders from exercising "due-on-sale" clauses, making the entire mortgage immediately come due upon the creation of a junior lien.[5] The provision was intended to deal with issues arising from novel financing arrangements, such as junior mortgages from sellers, that appeared in response to the inflation of the 1970s.[6] The prohibition prevents lenders from taking action upon the creation of a junior lien. Indeed, lenders do not even need to be informed of the junior lien's creation. Because lenders cannot adjust their pricing retroactively to account for the greater risk created by the increased leverage—and may not even know about it—they may underprice credit if they underestimate the likelihood of borrowers leveraging up with junior liens. What's more, because a rise in second-lien financing affects the risk-adjusted mortgage credit spread, the exercise of the leverage call option disguises the presence of the Pavlov-Wachter indictor, which frustrates attempts to identify a bubble in real time.

Ensuring the stability of the housing finance market requires unembedding the leverage put option from mortgages. The leverage call option should be unbundled from the mortgage and separately negotiated. Separating out the leverage call option would allow homeowners who value it to still be able to obtain it, while not forcing other homeowners to purchase an option that they may neither want nor need. Thus, mortgage prices should be lower with the leverage call option unbundled, as there will not be a cross-subsidy built into mortgage pricing from those who do not exercise the leverage call option to those who do.

Unembedding the option requires amending the Garn–St. Germain Act to allow lenders to enforce due-on-sale clauses on encumbrance of a property with a voluntary lien. Such an enforcement right would not be meaningful, however, unless a first-lien lender were to know of the junior lien. Accordingly, we also suggest that the Garn–St. Germain Act be amended to prohibit the enforcement of junior liens absent proof that the first lienholder has been notified of the junior lien. If the first lienholder does not exercise its due-on-sale power within a reasonable time after learning of the junior lien, then enforcement of the first lienholder's due-on-sale clause based on encumbrance by the junior lien should be prohibited. In essence, there should be a specifically enforceable, but waivable, negative pledge clause built into the first-lien mortgage. In such a situation, a potential junior lender will not actually lend until the first lienholder has been notified and consented by waiving its right to call the loan on account of the junior lien. Presumably, such consent would become a standard part of a second-lien mortgage's closing package.

What we are proposing with a repeal of Garn–St. Germain's prohibition of due-on-sale clauses triggered by encumbrances is that the mortgage contract contain an explicit and separate option for the homeowner to subsequently increase leverage via a junior lien either by an unlimited amount or up to a defined CLTV based on a new appraisal approved by the first mortgagee. The consumer would either pay for this optionality upfront or negotiate for it later. The key point is that it would not be automatically included in a mortgage.

The embedded leverage call option allows Americans to freely convert home equity into cash through second mortgages. Second mortgages enable homeowners to realize the benefits of home price appreciation without selling their properties. It is important to preserve this ability to tap home equity. Unembedding the leverage call option would not deprive homeowners of these important benefits. It would merely unwind the cross-subsidization of the leverage call option by homeowners who do not use it for those who do. Those who utilize the leverage call option would have to pay for it, but those who do not would benefit from lower costs of homeownership, and the possibility of refinancing rather than taking out a second mortgage ensures that all homeowners would still be able to access the appreciation in their home price.

Unembedding the leverage thus should actually make homeownership more affordable to those who do not purchase the leverage call option. Moreover, to the extent that a bargained-for leverage call option improves financial stability, there could be a market-wide stability dividend of lower interest rates and higher home prices, as borrowers would not pay a systemic risk premium.

Unembedding the leverage call option through an amendment of the Garn–St. Germain Act to make it a specifically bargained-for option would facilitate greater financial stability both by limiting unpriced leverage and by improving the ability to detect the Pavlov-Wachter indicator of mortgage spread compression. It can be done without any harm to consumers overall, merely an internalization of the costs of leverage for those who value it.

Stability Requires Eschewing Procyclical Risk-Based Pricing

The public interest in maximizing wide and deep homeownership means that it is imperative that housing finance markets *not* have substantial procyclical risk-based pricing. Risk-based pricing means that the marginal price of credit depends on the borrower's individual credit profile: riskier borrowers pay more. While the base price of credit is determined by the lender's cost of funds and operations, in risk-based pricing, the pricing at the margin depends on the borrower's risk.

Risk-based pricing is generally thought to be a good thing because it enables more efficient borrower-specific pricing by eschewing the one-size fits all pricing that imposes a cross-subsidization of high-risk borrowers by low-risk borrowers. Moreover, to the extent that some borrowers are low-risk because of more responsible behavior, risk-based pricing rewards such good behavior.

There is already some measure of risk-based pricing in housing finance, based on consumers' credit scores and LTV ratios and occupancy status. But credit scores and LTVs are not the only possible risk-measures. Geography, in particular, is an important risk component. Currently, however, geography is not reflected in risk-based pricing (excluding flood insurance requirements). Similar borrowers in South Carolina and Oregon end up paying similar rates; there is no location-based premium.

The flip-side of risk-based pricing is a cross-subsidy among borrowers. To the extent that pricing is not individualized but is instead one-size-fits-all, higher-risk borrowers (on any risk dimension) are subsidized by lower-risk borrowers. But this can be optimal for both. The pooling efficiencies from serving the entire market redound to the benefit of all borrowers, as does the insurance mechanism against random events that beset regional markets.

Risk-based pricing appears fairer and more efficient when viewed from the perspective of a single loan. But when viewed from a market-wide and cyclical perspective, it is actually inefficient because of the unique correlations of housing markets. Risk-based pricing over the cycle makes home-ownership more expensive at a time of market stress, and in some cases prohibitive, for higher-risk borrowers, and will thus reduce housing transactions, leading to downward pressure on home prices and make homes less liquid and harder to sell. Moreover, risk-based pricing makes it more likely that the market will "gap out" for high-risk segments when the market is stressed. When markets are shaken—which may be for reasons that have nothing to do with mortgages, such as geopolitical strife or a pandemic—the volatility in rates will be more extreme for particular risk segments, especially higher-risk borrowers. Risk-based-pricing results in higher rates for higher-risk borrowers and has the endogenous effect of increasing risk because it increases monthly mortgage payments.

Hence, risk-based pricing over the cycle, particularly on geography, will result in more volatile markets and local booms and busts. Risk-based pricing is a procyclical financial accelerant. For example, if there is a plant closure in a town, risk-based pricing will result in higher mortgage rates, driving down home prices, leading to a self-reinforcing decline in credit availability because of the correlated nature of home prices and the feedback loop between home prices and credit availability. This means that independent of the original decline in demand, a community may find itself in decline because an expected withdrawal of finance leads other lenders to withdraw funding. Given the correlated nature of housing prices, procyclical risk-based pricing will serve as rocket fuel for a much more volatile housing market.

The effects of risk-based pricing over the cycle will be felt particularly keenly in poorer communities. Because economic downturns affect the creditworthiness of less well-off borrowers more than others, risk-based pricing would cut off credit availability during a downturn for more vulnerable households more than for more secure households. Housing finance then becomes an automatic destabilizer, as it was in the Great Recession.

Moreover, procyclical risk-based pricing will lower homeownership in poorer communities. Because of the serial price correlation and feedback loop between housing prices and mortgage credit availability, there will be greater price volatility, higher foreclosure rates, and higher-risk-based pricing over the cycle with the result of a reduction in mortgage credit availability in LTMI communities. Resulting lower rates of homeownership will mean the loss of the positive social externalities of homeownership. Middle-class neighborhoods of people of color that are stable but just barely holding on will disintegrate as homeownership rates fall. The social effects from a risk-based pricing mortgage system will be noticeable and may have broad negative spillovers on the social fabric of many communities.

The risk from lower liquidity and increased procyclical volatility will all ultimately be embedded in the cost of funds. Thus, low-risk borrowers will be paying a premium for illiquidity, instability, and cyclicality. We do not ourselves attempt to estimate the systemic volatility premium, but one estimate has it at as much as 40–50 basis points system-wide.[7] Put another way, it is not only high-risk borrowers who benefit from avoiding procyclical risk-based pricing and cross-subsidization over the cycle. *We all benefit from cross-subsidization because it creates a stability dividend.* Countercyclical cross-subsidization creates a deeper and more stable housing market, and that results in lower costs of funds for everyone.

Affordability Requires Eschewing Risk-Based Pricing

Affordable housing can be supported in two ways: tax-and-transfer programs or mandatory housing outcome goals. A tax-and-transfer program accomplishes a cross-subsidy through the tax system, rather than through market pricing. Such a program might involve a set-aside fee on higher income borrowers that is then used to offset some of the credit risk premium on lower-income borrowers, such as through support of FHA. A tax-and-transfer program does not guarantee a particular outcome. Instead, it guarantees a finite level of financial commitment and takes whatever outcome that commitment ends up producing.

In contrast, housing goals have the effect of being outcome-based, encouraging the entities to expand markets through cross-subsidies as well as other efforts. In theory, both methods can achieve the same levels of support for LTMI homeownership, and at the same cost. But the advantage of housing goals is that they are likely to be more flexible and therefore cost effective. For example, a tax-and-transfer program will be fixed over the cycle. Thus, if tax-and-transfer is used to temper risk-based pricing, the resulting rates will be procyclical.—market gap outs and geographic procyclicality— will persist. The stability goals necessitate a cross-subsidy through housing outcome goals as a means of supporting affordable homeownership over the cycle, rather than a finite dollar amount of support through a tax-and-transfer program.

Evaluation of Existing Reform Proposals

With these objectives and design implications in mind, we now turn to existing housing finance reform proposals. Our goal here is not a detailed critique of any particular proposal. Rather, existing proposals fit into one of four basic structural models, and we evaluate each model for how well it addresses systemic stability, affordability, and efficiency of operations and execution.

Because all housing finance reform proposals assume, as do we, that securitization will be the main funding mechanism for US mortgages, there are only four basic models for reform. These models vary along two dimensions: first, whether the MBS that will finance US mortgages will be issued by a single issuer or by multiple competing issuers, and second, whether the credit risk on those MBS will be held by a single entity or by multiple competing entities. While credit risk can be held in many forms, for analytical simplicity, we will refer to it through the shorthand of a guarantee. Accordingly, we can categorize all of the proposals in these terms as falling into one of four categories: (1) multi-issuer/multi-guarantor; (2) single-issuer/multi-guarantor; (3) multi-issuer/single-guarantor; and (4) single-issuer/single-guarantor.

Obviously, there are features of particular proposals that blur this neat analytical division. For example, the same entity might be both an issuer and a guarantor. Likewise, multiple guarantors might shift credit risk derivatively to a single entity or a single entity might re-syndicate its credit risk to many investors. Moreover, some proposals attempt to split the difference between the single-multiple divide by allowing multiple issuer or guarantors, but limiting their number. Such proposals are, in our categorization, still multi-issuer or multi-guarantor as the case may be, but we recognize that two competing entities are different than two dozen, and that constrained competition among a very small number of entities is different than unfettered competition between numerous competitors.

Multi-issuer / Multi-guarantor

Multi-issuer/multi-guarantor is simply the private-label securitization model. In a multi-issuer/multi-guarantor model, interest rate risk tends to go to one set of investors through the MBS, and credit risk goes to another either through the tranching of the MBS or through guarantees of the MBS, although the demarcation of credit and interest rate risk is not complete. As the model's name implies, there would be multiple parties permitted to issue MBS, and multiple parties permitted to guarantee timely payment of principal and interest on those MBS or otherwise hold the credit risk on the MBS. These issuers and guarantors could be affiliated, but would not have to be.

The basic idea for multi-issuer/multi-guarantor is that there should be competition for issuance and for assumption of the credit risk on the MBS. Multi-issuer/multi-guarantor proposals vary in terms of eligibility requirements to be an issuer or guarantor, with the idea of imposing some minimum standards on the market. The leading examples of the multi-issuer/multi-guarantor model are the Protecting American Taxpayers and Homeowners (PATH) Act of 2013, a House Republican proposal,[8] and the American Enterprise Institute proposal by Peter Wallison, Alex Pollack, and Edward Pinto.[9]

A variation on the multi-issuer/multi-guarantor model would have a government backstop that would guarantee the deep credit risk, so that there would be competition solely for the first-loss risk. This sort of variation is closer to being a multi-issuer/single-guarantor structure and would produce a market of mini-Fannies and Freddies: private securitizers that hold first-loss risk but with a (now explicit) guarantee. Another variation is to have many issuers, but have the issuances all go through a central securitization utility that would impose eligibility standards on issuers and mortgages.

Multi-Issuer / Single-Guarantor

The multi-issuer/single-guarantor system is used in the Ginnie Mae model. In a multi-issuer/single-guarantor system, multiple parties would be permitted to issue MBS, but they would all have a common guarantee from a governmental entity for at least part of the credit risk. Eligibility to issue such guaranteed MBS would be set by the governmental guarantor entity, just as Ginnie Mae does today. Multi-issuer/single-guarantor proposals envision expanding the Ginnie Mae framework from the FHA/VA market to covering the entire conventional market. The leading examples of this approach are the Partnership to Strengthen Homeownership Act of 2015 (Delaney-Carney-Himes),[10] the Bipartisan Housing Reform Act of 2018 (Hensarling-Delaney-Himes),[11] and the Bright-DeMarco proposal.[12]

Notably, in the existing Ginnie Mae model, Ginnie Mae is actually holding the second-loss credit risk. In a Ginnie Mae securitization, if a mortgage defaults, the private firm that issued the Ginnie Mae-insured MBS is responsible for advancing the payments on the mortgage to the bondholders until it collects on the FHA/VA insurance; only if the issuer does not pay the bondholders does the Ginnie Mae guarantee kick in. Thus, the issuer's entire capital stands ahead of Ginnie Mae in terms of loss absorption. Because the VA guarantee is not for 100 percent of the loan amount, this structure means that the issuer bears the first-loss position, with some FHA/VA coverage, and Ginnie Mae holds the risk of issuer failures. The current prevalence among Ginnie Mae seller/servicers of thinly capitalized nonbanks has been the subject of concern. In adverse conditions, such firms may lose their bank lines of credit, resulting in a mass shutdown of loan insurers, which would have market-wide consequences.[13] Expansion of such a system would require far more regulatory attention to sufficiency of multiple firms' capitalization.

Presumably any expansion of Ginnie Mae coverage to conventional mortgages would operate with the issuer still holding the first-loss credit risk and being itself guaranteed by a governmental entity, rather than having all credit losses immediately paid out by the governmental entity. If so, this structure means that there is actually competition for credit risk in the multi-issuer/single-guarantor model. The MBS holders are ultimately assuming only the credit risk of the single-guarantor, but because the guarantee is a backstop for the issuer, there is competition for credit risk among the issuers. This competition could be held in check by the eligibility standards of the guarantor entity, but it will surely face pressure from issuers to loosen standards. While such controls could prevent races to the bottom if strictly enforced, they would necessarily obviate the expected benefit of rate competition that is the point of this structure.

Single-Issuer/Multi-Guarantor

Single-issuer/multi-guarantor is a model in which there would be a central securitization utility, with credit risk on MBS auctioned off to multiple guarantors. The single issuer would result in greater standardization of the terms of the MBS and of the mortgages that it would securitize, but there would still be competition for the credit risk. The leading examples of this model are the Johnson-Crapo (originally Corker-Warner) bill[14] and the Mortgage Bankers Association's proposal.[15]

The single-issuer/multi-guarantor model envisions a single securitization platform issuing MBS that vary solely based on the identity of the private guarantor and its pricing of the guarantee. These private guarantors would hold the first-loss credit risk, with an explicit and priced government backstop for catastrophic risk. Guarantors would control the terms of the mortgages that they would package and securitize. They would compete over such terms, inevitably introducing instability, unless they were carefully regulated to equate their risk. To do so, they would have to serve the same national market, in which case they would become equivalent to a single-issuer/single-guarantor.

Single-Issuer/Single-Guarantor

Single-issuer/single-guarantor or its functional equivalent—several guarantors operating under the same mandate and tight regulation to prevents races to the bottom—is a model in which all securitization issuance runs through a central governmental entity, a "Franny Mae," that sells off the interest rate risk and holds the credit risk. Such a model would ensure an internalization of systemic risk externalities.[16] Critically, the single-issuer/single-guarantor model could still have back-end credit risk transfers, as could all of the other models. The leading examples of a single-issuer/single-guarantor proposal are Rep. Maxine Waters' Housing Opportunities Move the Economy (HOME) Forward Act of 2014, the Jim Parrott et al. proposal,[17] the National Association of Realtors proposal,[18] and the PIMCO proposal.[19]

Comparing Housing Finance Reform Models

The devil is in the details for housing finance reform proposals, but it is impossible to get the details right without the correct big picture approach. In this regard, we believe that only one of the four basic approaches—single-issuer/single-guarantor (or its functional equivalent in several closely regulated entities)—meets the criteria of both stability and affordability.[20]

What is critical for our purposes is a recognition that only one of the four proposals rules out front-end competition for credit risk—that is mortgage underwriting competition. Systemic stability and affordability cannot be readily achieved without cabining competition for credit risk to the back end of the system in synthetic credit risk transfers where it can be divorced from prospective underwriting terms. If there is front-end competition for credit risk, there will be the pressure for underwriting races to the bottom and market fragmentation and loss of the TBA market, a return of balloon products, and a decline of the 30-year fixed. Moreover, competition for credit risk will virtually ensure the use of risk-based pricing, which will, in turn, undermine both affordability and stability.

Of the four models, only single-issuer/single-guarantor does not have front-end competition for credit risk. Multi-issuer/multi-guarantor and single-issuer/multi-guarantor have, by definition, competition for credit risk. All multi-guarantor models encourage price discovery through competition in the pricing of credit risk. This is both the virtue of these models and their fatal and overwhelming flaw.

Competition in front-end credit risk pricing is undesirable in a market with correlated asset prices, because in such a context competition produces systemic instability. Some variations of multi-guarantor models attempt to temper this problem through a government backstop for tail risk, but that actually exacerbates the problem by introducing moral hazard and exposing the public fisc to private-risk-taking activities.

Moreover, all multi-guarantor models prevent cross-subsidies among mortgage borrowers. That means that affordable housing must be achieved through direct tax-and-transfer, a system that is much more vulnerable to political pressure up or down, and which is by nature slow to respond to market shifts. As a result, multi-guarantor models are likely to see regional disparities in the availability of affordable housing finance.

Multi-issuer/single-guarantor would appear not to have competition for credit risk, but this is true only if a single governmental guarantor directly assumes all credit risk. All multi-issuer/single-guarantor proposals of which we are aware, however, involve multiple parties competing for first-loss credit risk, with a single-guarantor providing a secondary backstop.

This is a structure that has a built-in moral hazard because the issuer entities bear losses only up to their capital; they do not internalize the full costs of shoddy lending because of limited liability. Accordingly, they are incentivized to underprice risk to gain market share. A complete government backstop will add to market stability, and regulation by the guarantor can potentially keep underwriting standards in check, but the risk remains that issuers may fail.

The presence of multiple issuers means that no one issuer may appear to be too big to fail, but there can readily be correlated failures, not least because it is the MBS, not the issuers themselves, that are guaranteed. There is thus the result of a system-wide failure of firms, as in the case of the 2008 financial crisis, in which hundreds of firms failed, because the bust undid the unsustainable 100 percent rise in housing prices, induced by the very same perfusion of firms. This raises the question, then, whether any surviving firms can readily step up and fill the financing gap, or whether the government will have to step in, as it did in 2008, worsening moral hazard and setting the stage for future crises.

Thus, it is that we come now to our own single-issuer/single-guarantor reform proposal.

CHAPTER THIRTEEN

Meet Franny Meg

Franny Meg, the Federal Securitization Utility

This is our vision for a reformed housing finance system: we believe that the only way forward that guarantees stability and affordability is a single-issuer / single-guarantor system (or its functional equivalent), based around a regulated public utility.

Specifically, we envision a federally chartered securitization utility or perhaps a small number of closely regulated utilities that are subject to common underwriting standards. We'll call the utility the Federal Residential Mortgage Guaranty Corporation or "Franny Meg." Franny Meg would have private shareholders who would contribute its initial capital and select its board of directors, which would be responsible for its governance within the confines permitted by regulation. Franny Meg would also be backed (as the GSEs are currently) by a line of credit from the US Treasury, to be paid for by an explicit fee. Franny Meg would continue to be regulated by FHFA or a successor independent agency, as well as by the Federal Stability Oversight Counsel, as part of its macroprudential oversight for the US economy.

The Franny Meg would have a congressional charter providing limited corporate powers and would not be allowed to conduct business generally except as relates to the mortgage market. In particular, Franny Meg's charge would be to stand ready to purchase any and all mortgages that meet its underwriting criteria. For mortgage loans on one- to four-family residences, those underwriting criteria would include full amortization, a fifteen- or thirty-year term, free prepayment, a CLTV cap absent private mortgage insurance, conforming loan limits, and minimum documentation requirements. Regulatory oversight would ensure that these lending standards would not ease in good times and seize up in bad times. Franny Meg could purchase the mortgages on either a servicing-released or servicing-retained basis, but would always have a nominal call option on the servicing rights in order to strip problematic servicers of their servicing rights.

Franny Meg would buy mortgages at the face value of their unpaid principal balances, discounted by a service charge based on its operating costs and regulated by FHFA (the Fannie and Freddie's service fee is currently 8 basis points), as well as a guaranty fee for product-based credit risk. As we will explain in more detail, Franny Meg would (under FHFA guidance) set guaranty fees to vary countercyclically with provisioning in good times to insure against downturns and would reflect credit risk that was monitored and priced by private markets. Franny Meg would be allowed to vary the guaranty fee to facilitate access to the market under a statutory obligation to serve the national market. Thus, Franny Meg could meet all service obligations through a cross-subsidization among borrowers through variation in the guaranty fee.

The overall rate would be the sum of the service charge plus the guaranty fee, the Treasury line fee, and the MBS interest rate—as determined by the trading of interest rate risk in a standardized TBA market. The pass-through of the overall rate to the borrower would be similar to that paid today.

Franny Meg would securitize all the mortgages it purchases in nationally blended pools and sell those securities with a guaranty of timely payment and interest. The only standing distinctions among Franny securitization pools would be among vintages, with separate pools for one- to four-family mortgages and mortgages on multifamily residences.

Franny Meg would not maintain a portfolio of mortgage loans except to the extent of accumulating loans for securitization or in the event of an adverse market (requiring a formal regulatory finding by the FHFA). Franny Meg would also not maintain a securities or derivatives investment portfolio other than for the limited purpose of hedging pipeline risk.

Franny Meg would pay for the mortgages through a cash window but offer sellers an option of taking Franny Meg MBS in lieu of cash, with securities priced at market. The maintenance of a cash window would ensure access by originating institutions of all sizes, as smaller institutions are poorly equipped to handle the rate risk on MBS they receive in payment and lack the underwriting structures to move those securities to investors.

The Franny Meg structure would shift interest rate risk to capital markets through the MBS, while the credit risk would, in the first instance, be held by Franny Meg. Significantly, we would require Franny Meg to shift most of the credit risk to capital markets through back-end credit risk transfer transactions, except when adverse market conditions (as determined by FHFA) obtain.

We do not attempt to prescribe the precise details of the credit risk transfers transactions here, but we assume they would generally track the credit-linked note (CLN) structures used by Fannie and Freddie. This would produce a credit risk waterfall such that Franny Meg would be exposed to a limited level of initial losses, with second losses going to the CLN investors. Losses beyond those allocated to the CLN investors would again be borne by Franny Meg, meaning that they would be paid out of its capital. Only if Franny Meg's capital were exhausted would the catastrophic loss guaranty from Treasury kick in. Of particular importance, the CLN structure eliminates counterparty risk for Franny Meg because it is prefunded by the CLN investors. Key for making this structure work is a sufficiently large statutorily prescribed level of capital, which Franny Meg could obtain either through sales of stock, including an initial subscription from Treasury, or the retention of earnings.

Critically, any back-end credit risk transfers must come with a pair of substantive limitations. First, the reference pools for the CLNs must be national, blended pools without any differentiation except vintage and single versus multifamily mortgages. Mandating national, blended reference pools will protect against market fragmentation by ensuring the CLNs are priced based on nonfragmented markets. This is key for ensuring stable markets because the CLN pricing must reflect the risk of the entire market. Given the correlated nature of home prices and the endogeneity of credit and house prices, it is the risk of the overall market that determines the risk for individual mortgage lenders, homeowners, the taxpayer, and the system as a whole.

More importantly, the pricing of the CLNs must be separated from the pricing of the guaranty fee; that is, there must be no automatic passthrough of the pricing of the CLNs to the pricing of the mortgages. If such pricing were to occur, then all the benefits of reduced credit-risk competition would be lost, and we would be right back to the problem of flighty, procyclical markets.

Using synthetic credit risk transfers through CLNs would not only help inject private risk capital ahead of the government (but without the dangers of private underwriting). It would also generate information about credit risk. The private market trading, pricing, and provisioning through the CLNs against transparently observable credit risk in the reference pools would reveal the credit risk of the mortgages in these pools. The credit spreads on the CLNs—the amount private markets charge for credit risk—can be used to test for the Pavlov-Wachter bubble indicators. Thus, should spreads on the CLNs widen, it would signal to FHFA the need to restrict dividends to Franny Meg's shareholders in order to accumulate capital through retained earnings.

Using the CLN structure with Franny Meg completes housing markets. It provides a source of information about the level of risk in mortgage lending and home prices and a liquid vehicle for expressing long and short positions on the housing market. Importantly, the information provided by the CLN structure is purely about mortgage risk; it is not contaminated by counterparty risk like the ABX indices that track the price of credit default swaps in the dealer markets because the CLN would be free of counterparty risk—the GSEs would pay up front for the swap protection from the special-purpose vehicle, which would be prefunded by the CLN investors. Using Franny Meg with an appropriate CLN structure would ensure that there would, in fact, be effective market discipline in the housing markets.

How Many Franny Megs?

While we are proposing a single-issuer/single-guarantor system, we believe that the role of Franny Meg could in fact be performed by *multiple* Franny Meg entities, *provided that they would complete only on operational efficiency and not on underwriting or pricing.* This could be achieved if all underwriting were subject to the same national standards, and guaranty fees were standardized by regulation across Franny Megs.

There are trade-offs between having a single Franny Meg and multiple ones. (If multiple, we envision not more than three or four.) On the one hand, a single-issuer/single-guarantor model involving multiple Franny Megs would benefit from competition on operational efficiency in prospecting for and processing loans, as this would encourage borrower-friendly technological innovations and better customer service. Multiple Franny Megs would also create some protective redundancy against non-systematic operational failures.

On the other hand, multiple Franny Megs would create some inefficiencies through duplication. Their CLNs would be inherently less liquid because they would not be good delivery for each other. Importantly, however, their MBS would have to be uniform and accepted as good delivery for each other in order to enable a TBA market. Additionally, having multiple guarantor entities is unlikely to protect against systemic failure. While no single Franny Meg would be too big to fail, they would face common risks, so there would be a chance of a correlated failure or at least a panic due to fear of a correlated failure. Having multiple guarantor entities does not really solve the too-big-fail problem because what we are concerned about is the stability of the *market, not individual firms.*

Ultimately, we are agnostic about whether there should be one or multiple Franny Megs. The point here is simply that it is possible to have multiple Franny Megs that compete on the limited dimension of operational efficiency and not credit risk, while staying within the single-issuer/single-guarantor paradigm.

To be sure, even if there is only one Franny Meg, it need not be the only game in town. Under our proposal, portfolio lending would continue, as would FHLB advances. So, too, would private securitization (particularly of jumbos) outside the regulated utility. We would, however, require PLS to go through Securities Act registration, which means that Reg AB II would apply, so that investors would benefit from the protections of pre-purchase disclosures and the ability to ensure representation and warranty enforcement.

Likewise, the FHA/VA/Ginnie Mae system would continue to operate as before. Franny Meg would be a self-contained structure for cross-subsidization rather than drawing on taxpayer dollars except in the situation of a catastrophic market meltdown. It would not, however, be asked to support borrowers who need substantial assistance in achieving home-ownership. Those borrowers would continue to be supported through the tax-and-transfer system of FHA/VA/Ginnie Mae.

Benefits from the Franny Meg Structure

The Franny Meg structure would have several immediate stability benefits. First, the standing offer to purchase any and all mortgages that meet underwriting criteria would ensure a constant supply of liquidity to the housing market across the cycle. This standing purchase offer is available solely because of the federal government's assumption of catastrophic credit risk, which leverages the government's unique ability to bear risk to ensure that markets will not gap out when stressed.

Second, because the guaranty fee would be priced on a national portfolio and would consider portfolio-wide risk, it would account for systemic externalities. Only a single-issuer/single-guarantor structure, such as a regulated utility, is able to price in the systemic externality. In practical terms, this will mean a lower guaranty fee for products that have more positive systemic stability effects, such as the 30-year fixed.

Third, a single-issuer/single-guarantor model eliminates competition for market share through the erosion of mortgage underwriting standards. By eliminating credit risk competition in the secondary market, a single-issuer/single-guarantor model would ensure that there would not be rate wars for market share. Instead, the only competition for credit risk would be in the tertiary CLN market, and that competition would simply be in terms of the price investors are willing to pay for the CLNs, which would be delinked from mortgage underwriting or guaranty fees.

Fourth, channeling all mortgage credit through a single CLN channel will facilitate the monitoring of credit risk spreads so that bubbles can be caught as soon as they start to form. The single channel will facilitate standardization of mortgages themselves and of secondary market products, which will make CLN pricing an indicator of the risk of the mortgage market to the overall economy. In this way, the trading of CLN completes the market, preventing credit-induced housing price bubbles from going unchecked. This would make credit risk spreads comparable over time without risk adjustment.

Fifth, if there were only a single Franny Meg, there would be only a single, and therefore larger, more liquid, and more efficient, market for the pricing of back-end credit-risk transfers. Maximizing the efficiency of this market is critical because the pricing of the CLNs issued by Franny Meg would be the tell-tale indicator of market-wide mortgage credit risk. Because Franny Meg would be most of the market, it would internalize the systemic risk externalities in the market, which would be passed on in the pricing of the CLNs. The Franny Meg structure thus enables the pricing of the systemic risk externality. Franny Meg would make all the relevant data available on the risk characteristics of their MBS, thus enabling the CLN to evaluate the credit risk of the entire market.

Finally, by eliminating credit risk competition by entities whose role should be the monitoring of standards, the Franny Meg structure would maintain a national, unfragmented MBS market. This means that the TBA market can be preserved, that there will be greater liquidity in the market, and that there will not be regional disparities in credit pricing or the resulting volatility. Even with multiple Franny Megs, the TBA market could be preserved if they issued Uniform MBS as Fannie and Freddie currently do.

In addition to stability benefits, the Franny Meg structure would also have affordability benefits. The systemic stability engendered by Franny Mae would translate into lower guaranty fees and thus lower mortgage rates. Borrowers would not be paying a systemic risk premium. Systemic stability is a dividend for all borrowers.

In addition, because Franny Meg would commit to purchase all mortgages that meet its underwriting requirements but would charge a guaranty fee that would vary on only a few dimensions, there would be automatic cross-subsidization within the Franny Meg structure. The cross-subsidization, in turn, would contribute to affordability and stability in the system. Just as credit terms affect housing prices and vice versa, so too does afford-ability affect stability and vice versa. By recognizing these interlinked rela-tionships that make housing finance markets fundamentally different from other markets, the Franny Meg structure will secure both affordability and stability.

Formalizing Franny Meg

The current situation has many of the characteristics we think are desirable for a housing finance system. While there is still a Fannie/Freddie duopoly, it is effectively a type of single-issuer/single-guarantor system, particularly because of the convergence of Fannie and Freddie through the common support from Treasury and the adoption of the Uniform MBS. The current system has also substantially derisked Fannie and Freddie. Nonetheless, it is not ideal.

Most importantly, the system is not in a legal equilibrium because of the continuing uncertainty of the conservatorship. Changing from a de facto system to a de jure Franny Meg will result in a greater certainty about the future of housing finance.

Many of the positive reforms of Fannie Mae and Freddie Mac have also been done either informally, through FHFA suasion, or through contract, namely, the Senior Preferred Stock Purchase Agreements. Moving to a de jure Franny Meg system would give Congress an opportunity to set up and formalize reform. In particular, it is necessary to legislate governance and to place limitations on the design and pricing of synthetic credit risk transfer transactions. We cannot predict when there will be a political path forward, but we believe that whenever such a path arises, our Franny Meg proposal will provide the blueprint for reform to ensure a stable and affordable housing finance system.

Conclusion

IN THE PAST century, the American housing finance system has been thoroughly transformed from a volatile market to a stable market, only to relapse and then repeat the transition. Both times, the transformation was spurred by the traumatic collapse of the private mortgage market after an unsustainable boom. The first episode was part of the Great Depression, and the reforms that followed created a home mortgage market that was the economic cornerstone of the American Middle Class. Yet those reforms were consistently eroded and eventually led to the most recent episode, when excessive mortgage credit caused housing prices to increase over 50 percent in a matter of a few years, with no changes in fundamentals. The bust that followed led to the Great Financial Crisis and worldwide turmoil, with consequences that persist today. Both times the collapse was devastating to households, to the economy, and to social stability.

It is time to finally learn from the mistakes of the past century and move to a stable housing finance system based on sustainable standards in lending and layered cushions of private capital. A reformed housing finance system that would securitize mortgages and transfer credit risk to capital markets without a feedback loop to prospective mortgage underwriting is the only model that can provide systemic stability and support affordability, along with mortgage rate determination through global capital markets and access to homeownership. Reforming the housing finance system will ensure that American housing sits on a sound and stable financial foundation and that American families will be able to afford a place called home.

Appendix A:
The Pre–New Deal Farm Finance System

Appendix B:
The Levitin-Wachter Subprime PLS Dataset

Appendix C:
CDO Manager Compensation

Glossary

Notes

Acknowledgments

Index

The Pre–New Deal Farm
Finance System

WHILE AN ENDURING secondary market for *home* mortgage loans did not develop before the New Deal, it did for farm finance. Farms, of course, are not just commercial units, but also include residences. Prior to 1920, the US population was primarily rural, so farm finance was also housing finance. In 1916, responding to long-standing agrarian complaints about difficulties in accessing affordable, long-term credit, Congress passed the Federal Farm Loan Act, which created a pair of lending facilities for farm mortgages—the public Federal Land Bank system (later supplemented by the Federal Intermediate Credit Banks) and the private Joint Stock Land Banks. The Federal Land Bank system arguably represents the first federal foray into housing finance, although it was never conceived of as a housing finance program, but rather meant to be an agricultural finance program. While all but forgotten today, the pre–New Deal federal *farm* finance system is important in the story of *housing* finance because it established several of the precedents for New Deal housing finance reform.

The Federal Land Bank system was modeled after the Federal Reserve System. It consisted of twelve regional federally chartered but privately owned Federal Land Banks, regulated by a Federal Farm Loan Board, which conducted examinations and engaged in prudential rulemaking. The Federal Land Banks raised capital through stock subscriptions and through the issuance of bonds backed by farm mortgage loans.[1]

The Federal Land Bank stock subscriptions were open to the public, but with the initial offering backstopped by the federal government,[2] which provided almost all the original capital.[3] The bonds were what we would now call "covered bonds": multiple issuances were backed by a common "cover pool" of mortgages, rather than specific pools of mortgages backing specific bonds. The bond issuances were done centrally under the auspices of the Federal Farm Loan Board, and all the Federal Land Banks were jointly liable for the bonds.[4] Bond issuance for each Federal Land Bank was limited to twenty times the bank's paid-in capital and surplus—a leverage ratio of 5 percent. The interest rate on the bonds was limited to no more than 1 percent less than the rate on the mortgages.[5] Given that 25 basis points was committed as a servicing spread,[6] the Federal Land Banks were able to make roughly 75 basis points on a loan. The Federal Land Banks' bonds were not expressly guaranteed by the federal government, but there was an implicit guaranty, as it turned out.

The Federal Land Banks made loans to borrowers through the National Farm Loan Associations (NFLAs), federally chartered cooperative corporations owned by farm loan borrowers and regulated by the Federal Farm Loan Board.[7] The NFLAs acted as exclusive correspondents for the Federal Land Banks, a structure copied from the German *Landschaften* system.[8] A farmer who wanted to borrow had to apply to the NFLA for a loan.[9] The NFLA's directors had to approve the loan by a two-thirds vote.[10]

If the NFLA approved the loan application, it was then passed along to a Federal Land Bank for approval, which entailed an appraisal of the property by the Federal Land Bank.[11] If the Federal Land Bank approved the loan, the NFLA was required to endorse the note, making it jointly liable with the farmer.[12] Thus, the correspondent had "skin in the game." The farmer, then, was required to take out a stock subscription in an NFLA equal to 5 percent of the loan amount, to be held by the NFLA as collateral for the loan,[13] and the NFLA had to purchase stock in the Federal Land Bank equal to 5 percent of the loan, which was also held as collateral by the Federal Land Bank.[14] This stock could pay dividends, however, thereby defraying its cost to the borrower. Additionally, all NFLA members were liable to the NFLA for double the amount of their paid-in stock subscription.[15] Thus, any loans made by a Federal Land Bank were backed first by the individual farmer's repayment ability, then by the individual farmer's stock subscription in the NFLA, then by the mortgaged farmland, then by the NFLA's stock subscription in the Federal Land Bank, then by the assets of the NFLA, and finally by the liability of the NFLA's members up to the amount of their stock subscription in the NFLA. These multiple layers of capital were supposed to ensure that the Federal Land Banks were protected from defaults on the loans. The NFLAs also serviced the Federal Land Bank loans they facilitated, for which they were compensated a fee of 25 basis points per year on the loan balance,[16] but they were also responsible for advancing payments in the event of defaults.[17]

The use of the NFLAs was key to the Federal Land Bank system. Although the Federal Land Banks were required to conduct their own appraisals before making loans,[18] the initial screening of the loan application was done by the NFLA.[19] The use of the NFLA helped address the local appraisal problem: the local farmers who made up the NFLA had the best sense of the value of their neighbors' properties and were incentivized against aggressive valuations because of their own shared liability on the loans. The system did leave the NFLA approval process vulnerable to groupthink: if the farmers in a region were overly optimistic about the future of the agricultural market, there was no check on their approval.

The Federal Farm Loan Act also regulated the terms of loans made by the Federal Land Banks to ensure that the system provided stable, long-term loans to farmers. Federal Land Banks were limited to lending only in their own district,[20] only to owners engaged in the cultivation of loans,[21] and only against first mortgages,[22] at no more than 50 percent LTV,[23] with interest rates capped at 6 percent.[24]

Long-term credit was particularly important to farmers because if they had short-term credit, they faced the risk of needing to refinance at a time of a bad harvest or economic depression, that could severely depress their property's value and limit their ability to get enough new credit to pay off the old loan.[25] Thus, Federal Land Banks were allowed to make loans only with terms of between five and forty years' duration.[26] All the loans were required to be fully amortized at a rate of at least 1 percent annually,[27] which meant that practically speaking, loans were no longer than thirty-six years. The required amortization of loans was a controversial feature of the Federal Land Bank loans.[28] Opponents argued that forced principal repayments over time deprived farmers of the ability to make better investments, while proponents noted the benefits of enforced thrift for farmers and better security for lenders.[29]

In addition to the Federal Land Bank system, the Federal Farm Loan Act also created a parallel Joint Stock Land Bank system. The "joint stock" designation merely means that these were shareholder-owned banks. The Joint Stock Land Banks were federal corporations modeled on national banking associations.[30] Some eighty-eight Joint Stock Land Banks were ultimately chartered by 1931.[31] They were privately capitalized (with double shareholder liability like national banks) and issued bonds individually, with their own servicing arrangements. The terms of their lending, however, were restricted along the lines of the Federal Land Banks' lending,[32] making them monoline agricultural lending banks. The Joint Stock Land Banks were also subject to some prudential regulation by the Federal Farm Loan Board, including on loan appraisals, and their bonds were limited to fifteen times their paid-in capital and surplus, a maximum leverage ratio of 6.67 percent equity to liabilities.[33] Whereas Federal Land Banks could only loan within their particular district, however, Joint Stock Land Banks could loan in their own state and a contiguous one.[34]

The creation of the two systems was a matter of political compromise between those who wanted more "private" capital in the system and those who wanted less.[35] Ironically, however, even though the Joint Stock Land Banks were a more "private" system than the Federal Land Banks (which only had government ownership initially),[36] they were still heavily favored by federal regulation (as were Federal Land Banks): they had federal chartering and exemption from all nonreal estate taxes,[37] and their bonds were deemed appropriate investments for fiduciaries.[38] The distinction between the Federal Land Banks and the Joint Stock Land Banks was not so much public versus private as that between a mutual or cooperative and a regular for-profit corporation, as the profits of the Federal Land Banks, such as they were, largely went back to the NFLAs, and thus to the borrowers in the form of dividend payments.

The Federal Land Banks and Joint Stock Land Banks competed to some degree. Because the Federal Land Banks were mutuals, they were often able to offer lower interest rates than the Joint Stock Land Banks, which had to make higher returns in order to attract capital, especially given their lower leverage limitation. Federal Land Bank system loans were usually 50 to 100 basis points cheaper than Joint Stock Land Bank loans, although this was offset somewhat by the stock purchase requirement.[39]

Neither the Federal Land Banks nor the Joint Stock Land Banks ever occupied an especially important position in the agricultural-financing system. Prior to their New Deal reorganization, they never accounted for more than a quarter of the agricultural finance in any year; on average, they provided only 8 percent of the financing in the market.[40] Instead, the farm finance market remained dominated by individual lenders. The main contribution that the Federal Land Banks and Joint Stock Land Banks made to the farm finance market was to offer products with longer terms than those of other lenders. While the longer terms might have been appealing to farmers, the mandatory amortization of the loans may have been off-putting to those who wanted the cash-flow flexibility offered by nonamortizing loans. Notably, the Federal Land Banks and Joint Stock Land Banks were not capable of engaging in countercyclical lending; they were procyclical like the rest of the market because they lacked any formal federal support.

The Federal Land Banks and Joint Stock Land Banks met their end with the Great Depression. Agricultural commodity prices had declined after World War I, but the decline accelerated during the Depression. This wreaked havoc on the farm finance system. Farmers were unable to make the payments on their fixed-rate loans, and many simply abandoned their properties. The result was that nearly half of NFLAs failed by 1933.[41] The farm finance system was simply not capable of handling a market-wide downturn.

The primary protection for the farm finance system was the farmers' equity stake in the property, but the collateral was undiversified in the sense that it was all agricultural land, and thus it was an inadequate protection when faced with a market-wide decline. The Federal Farm Loan Act required initial LTV ratios on loans for both Federal Land Banks and Joint Stock Land Banks of no more than 50 percent (and declining thereafter because of amortization). Thus, LTVs on Federal Land Bank loans should never have been more than 47.5 percent because of the additional stock subscription collateral of 5 percent of loan value or up to 2.5 percent of LTV, while the LTVs on Joint Stock Land Bank loans should never have been more than 50 percent. Even these very low LTVs (by contemporary standards), however, were of little protection when faced with mass defaults. The crash in agricultural prices severely depressed the value of farmland, and mass defaults and foreclosures furthered a downward cycle, resulting in a glut of properties on the market. At the same time, frozen capital markets meant that the Federal Land Banks and the Joint Stock Land Banks could not roll over their own debt.

State foreclosure moratoria and federal farm bankruptcy laws attempted to protect farmers' tenancy until prices could rebound.[42] Similarly, the federal Emergency Farm Mortgage Act of 1933 extended repayment terms and offered emergency financing to strapped farmers,[43] but the heavily leveraged pre–New Deal farm finance system lacked the capital to weather the storm.

Congress bailed out the Federal Land Banks in 1932 with an investment of $125 million in Federal Land Bank stock, which almost tripled the system's capital.[44] The federal government put another $189 million into the system in 1933.[45] Whereas the mutual system of Federal Land Banks was bailed out, Congress pulled the plug on the Joint Stock Land Banks. The Emergency Farm Mortgage Act of 1933 prohibited Joint Stock Land Banks from further tax-exempt bond issuance or further loan origination except to refinance existing ones.[46] The existing Joint Stock Land Banks all went into wind-down or liquidation, and by 1951 all the Joint Stock Land Banks had been liquidated.[47]

The 1916 farm finance system was never understood as housing policy, but rather was seen as support for America's agricultural sector. Despite the failure of both the mutual and private farm finance systems that were created in 1916, both systems did create three important precedents for the housing finance system that bore fruit in the New Deal. First, they pioneered the use of both mutual and joint stock structures for federal financing entities. Both structures have subsequently been used with the FHLB system and the original design of Freddie Mac being mutuals, while Fannie Mae and the current Freddie Mac are joint stock entities. Second, the farm finance system helped establish the regulatory preference for long-term, amortized loan products. And third, the farm finance system helped normalize federal regulatory intervention in real estate finance markets more generally.

The Levitin-Wachter Subprime
PLS Dataset

MUCH OF THE DATA in Chapter 7 comes from the Levitin-Wachter Subprime PLS Dataset, an original, hand-coded dataset of the aggregate loan terms of mortgages securitized in subprime PLS deals from 2001 to 2007. We assembled the dataset specifically for this book. The dataset provides data, not just on mortgage interest rates, but also on key risk factors that can be used to evaluate risk-adjusted pricing. This additional data is critical because mortgage pricing needs to be evaluated on a risk-adjusted basis in order to be meaningful. Such additional data on risk factors is missing from more readily available datasets, which generally only have interest rate data, not key risk factors.

The dataset consists of 361 private-label subprime mortgage securitization deals from between 2001 and 2007. There are at least 50 deals represented in every year. The deals contain a total of 686 loan groups, with at least 87 loan groups per year. Collectively, these deals contain nearly 2 million mortgage loans, with a total principal balance at the time of securitization of over $313 billion. (See Table B.1.) For each deal, we tracked the average loan size and weighted-average LTV, FICO, owner-occupied percentage, full documentation percentage, interest-only percentage, balloon loan percentage, and percentage of second liens included in each loan group in the deal.

Table B.2 summarizes the coverage of the dataset. We cannot claim the dataset to be statistically significant in the technical sense,[1] because we do not

Table B.1. Summary Statistics for Levitin-Wachter Subprime PLS Dataset

Deal Year	# of Deals	# of Loan Groups	# of Mortgage Loans	Total Principal of Mortgages
2001	50	91	371,686	$35,759,498,078.07
2002	50	95	203,837	$27,955,236,346.43
2003	50	105	262,539	$38,889,443,315.46
2004	54	109	314,596	$53,143,010,161.73
2005	50	95	297,380	$53,830,287,036.50
2006	50	87	270,980	$53,010,436,109.15
2007	57	104	256,564	$50,662,820,346.89
Total	**361**	**686**	**1,977,582**	**$313,250,731,394.23**

Table B.2. Coverage of Levitin-Wachter Subprime PLS Dataset

Deal Year	Mortgage Volume in Sample	Total Subprime Originations[a]	% of Subprime Originations in Sample
2001	$35,759,498,078	$160,000,000,000	22.3%
2002	$27,955,236,346	$200,000,000,000	14.0%
2003	$38,889,443,315	$310,000,000,000	12.5%
2004	$53,143,010,162	$540,000,000,000	9.8%
2005	$53,830,287,037	$625,000,000,000	8.6%
2006	$53,010,436,109	$600,000,000,000	8.8%
2007	$50,662,820,347	$191,000,000,000	26.5%
Total	**$313,250,731,394**	**$2,626,000,000,000**	**11.9%**

[a] Inside Mortgage Finance, "Mortgage Originations by Product," *2015 Mortgage Market Statistical Annual.*

know the total universe of subprime securitization deals.[2] But what we can say is this: the mortgages in the dataset comprise 12 percent of the $2.626 trillion in subprime mortgage origination during this period. Therefore, even if the precise measurements might differ from the complete market data, we do not believe that they would be materially or directionally different.

Given that our argument depends on these figures being directionally correct rather than on their ultimate statistical precision, we believe that the subprime PLS we have collected provides a strong basis for evaluating the source of the housing bubble.[3] We also note that our findings from the dataset are consistent with our analysis in other work of the Columbia Collateral File, a data source on all the loans in private-label securitizations (prime and nonprime) for which Wells Fargo is trustee.[4]

CDO Manager Compensation

CDO APPETITE FOR B-PIECES of PLS (and similarly for B-pieces of CMBS) was whetted in part by CDO manager compensation structures. CDO managers were typically compensated with two standard types of fees. Additionally, a substantial minority of CDOs compensated managers with at least one additional type of fee. First, CDO managers would receive a senior asset management fee based on the par value of assets under management (AUM).[1] This fee was in the range of 5–20 basis points annually on the AUM.[2] So-called high-grade CDOs, which were resecuritizations of more senior PLS tranches—and generally AAA- to A-rated—had lower fees than so-called mezzanine CDOs, which were resecuritizations of the more junior PLS tranches (BBB to not rated),[3] but because high-grade deals tended to be about twice as large as mezzanine deals, the total compensation from the senior management fees in both types of deals would be around the same.[4]

Second, CDO managers would receive a subordinated asset management fee, also based on the face value of AUM. This fee would be in the range of 2–14 basis points (smaller in high-grade deals and larger in mezzanine deals) and would be subordinated to all the CDO tranches except the "equity" tranche. Together the senior and subordinated asset management fees might be 10–30 basis points annually on AUM.

In some deals, the CDO manager would also receive an upfront fee for expenses of assembling the deal. This fee would usually be around $1 million, roughly equal to a year's worth of management fees.[5] In other deals, the CDO manager would receive a performance-based fee that was typically equal to 20 percent of the returns on the equity tranche once the equity tranche had achieved a specified internal rate of return, perhaps 12–15 percent.[6] Finally, in some deals the CDO manager would hold part of the equity tranche itself.[7]

This compensation structure did not properly incentivize CDO managers to be diligent about credit risk for several reasons.

Asset-Under-Management-Based Compensation Made CDO Managers Indifferent to Marginal Investment Returns

The senior AUM-based compensation component (as well as any upfront fees) made CDO managers somewhat indifferent to the CDOs' performance; they did not incur any downside exposure for this fee because the senior AUM-based compensation was paid off the top of any returns. Thus, on a CDO with $500 million in AUM and a senior fee of 20 basis points, the manager would receive $1 million per year, irrespective of the CDO's performance in most instances.[8]

In such a situation, the CDO manager has no incentive to spend time and effort diligencing particular asset purchases because it is not compensated for the costs of such diligence. Instead, the manager is incentivized to simply "buy the market."[9] This is particularly true if the CDO manager lacks the expertise to undertake the credit analysis itself, as may well have been the case, at least in some instances.[10]

The subordinated AUM-component was meant to offset the incentive problem of the senior management fee by making the largest component of compensation subordinated to most of the CDO investors, but the subordination was limited: it was only a subordination of payment in any given time period, but there was no temporal subordination between payments made in different time periods. Thus, if in months 1 through 4 there were no defaults on the underlying PLS, cash would flow down to the subordinated management fee, while if in month 5 the underlying PLS defaulted and paid nothing, cash would not flow to anyone in the CDO. The CDO manager's subordinated management fee in months 1 to 4 would therefore have been paid before the supposedly senior CDO investors in month 5. Only the CDO manager's fee for month 5 would not be paid. Therefore, while the CDO manager's subordinated management fee was subordinated in terms of liquidation priority, it was not subordinated temporally in terms of right to payment.

This distinction between liquidation priority and temporal payment priority is important because the AUM-based fee meant that only actual losses, not market value declines of the PLS based on anticipation of future losses, affected CDO managers' compensation. Given that most mortgage defaults and therefore actual realized losses on PLS were in 2009 or later, CDO managers were able to collect substantial subordinated fees for the 2004–2007 period, even once market values fell in 2007–2008.[11] Thus, until there were defaults on the PLS, the CDO manager with $500 million of par value in AUM and a subordinated fee of 14 basis points would be receiving another $700,000 annually in addition to its $1 million senior fee. This structure reduced CDO managers' incentive to take care regarding their investments beyond ensuring that defaults would not be immediate. Any delay in loss realization would extend the period for which CDO managers could receive their senior and subordinated fees on the asset.

AUM-Based Compensation Incentivized the Purchase of Discounted Assets

The fact that much of CDO managers' compensation was based on an AUM-based formula incentivized them to invest in B-pieces irrespective of risk. We have only been able to locate a limited number of CDO management contracts, but the ones we have examined compute CDO managers' fees based on the principal balance of AUM, rather than fair market value of AUM. This formula would have incentivized CDO managers to purchase assets that sell at a discount from par in order to increase their guarantied compensation. As it happened, no class of securities sold with discounts as deep from par as junior tranches of PLS, and that is where CDOs concentrated their investment.[12]

Purchasing discounted securities had the effect of goosing the CDO manager's AUM-based compensation because the CDO can, for the same amount of funds, purchase more assets. For example, imagine that a CDO manager has $500 million in funds to invest. If the manager invests solely in par securities, the annual management fee (20 bps of senior and 14 bps of subordinated) is $1.7 million (0.34 percent of $500 million). But if the manager purchases only securities discounted to 80 percent, the manager could purchase $625 million in par value for $500 million, which would increase the annual management fee to $2.125 million (0.34 percent of $625 million). And if the manager purchases only securities discounted to 20 percent, the manager could purchase $2.5 billion in par value for $500 million, which would increase the annual management fee to $8.5 million.

Basing CDO management fees on the principal amount of AUM, rather than on fair market value, incentivized managers to invest in deeply discounted securities, which dictated investment in a very particular asset class, namely junior tranches of PLS.[13] Junior tranches of PLS usually sold at substantial original issue discounts, often as low as 15¢ or 20¢ on the dollar in deals without excess spread or net interest margin securities.[14]

Junior tranches sold at this sort of a discount because discounted issuance is the only way to increase the yield on the junior tranches without excess spread (typical for adjustable rate mortgage securitizations) or net interest margin securities. Short of using these structuring devices, the yield on junior tranches cannot be increased by offering a higher coupon on the bonds when mortgages of different interest rates are pooled together (so the bonds are not pure pass-throughs of the payments on the mortgages).[15] Instead, original issue discounting is the only way to increase the yield.

Normally, increasing risk on the mortgages would have resulted in ever deeper discounts on the junior tranches of PLS, which would have had the effect of raising the cost of mortgages and pushing home prices down. But the discounting actually *increased* CDOs' demand for the junior tranches of PLS because of the way CDO managers were compensated. As a result, even when risk on mortgages increased, there was not a concomitant increase in the cost of mortgage funding.

Equity Tranche Compensation Incentivized Purchases of Riskier Securities

Additionally, compensating the CDO manager with part of the equity tranche, which occurred in a substantial minority of deals, meant that the CDO manager was incentivized to take on more risk because the higher returns on riskier assets increased the likelihood that the fees would trickle down the CDO's cash-flow waterfall to the equity tranche. If the CDO manager invested solely in safe securities, the CDO's equity tranche would be unlikely to hit the investment return hurdle that would allow excess returns to flow to the CDO manager. In 2006–2007 in particular, the projected earnings on safer securities were declining, so the incentive for CDO managers to purchase riskier securities increased.[16]

CDO managers' incentive to invest in riskier assets also created an "asset substitution" problem. There were two times when this problem could manifest itself.[17] First, CDOs had a "ramp-up" period when they assembled the collateral securities. While the assets had to be assembled according to investment guidelines, managers could seek out the riskiest assets that complied with the guidelines. Second, there is a "reinvestment" period for CDOs, enabling managers to purchase new collateral as old collateral is paid off. Managers could substitute riskier assets for less risky ones as the original ones matured.[18] In both cases, managers were able to maximize the riskiness of the CDO's assets within the investment guidelines.

The result was that if the CDO's investments paid off, the manager would reap handsome rewards, while if it did not, it would at least make the none-too-shabby management fees in the interim. Indeed, as a general matter all else being equal, an equity holder in a limited liability entity benefits from greater volatility in a firm's value, because the equity holder has all of the upside and limited downside. This means that CDO managers were incentivized to create investment portfolios with more concentrated risk—and thus more volatility. A portfolio of assets with high default correlation, such as junior tranches of PLS, fit this bill perfectly.

The performance-based component of CDO managers' compensation also incentivized them to purchase discounted assets like the junior tranches of PLS. While the coupons on junior tranches were not particularly high, the original issue discount on junior tranches functions as a type of yield thereby increasing the performance-based fee.

In some instances, the CDO manager's compensation structure was further complicated by an affiliation with a hedge fund that invested in the CDO's junior-most "equity" tranche. In such a situation, the CDO manager (or its affiliate) would also receive a hedge fund asset management fee (typically 2 percent of AUM) and a performance-based fee of 20 percent of returns. This type of double-dipping arrangement meant that the CDO manager was both more invested in the equity tranche than otherwise (and thus more inclined to create a more volatile portfolio) and increased the AUM-based fees, encouraging the manager to maximize AUM.

CDO manager compensation thus created a set of misaligned incentives that discouraged careful investment diligence and encouraged investment particularly in PLS and PLS-based derivatives (that is, selling CDS protection on PLS to achieve a synthetic long investment in PLS).

Glossary

There are many acronyms used throughout the text. They are part of the jargon of housing finance and are unfortunately unavoidable. This glossary spells out those terms that appear repeatedly in the text along with a very brief explanation.

ABCP—asset-backed commercial paper. A securitization of long-term assets that is funded through the issuance of commercial paper (short-term debt obligations with a term of under one year).

ABS—asset-backed security or asset-backed securities. A securitization of debt obligations. The underlying obligations can be from a wide variety of asset classes, but ABS generally exclude mortgages. Home equity loan securitizations, however, are usually categorized as ABS, not MBS. The acronym is used for both singular (security) and plural (securities), as indicated by context.

ARM—adjustable-rate mortgage. A mortgage whose interest rate changes periodically based on a margin over a referenced index rate.

AUM—assets under management. The total amount of assets in an investment fund managed by an investment manager.

CDO—collateralized debt obligation. A securitization of other securities, that is, generally, a resecuritization of PLS.

CDS—credit default swap. A contract in which, in exchange for protection premiums, a protection seller promises to pay the protection buyer a certain amount in the event of a defined credit event on a referenced asset.

CFPB—Consumer Financial Protection Bureau. A new federal regulator for consumer financial products that was created in 2010.

CLN—credit-linked note. A securitization of CDS, the payments on the CLN depend on the performance of the assets referenced by the CDS.

CLTV—combined-loan-to-value. The ratio of the aggregate mortgage debt on a property to the value of the property.

CMBS—commercial mortgage-backed security. A securitization of mortgage loans on commercial properties, including multifamily housing.

CRA—Community Reinvestment Act. A 1977 federal law that encourages federally insured banks and savings associations to provide credit and other financial services in underserved markets.

DTI—debt-to-income. The ratio of the borrower's debts to the borrower's income.

FDIC—Federal Deposit Insurance Corporation. A federal government corporation that provides deposit insurance and regulates insured institutions. Historically, only banks, not savings and loans, were eligible for FDIC insurance; savings and loans were insured by FSLIC.

FHA—Federal Housing Administration. An office within HUD that provides partial insurance to low–down payment mortgage loans.

FHFA—Federal Housing Finance Agency. A new regulator for Fannie Mae, Freddie Mac, and the FHLBs that was created in 2008.

FHLB—Federal Home Loan Bank. A system of twelve privately owned, federally chartered banks that provide liquidity to the mortgage market.

FHLBB—Federal Home Loan Bank Board. The now-defunct regulator of federally chartered thrifts and the GSEs.

FICO—Fair, Isaac and Company. The creator of some of the most commonly used models of credit scoring. A FICO score is a credit score created by FICO. Several models of FICO scores are used, but the mortgage industry has long used the FICO 4 model, even as newer models have come out.

FRM—fixed-rate mortgage. A mortgage whose interest rate is set contractually at the same absolute rate for its entire term.

FSLIC—Federal Savings and Loan Insurance Corporation. A now-defunct federal government corporation that provided deposit insurance and regulated insured S&L institutions.

GSE—government-sponsored enterprise; generally used to refer to Fannie Mae and Freddie Mac. (The FHLBs are also GSEs, but we usually use the term to refer just to Fannie Mae and Freddie Mac.) Ginnie Mae is not a GSE, but a government agency.

HAMP—Home Affordable Mortgage Program. A federal program that ran from 2009 to 2016 and that subsidized the modification of distressed mortgage loans.

HARP—Home Affordable Refinance Program. A federal program that ran from 2009 to 2018 and that allowed underwater homeowners whose mortgages were held by the GSEs to refinance without purchasing private mortgage insurance.

HERA—Housing and Economic Recovery Act. A 2008 law that most significantly created a new regulator for the GSEs, replacing OFHEO with FHFA, and provided a framework for the GSEs to be placed into conservatorship.

HOEPA—Home Ownership and Equity Protection Act. A 1994 federal law that prohibited certain predatory lending practices. A "HOEPA loan" is a high-cost loan that is subject to certain additional regulatory requirements under the law.

HOLC—Home Owners Loan Corporation. A New Deal–era government corporation created to refinance troubled residential mortgages.

HUD—Department of Housing and Urban Development. The federal agency in charge of affordable housing programs and with enforcement authority for fair housing laws.

LLPA—loan-level pricing adjustment. A type of fee charged by the GSE, over and above the standard guaranty fee. The LLPA varies by loan characteristics in the form of a discount from the amount a GSE will pay to purchase a mortgage.

LTMI—low- to moderate-income. LTMI borrowers are borrowers with below-median income. They are not necessarily borrowers of poor credit quality.

LTV—loan-to-value ratio. The ratio of a single mortgage debt on a property to the value of the property.

MBS—mortgage-backed security or mortgage-backed securities. A securitization of mortgage loans. The acronym is used for both singular (security) and plural (securities), as indicated by context.

NFLA—National Farm Loan Association. A federally chartered cooperative corporation owned by farm loan borrowers that acted as a correspondent for Federal Land Banks.

OCC—Office of the Comptroller of the Currency. A federal bank regulator with authority over federally chartered banks.

OFHEO—Office of Federal Housing Enterprise Oversight. The now defunct regulator of the GSE from 1992 to 2008, OFHEO was the partial successor to the FHLBB and was succeeded by FHFA.

PLS—private-label security or private-label securities or private-label securitization. This acronym refers to both an MBS that is not guarantied by a GSE or by Ginnie Mae—that is a private-label security—and to the process of creating such private-label securities—that is private-label securitization. The distinction is generally clear from both context and the use of an article (definite or indefinite) when referring to the securitization product, as opposed to the lack of any article when referring to the securitization process. Additionally, when the acronym refers to the securitization product, rather than the process, it is used for both singular (security) and plural (securities), as indicated by context.

PMI—private mortgage insurance. Insurance provided by private companies that pays the lender (typically) in the event of the borrower default. Required by law for loans purchased by the GSEs that have an LTV of over 80 percent.

QM—Qualified Mortgage. A Qualified Mortgage is one that qualifies for a regulatory safe harbor from the Dodd-Frank Act's Ability-to-Repay requirement.

REO—real estate owned. Real properties a lender has purchased in foreclosure that it holds on its balance sheet until it is able to resell them.

RFC—Reconstruction Finance Corporation. A New Deal–era government corporation that purchased troubled assets.

RTC—Resolution Trust Corporation. A government corporation created in 1989 to hold and resolve the assets of troubled S&Ls.

S&L—saving & loan. A financial institution whose charter limits it to making primarily consumer loans, funded through savings deposits.

SIV—structured investment vehicle. An actively managed securitization that funded long-term assets through the issuance of medium-term notes and commercial paper. SIVs were often used to provide warehouse financing for mortgages that were being assembled for securitization into PLS.

SPV—special purpose vehicle. A legal entity created for securitization transactions that is highly restricted in the type of business it can do, so that its counterparty's risks are more limited than if it were a general purpose business entity.

TBA—To-Be-Announced. The TBA market is a forward contract market in GSE and Ginnie Mae MBS.

VA—Veterans Agency. Federal agency that guaranties certain mortgage loans made to veterans.

Notes

Introduction

1. *See, e.g.,* Catherine Rampell, "Millennials Aren't Buying Homes. Good for Them," *Washington Post*, Aug. 22, 2016; Richard Florida, "Why the U.S. Needs to Fall Out of Love with Homeownership," *Citylab*, Sept. 17, 2013, *at* https://www.citylab.com/equity/2013/09/why-us-needs-fall-out-love-home ownership/6517/.

2. FRED, "Real Median Household Income in the United States," *at* https://fred .stlouisfed.org/series/MEHOINUSA672N/, showing the 2018 real median household income as $63,179.

3. FRED, "Personal Saving Rate," *at* https://fred.stlouisfed.org/series/PSAVERT, showing the average annual personal savings rate over the quarter-century from 1994 to 2018 as 6.08%, and the average annual personal savings rate for the decade from 2009 to 2018 as 7.14%).

4. Milton Friedman, "The Permanent Income Hypothesis," in *A Theory of the Consumption Function* 20 (Milton Friedman, ed., 1957); Franco Modigliani & Richard H. Brumberg, "Utility Analysis and the Consumption Function: An Interpretation of Cross-Section Data," in *Post-Keynesian Economics* 388 (K. K. Kurihara, ed., 1954).

5. *See* the discussion of homeownership and civic engagement later in this chapter, in the section on the social benefits of homeownership.

6. Jesse Bricker *et al.*, "Changes in U.S. Family Finances from 2013 to 2016: Evidence from the Survey of Consumer Finances," 103 *Fed. Res. Bull.* 1, 18 (2017). Bricker and colleagues also note that a higher percentage of households have home equity than any other type of asset excluding bank

accounts and vehicles, and the median value of that home equity ($185,000) is higher than that of any other type of asset.

7. A home purchase is one of the few leveraged investments available to consumers. It is very possible to purchase a home with only 20 percent down, and frequently with as little as 3 percent down. Such financed purchases provide consumers with a degree of leverage not available in any other market and on a scale they could not otherwise obtain. It is possible to purchase stock or commodities on margin, but regulatory margin limits cap leverage at 50 percent, rather than at 80 or 97 percent. Moreover, the amount of margin credit one can obtain for stocks is likely to be far less than for a home purchase, margin limits aside.

8. *See, e.g.*, Laurie Goodman & Christopher Mayer, "Homeownership and the American Dream," 32 *J. Econ. Perspectives* 31, 43–48 (2018), which shows that the financial returns on homeownership from 2002 to 2016 were generally superior to those from renting and investing.

9. Eli Beracha & Ken H. Johnson, "Lessons from Over 30 Years of Buy versus Rent Decisions: Is the American Dream Always Wise?" 40 *R.E. Econ.* 217 (2012).

10. *Ibid.*

11. Eli Beracha *et al.*, "A Revision of the American Dream of Homeownership," 26 *J. Housing Research* 1 (2017). *See also* Zhu Xiao Di *et al.*, "Do Homeowners Achieve More Household Wealth in the Long Run?" 16 *J. Housing Econ.* 274 (2007), which finds that homeowners accumulate more wealth than renters.

12. Todd Sinai & Nicholas Souleles, "Owner-Occupied Housing as a Hedge against Rent Risk," 120 *Q. J. Econ.* 763 (2005); Todd Sinai & Nicholas Souleles, "Can Owning a Home Hedge the Risk of Moving?" 5 *Am. Econ. J: Econ. Pol'y.* 282 (2013).

13. While a home is not a diversified asset, the hedging benefits of homeownership can only be achieved through a single, large asset.

14. Peter Linneman, "An Economic Analysis of the Homeownership Decision," 17 *J. Urban Econ.* 230 (1985).

15. J. Vernon Henderson & Yannis M. Ioannides, "A Model of Housing Tenure Choice," 73 *Am. Econ. Rev.* 98 (1983). Presumably rents are higher when there are limitations on security deposits.

16. *See* Deborah Page-Adams & Nancy Vosler, "Homeownership and Well-Being among Blue-Collar Workers," Washington University Center for Social Development, Working Paper No. 97-5 (1997), which finds that homeowners are better able to adjust to layoffs than renters because of their access to home equity lines of credit.

17. *See* Matthew Desmond, *Evicted: Poverty and Profit in the American City* (2016).

18. 12 C.F.R. § 1024.41(f)(1) (2018).

19. *See* Desmond, *Evicted*, which describes the vulnerability of renters.

20. Bricker *et al.*, "Changes in U.S. Family Finance," at 22. Other than credit card balances, a higher percentage of households have mortgage debt than any

other type of debt, and the median amount owed, $111,000, is a magnitude larger than the median amount owed for any other type of debt. *See ibid.*

21. Bd. of Gov. of the Fed. Res. Sys., "Mortgage Debt Outstanding by Type of Property: One- to Four-Family Residences [MDOTP1T4FR]," June 17, 2019, retrieved from FRED, Federal Reserve Bank of St. Louis, *at* https://fred.stlouisfed.org/series/MDOTP1T4FR.

22. *See ibid.*, concerning the $10.9 trillion in mortgage debt; *see* Bd. of Gov. of the Fed. Res. Sys. (US), "Households and Nonprofit Organizations; Total Liabilities, Level [TLBSHNO]," June 17, 2019, retrieved from FRED, *at* https://fred.stlouisfed.org/series/TLBSHNO, concerning the $16 trillion in household liabilities.

23. Bd. of Gov. of the Fed. Res. Sys., Nonfinancial Corporate Business; Debt Securities and Loans; Liability, Level [BCNSDODNS]," June 17, 2019, retrieved from FRED, *at* https://fred.stlouisfed.org/series/BCNSDODNS.

24. Nat'l. Ass'n. of Realtors, "Jobs Impact of an Existing Home Sale," (2011) *at* https://www.nar.realtor/jobs-impact-of-an-existing-home-purchase.

25. Karen Dynan, "Is a Household Debt Overhang Holding Back Consumption?" Brookings (2012); International Monetary Fund, *Dealing with Household Debt* (2011); Atif Mian & Amir Sufi, "What Explains High Unemployment? The Aggregate Demand Channel," Unpublished Paper, University of Chicago (2011); Atif Mian *et al.*, "Household Balance Sheets, Consumption, and the Economic Slump," Unpublished Paper, University of Chicago (2011).

26. *E.g.*, Ben S. Bernanke, "Bankruptcy, Liquidity, and Recession," 71 *Am. Econ. Rev.* 155 (1981); Ben S. Bernanke, "Nonmonetary Effects of the Financial Crisis in the Propagation of the Great Depression," 73 *Am. Econ. Rev.* 257 (1983); Ben S. Bernanke & Mark Gertler, "Agency Costs, Net Worth, and Business Fluctuations," 79 *Am. Econ. Rev.* 14 (1989).

27. Regional clustering of foreclosures makes the effect more marked. One study found that a 1 percent increase in foreclosures in a given region increased the odds of default for surrounding homeowners by 2.9 percent. Sumit Agarwal *et al.*, "Thy Neighbor's Mortgage: Does Living in a Subprime Neighborhood Affect One's Probability of Default?" 40 *R. E. Econ.* 1 (2012). Concentrated foreclosures can produce lasting blight. Foreclosed properties fall into a state of disrepair when the owners leave, casting a pall on the neighborhood that depresses surrounding house prices.

28. Here we are using the securities-market phrase "selling short," which refers to selling an asset in anticipation of its price dropping. It means something entirely different than the housing market jargon of a "short sale," which refers to the sale of a mortgaged property for less than is owed on the mortgage, with the sale proceeds taken by the lender in satisfaction of the mortgage.

29. Adam J. Levitin & Tara Twomey, "Mortgage Servicing," 28 *Yale J. Reg.* 1, 5–6, 84 (2011).

30. Crime can negatively impact the property values of a neighborhood. Because homeowners are financially more invested in a community than renters, they have more to lose from increased crime rates and thus greater incentive to

take up and support crime prevention programs. Accordingly, there are lower crime rates in communities with higher homeownership and homeowners are less likely to be crime victims. Richard D. Alba *et al.*, "Living with Crime: The Implications of Racial/Ethnic Differences in Suburban Location," 73 *Social Forces* 395 (1984). *See also* Edward Glaeser & Bruce Sacerdote, "Why Is There More Crime in Cities?" 107 *J. Pol. Econ.* s225 (1999). Indeed, one study found that a 1 percent rise in the homeownership rate is associated with a fall in the property crime rate of more than 1 percent and a fall in the violent crime rate of nearly 1 percent. *See* Jinlan Ni & Christopher Decker, "The Impact of Homeownership on Criminal Activity: Empirical Evidence from United States' County Level Data," 2 *Econ. & Bus. J.: Inquiries & Perspectives* 17, 24 (2009). *See also* Daniel MacDonald & Yasemin Dildar, "The Relationship between Homeownership and Sociological Factors in California: A County-Level Study," *Cal. State Univ. San Bernadino Dep't. of Econ.* 23 (2017), which presents a similar finding; and Terrance James Rephann, "Rental Housing and Crime: The Role of Property Ownership and Management," 43 *Annals of Regional Sci.* 435 (2008).

31. Nearly a third of renters move in any given year, whereas only 7 percent of homeowners do the same. *See* David K. Ihrke *et al.*, "Geographical Mobility: 2008 to 2009," in US Census Bureau, *Current Population Reports*, Nov. 2011, P20-565, 9, *at* https://www.census.gov/content/dam/Census/library/publications/2011/demo/p20-565.pdf. Over a five-year window, two-thirds of renters move whereas only one-quarter of homeowners do so. David K. Ihrke & Carol S. Faber, "Geographical Mobility: 2005 to 2010," in US Census Bureau, *Current Population Reports*, Dec. 2012, P20-567, 4, *at* https://www.census.gov/content/dam/Census/library/publications/2012/demo/p20-567.pdf. In large measure this is because renters are younger than homeowners and not as settled in their careers and family lives, but it is also in part because homeowners do not get priced out of neighborhoods by gentrification. Accordingly, the isolated effect solely of renting is to make moving within a year 162 percent more likely. *See* Ihrke *et al.*, "Geographical Mobility," at 14, tbl. 5.

32. Barbara D. Warner & Pamela Wilcox Roundtree, "Local Social Ties in a Community and Crime Model: Questioning the Systematic Nature of Informal Social Control," 44 *Social Problems* 521 (1997). *See also* Robert J. Sampson *et al.*, "Neighborhoods and Violent Crimes," 277 *Sci.* 918 (1997).

33. Richard K. Green & Michelle J. White, "Measuring the Benefits of Homeowning: Effects on Children," 41 *J. Urban Econ.* 441 (1997); Daniel Aaronson, "A Note on the Benefits of Homeownership," 47 *J. Urban Econ.* 356 (2000).

34. Lisa L. Mohanty & Lakshmi K. Raut, "Home Ownership and School Outcomes of Children: Evidence from the PSID Child Development Supplement," 68 *Am. J. Econ. & Sociology* 465 (2009).

35. Eric A. Hanushek *et al.*, "The Cost of Switching Schools," Working Paper, University of Texas (1999).

36. Joseph Harkness & Sandra J. Newman, "Effects of Homeownership on Children: The Role of Neighborhood Characteristics and Family Income," 9 *Fed. Res. Bank of N.Y. Econ. Pol'y Rev.* 87 (2003).

37. Kevin R. Cox, "Housing Tenure and Neighborhood Activism," 18 *Urban Affairs Quarterly* 107 (1982).

38. *Ibid.*

39. *See* Denise DiPasquale & Edward Glaeser, "Incentives and Social Capital: Are Homeowners Better Citizens?" 45 *J. Urban Econ.* 354 (1998), which found a 77 percent local election voting rate for homeowners versus 52 percent for renters.

40. *Ibid.*

41. James L. Sweeney, "Housing Unit Maintenance and the Mode of Tenure," 8 *J. Econ. Theory* 111 (1974).

42. J. Vernon Henderson & Yannis M. Ioannides, "A Model of Housing Tenure Choice," 73 *Am. Econ. Rev.* 98 (1983).

43. *See* Thomas Piketty, *Capital in the 21st Century* (2014).

44. Matthew Rognlie, "Deciphering the Fall and Rise in the Net Capital Share: Accumulation or Scarcity?" 46 *Brookings Papers on Econ. Activity* 1, 2 (2015).

45. *Ibid.*

46. Gianna La Cava, "Housing Prices, Mortgage Interest Rates and the Rising Share of Capital Income in the United States," BIS Working Paper, No. 572 (July 2016).

47. Of course, some peer countries, notably Germany, have a lower rate of homeownership. Countries can achieve social benefits through universal access to housing subsidies and through a web of rental regulations, but rental regulations are also likely to reduce mobility and raise the cost of housing overall because they reduce supply.

48. 12 C.F.R. § 1026.19(e)(1)(iii) (2018), which requires the loan estimate to be delivered to the borrower at least three days before closing and the closing disclosure to be delivered at least three days before closing.

49. Atif Mian *et al.*, "Foreclosures, House Prices, and the Real Economy," 70 *J. Fin.* 2587 (2015). *See also* Kristopher Gerardi *et al.*, "Foreclosure Externalities: Some New Evidence," 87 *J. Urban Econ.* 42 (2015); Elliot Anenberg & Edward Kung, "Estimates of the Size and Source of Price Declines Due to Nearby Foreclosures," 104 *Am. Econ. Rev.* 2527 (2014); John Campbell *et al.*, "Forced Sales and House Prices," 101 *Am. Econ. Rev.* 2108 (2011); John P. Harding *et al.*, "The Contagion Effect of Foreclosed Properties," 66 *J. Urban Econ.* 164 (2009); Zhenguo Lin *et al.*, "Spillover Effects of Foreclosures on Neighborhood Property Values," 38 *J. R. E. Fin. & Econ.* 387 (2009); Dan Immergluck & Geoff Smith, "The External Costs of Foreclosure: The Impact of Single-Family Mortgage Foreclosures on Property Values," 17 *Housing Pol'y Debate* 57 (2006).

50. In the first quarter of 2018, all-cash purchases were 30 percent of single-family and condo sales; all other purchases involved financing. *See* ATTOM Data Solutions, "54 Percent of U.S. Metros Post Median Home Prices Above Pre-

Recession Peaks in Q1 2018," Apr. 17, 2018, *at* https://www.attomdata.com
/news/market-trends/home-sales-prices/q1-2018-u-s-home-sales-report/.

51. *See* Thorstein Veblen, *The Theory of Business Enterprise* 105–6, 112–13
(1904), which notes that a cycle in which an increase in collateral value increases credit availability, which then further increases collateral value; Nobuhiro Kiyotaki & John Moore, "Credit Cycles," 105 *J. Pol. Econ.* 211,
212–13 (1997), which theorizes that there is a cycle in which increasing collateral value increases credit availability, which then further increases collateral value; and Atif Mian & Amir Sufi, "The Consequences of Mortgage
Credit Expansion: Evidence from the U.S. Mortgage Default Crisis," 124 *Q. J.
Econ.* 1449, 1490–92 (2009), which finds support for the Kiyotaki & Moore
model in housing price and credit growth.

52. *See* Susan M. Wachter, "The Market Structure of Securitisation and the US
Housing Bubble," 230 *Nat'l. Instit. Econ. Rev.* 34 (2014), which shows that
a monopolist will internalize systemic externalities.

1. Housing Finance before the New Deal

1. US Census Bureau, *Report on Farms and Homes: Proprietorship and Indebtedness in the United States*, at 19, tbl. 7 (1890). *See also* George K. Holmes,
"Investigations of Mortgages and Farm and Home Proprietorship in the United
States," 56 *J. Royal Stat. Soc.* 443, 466 (1893), which found a 43 percent
homeownership rate.

2. US Census Bureau, *Report on Farms and Homes: Proprietorship and Indebtedness in the United States*, at 21, diagram 1 (1890).

3. *Ibid.*, at 169, diagram 21.

4. *Ibid.*, at 19, tbl. 7.

5. *Ibid.*, at 169, diagram 210.

6. *Ibid.*, at 24.

7. *Ibid.*, at 19; Holmes, "Investigations of Mortgages," at 466.

8. US Census Bureau, *Report on Farms and Homes*, at 19 (1890).

9. US Census Bureau, "Historical Survey of Housing Tables: Units," Oct. 31,
2011, *at* http://www.census.gov/hhes/www/housing/census/historic/units
.html.

10. US Census Bureau, "Historical Survey of Housing Tables: Plumbing Facilities,"
Oct. 31, 2011, *at* http://www.census.gov/hhes/www/housing/census/historic
/plumbing.html.

11. *Ibid.*

12. Steve Kerch, "1900 to 2010: Evolution of the American Home Today: Fun
Housing Facts," *Chicago Tribune*, June 18, 2000, *at* http://articles.chicagotri
bune.com/2000-06-18/business/0006180063_1_single-family-homes-two-or
-three-bedrooms-new-housing-units.

13. US Census Bureau, "Median and Average Square Feet of Floor Area in New
Single-Family Houses Completed by Location," (2018) *at* https://www.census
.gov/construction/chars/xls/sewer_cust.xls, which reports a median of 2,386

square feet and an average of 2,588 square feet for new single-family home completions in 2018.

14. US Census Bureau, "Historical Census of Housing: Crowding," *at* http://www .census.gov/hhes/www/housing/census/historic/crowding.html; Christopher Mazur and Ellen Wilson, "Housing Characteristics: 2010," 2010 Census Briefs, Oct. 2011, *at* https://www.census.gov/prod/cen2010/briefs/c2010br-07 .pdf; F. John Devaney, "Tracking the American Dream, 50 Years of Housing History from the Census Bureau: 1940 to 1990," *Current Housing Reports* H121/94-1, May 1994, *at* http://www.huduser.org/portal//Publications/pdf /HUD-7775.pdf.

15. FRED, "Real Median Household Income in the United States," *at* https://fred .stlouisfed.org/series/MEHOINUSA672N/.

16. Press release, National Association of Realtors, "Existing-Home Sales Slip 0.7 Percent in July," Aug. 22, 2018. New homes sold in 2018 for a median price of $326,400. *See* US Census Bureau, "Median and Average Sales Prices of Houses Sold by Region," data for 1963–2018, *at* https://www.census.gov /construction/nrs/pdf/pricerega.pdf.

17. Leo Grebler *et al.*, *Capital Formation in Residential Real Estate: Trends and Prospects*, at 232 (1956); Richard H. Keehn & Gene Smiley, "Mortgage Lending by National Banks," 51 *Bus. His. Rev.* 474, 478–79 (1977); Allan G. Bogue, *From Prairie to Corn Belt* 176 (1963), which states: "Most loans were repayable at the end of five years or by installments over a short term of years. The long-term amortized loan was not common in this period." *See also* Richard Green & Susan M. Wachter, "The American Mortgage in Historical and International Context," 19 *J. Econ. Perspectives* 93, 94 (2005). Building and loan associations did offer amortizing mortgages as early as the 1880s, but prior to the New Deal, these were not standard products. *See* Jonathan Rose & Kenneth A. Snowden, "The New Deal and the Origins of the Modern American Real Estate Loan Contract," NBER Working Paper 18388, Sept. 2012, *at* http://www.nber.org/papers/w18388. The only cross-institutional-type data on longer-term amortizing loans comes from an out-of-print study, J. E. Morton, "Appendix C: Periodic Data of Institutionally Held Nonfarm Mortgage Debt, Loan Characteristics, and Credit Experience," in *Urban Mortgage Lending: Comparative Markets and Experience* (1956), *available at* http://www.nber.org/chapters/c2854.pdf. Morton's duration data is weighted by dollar volume, covers only urban, nonpurchase money loans with unclear geographic coverage, and is based on very small samples, with $n < 150$ and as small as 18 for some years.

18. D. M. Frederiksen, "Mortgage Banking in America," 2 *J. Pol. Econ.* 203, 204–5 (1894).

19. H. Morton Bodfish & A. C. Bayless, "Costs and Encumbrance Ratios in a Highly Developed Real Estate Market," 4 *J. L. & Pub. Utility Econ.* 125, 131 (1928).

20. *Ibid.*, at 131.

21. Holmes, "Investigations of Mortgages," at 471.

22. Frederiksen, "Mortgage Banking in America," at 204–5.

23. H. Morton Bodfish & A. C. Bayless, "Costs and Encumbrance Ratios in a Highly Developed Real Estate Market," 4 *J. L. & Pub. Utility Econ.* 125, 127 (1928).

24. *Ibid.*, at 133.

25. *See* Leo Grebler *et al.*, *Capital Formation in Residential Real Estate* 127, tbl. 2 (1956).

26. *See ibid.*

27. Bodfish & Bayless, "Costs and Encumbrance Ratios," at 134 n.6 (1928). *But see ibid.*, at 131, n.17, where the authors note that amortization was more common with loans from institutional lenders. Curiously, unlike first-lien mortgages, most second-lien mortgages were amortized. *See ibid.*, at 134.

28. John M. Gries with James Ford, "Home Finance and Taxation," Vol. 2 of *President's Conference on Home Building and Home Ownership, Final Report* 26 (1932).

29. Marc A. Weiss, "Marketing and Financing Home Ownership: Mortgage Lending and Public Policy in the United States, 1918–1989," 18 *Bus. & Econ. Hist.* (2d Series), 109, 111 (1989).

30. Grebler *et al.*, *Capital Formation in Residential Real Estate*, at 234, tbl. 67.

31. *See ibid.*, at 228, tbl. 64.

32. *See* Raymond J. Saulnier, *Urban Mortgage Lending by Life Insurance Companies* 83, 85 (1950), which also notes that "Amortization provisions are of most importance on loans made sufficiently long before a period of mortgage distress to permit repayments to reduce the principal substantially."

33. Saulnier, *Urban Mortgage Lending by Life Insurance Companies*, at 80.

34. MBA National Delinquency Surveys.

35. Lance Davis, "The Investment Market, 1870–1914: The Evolution of a National Market," 33 *J. Econ. Hist.* 355, 371–72 (1961).

36. Kenneth A. Snowden, "Mortgage Lending and American Urbanization, 1880–1890," 48 *J. Econ. Hist.* 273, 275 (1988).

37. Fredricksen, "Mortgage Banking in America," at 209.

38. US Census Bureau, *Report on Farms and Homes: Proprietorship and Indebtedness in the United States*, at 47–48.

39. US Census Bureau, Selected Historical Decennial Census Population and Housing Counts, Urban and Rural Populations, *at* http://www.census.gov /population/www/censusdata/files/table-4.pdf. The Census Bureau changed its definition of "urban" in 1950. This table uses the old definition for 1790–1940 and the new definition for 1950–present.

40. Rural markets tend to be less liquid than urban markets. While this should merely reduce property values, it may also make lenders less eager to lend because of the possibility that they will end up with a hard-to-dispose-of property in the event of a foreclosure.

41. Davis, "The Investment Market," at 392, which found empirical confirmation of regional interest rate differentials for both short-term and long-term capital; Kenneth A. Snowden, "Mortgage Rates and American Capital Market Development in the Late Nineteenth Century," 47 *J. Econ. Hist.* 671, 688–89

(1987), which found variation in regional home and farm mortgage interest rates in excess of predicted risk premia; Snowden, "Mortgage Lending and American Urbanization," at 285; US Census Bureau, *Report on Farms and Homes: Proprietorship and Indebtedness in the United States*, at 116–17.

42. Louis Winnick, "The Burden of the Residential Mortgage Debt," 11 *J. Fin.* 166, 168 (1956); Grebler *et al.*, *Capital Formation*, at 468–71, tbl. N-2 (1956). *But see* Frederiksen, "Mortgage Banking in America," at 204–5, which gives a figure of 73 percent for individual mortgage holdings.

43. John H. Fahey, "Competition and Mortgage Rates," 15 *J. Land & Pub. Utility Econ* 150 (1939). Fahey was chairman of the Federal Home Loan Bank Board.

44. Bodfish & Bayless, "Costs and Encumbrance Ratios," at 133.

45. Frederiksen, "Mortgage Banking in America," at 205.

46. *Ibid.*

47. Significant branch banking restrictions remained in place until 1994. *See* Riegle-Neal Interstate Banking and Branching Efficiency Act of 1994, Pub. L. 103-328, § 101, 108 Stat. 2338, 2339 (Sept. 29, 1994), which repealed the restrictions on interstate branch banking.

48. Kenneth A. Snowden, "Mortgage Securitization in the United States: Twentieth Century Developments in Historical Perspective," in *Anglo-American Financial Systems: Institutions and Markets in the Twentieth Century*, at 261 (Michael D. Bordo & Richard Sylla, eds., 1995). *See also* Kenneth A. Snowden, "The Evolution of Interregional Mortgage Lending Channels, 1870–1940: The Life Insurance-Mortgage Company Connection," in *Coordination and Information: Historical Perspectives on the Organization of Enterprises*, at 209 (Naomi R. Lamoreaux & Daniel M.G. Raff, eds. 1995), *available at* http://www.nber.org/chapters/c8755.pdf.

49. National Bank Act, § 8, 13 Stat. 99, 101 (Jun. 3, 1864), *codified as amended at* 12 U.S.C. § 24(7) (2018). *See also Nat'l Bank v. Matthews*, 98 U.S. 621, 626 (1878).

50. *See* Richard H. Keehn & Gene Smiley, "Mortgage Lending by National Banks," 51 *Bus. His. Rev.* 474 (1977), which discusses the literature.

51. Federal Reserve Act, Pub. L. 63-43, § 24, 38 Stat. 251, 273 (Dec. 23, 1913), *codified at* 12 U.S.C. § 371. On the history of restrictions on real estate investment by national banks, *see* John A. Deangelis, "Riches Do Not Last Forever: Real Estate Investment by National Banks," 1991 *U. Ill. L. Rev.* 777, 779–784.

52. McFadden Act, Pub. L. 69-639, § 16, 44 Stat. 1224, 1232–33 (Feb. 25, 1927). *See also* Gries with Ford, "Home Finance and Taxation," at ix (1932).

53. Garn–St. Germain Depository Institutions Act of 1982, Pub. L. 97-320, § 403(a), 96 Stat. 1469, 1510–11 (Oct. 15, 1982), *codified as amended at* 12 U.S.C. § 371 (1988). *See also* 48 Fed. Reg. 40,699 (Sept. 9, 1983), *codified at* 12 C.F.R. § 34.1 [1990]). National banks appear to still be forbidden from entering partnerships whose stated purpose is to invest in real estate; *Merchants' Nat'l Bank v. Wehrmann*, 202 U.S. 295, 301 (1906); OCC Interp.

Ltr. 435, [1988–89 Transfer Binder] Fed. Banking L. Rep. (CCH) ¶ 85,659 (June 30, 1988).

54. Riegle-Neal Interstate Banking and Branching Efficiency Act of 1994, § 101.

55. H. Peers Brewer, "Eastern Money and Western Mortgages in the 1870s," 50 *Bus. Hist. Rev.* 356, 358–59 (1976); Snowden, "The Evolution of Interregional Mortgage Lending Channels," at 219.

56. Paul M. Gregory, "The Mortgage Portfolio of Mutual Savings Banks," 61 *Q. J. Econ.* 232, 249, 249 nn.8–9 (1947).

57. *Ibid.*, at 253.

58. Gries with Ford, "Home Finance and Taxation," at ix (1932).

59. Davis, "The Investment Market," at 381, 383; *see also* Snowden, "The Evolution of Interregional Mortgage Lending Channels," at 235.

60. Saulnier, *Urban Mortgage Lending by Life Insurance Companies*, at 22–23.

61. *Ibid.*, at 20–21.

62. Earl Sylvester Sparks & Thomas N. Carver, *History and Theory of Agricultural Credit in the United States* 57 (1932).

63. James Grant, *Money of the Mind: Borrowing and Lending in American from the Civil War to Michael Milken* 296 (1992).

64. James Fenimore Cooper, *Home as Found* (1838); Charles Dickens, *Martin Chuzzlewit* (1844); Mark Twain and Dudley Warner, *The Gilded Age* (1873).

65. Fredricksen, "Mortgage Banking in America," at 210.

66. Snowden, "Mortgage Securitization in the United States," at 270.

67. *Ibid.*, at 279. *See* George A. Akerlof, "The Market for 'Lemons': Quality Uncertainty and the Market Mechanism," 84 *Q. J. Econ.* 488 (1970). *See also* Claire A. Hill, "Securitization: A Low-Cost Sweetener for Lemons," 74 *Wash. U. L.Q.* 1061 (1996).

68. *Ibid.*, at 271–73.

69. The 1870s saw a 44 percent increase in farm acreage and a 54 percent increase in the number of farms in the mid-continent states near the frontier. *See* Brewer, "Eastern Money and Western Mortgages in the 1870s," at 356–57.

70. Snowden, "Mortgage Securitization in the United States," at 274–77.

71. *Ibid.*, at 277. *See also* Brewer, "Eastern Money and Western Mortgages in the 1870s," at 372, 378–79.

72. Snowden, "Mortgage Securitization in the United States," at 278–80.

73. *Ibid.*, at 279.

74. *Ibid.*, at 278.

75. *Ibid.*

76. *Ibid.*, at 279–80.

77. J. W. Brabner Smith, "The Financing of Large-Scale Rental Housing," 5 *Law & Contemp. Problems* 608 (1938).

78. *See also* James Graaskamp, "Development and Structure of Mortgage Loan Guaranty Insurance in the United States," 34 *J. Risk and Ins.* 47, 49 (1967). Some title companies had been engaged in insuring prompt payment of interest on mortgages since at least 1895, utilizing loose wording in the title insurance statute. The 1904 law ratified their actions and gave them expanded authority. *See ibid.*

79. Snowden, "Mortgage Securitization in the United States," at 283–84; *see also* Graaskamp, "Development and Structure of Mortgage Loan Guaranty Insurance," at 48. For a detailed history of the mortgage guaranty industry, *see* George Alger, *Report on the Operation, Conduct, and Management of Title and Mortgage Guarantee Corporations* (1934), *available at* https://www.aei.org/wp-content/uploads/2012/05/-alger-commission-report_13595669733.pdf.

80. Graaskamp, "Development and Structure of Mortgage Loan Guaranty Insurance," at 49.

81. *Ibid.*, at 49–50; Snowden, "Mortgage Securitization in the United States," at 284.

82. Snowden, "Mortgage Securitization in the United States," at 285.

83. *See also* Graaskamp, "Development and Structure of Mortgage Loan Guaranty Insurance," at 49.

84. Snowden, "Mortgage Securitization in the United States," at 285; Graaskamp, "Development and Structure of Mortgage Loan Guaranty Insurance," at 49.

85. Graaskamp, "Development and Structure of Mortgage Loan Guaranty Insurance," at 51.

86. Snowden, "Mortgage Securitization in the United States," at 285.

87. Graaskamp, "Development and Structure of Mortgage Loan Guaranty Insurance," at 50.

88. *Ibid.*

89. *Ibid.*

90. Wisc. Admin. Code, Ins. § 3.09 (Register Mar. 1957 at 8d–8e). *See also* Graaskamp, "Development and Structure of Mortgage Loan Guaranty Insurance," at 47, 55.

91. Single-property commercial-mortgage backed securities exist.

92. Snowden, "Mortgage Securitization in the United States," at 286.

93. *Ibid.*, at 287.

94. *Ibid.*

95. *Ibid.*

96. *Ibid.*

97. *Ibid.*

98. *Ibid.*

99. *Ibid.*

100. *Ibid.*

101. *Ibid.*

102. Grant, *Money of the Mind*, at 162.

103. Snowden, "Mortgage Securitization in the United States," at 278–88; Grant, *Money of the Mind*, at 164.

104. Snowden, "Mortgage Securitization in the United States," at 286.

105. *Ibid.*, at 288.

106. Grant, *Money of the Mind*, at 165–67.

107. *Ibid.*, at 169.

108. Snowden, "Mortgage Securitization in the United States," at 288.

109. Grant, *Money of the Mind*, at 171.

110. Snowden, "Mortgage Securitization in the United States," at 263.
111. Of course, federal land policy had an indirect impact on housing by encouraging frontier settlement.
112. William J. Williams, "Accommodating American Shipyard Workers, 1917–1918: The Pacific Coast and the Federal Government's First Public Housing and Transit Programs," 84 *Pac. Nw. Q.* 51 (1993).
113. Frederick Law Olmsted [Jr.], "Lessons from Housing Developments of the United States Housing Corporation," 8 *Monthly Labor Rev.* 27 (1919).
114. Williams, "Accommodating American Shipyard Workers," at 54.
115. Act of Mar. 1, 1918, Pub. L. 65-102, 40 Stat. 438 (1918).
116. Act of Mar. 1, 1918, which authorized a $50 million appropriation; *see also* Act of July 1, 1918, Pub. L. 65-181, 40 Stat. 634, 651 (Jul. 1, 1918), which authorized a $75 million appropriation.
117. *See also* John L. Tierney, "War Housing: The Emergency Fleet Corporation Experience," 17 *J. Land & Pub. Utility Econ.* 151, 155 (1941).
118. Williams, "Accommodating American Shipyard Workers," at 55.
119. *Ibid.*, at 57. The Ordnance Department also engaged in some housing construction for munitions plant workers. *See also* Curtice N. Hitchcock, "The War Housing Program and Its Future," 27 *J. Pol. Econ.* 241, 252 (1919).
120. Williams, "Accommodating American Shipyard Workers," at 56, 59.
121. Olmsted, "Lessons from Housing Developments," at 30.
122. Williams, "Accommodating American Shipyard Workers," at 58.
123. Henry E. Hoagland, "Housing and National Defense," 16 *J. Land & Pub. Utility Econ.* 377, 378 (1940).
124. *Ibid.*
125. John L. Tierney, "War Housing: The Emergency Fleet Corporation Experience," 17 *J. Land & Pub. Utility Econ.* 303, 305–6 (1941).
126. *Ibid.*, at 305.
127. *See, e.g.*, Hitchcock, "The War Housing Program."
128. In this regard, they resemble the federal government's first foray into consumer credit regulation, which was motivated by a concern about war production in the lead-up to World War II. *See* Adam J. Levitin, "The Consumer Financial Protection Bureau: An Introduction," 32 *Rev. Banking & Fin. L.* 321, 325 (2013). Similarly, the federal government's regulation of short-term, small-dollar lending, with the Military Lending Act, was motivated as much by national security concerns as concerns for consumer protection.
129. *See* Stephen Daggett, "Costs of Major U.S. Wars," Congressional Research Service Report, June 29, 2010, at 2, which gave the cost of World War I in current year dollars as $20 billion.
130. Bruce I. Bustard, "Homes for War Workers: Federal Housing Policy during World War I," 24:1 *Prologue* 33, 42 (Spring 1992).
131. D. C. Willis, chairman of the Board of the Cleveland Federal Reserve Bank, Home Building and Thrift, at the convention of the Ohio Building Association League, Oct. 15, 1919, printed in 40:1 *Am. Bldg. Ass'n News* 28 (Jan. 1920)

132. "Ants and Crickets," 40:4 *Am. Bldg. Ass'n News* 152 (Apr. 1920).
133. Raymond F. Frazier, "Amortization of Savings Bank Loans, Before the Convention of the American Bankers' Association, St. Louis, MO, Sept. 29, 1919," in 40:1 *Am. Bldg. Ass'n News* 32, 33 (Jan. 1920).
134. *See, e.g.,* 40:1 *Am. Bldg. Ass'n. News* 1 (Jan. 1920); 40:7 *Am. Bldg. Ass'n News* 289 (July 1920).
135. Olmsted, "Lessons from Housing Developments," at 33.
136. *Ibid.*
137. *Ibid.*, at 32.
138. Paul Matthew Stoner, "The Mortgage Market—Today and after World War I," 19 *J. of Land & Pub. Utility Econ.* 224, 225 (1943), which explains that the housing shortage of 1919–1922 was perceived as a public health issue.
139. K. V. Haymaker, "Financing Home Building," 40:3 *Am. Bldg. Ass'n News* 113–14 (Mar. 1920).
140. "Annual Report of the New York League of Savings and Loan Associations," 40:7 *Am. Bldg. Ass'n News* 316 (July 1920).
141. *See* Weiss, "Marketing and Financing Home Ownership," at 109, which states that "The government's objective [in the 1918 "Own Your Own Home" campaign by the Department of Labor] was to defeat radical protest and restore political stability by encouraging urban workers to become home owners."
142. Marc A. Weiss, "Own Your Own Home: Housing Policy and the Real Estate Industry," paper presented to the Conference on Robert Moses and the Planned Environment, Hofstra University, June 11, 1998, at 6.
143. David T. Rowlands, "Urban Housing Activities of the Federal Government," 190 *Annals of the Am. Aca. of Poli. & Soc. Sci.* 83 (1937).
144. Edward L. Schaub, "The Regulation of Rentals during the War Period," 28 *J. Pol. Econ.* 1 (1920).
145. "Statutes Relating to the Housing Shortage," 23 *Colum. L. Rev.* 583, 585 (1923).
146. Stoner, "The Mortgage Market," at 225.
147. *Ibid.*, at 226.
148. *Ibid.*, at 226–27.
149. *Ibid.*, at 227.
150. Eugene N. White, "Lessons from the Great American Real Estate Boom and Bust of the 1920s," NBER Working Paper 15573, 12–14, *at* http://www.nber.org/papers/w15573.
151. *Ibid.*, at 14–46.
152. *See* Frederick M. Babcock, "Influence of the Federal Housing Administration on Mortgage Lending Policy," 15 *J. Land & Pub. Utility Econ.* 1 (1939).

2. The New Deal Mortgage

1. *See* Kenneth T. Jackson, *Crabgrass Frontier: The Suburbanization of the United States* 193 (1985).
2. *See* Bd. of Gov. of Fed. Res. Sys., *Financial Accounts of the United States, Statistical Release Z.1,* tbls. 218 and 219 (1952–2008); and Leo Grebler

et al., *Capital Formation in Residential Real Estate: Trends and Prospects* 468–71, tbl. N-2 (1956), which covers the years 1896–1951.

3. *See ibid.*, at 468–71, tbl. N-2.

4. Maureen O'Hara & David Easley, "The Postal Savings System in the Depression," 29 *J. Econ. Hist.* 741, 745–50 (1979).

5. Josephine H. Ewalt, *A Business Reborn: The Savings and Loan Story, 1930–1960* 178 (1962).

6. O'Hara & Easley, "The Postal Savings System," at 746–47.

7. Horace Russell, *Savings and Loan Associations* 462 (1956).

8. O'Hara & Easley, "The Postal Savings System," at 748.

9. Paul Matthew Stoner, "The Mortgage Market—Today and after World War I," 19 *J. of Land & Pub. Utility Econ.*, 224, 227 (1943). Starting in 1974, the Federal Reserve was permitted to rediscount mortgages, like the FHLBs. *See* The Emergency Home Purchase Assistance Act of 1974, Pub. L. 93-449, § 5, 88 Stat. 1364, 1368 (Oct. 18, 1974), *codified at* 12 U.S.C. § 347b(a), 2nd para.

10. Federal Home Loan Bank Board, *Sixth Annual Report* 21 (1938).

11. *Ibid.*

12. David A. Bridewell, *The Federal Home Loan Bank Board and Its Agencies: A History of the Facts Surrounding the Passage of the Creating Legislation, the Establishment and Organization of the Federal Home Loan Bank Board and the Bank System, the Savings and Loan System, the Home Owners' Loan Corporation, and the Federal Savings and Loan Insurance Corporation* 172 (1938). *See also* Marc A. Weiss, "Marketing and Financing Home Ownership: Mortgage Lending and Public Policy in the United States, 1918–1989," 18 *Bus. & Econ. Hist.* (2nd Series), 109, 112 (1989).

13. *See* Jonathan D. Rose, "A Primer on Farm Debt Relief Programs during the 1930s," Fed. Res. Bd. Finance and Economic Discussion Series, No. 2013-33, Apr. 22, 2013, at 4, *available at* https://www.federalreserve.gov/pubs/FEDS /2013/201333/201333pap.pdf; David C. Wheelock, "Changing the Rules: State Mortgage Foreclosure Moratoria during the Great Depression," *Fed. Res. Bank of St. Louis Rev.*, 569 (2008).

14. *Historical Statistics of the United States: Millennial Edition on Line* (2006), Series Dc 1257.

15. Weiss, "Marketing and Financing Home Ownership," at 112.

16. *Historical Statistics of the United States: Millennial Edition On Line* (2006), Series Dc 510.

17. In 1931, the Hoover administration convened a major conference on home building and homeownership. *See* Kenneth A. Snowden, "Mortgage Securitization in the United States: Twentieth Century Developments in Historical Perspective," in *Anglo-American Financial Systems: Institutions and Markets in the Twentieth Century* 261, 290 (Michael D. Bordo & Richard Sylla, eds., 1995). While there was broad consensus that some sort of secondary housing financing system needed to be created, there was little consensus on its shape. There were three primary proposals on the table. First was a proposal to create a central mortgage bank that would purchase loans from local, federally char-

tered mortgage banks and issue debentures on the collateral. Any qualified mortgage originator could join the system by contributing capital to a local federally chartered mortgage bank. This proposal was pushed by the National Association of Real Estate Builders. *See ibid.*

   A second proposal was to create a home mortgage reserve bank that would provide temporary liquidity for all qualified residential mortgage lenders just as the Federal Reserve did for commercial banks. The third proposal, which was supported by the US Building and Loan League and strongly opposed by commercial banks, was to create a home mortgage reserve bank solely for savings and loan institutions. *See ibid.; see also* Marc A. Weiss, "Own Your Own Home: Housing Policy and the Real Estate Industry," paper presented to the Conference on Robert Moses and the Planned Environment, Hofstra University, June 11, 1998, at 6.

18. This is not meant to imply that these four pieces were the entirety of federal involvement in the housing market. For example, the Emergency Relief and Construction Act of 1932 authorized the Reconstruction Finance Corporation to make loans to corporations formed to provide low income housing or urban renewal. *See* Emergency Relief and Construction Act of 1932, Pub. L. 72-302, § 201(a)(2), 47 Stat. 709, 711 (Jul. 21, 1932).

19. Federal Home Loan Bank Act, Pub. L. 72-304, 47 Stat. 725 (Jul. 22, 1932).

20. Weiss, "Own Your Own Home," at 6.

21. Federal Home Loan Bank Act, § 4(a).

22. *Ibid.*, § 6(f).

23. *Ibid.*, § 13.

24. *Ibid.*, § 11(f), *codified at* 12 U.S.C. § 1431(b)–(c) (2018). The joint and several liability creates a danger of individual FHLBs attempting to free ride by engaging in riskier lending activities, as the costs are borne by the other banks in the system. Moreover, because financial institutions that operate across state lines are often eligible to be members of more than one FHLB, they are able to direct business to those with the laxest lending standards. *See* Mark J. Flannery and W. Scott Frame, "The Federal Home Loan Bank System: The "Other" Housing GSE," *Fed. Res. Bank of Atlanta Econ. Rev.*, 33 (3rd quarter 2006).

25. Federal Home Loan Bank Act, § 15, *codified at* 12 U.S.C. § 1435 (2018). ("All obligations of Federal Home Loan Banks shall plainly state that such obligations are not obligations of the United States and are not guarantied by the United States.")

26. Ernest M. Fisher, "Changing Institutional Patterns of Mortgage Lending," 5 *J. Fin.* 307, 311 (1950).

27. *See* 12 U.S.C. § 1421(a)(1)(C), which restructured FHLB membership eligibility to institutions making long-term loans, and deferring to Federal Home Loan Bank Board discretion on what is long-term; 12 C.F.R. § 925.1, which defined "long term" as longer than five years; Federal Home Loan Bank Act, § 10(a)(1), which defined the size limit; and *ibid.*, § 10(b), which stated that mortgages with more than fifteen years remaining to maturity were ineligible as collateral for FHLB advances.

The fifteen-year limit was gradually extended to thirty years and then abolished. *See* Pub. L. 74-76, § 4, 49 Stat. 293, 295 (May 28, 1935), which extended the term to twenty years; Pub. L. 80-311, 61 Stat. 714 (Aug. 1, 1947), which extended the term to twenty-five years; Housing Act of 1964, Pub. L. 88-560, § 906, 78 Stat. 769, 805 (Sep. 2, 1964), which extended the term to thirty years; and Garn–St. Germain Depository Institutions Act of 1982, Pub. L. 97-320, § 352, 96 Stat. 1469, 1507 (Oct. 15, 1982), which abolished the term limitation.

28. Federal Home Loan Bank Act, §§ 10(a)(1)–(2), 725, 731–32.
29. For example, the National Housing Act reduced the term length for amortized loans to six years and raised the advancing limits to 65 percent of the principal, capped at 60 percent LTV, for amortized loans, and to 50 percent of principal, capped at 40 percent LTV, for other loans. *See* National Housing Act of 1934, Pub. L. 73-479, § 501, 48 Stat. 1246, 1261 (Jun. 27, 1934).
30. Federal Home Loan Bank Act, § 10(c).
31. *Ibid.*, § 11(i).
32. *Ibid.*, § 4(d), *repealed by* Home Owners' Loan Act of 1933, Pub.L. 73–43, § 3, 48 Stat. 128 (Jun. 13, 1933).
33. Federal Home Loan Bank Act, § 16.
34. *Ibid.*, § 11(e).
35. *Ibid.*, § 4(e).
36. Home Owners' Loan Act of 1933, § 5(c).
37. *Ibid.*, § 5.
38. *Ibid.*, § 5(d).
39. National Housing Act, § 402.
40. Weiss, "Marketing and Financing Home Ownership," at 113.
41. Federal Home Loan Bank Act, § 4(d), which provided that direct lending authority would expire when government-owned stock was retired.
42. Peter M. Carrozzo, "A New Deal for the American Mortgage: The Home Owners' Loan Corporation, the National Housing Act, and the Birth of the National Mortgage Market," 17 *U. Miami Bus. L. Rev.* 1, 9 (2008), which ascribed limited FHLB direct mortgage lending to the FHLB's conservative nature as reserve banks.
43. Home Owners' Loan Act of 1933, § 4(a)–(b).
44. *Ibid.*, § 3.
45. C. Lowell Harriss, *History and Policies of the Home Owners' Loan Corporation* 11, 35 (1951). *See also* Home Owners' Loan Act of 1933, § 4(d).
46. Snowden, "Mortgage Securitization in the United States," at 291; Harriss, *History and Policies of the Home Owners' Loan Corporation*, at 1; Home Owners' Loan Act of 1933, § 4(d).
47. Harriss, *History and Policies of the Home Owners' Loan Corporation*, at 1; Home Owners' Loan Act of 1933, § 4(d). The interest rate on all HOLC loans was originally 5 percent, but it was reduced in October 1939 to 4.5 percent. *See* Leo Grebler *et al.*, *Capital Formation in Residential Real Estate: Trends and Prospects* 257 (1956).
48. Snowden, "Mortgage Securitization in the United States," at 292; Harriss, *History and Policies of the Home Owners' Loan Corporation*, at 1.

49. Harriss, *History and Policies of the Home Owners' Loan Corporation*, at 1–2; Ellen Seidman & Andrew Jakabovics, "Learning from the Past: The Asset Disposition Experiences of the Home Owners Loan Corporation, the Resolution Trust Corporation and the Asset Control Area Program," *at* http://www.americanprogress.org/issues/2008/09/pdf/econ_memo.pdf.
50. David M. French, "The Contest for a National System of Home-Mortgage Finance," 35 *Am. Pol. Sci. Rev.* 53, 54 (1941).
51. *Ibid.*
52. Snowden, *History and Policies of the Home Owners' Loan Corporation*, at 291–92.
53. Home Owners' Loan Act of 1933, § 4(c), which specified the guaranties concerning interest; Pub. L. 73-178, 48 Stat. 643 (Apr. 27, 1934), which specified the guaranties concerning principal and interest.
54. Snowden, *History and Policies of the Home Owners' Loan Corporation*, at 291–92.
55. *Ibid.*, at 292.
56. Jackson, *Crabgrass Frontier*, at 196.
57. Weiss, "Marketing and Financing Home Ownership," at 15.
58. *Ibid.*
59. Carrozzo, "A New Deal for the American Mortgage," at 23; Harriss, *History and Policies of the Home Owners' Loan Corporation*, at 2, which discusses the use of credit reports.
60. *Ibid.*, at 2.
61. Jackson, *Crabgrass Frontier*, at 197–203.
62. Amy Hillier, "Redlining and the Homeowners' Loan Corporation," 29 *J. Urban Hist.* 394, 395 (2003).
63. *Ibid.*, at 398.
64. *Ibid.*, at 397.
65. Jackson, *Crabgrass Frontier*, at 198.
66. Hillier, "Redlining and the Homeowners' Loan Corporation," at 395.
67. *Ibid.*, at 401–2.
68. *Ibid.*, at 402–4.
69. *Ibid.*, at 403.
70. Thomas J. Sugrue, *Origins of the Urban Crisis: Race and Inequality in Postwar Detroit* 65 (2005). *See also* Daniel Aaronson *et al.*, "The Effects of the 1930s HOLC 'Redlining' Maps," Fed. Res. Bank of Chic. Working paper, WP 2017-12 (Feb. 2019 revision), which found that the HOLC redlining maps served to create the long-term reinforcement of segregation.
71. Jackson, *Crabgrass Frontier*, at 203.
72. National Housing Act, § 402.
73. 12 U.S.C. § 1710(d) (2018).
74. *Ibid.*
75. French, "The Contest for a National System of Home-Mortgage Finance," at 65; Federal Housing Administration (FHA), *The FHA Story in Summary* 7 (1959).
76. FHA, *The FHA Story in Summary*; Carrozzo, "A New Deal for the American Mortgage," at 41.

77. Grebler *et al.*, "Capital Formation in Residential Real Estate," at 257. FHA authority to restrict maximum interest rates of FHA-insured loans lapsed in 1983. *See* Supplemental Appropriations Act, Pub. L. 98-181, § 404(a), 97 Stat. 1208 (Nov. 30, 1983), *codified at* 12 U.S.C. § 1709-1 (2018). It was later reduced to 4.5 percent and then 4 percent, and then raised back to 4.5 percent. *See* Grebler *et al.*, "Capital Formation in Residential Real Estate," at 257.

78. French, "The Contest for a National System of Home-Mortgage Finance," at 63. *See* Housing Act of 1948, Pub. L. 80-901, § 101(j)(2), 62 Stat. 1268, 1272 (Aug. 10, 1948), which extended the maximum term of loans for insurance to thirty years); Housing Act of 1954, Pub. L. 83-560, § 104, 68 Stat. 590 (Aug. 2, 1954), which raised the maximum LTV to 95 percent for loans up to $9,000 and 75 percent LTV for larger loans; Housing Act of 1957, Pub. L. 85-104, § 101, 71 Stat. 294 (Jul. 12, 1957), which raised the maximum LTV to 97 percent; Housing Act of 1961, Pub. L. 87-70, § 605, 75 Stat. 149, 178 (Jun. 30, 1961), which extended the maximum term to thirty-five years; and Omnibus Budget Reconciliation Act of 1990, Pub. L. 101-508, § 2102, 104 Stat. 1388 (Nov. 5, 1990), which raised the maximum LTV to 98.75 percent.

79. 12 U.S.C. § 1709(b)(4) (2018); 24 C.F.R. § 203.17(c)(2), on amortization; and 12 C.F.R. § 203.49, which permitted the insurance of adjustable rate mortgages, but only as of June 6, 1984; *see* 49 Fed. Reg. 23584.

80. Grebler *et al.*, "Capital Formation in Residential Real Estate," at 257–58.

81. *Ibid.*, at 246.

82. *Ibid.*

83. *See* Frederick M. Babcock, "Influence of the Federal Housing Administration on Mortgage Lending Policy," 15 *J. Land & Pub. Utility Econ.* 1 (1939). Babcock is hardly a neutral observer, as he was the author of the first general appraisal methodology book in the United States and went on to work for the FHA.

84. Fisher, "Changing Institutional Patterns of Mortgage Lending," at 311.

85. Miles L. Colean, "A Review of Federal Mortgage Lending and Insuring Practices," 8 *J. Fin.* 249, 251 (1953).

86. *Ibid.*, at 250.

87. To be sure, the encouragement of easy credit terms likely exerted upward pressure on real estate prices, thereby at least partially canceling the benefits of easy credit. *See* Grebler *et al.*, "Capital Formation in Residential Real Estate," at 260.

88. *Ibid.*, at 246–47.

89. Adam Gordon, "Note: The Creation of Homeownership: How New Deal Changes in Banking Regulation Simultaneously Made Homeownership Accessible to Whites and Out of Reach for Blacks," 115 *Yale L.J.* 186, 194–95, 224 (2005). The authors know of no parallel situation in which a federal program necessitated the revision of all states' laws.

90. 12 U.S.C. § 1463(g) (2018).

91. Some flexibility was involved with the FHA rate cap in regard to fees. *See* John H. Fahey, "Competition and Mortgage Rates," 15 *J. Land & Pub. Util. Econ.* 150, 152 (1939).

92. James Gillies & Clayton Curtis, "The Structure of Local Mortgage Markets and Government Housing Finance Programs," 10 *J. Fin.* 363, 365 (1955).
93. *Ibid.*, at 365–66.
94. *Ibid.*
95. *Ibid.*
96. James Graaskamp, "Development and Structure of the Mortgage Loan Guaranty Insurance in the United States," 34 *J. Risk & Ins.* 47, 49–52 (1967).
97. *Ibid.*, at 47.
98. French, "The Contest for a National System of Home-Mortgage Finance," at 55 (emphasis in the original).
99. Snowden, "Mortgage Securitization in the United States: Twentieth Century Developments in Historical Perspective," at 266.
100. Stoner, "The Mortgage Market—Today and after World War I," at 228.
101. French, "The Contest for a National System of Home-Mortgage Finance," at 63.
102. Grebler *et al.*, *Capital Formation in Residential Real Estate: Trends and Prospects at* 252–53.
103. FHA loans were eligible for advancing at a 90 percent rate by the FHLBs. National Housing Act of 1934, § 501.
104. *Ibid.*, at § 402.
105. James S. Olson, *Saving Capitalism: The Reconstruction Finance Corporation and the New Deal, 1933–1940,* 196 (1988). The RFCMC was intended to make loans against income producing properties, like hotels and apartment complexes, as well as to support a market in FHA-insured loans. *See* Carol Aronvici, *Catching Up with Housing* 88 (1936); Office of War Information, Division of Public Inquiries, in *United States Government Manual* 435–36 (1945), *available at* http://ibiblio.org/hyperwar/ATO/USGM/index.html#contents.
106. *See* 12 U.S.C. § 1716 (2018), which lists the purposes of Fannie Mae according to the charter as:
    (1) provide stability in the secondary market for residential mortgages;
    (2) respond appropriately to the private capital market;
    (3) provide ongoing assistance to the secondary market for residential mortgages (including activities relating to mortgages on housing for low- and moderate-income families involving a reasonable economic return that may be less than the return earned on other activities) by increasing the liquidity of mortgage investments and improving the distribution of investment capital available for residential mortgage financing;
    (4) promote access to mortgage credit throughout the Nation (including central cities, rural areas, and underserved areas) by increasing the liquidity of mortgage investments and improving the distribution of investment capital available for residential mortgage financing; and
    (5) manage and liquidate federally owned mortgage portfolios in an orderly manner, with a minimum of adverse effect upon the residential mortgage market and minimum loss to the Federal Government.
107. Olson, *Saving Capitalism*, at 196.
108. R. W. Lindholm, "The Federal National Mortgage Association," 6 *J. Fin.* 54, 56 (1951).

109. *Historical Statistics of the United States, Millennium Edition* (2006), tbl. Dc983.

110. *Ibid.*

111. Colean, "A Review of Federal Mortgage Lending," at 252.

112. Lindholm, "The Federal National Mortgage Association," at 56.

113. *Ibid.*, at 56–57.

114. George W. McKinney, Jr., "Residential Mortgage Lenders," 7 *J. Fin.* 28, 42 (1952).

115. Lindholm, "The Federal National Mortgage Association," at 56–57.

116. McKinney, "Residential Mortgage Lenders," at 40.

117. *Ibid.*

118. Servicemen's Readjustment Act of 1944, Pub. L. 78-346, §§ 500–505, 58 Stat. 284, 291–93 (Jul. 22, 1944), *codified as amended* in scattered sections of 38 U.S.C., which allowed the VA to extend mortgage loan guaranties.

119. Ben S. Bernanke, "Housing, Housing Finance, and Monetary Policy," Speech at the Federal Reserve Bank of Kansas City's Economic Symposium, Jackson Hole, Wyoming, Aug. 31, 2007, n.5, *at* http://www.federalreserve.gov/news events/speech/Bernanke20070831a.htm.

120. Pub. L. 80-864, 62 Stat. 1206-1210 (Jul. 1, 1948). *See also* Lindholm, "The Federal National Mortgage Association," at 58. VA-guarantied mortgages originally differed from FHA-insured mortgages in that there is no cost to the borrower for the VA-guaranty, whereas FHA administers a mutual insurance fund, in which the borrowers pay an insurance premium for the insurance on their loans. Since 1982, however, the VA has charged a guaranty fee. *See* Tax Equity and Fiscal Responsibility Act of 1982, Pub. L. 97-523, § 406(a)(1), 96 Stat. 605 (Sep. 8, 1982), *codified at* 38 U.S.C. § 3729 (2018).

121. Lindholm, "The Federal National Mortgage Association," at 56–57.

122. Grebler *et al.*, "Capital Formation in Residential Real Estate," at 253.

123. *Ibid.*, at 260.

124. Andrey Pavlov *et al.*, "Transparency in the Mortgage Market," 49 *J. Fin. Serv. Research* 265 (2015).

125. *Ibid.*, at 255.

126. Jack M. Guttentag, "The Short Cycle in Residential Construction, 1946–1959," 51 *Am. Econ. Rev.* 275, 289 (1961).

127. *Ibid.* Because construction is often inverse with the general business cycle, Fannie Mae activities might have actually fueled overall economic procyclicality.

128. *Ibid.*, at 290.

129. Weiss, "Marketing and Financing Home Ownership," at 114.

130. *Ibid.*, at 289 n.77 (1961).

131. *Ibid.*

132. *Ibid.*

133. Housing Act of 1954, § 303(a).

134. *Ibid.*, § 304(c).

135. *Ibid.*, § 303.

136. *Ibid.*, § 308.

137. *Ibid.,* § 304(d).
138. Housing Act of 1956, Pub. L. 1020, § 204, 70 Stat. 1096 (allowing precommitments).
139. Housing Act of 1954, § 304(a).
140. *Ibid.,* § 304(b).
141. *Ibid.,* §§ 301(b), 305.
142. *Ibid.,* § 305(c).
143. *See* Saul B. Klaman, *The Volume of Mortgage Debt in the Postwar Decade,* at 38, tbl. 1 (1958).
144. Through historical and international perspectives, Richard Green & Susan M. Wachter identify the unique characteristics of this product in "The American Mortgage in Historical and International Context," 19 *J. Econ. Perspectives* 93, 94 (2005).
145. *See* Michael H. Schill & Susan M. Wachter, "Housing Market Constraints and Spatial Stratification by Income and Race," 6 *Housing Pol'y. Debate* 141, 151, 155–56 (1995).
146. *See* Fair Housing Act of 1968, Pub. L. 90-284, §§ 801–819, 82 Stat. 73, 81–89 (Apr. 11, 1968), *codified at* 42 U.S.C. §§ 3601–3619 (2018).
147. *See* Equal Credit Opportunity Act, Pub. L. 93-495, §§ 701–7, 88 Stat. 1500, 1521–25 (Oct. 28, 1974), *codified at* 15 U.S.C. § 1691 (2018). The Equal Credit Opportunity Act did not originally cover race, ethnicity, or age. It was amended in 1976 to include these protected classes. Pub. L. 94-239, § 2, 90 Stat. 251 (Mar. 23, 1976).
148. *See* Home Mortgage Disclosure Act, Pub. L. 94-200, §§ 301–10, 89 Stat. 1124, 1125 (Dec. 31, 1975), *codified at* 12 U.S.C. §§ 2801–10 (2018).
149. *See* Community Reinvestment Act of 1977, Pub. L. 95-128, §§ 801–6, 91 Stat. 1111, 1147, 1148 (Oct. 12, 1977), *codified at* 12 U.S.C. §§ 2901–2908 (2018). Performance under the Community Reinvestment Act was incorporated into the standard for eligibility for FHLB advances in 1989. *See* Financial Institutions Reform, Recovery, and Enforcement Act of 1989, Pub L. 101-73, § 710, 103 Stat. 183, 418–19 (Aug. 9, 1989), *codified at* 12 U.S.C. § 1430(g) (2018).
150. Saul B. Klaman, *The Postwar Residential Mortgage Market* 163–65 (1961).
151. 12 C.F.R. pt. 526 (1978), which set return rate limits on Federal Home Loan Bank members and FSLIC-insured nonmember thrifts. Formally, Regulation Q only refers to the parallel Federal Reserve regulation for Federal Reserve member institutions. *See* Regulation Q, 12 C.F.R. pt. 217 (1978).
152. *See* Thomas F. Cargill, "Disintermediation," in *Business Cycles and Depressions: An Encyclopedia* 164, 164–65 (David Glasner, ed., 1997).
153. Prior to 1979, federal regulations permitted federally chartered thrifts to make "installment loans"; *see* 12 C.F.R. § 545.6-1 (1979), *repealed by* 82 Fed. Reg. 47083, 47084 (Oct. 11, 2017). The definition of these loans included the requirement that "no required payment after the first shall be more, but may be less, than any preceding payment"; *see* 12 C.F.R. § 541.14(a) (1979), *repealed by* 82 Fed. Reg. 47083, 47084 (Oct. 11, 2017). The FHLBB bruited about the idea of permitting ARMs in 1971 and 1974 but backed down in

the face of congressional opposition; *see* Joe Peek, "A Call to ARMs: Adjustable Rate Mortgages in the 1980s," *New England Econ. Rev.*, Mar.–Apr. 1990, at 47, 48. In 1978, however, the FHLBB permitted federal thrifts in California to make ARMs in order to compete with state-chartered institutions, and the authority was expanded nationally as of June 5, 1979; *see* "Variable Rate Mortgages," 44 Fed. Reg. 32,199, 32,200 (June 5, 1979); *see also* "Federal Savings and Loan System, Reduction and Simplification of Regulations," 44 *Fed. Reg.* 39,108, 39,122 (Jul. 3, 1979). The ARMs that were permitted, however, allowed only for upward rate (and payment) adjustments; *see* "Variable Rate Mortgages," at 32,200; *see also* "Federal Savings and Loan System, Reduction and Simplification of Regulations," at 39,122. The Federal Register notice states that "the Bank Board believes such investment authority is necessary to offset the costs of paying higher interest rates on savings accounts and to allow a variable rate on a portion of an association's loans just as variable rates are allowed for certain savings instruments"; *see* "Variable Rate Mortgages," at 32,199. Under the 1979 regulations, S&Ls' ARMs were limited to rate increases to half a percentage point per year, with a maximum aggregate rate change of 2.5 percent for ARMs and of 5 percent for renegotiable rate mortgages. Also, S&Ls offering ARMs had to also offer an FRM alternative to the buyer—a precursor, as it were, to the ill-fated "plain vanilla" proposal for the Consumer Financial Protection Bureau; *see* "Adjustable Rate Mortgages," 45 Fed. Reg. 79,493, 79,494 (Dec. 1, 1980); *see also* 12 C.F.R. § 545.6-4(a) (1980), *repealed by* 82 Fed. Reg. 47083, 47084 (Oct. 11, 2017). As of 1979, sixteen states had regulations specifically authorizing ARMs, while six states prohibited at least some forms of ARMs; *see* "Adjustable Rate Mortgages," 45 Fed. Reg. 64,196, 64,198 (Sept. 29, 1980).

Federal law for national banks was quiet on the issue of ARMs, leaving federally chartered lenders free to make ARMs, if state law permitted; *see* "Adjustable Rate Mortgages," 45 Fed. Reg., at 64,198, which describes the ARM rules proposed by the Office of the Comptroller of the Currency. In 1980, federal banking regulators—the Office of the Comptroller of the Currency, the FHLBB, and the National Credit Union Administration—all passed preemptive regulations on ARM lending; *see* "Adjustable Mortgage Loan Instruments," 46 Fed. Reg. 24,148, 24,149 (Apr. 30, 1981), which permits the use of ARMs for federal S&Ls and mutual savings banks; upheld by *Conference of State Bank Supervisors v. Conover*, 710 F.2d 878 (D.C. Cir. 1983); *see also* Alternative Mortgage Transactions Parity Act of 1982, Pub. L. 97-320, § 804(a), 96 Stat. 1469, 1545–48 (Oct. 15, 1982), which preempts state regulation prohibiting adjustable-rate mortgages; *cf.* "Adjustable Rate Mortgages," 46 Fed. Reg. 18,932 (Mar. 27, 1981), which grants ARM authority to national banks; "Graduated Payment Adjustable Mortgage Loan Instruments," 46 Fed Reg. 37,625 (Jul. 22, 1981), which permits federal S&Ls and mutual savings banks to make graduated payment adjustable mortgage loans, such as payment option ARMs; and "Adjustable Rate Mortgage Loans,"

46 Fed. Reg. 38,669 (July 29, 1981), which describes National Credit Union Administration regulations granting ARM authority for federal credit unions).

154. Prior to 1980, fixed-rate first-lien mortgage products were subject to state usury laws; *see* Depository Institutions Deregulation and Monetary Control Act of 1980, Pub. L. 96-221, § 501, 94 Stat. 132,161 (Mar. 31, 1980); *codified as amended at* 12 U.S.C. § 1735f–7a (2006), which preempts state usury laws for first-lien mortgage loans that meet certain consumer protection requirements. Starting in 1980, federal thrifts were permitted to make junior-lien (second) mortgages; *see ibid.*, § 5(c), *codified as amended at* 12 U.S.C. § 1464(c) (2006), which authorizes mortgage lending without including first-lien requirements; "Revision of Real Estate Lending Regulations," 45 Fed. Reg. 76,095, 76,906 (Nov. 18, 1980), which explicitly authorizes junior-lien lending. Prior to 1982, state laws often prevented the enforcement of due-on-sale clauses, which prevented assumable mortgages from being transferred along with properties, thus keeping the S&L locked into loans at below the market interest rate loans; *see* Thrift Institutions Restructuring Act, Pub. L. 97-320, § 341(b), 96 Stat. 1469, 1505–8 (Oct. 15, 1982), which preempts state law on due-on-sale clauses.

155. *See, e.g.,* 12 U.S.C. § 371 (1970), which sets national bank LTV limits; 12 C.F.R. § 545.6-1 (1976), *repealed by* 82 Fed. Reg. 47083, 47084 (Oct. 11, 2017), which set LTV restrictions. Thrift LTV limits were generally regulatory, but there were also statutory LTV limits from 1980 to 1982; *see* Depositary Institutions Deregulation and Monetary Control Act of 1980, § 401, which sets statutory LTV limits; and Thrift Institutions Restructuring Act, § 322, which repeals statutory LTV limits that were set in 1980.

156. 12 U.S.C. § 1464(c) (1976), which sets geographic restrictions on lending; Emergency Home Finance Act of 1970, Pub. L. 91-351, § 706, 84 Stat. 450, 462 (Jul. 24, 1970), which grants statewide lending authority; 12 C.F.R. § 545.6-6 (1963), which sets a fifty-mile lending radius from headquarters; "Lending Area," 30 Fed. Reg. 826, 827 (Jan. 27, 1965), which increases the lending radius to one hundred miles from headquarters; and "Lending Area," 36 Fed. Reg. 2,912, 2,912 (Feb. 12, 1971), which establishes a statewide or one hundred–mile lending radius from headquarters or branches.

157. *See* 12 C.F.R. § 541.14(b) (1976), *repealed by* 82 Fed. Reg. 47083, 47084 (Oct. 11, 2017), which defined partial amortization as having a maximum thirty-year amortization schedule, but with a shorter term; and 12 C.F.R. § 545.6-1, *repealed by* 82 Fed. Reg. 47083, 47084 (Oct. 11, 2017), which detailed LTV and amortization restrictions.

158. Thrift Institutions Restructuring Act, § 352, *codified at* 12 U.S.C. § 1430(a) (1) (2018), which gives each FHLB discretion about the amount and type of collateral that is necessary to fully secure advances.

159. Federal Home Loan Bank Act, §§ 2(6), 2(8), 10(a)(1), *codified as amended at* 12 U.S.C. §§ 1422(2), 1422(6), 1430(a)(2) (2018), which defines "home mortgage" and "amortized" and sets LTV limits.

160. *Ibid.*, § 10(a)(2), *codified as amended at* 12 U.S.C. § 1430(a)(3) (2018).

161. *Ibid.*, § 10(b), *codified as amended at* 12 U.S.C. § 1430(b) (2018).

162. *See supra* note 27 and sources therein.

163. 12 U.S.C. § 1430(a)(1)–(2), (b) (1976).

164. *Ibid.*, § 1430(a)(3), (b).

165. Daniel K. Fetter, "How Do Mortgage Subsidies Affect Home Ownership? Evidence from the Mid-Century GI Bills," 5 *Am. Econ. J: Econ. Pol'y.* 111, 144 (2013).

166. US Census Bureau, "Historical Census of Housing Tables: Crowding," Oct. 31, 2011, *at* http://www.census.gov/hhes/www/housing/census/historic /crowding.html.

167. *Ibid.*

168. US Census Bureau, Historical Census of Housing Tables: Plumbing Facilities, Oct. 31, 2011, *at* http://www.census.gov/hhes/www/housing/census/historic /plumbing.html. Complete plumbing is defined as having hot and cold piped water, a bathtub or shower, and a flush toilet.

169. US Census Bureau, Historical Census of Housing Tables: Home Values, June 6, 2012, *at* http://www.census.gov/hhes/www/housing/census/historic /values.html.

170. *See Jones v. Alfred H. Mayer Co.*, 392 U.S. 409 (1968).

171. *Buchanan v. Warley*, 245 U.S. 60 (1917).

172. *Shelley v. Kramer*, 334. U.S. 1 (1948). *See also Hansberry v. Lee*, 311 U.S. 32 (1940).

173. Rose Helper, *Racial Policies and Practices of Real Estate Brokers* 39 (1969).

174. *See* Robert C. Weaver, "Race Restrictive Housing Covenants," 20 *J. Land & Pub. Utility Econ.* 183, 190 (1944), which quotes an FHA official as saying that FHA's "experience with Negro mortgagors has been good, and on the basis of credit analysis we consider them as good or better risk than white mortgagors."

175. The President's Conference on Home Building and Home Ownership, *Negro Housing: Report of the Committee on Negro Housing* 97 (1932).

176. *Ibid.*, at 94–95 (1932).

177. U.S. Housing and Home Finance Agency, *Housing of the Nonwhite Population, 1940 to 1950* 14 (1952).

178. Preston H. Smith, *Racial Democracy and the Black Metropolis: Housing Policy in Postwar Chicago* 230–31 (2012).

179. Robert C. Weaver, "The Relative Status of the Housing of Negroes in the United States," 22 *J. Negro Ed.* 343, 349 (1953).

180. Sophonisba P. Breckinridge, "The Color Line in the Housing Problem," 29 *The Survey* 575 (Feb. 1913).

181. Weaver, "Race Restrictive Housing Covenants," at 190.

182. *Ibid.*

183. *Ibid.*

184. *Ibid.*

3. The Rise of Securitization

1. Saul B. Klaman, "Public/Private Approaches to Urban Mortgage and Housing Problems," 32 *L. & Contemp. Prob.* 250 (1967).

2. Albert E. Burger, "A Historical Analysis of the Credit Crunch of 1966," *Fed. Res. Bank of St. Louis Rev.* 13 (Sept. 1969).

3. Reg Q, 12 C.F.R. Part 217. Reg Q was relaxed for various types of savings accounts in 1980, with the relaxation phased in between 1981 and 1986. Depository Institutions Deregulation and Monetary Control Act of 1980, Pub. L. 96-221, 94 Stat. 132, 142–45 (Mar. 31, 1980). Reg Q was effectively repealed for demand deposit accounts, effective July 21, 2011. Dodd-Frank Wall Street Reform and Consumer Protection Act of 2010, Pub. L. 111-203 § 627, 124 Stat. 1376, 1640 (Jul. 21, 2010).

4. *See* Burger, "A Historical Analysis of the Credit Crunch of 1966," at 13, 24.

5. *Ibid.*, at 25–27, which discusses the impact on municipal bond and business lending markets.

6. Ben S. Bernanke, chairman, Fed. Res., Speech at the Federal Reserve Bank of Kansas City's Economic Symposium, Jackson Hole, Wyoming (Aug. 31, 2007), *available at* http://www.federalreserve.gov/newsevents/speech/Bernanke 20070831a.htm.

7. *Cf.* Edwin L. Dale, Jr., "Fanny May Notes to Retain Status," *New York Times*, Feb. 5, 1968, at 49 (noting that a newly privatized Fannie Mae would operate outside the federal budget). Prior to 1968, Fannie Mae's secondary market operations had not been included in the federal budget on the grounds that the financing was not provided through taxation. A 1967 report of a presidential budget commission, however, recommended that the secondary market operations be included in the budget, with an estimated first-year impact of $2.5 billion dollars—approximately 1.5 percent of the $178.1 billion in federal expenditures in 1968. *See* Richard W. Bartke, "Fannie Mae and the Secondary Mortgage Market," 66 *Nw. L. Rev.* 1, 31 (1971).

8. Housing and Urban Development Act of 1968, Pub. L. 90-448, § 801, 82 Stat. 476, 536 (Aug. 1, 1968), *codified at* 12 U.S.C § 1719 (2018).

9. *Ibid.*, § 802(c), *codified at* 12 U.S.C. § 1718 (2018).

10. *Ibid.*, § 802(y), *codified at* 12 U.S.C. § 1723 (2018).

11. *Ibid.*, § 802(ee), *codified at* 12 U.S.C. § 1723A (2018), which requires the HUD secretary's approval for the issuance of securities; *see also ibid.*, § 804(a), *codified at* 12 U.S.C. § 1719, which requires the Treasury secretary's approval for the issuance of mortgage-backed securities.

12. *Ibid.*, § 802, *codified at* 12 U.S.C § 1717 (2018).

13. *Ibid.*, § 804(b), *codified at* 12 U.S.C. § 1721(g) (2018).

14. *See* Vinod Kothari, *Securitization: The Financial Instrument of the Future* 628 (2008).

15. Covered bonds are also securitizations but differ in that originating entities are also responsible for covering losses. The European countries' banks often use covered bonds for mortgage securitization. Despite their seeming greater investor protection, they too experienced significant losses during the bubbles

in various countries, as discussed here. *See* Susan M. Wachter, "The Housing and Credit Bubbles in the US and Europe: A Comparison," 47 *J. Money, Credit & Banking* 1, 37–42 (2015).

16. Thus, there is no special-purpose entity used in a Ginnie Mae securitization. The loan documentation, which may or may not consist of negotiable documents, are transferred to a document custodian, but it is unclear whether this transfer of documentation is also meant to serve as a transfer of legal title to the mortgages.

17. Indeed, although Ginnie Mae transactions are commonly referred to as securitizations and Ginnie Mae is generally credited with having undertaken the first modern securitization, Ginnie Mae transactions are, in fact, best described as covered bonds and not securitizations because the mortgage loans are not transferred by the issuer to a separate issuance entity.

18. The word "repurchase" is used in Ginnie Mae transactions, but given the lack of clarity about whether there is an initial sale in a Ginnie Mae transaction, the term is used with quotation marks. At the very least, it signifies that a loan is moved out of the cover pool and cash is placed in the cover pool

19. Hence the recent discussions around the stability of the nonbanks, who lack capital and who are the predominant suppliers of mortgage capital in the aftermath of the crisis. *See* the discussion here and in You S. Kim *et al.*, "Liquidity Crises in the Mortgage Market," *Brookings Papers on Econ. Activity*, 347–413 (Spring 2018) and associated comment there by Susan M. Wachter, 420–23.

20. Department of Housing and Urban Development, "Salaries and Expenses, Government National Mortgage Association," *at* https://www.hud.gov/sites/dfiles/CFO/documents/31%20-%20FY19CJ%20-%20GNMA%20-%20Mortgage-Backed%20Securities%20Program.pdf at 29-1 (2018).

21. Jonathan Tower, "Ginnie Mae Pool No. 1: A Revolution Is Paid Off," *Seattle Times*, Sept. 19, 1999.

22. Susan Woodward & Robert Hall, "What to Do about Fannie Mae and Freddie Mac," *RGE Monitor*, Feb. 3, 2009, *at* http://www.rgemonitor.com/finance markets-monitor/255401/what_to_do_about_fannie_mae_and_freddie_mac. It appears that Ginnie was able to produce a significant drop in the cost of funds for FHA/VA, not by creating a secondary market, as Fannie had already done, but by making a much larger secondary market. Ginnie Mae MBS accounted for a much larger share of FHA/VA mortgages than Fannie's portfolio holdings had. Greater market share meant more liquidity, and this resulted in a lower cost of funds.

23. Housing and Urban Development Act of 1968, § 804, *codified at* 12 U.S.C. §1719(d) (2018).

24. Congressional Budget Office, "Assessing the Public Costs and Benefits of Fannie Mae and Freddie Mac," May 1996, at 5, *available at* https://www.cbo.gov/sites/default/files/104th-congress-1995-1996/reports/10339.pdf.

25. Peter M. Carrozzo, "Marketing the American Mortgage: The Emergency Home Finance Act of 1970, Standardization, and the Secondary Market Revolution," 39 *Real Prop., Prob. & Tr. J.* 765, 768–70 (2005).

26. Emergency Home Finance Act of 1970, Pub. L. No. 91-351, § 201, 84 Stat. 450-51 (Jul. 24, 1970).

27. *Ibid.*, § 201(a)(2), which authorized Fannie Mae; *ibid.*, § 305(a), which authorized Freddie Mac.

28. *See* Edwin L. Dale, Jr., "Fanny May to Buy Regular Mortgages," *New York Times*, Dec. 3, 1970, at 73.

29. Douglas W. Cray, "5% Down Payment on Home Allowed," *New York Times*, Aug. 20, 1971, at 43; "Fanny May Adding 95% Mortgages," *New York Times*, Sept. 9, 1972, at 32.

30. *See* Carrozzo, "Marketing the American Mortgage," at 773–74.

31. Saul B. Klaman, *The Postwar Residential Mortgage Market* 163–65 (1961), which notes the S&Ls' avoidance of FHA loans but not VA loans; Richard W. Bartke, "Fannie Mae and the Secondary Mortgage Market," 66 *Nw. Univ. L. Rev.* 1, 13 (1971), which notes the S&Ls' preference for conventional loans over FHA/VA loans; Richard W. Bartke, "Home Financing at the Crossroads—A Study of the Federal Home Loan Mortgage Corporation," 48 *Ind. L.J.* 1, 11 (1972), which describes Fannie Mae's domination of the mortgage banks.

32. *See* Carrozzo, "Marketing the American Mortgage," at 772–97, which describes the Emergency Home Finance Act as a compromise between a bill expanding Fannie Mae's authority and a bill creating Freddie Mac. FHLB membership was opened to commercial banks in 1989; *see* the Financial Institutions Reform, Recovery, and Enforcement Act of 1989, Pub L. 101–73, § 704(a), 103 Stat. 183, 415–16 (Aug. 9, 1989), *codified at* 12 U.S.C. § 1424(a) (2018).

33. Edwin L. Dale, Jr., "A New Mortgage Venture Enters Housing Markets," *New York Times*, Sept. 2, 1970, at 47.

34. Marc A. Weiss, "Marketing and Financing Home Ownership: Mortgage Lending and Public Policy in the United States, 1918–1989," 18 *Bus. & Econ. Hist.* (2d Series), 109, 113 (1989).

35. Emergency Home Finance Act of 1970, Pub. L. 91–351, § 305, 84 Stat. 450, 454–55 (Jul. 24, 1970), *codified as amended at* 12 U.S.C. § 1454 (2018), which describes the Freddie Mac MBS; Housing and Urban Development Act of 1968, § 804(a), *codified at* 12 U.S.C § 1719 (2018), which describes the Fannie Mae MBS.

36. Indeed, Freddie Mac purchased very few FHA/VA mortgages as compared to conventional mortgages.

37. James R. Hagerty, *The Fateful History of Fannie Mae: New Deal Birth to Mortgage Crisis Fall* 57 (2012).

38. *See* Richard K. Green & Ann B. Schnare, "The Rise and Fall of Fannie Mae and Freddie Mac: Lessons Learned and Options for Reform," Lusk Ctr. for Real Estate Working Paper No. 2009-1001 (2009), at 17, *available at* http://www.usc.edu/schools/sppd/lusk/research/pdf/wp_2009–1001.pdf.

39. Dwight M. Jaffee & Kenneth T. Rosen, "Mortgage Securitization Trends," 1 *J. Hous. Research* 117, 122 (1990).

40. Jeffrey Carmichael & Michael Pomerleano, *The Development and Regulation of Non-Bank Financial Institutions* 182 (2002).

41. *See* Dale, "Fanny May to Buy Regular Mortgages," at 73.

42. The Uniform MBS are issued separately by both Fannie and Freddie through the Common Securitization Platform owned by Common Securitization Solutions, LLC, a joint venture of Fannie Mae and Freddie Mac. The Uniform MBS is structured like the Fannie Mae MBS (with a fifty-five-day investor payment delay), but with Freddie Mac–style disclosures. The guaranties on Fannie Mae Uniform MBS continue to be obligations solely of Fannie Mae and the guaranties on Freddie Mac Uniform MBS continue to be obligations of solely Freddie Mac, but Fannie and Freddie Uniform MBS will be good delivery for each other in the To Be Announced forward contract market (meaning that a contract for a Uniform MBS can be satisfied by delivery of either a Fannie Mae Uniform MBS or a Freddie Mac Uniform MBS), and indication of the implicit government guaranty of Fannie and Freddie. Indeed, part of the goal of the Uniform MBS initiative was to enable Freddie Mac to cease subsidizing its securitizations to offset their lower liquidity relative to Fannie's, as the cost reduces the profit that Treasury can sweep from Freddie under its Capital Support Agreement.

43. 12 U.S.C. § 4612(a) (2018).

44. *See* 12 U.S.C. § 1717(b) (2018), addressing Fannie Mae; and § 1454 (2018), addressing Freddie Mac.

45. *See* Saul B. Klaman, *The Volume of Mortgage Debt in the Postwar Decade* 40–41, tbl.2 (1958).

46. *See* Figure 3.1.

47. *See, e.g.*, Carl F. Behrens, *Commercial Bank Activities in Urban Mortgage Financing* 1 (1952), which describes the "severe limitations" on commercial banks operating in the real estate market.

48. *See* David L. Mason, *From Building and Loans to Bail-Outs: A History of the American Savings and Loan Industry, 1831–1995*, 12 (2004).

49. *Ibid.*

50. Kenneth A. Snowden, "The Evolution of Interregional Mortgage Lending Channels, 1870–1940: The Life Insurance-Mortgage Company Connection," in *Coordination and Information: Historical Perspectives on the Organization of Enterprises* 209 (Naomi R. Lamoreaux & Daniel M. G. Raff, eds., 1995), *available at* http://www.nber.org/chapters/c8755.pdf.

51. Saul B. Klaman, *The Postwar Rise of Mortgage Companies* 5–13 (1959).

52. *See* Bartke, *Fannie Mae and the Secondary Mortgage Market*, at 13, which notes the S&Ls' preference for conventional loans over FHA/VA loans. The S&Ls did in fact purchase VA loans, but they eschewed FHA loans, having historically been opposed to FHA insurance; Klaman, *The Postwar Rise of Mortgage Companies*, at 163–65.

53. Kenneth T. Jackson, *Crabgrass Frontier: The Suburbanization of the United States* 232–34, 238 (1985).

54. Here we do not mean money market mutual funds, which were in their infancy, but rather investments such as Treasuries, certificates of deposit, and corporate commercial paper.

55. *Fidelity Federal Savings and Loan Association v. de la Cuesta*, 458 U.S. 141 (1982); *California v. Coast Federal Savings and Loan Association*, 98 F. Supp. 311 (S.D. Cal. 1951).

56. Depository Institutions Deregulation and Monetary Control Act of 1980, Pub. L. 96-221, § 501, 94 Stat. 132, 161 (Mar. 31, 1980), *codified at* 12 U.S.C. § 1735f–7a (2018). Prior to 1980, Congress preempted state usury caps for FHA and VA loans; *see* Cathy Lesser Mansfield, "The Road to Subprime 'HEL' Was Paved with Good Congressional Intentions: Usury Deregulation and the Subprime Home Equity Market," 51 *S.C. L. Rev.* 473, 484–92 (2000). By 1983, all interest rate caps on FHA loans had been effectively removed; *see* Mansfield, "The Road to Subprime 'HEL,'" at 483.

57. The FHLBB disastrously widened this expansion by permitting the S&Ls to invest up to 11 percent of their assets in junk bonds, rather than the 1 percent permitted by statute, by allowing junk bonds to be counted as both "corporate loans" and noninvestment grade securities; *see* William W. Bratton & Adam J. Levitin, "A Transactional Genealogy of Scandal: From Michael Milken to Enron to Goldman Sachs," 86 *S. Cal. L. Rev.* 783, 798–99 n.43 (2013).

58. Depository Institutions Deregulation and Monetary Control Act of 1980, § 501. States can, however, opt out of the deregulation provisions of this act by passing a law to that effect; *see ibid.*, § 501(b)(2), *codified at* 12 U.S.C. § 1735f–7a(b)(2) (2018).

59. Leo Grebler *et al.*, *Capital Formation in Residential Real Estate* 257 (1956). The FHA rate cap was originally 5 percent, later reduced to 4.5 percent and then 4 percent, and then raised back to 4.5 percent.

60. 12 U.S.C. § 1709–1 (1982), *repealed by* Pub. L. 98–181, § 404(a), 97 Stat. 1208 (Nov. 30, 1983).

61. The story of mortgage usury laws is distinct from that of usury laws generally. In 1978, the Supreme Court held that a national bank could export the usury rate of its home state when it made loans in other states; *see Marquette Nat'l Bank of Minneapolis. v. First of Omaha Serv. Corp.*, 439 U.S. 299, 313–15, 318 (1978). States responded by enacting parity laws to protect their state-chartered institutions by giving them the right to charge whatever rate a national bank could charge. *See* Elizabeth Renuart & Kathleen E. Keest, *The Cost of Credit: Regulation, Preemption, and Industry Abuses*, at 3.14 (3rd ed. 2005; Supp. 2008).

    Almost every state has enacted some form of parity provision; *see* John J. Schroeder, "'Duel' Banking System? State Bank Parity Laws: An Examination of Regulatory Practice, Constitutional Issues, and Philosophical Questions," 36 *Ind. L. Rev.* 197, 202 (2003). Congress also extended national banks' "most favored lender" status to other depository institutions, enabling them to select between a federal and a state maximum applicable rate for their other transactions; *see* 12 U.S.C. § 1463(g) (2018), which addresses federal S&Ls; § 1785(g) (2018), which addresses federal credit unions; and § 1831d(a) (2018), which addresses state-chartered banks and savings banks. Under federal law, states still have the ability to opt out of the most favored lender preemption. The result of this regulatory race was the substantial evisceration of usury laws for transactions by depositories other than first-lien mortgage lending.

62. *See* Alternative Mortgage Transactions Parity Act of 1982, Pub. L. 97–320, §§ 801–7, 96 Stat. 1545–48 (Oct. 15, 1982), *codified at* 12 U.S.C. § 3801 *et seq.* (2018). Six states—Arizona, Maine, Massachusetts, New York, South

Carolina, and Wisconsin—opted out of preemption in a timely way; *see* Renuart & Keest, *The Cost of Credit*, at 3.10.1, 3.10.2 n.664.

63. Garn-St. Germain Depository Institutions Act of 1982, Pub. L. 97–320, § 341, 96 Stat. 1469, 1505 (Oct. 15, 1982), *codified at* 12 U.S.C. § 1701j–3 (2018).

64. *See* 12 C.F.R. § 541.14(b) (1976), *repealed by* 82 Fed. Reg. 47083, 47084 (Oct. 11, 2017), which defined partial amortization as having a maximum thirty-year amortization schedule, but with a shorter term; and 12 C.F.R. § 545.6-1 (1976), *repealed by* 82 Fed. Reg. 47083, 47084 (Oct. 11, 2017), which detailed LTV and amortization restrictions.

4. The Boom and the Bubble

1. *See supra* Chapter 2, note 153 and accompanying text.

2. Joe Peek, "A Call to ARMs: Adjustable Rate Mortgages in the 1980s," *New. Eng. Econ. Rev.*, Mar./Apr. 1990, at 47, 49 chart 1 (1990).

3. *Ibid.*

4. *Ibid.*, *at* 48.

5. *See ibid.*, at 56.

6. *See ibid.*, at 56, 59 chart 3.

7. *See* Richard Green & Susan M. Wachter, "The American Mortgage in Historical and International Context," 19 *J. Econ. Persp.* 93, 101 (2005); *see also* "Housing Finance Reform: Should There Be a Government Guarantee? Hearing before the S. Comm. on Banking, Hous. & Urban Affairs," 112th Cong., Sept. 13, 2011 (statement of Adam J. Levitin, Professor of Law, Georgetown University Law Center), CIS No.: 2012-S241-30) *available at* http://www .law.georgetown.edu/faculty/faculty-webpags/adam-levitin/upload/levitin -senate-banking-testimony-9_13_11-1.pdf, which discusses government support for mortgage markets in Germany and Denmark, the other two countries where long-term FRMs are widely available).

8. *See* Emanuel Moench *et al.*, "Why Is the Market Share of Adjustable-Rate Mortgages So Low?" 16 *Fed. Res. Bank of N.Y. Current Issues in Economics and Finance* (2010).

9. *See* Matthew L. Wald, "Sorting Out a New World of Mortgage Possibilities," *New York Times*, Jul. 25, 1993, sec. 10, p. 1, which describes an experiment in which subjects overwhelmingly chose an FRM over a substantially cheaper ARM (on an option-adjusted basis).

10. *Refer back* to Figure 3.1, "Residential Mortgage Market Share by Institution Type, 1948–2008."

11. Bd. of Gov. of the Fed. Res. Sys., *Statistical Release Z.1, Financial Accounts of the United States*, tbl. L.218.

12. *Ibid.*

13. *Ibid.*

14. U.S. Census Bureau, Homeownership Rate for the United States [USHOWN], retrieved from FRED, Fed. Res. Bank of St. Louis, *at* https://fred.stlouisfed.org /series/USHOWN, Nov. 24, 2019.

15. U.S. Census Bureau, Homeownership Rate for the United States: Non-Hispanic White Alone [NHWAHORUSQ156N], retrieved from FRED, Fed. Res. Bank of St. Louis, *at* https://fred.stlouisfed.org/series/NHWAHORUSQ 156N, Nov. 24, 2019. (1994-2018).

16. U.S. Census Bureau, Homeownership Rate for the United States: Black or African American Alone [BOAAAHORUSQ156N], retrieved from FRED, Fed. Res. Bank of St. Louis, *at* https://fred.stlouisfed.org/series/BOAAAHORU SQ156N, Nov. 23, 2019.

17. Federal Housing Enterprises Financial Safety and Soundness Act of 1992 (the "GSE Act"), 102 P.L. 550, § 1331, 106 Stat. 3672, 3956 (Oct. 28, 1992), *codified at* 12 U.S.C. § 4561 (2018). From 1993 to 2008, the affordable housing goals were supervised by the HUD secretary.

18. David W. McDonald *et al.*, "Desktop Underwriter: Fannie Mae's Automated Mortgage Underwriting Expert System," (Jan. 1997) *at* https://www .researchgate.net/profile/Henry_Bowers2/publication/221606587_Desktop _Underwriter_Fannie_Mae's_Automated_Mortgage_Underwriting_Expert _System/links/5bce355b92851c1816ba3914/Desktop-Underwriter-Fannie -Maes-Automated-Mortgage-Underwriting-Expert-System.pdf; M. Lynne Markus *et al.*, "The Computerization Movement in the US Home Mortgage Industry, 1980-2004," 15 (Feb. 2005), *at* https://www.researchgate.net/profile /Rolf_Wigand/publication/228813098_The_Computerization_Movement _in_the_US_Home_Mortgage_Industry_1980-2004/links/0912f5058b45 8def64000000.pdf.

19. Peter E. Mahoney & Peter M. Zorn, "The Promise of Automated Under-writing: Freddie Mac's Loan Prospector," 13:3 *Secondary Mortgage Markets* 1, 14 (1996), *at* http://www.housingfinance.org/uploads/Publicationsmanager /9706_Aut.pdf.

20. *Ibid.*, at 17.

21. *Ibid.*

22. *Ibid.*, at 19.

23. Mortgage Bankers Association, "National Delinquency Survey," (2019) which reports foreclosure rates as ranging between 0.86 percent in 1995 and 1.51 percent in 2002 (in the wake of the 2001 recession), as compared to a high of 4.64 percent in 2010.

24. The GSEs did engage in interest rate hedging on noncallable debt through swaps and swaptions, which discusses options to engage in a swap on speci-fied terms.

25. The GSEs prefer to deal with larger sellers, both because of the economies of scale and because of the greater financial strength larger sellers have to back up the representations and warranties they make regarding the mortgages they sell to the GSEs.

26. The trusts pay the GSEs in the form of the MBS, which the GSEs then use to pay the sellers.

27. The FHA and the VA guaranty the repayment of principal and accrued in-terest, but not necessarily in a timely fashion. They only pay out after foreclo-sure, which can mean that the insurance payments are considerably delayed.

28. *See* 12 C.F.R. §§ 220.4, 220.12 (2018), which sets a 50 percent margin for the long position in equity securities. Further limitations come from the Financial Industry Regulatory Authority (FINRA) Rule 4210 and exchange rules, as well as contract.

29. Fannie Mae and Freddie Mac began to issue Uniform Notes and Uniform Security Instruments in 1975. The Uniform Instruments have undergone several revisions since then, and today, virtually all mortgages still outstanding today are written using some iteration of the Uniform Notes and Security Instruments. Fannie Mae and Freddie Mac mandate the use of the Uniform Notes or Uniform Security Instruments in most circumstances, and even lenders that do not contemplate selling their notes to Fannie Mae and Freddie Mac use the latter. *See* Julia Patterson Forrester, "Fannie Mae/Freddie Mac Uniform Mortgage Instruments: The Forgotten Benefit to Homeowners," 72 *Univ. Missouri L. Rev.* 1077, 1085 (2007).

30. Eric S. Belsky & Nela Richardson, "Understanding the Boom and Bust in Nonprime Mortgage Lending," *at* 18, *at* http://www.jchs.harvard.edu/sites /jchs.harvard.edu/files/ubb10-1.pdf.

31. *See, e.g.*, Peter G. Miller, "Arbitration Clauses Blocked by Fannie Mae & Freddie Mac," RealtyTimes.com. Feb. 10, 2004, *at* http://realtytimes.com /rtpages/20040210arbitration.htm, which describes how arbitration provisions help poor or credit-challenged borrowers, while refusing to allow arbitration provisions favoring wealthier people or mortgage lenders. As a result of the absence of these clauses, mortgage-related consumer class action suits remained possible even as they generally ceased to be possible for other consumer financial products. Congress subsequently prohibited arbitration clauses in mortgage by statute as part of the Dodd-Frank Wall Street Reform and Consumer Protection Act of 2010; *see* 15 U.S.C. § 1639c(e) (2018).

32. The possibility of needing a federal bailout by virtue of being too big to fail raised moral-hazard problems for the GSEs and could have undermined their underwriting quality. The GSEs only invested in highly rated tranches of subprime and alt-A MBS, and these tranches were vulnerable to ratings downgrades. As AAA-subprime MBS were downgraded, the GSEs were forced to recognize large losses in their trading portfolios. Because the GSEs were highly leveraged, these losses ate heavily into the GSEs' capital, which undermined their MBS guaranty business (the GSEs' guaranty is only valuable to the extent that they are solvent).

33. *See* 12 U.S.C. §§ 1454(a)(2), 1717(b)(2) (2018).

34. Title I, Subtitle B of the Riegle Community Development and Regulatory Improvement Act of 1994, Pub. L. 103–325, §§ 151–158 (1994).

35. *See, generally,* Kathleen C. Engel & Patricia A. McCoy, *The Subprime Virus: Reckless Credit, Regulatory Failure, and Next Steps* 157–87 (2011), which details the increase in preemption laws that were created and enforced and the devastating results of the federal regulators' failure to fill in the gaps left by such preemption.

36. *Watters v. Wachovia Bank, N.A.*, 550 U.S. 1, 18–19 (2007); *see* Patricia A. McCoy & Elizabeth Renuart, "The Legal Infrastructure of Subprime and

Nontraditional Home Mortgages," in *Borrowing to Live: Consumer and Mortgage Credit Revisited* 110, 120–21 (Nicolas P. Retsinas & Eric S. Belsky, eds., 2008).

37. 2003 OCC Enf. Dec. Lexis 291; OCC NR 2003–21, OCC NR 2003–21 (the OCC was the only agency to use its UDAP power to prohibit unfair and deceptive acts and practices); *see also* Todd Davenport, "Too Vague for Both Sides; FTC Act Enforcement Worries Banks, Activists," *Am. Banker*, Dec. 16, 2004, which notes seven OCC actions by the Office of the Controller of the Currency (OCC) in the previous four years, none of which involved mortgages.

38. Home Ownership and Equity Protection Act (HOEPA) of 1994, *codified at* 15 U.S.C. § 1639 (2018).

39. *Ibid.*, § 1639(c)–(i) (2018).

40. *See ibid.*, § 1640(a) (2018); 12 C.F.R. §§ 226.32, 226.34 (2018). Holders of HOEPA loans are "subject to all claims and defenses . . . that the consumer could assert against the creditor of the mortgage." *See* 15 U.S.C. § 1641(d) (1) (2018).

41. *See* 15 U.S.C. § 1635 (2018).

42. *Ibid.*, § 1639(l) (2018).

43. *See* Engel & McCoy, *The Subprime Virus*, at 194–96.

44. *See* McCoy & Renuart, "The Legal Infrastructure of Subprime and Nontraditional Home Mortgages," at 119–20. By 2007, only six states—Arizona, Delaware, Montana, North Dakota, Oregon, and South Dakota—had failed to regulate any of the most troublesome subprime loan terms: prepayment penalties, balloon clauses, and mandatory arbitration clauses. Raphael W. Bostic *et al.*, "State and Local Anti-Predatory Lending Laws: The Effect of Legal Enforcement Mechanisms," 60 *J. Econ. & Bus.* 47, 49, 55–58 (2008).

45. *See* the section, "The S&Ls" in Chapter 3.

46. *See* Engel & McCoy, *The Subprime Virus*, at 157–66.

47. *See* Brent W. Ambrose & Arthur Warga, "Measuring Potential GSE Funding Advantages," 25 *J. Real Est. Fin. & Econ.* 129, 146 (2002), which found that the GSE-to-Treasuries spread was 25 to 29 basis points less than AA-rated banking-sector bonds; and Frank E. Nothaft *et al.*, "Debt Spreads between GSEs and Other Corporations," 25 *J. Real Est. Fin. & Econ.* 151 (2002), which found that GSEs had a funding advantage of 22 to 30 basis points relative to AA-rated bonds. The GSEs are now in federal conservatorship, and their obligations carry an "effective guaranty" from the federal government but do not enjoy a "full faith and credit" backing. *See* Dawn Kopecki, "Fannie, Freddie Have 'Effective' Guarantee, FHFA Says," Bloomberg, Oct. 23, 2008, 14:06 EDT, *at* http://www.bloomberg.com/apps/news?pid=20601087&sid=aO5XSFgEISZA&refer=home, which describes the director of the Federal Housing Finance Agency as saying that GSEs have an "effective" federal guaranty; and 12 U.S.C. § 1719(e) (2018), which explicitly states that GSE debts are not government debts. The difference, if any, between "full faith and credit" and an "effective guaranty" is unclear.

48. Investors would be concerned only to the extent that defaults affected prepayment speeds.

49. Admittedly, defaults affect prepayment speed, but in GSE securitized pools, the GSEs replace defaulted loans with performing ones so prepayment speed should be largely unaffected.

50. We note that the work of Edward Pinto, a fellow at the American Enterprise Institute think tank, claims otherwise. While Pinto's work has been embraced by some ideologues who favor the complete privatization of the housing finance market, it has generally been discounted within the scholarly community as based on a tendentious and idiosyncratic interpretation of GSE loan data. *See* David Min, "Faulty Conclusions Based on Shoddy Foundations: FCIC Commissioner Peter Wallison and Other Commentators Rely on Flawed Data from Edward Pinto to Misplace the Causes of the 2008 Financial Crisis," Ctr. for Am. Progress, Feb. 2011, *at* https://cdn.americanprogress.org/wp-content/uploads/issues/2011/02/pdf/pinto.pdf, which explains some of the problems with Pinto's empirical work and the conclusions Pinto draws from this data. *See also* Financial Crisis Inquiry Commission, "The Financial Crisis Inquiry Report: Final Report of the National Commission on the Causes of the Financial and Economic Crisis in the United States," 219–220 (Jan. 2011), which explains some of the flaws in Pinto's work.

    Ironically, some of the best evidence that the GSEs were *not* the source of the bubble comes from other American Enterprise Institute work, which calculates the "stressed default rates": the default rate that would be anticipated for loans of a particular vintage in the face of 2008 financial crisis conditions. *See* Morris A. Davis *et al.*, "A Quarter Century of Mortgage Risk," at 41, fig. 3, AEI Economics Working Paper 2019-04, Oct. 2019, *at* https://www.aei.org/wp-content/uploads/2019/02/Mortgage-Risk-WP.pdf. The stressed default rates on all types of loans soars for the 2003–2007 vintages, but the default rates on PLS are more than double that of the GSE loans. As the study notes, " Enterprise loans consistently have had lower risk than the market as a whole"; *see ibid.* at 18. Indeed, the data supporting Davis *et al.* show that the GSEs maintained much higher underwriting standards overall than PLS other than on debt-to-income ratios.

51. Individual deals would have minimum underwriting requirements, but they were much looser than the GSEs and were often violated.

52. Financial institutions' ability to make nontraditional loans was facilitated by federal legislation and regulations. Congressional legislation began the deregulation of mortgages in the 1980s with two key federal statutes: the Depository Institutions Deregulation and Monetary Control Act of 1980, 12 U.S.C. § 1735f-7a (2018), and the Alternative Mortgage Transaction Parity Act of 1982, 12 U.S.C. § 3803(a)(3) (2018). These statutes preempted state usury laws for first-lien mortgages and state regulation of nontraditional mortgages. Federal regulatory agencies expanded the scope of federal preemption of state regulations again without substituting federal regulation. *See* Adam J. Levitin, "Hydraulic Regulation: Regulating Credit Markets Upstream," 26 *Yale J. on Reg.* 143, 154 (2009). The Federal Reserve also failed to act on its regulatory authority under the Home Ownership and Equity Protection Act (HOEPA) to regulate high-cost mortgages. *See* Patricia A. McCoy *et al.*, "Systemic Risk

through Securitization: The Result of Deregulation and Regulatory Failure," 41 *Conn. L. Rev.* 1327, 1334 (2009).

53. The first private-label mortgage-securitization deal is often dated to 1977, with credit being awarded to a $150 million Bank of America deal issued on Sept. 21, 1977. *See* Bank of America National Trust & Savings Assoc., SEC No-Action Letter, 1977 SEC No-Act. LEXIS 1343, at 5–10 (May 19, 1977), which describes Bank of America's first PLS transaction; Michael D. Grace, "Alternative Mortgages Instruments and the Secondary Market," *Am. Banker*, Oct. 13, 1982. It appears that this deal was, in fact, the third mortgage securitization, but the first true private pass-through securitization. The first modern private mortgage bond appears to have been the California Federal Savings and Loan's September 25, 1975, $50 million bond issuance, which was secured by FHA-insured/VA-guarantied mortgages. *See* Grace, "Alternative Mortgages Instruments and the Secondary Market"; "Mortgage Bonds," *U.S. News & World Report*, Oct. 13, 1975, at 86. The second private-label deal was a $200 million bond issuance by the Home Savings and Loan Association (Los Angeles, California) on June 23, 1977, which was secured by conventional mortgages. The Bank of America deal was a true pass-through; the prior deals appear to have been secured bonds, meaning that the revenue to pay the bondholders was not necessarily from the mortgages in the first instance.

54. *See* David Murphy, *Unravelling the Credit Crunch* 133 (2009), which explains, "The first private label MBS deals were backed by very high quality mortgages: it took some years for investors to become comfortable with lower quality pools."

55. *See* MBS Basics, "Nomura Fixed Income Res." (Nomura, New York, NY), Mar. 31, 2006, at 22 exhibit 12, *available at* http://www.securitization.net/pdf/Nomura/MBSBasics_31Mar06.pdf.

56. *See ibid.*, at 22–23.

57. In the TBA market, a mortgage originator enters into a forward contract with a GSE or Ginnie Mae in which the originator promises to deliver, in the future, a package of loans meeting the GSE's or Ginnie Mae's requirements in exchange for GSE or Ginnie Mae MBS being identified in the future. *See* Office of Fed. House Enter. Oversight, "Mortgage Market Note 08-3," A Primer on the Secondary Mortgage Market (2008), *available at* https://www.fhfa.gov/PolicyProgramsResearch/Research/PaperDocuments/20080721_MMNote_08-3_N508.pdf. Because the originator is able to resell the loan to the GSE or Ginnie Mae for a guaranteed rate *before* the closing of the loan, the originator is not exposed to interest-rate fluctuations between the time it quotes a rate and closing. Without the TBA market, originators would have to bear the risk that the market value of the loan would change before closing due to fluctuations in market rates. The commodity nature of GSE and Ginnie Mae MBS means that they are sufficiently liquid to support a TBA market that allows originators to offer borrowers locked-in rates in advance of closing. Originators of nonconforming (non-GSE-eligible) loans, particularly prime jumbos, are able to piggyback on the TBA market to hedge their interest rate

risk by purchasing in the TBA market. For a fuller discussion of the TBA market, *see* the section on the Common Securitization Platform in Chapter 11.

58. *See* Ricardo J. Caballero, "The 'Other' Imbalance and the Financial Crisis," at 13–14, Nat'l. Bureau of Econ. Research, Working Paper No. 15636, 2010, *available at* http://www.nber.org/papers/w15636.

59. For example, for the Wells Fargo Mortgage Backed Securities 2003-2 Trust, a jumbo deal consisting mainly of prime or near-prime (alt-A) jumbos, 98.7 percent of the securities, by dollar amount, were rated AAA. *See* Wells Fargo Asset Sec. Corp., "Mortgage Pass-Through Certificates, Series 2003-2" Form 424(b)(5), Feb. 27, 2003, *available at* http://www.secinfo.com/dsVsn .2h2.htm.

60. "RTC Offering $750MM Servicing," *Nat'l Mortg. News*, Dec. 2, 1991.

61. *See* "Advanta Securitizing 'B&C' Loans," *Nat'l Mortg. News*, May 24, 1993.

62. Manuel Adelino, "Do Investors Rely Only on Ratings? The Case of Mortgage-Backed Securities," at 42, Nov. 24, 2009 (unpublished manuscript), *available at* http://citeseerx.ist.psu.edu/viewdoc/download?doi=10.1.1.156.989&rep =rep1&type=pdf.

63. Overcollateralization means that the initial principal balance of the mortgages supporting the MBS is greater than the principal balance on the MBS. *See* Richard J. Rosen, "The Role of Securitization in Mortgage Lending," *Chi. Fed Letter* (Fed. Reserve Bank of Chi.), Nov. 2007, which notes that 61 percent of private-label PLS products issued in 2006 were overcollateralized. The cash flows generated by a larger pool balance are available to absorb losses from mortgage defaults. Overcollateralization is an expensive form of credit enhancement because it ties up collateral that could otherwise be used for other deals, so PLS indentures sometimes provide for the periodic release of collateral if performance thresholds are met. Note that pool overcollateralization is done in addition to the overcollateralization of mortgages with a less than 100 percent LTV ratio.

64. Excess spread is the difference between the income of the special purpose vehicle (SPV) in a given period and its payment obligations on the MBS in that period—essentially the SPV's periodic profit. Excess spread is accumulated to supplement future shortfalls in the SPV's cash flow but is periodically released to the residual tranche holder. Excess spread generally cannot be released if certain triggers are tripped, such as a decline in the amount of excess spread trapped during a specified period.

65. Shifting interest involves the reallocation of subordinate tranches' share of prepayments (both voluntary prepayments and the proceeds of involuntary liquidations) to senior tranches. Shifting-interest arrangements are often stepped down over time, with a decreasing percentage of prepayments being shifted. *See* Sunil Gangwani, "MBS Structuring: Concepts and Techniques," *Securitization Conduit*, Autumn 1998, 26, 33. The effect is to make senior tranches' share of a securitization larger at the beginning of the deal and smaller thereafter. *See* Manus J. Clancy & Michael Constantino, III, "Understanding Shifting Interest Subordination," in *The Handbook of Nonagency Mortgage-Backed Securities* 39, 42 exhibit 4 (Frank J. Fabozzi *et al.*, eds., 2nd ed. 2000).

Credit subordination is almost always accompanied by shifting interest. *See* Frank J. Fabozzi and David Yuen, *Managing MBS Portfolios* 94 (1998).

66. A reserve account is a segregated trust account that is typically invested in highly liquid, investment-grade investments (for example, commercial paper). It provides a cushion for losses caused by defaults on the underlying mortgage loans. Reserve accounts come in two types: prefunded cash reserves and excess spread. Prefunded reserve accounts are funded in full at the closing of the deal; the arranger of the deal typically funds the account with a share of the deal proceeds. The reserve account thus is a holdback or discount on the SPV's purchase price of the loans. This type of prefunded reserve account is known as a cash collateral account. Reserve accounts either are required to be maintained at a specified level regardless of losses or are permitted to be drained in accordance with losses. In the former case, the credit enhancement of the reserve account actually *increases* as the principal and interest due on the PLS decreases.

67. Pool-level insurance either covers losses or provides cash-flow maintenance up to specified levels for the entire pool owned by the SPV. It insurance is typically provided by private mortgage-insurance companies. Bond-level insurance involves the guaranty by a monoline bond insurer on the timely payment of principal and interest on a tranche of bonds; *see* Gangwani, "MBS Structuring," at 35.

68. *See* Gary B. Gorton, *Slapped by the Invisible Hand: The Panic of 2007*, 87 (2010).

69. Regulation AB, 70 *Fed. Reg.* 1506, Jan. 7, 2005, *codified throughout* title 17 of the Code of Federal Regulations.

70. Inside Mortgage Finance, *2019 Mortgage Market Statistical Annual*.

71. *See ibid.*

72. *See ibid.*

73. *See ibid.*

74. *See* William W. Bratton & Michael L. Wachter, "The Case against Shareholder Empowerment," 158 *U. Pa. L. Rev.* 653, 719 n.198 (2010).

75. *See* Fernando Ferreira & Joseph Gyourko, "Anatomy of the Beginning of the Housing Boom across U.S. Metropolitan Areas," working paper, Feb. 2, 2018, which found that the local real estate price increases—which, as we explain in Chapter 6, is not necessarily a bubble—were initially financed by conventional mortgages, with subprime financing arriving later.

76. *See* Whitney Tilson, "Value Investing Website," T2 Partners LLC, *at* http://www.t2partnersllc.com, accessed Mar. 16, 2012. These figures reflect all mortgages, not just those that are subprime. The LTVs are arguably understated relative to fundamentals because of the housing-price inflation of the bubble. Determining true LTVs, however, is impossible due to the endogeneity problem.

77. *See* Michael Tucker, "Adjustable-Rate and Fixed-Rate Mortgage Choice: A Logit Analysis," 4 *J. R. E. Res.* 81, 86 (1989), which states, "Higher T-bill rates are associated with a decrease in the probability of borrowers selecting ARMs."

78. *See* Andrey Pavlov & Susan Wachter, "Mortgage Put Options and Real Estate Markets," 38 J. *R.E. Fin. & Econ.* 89, 92 (2009).

79. Although housing economists have noted that interest rate changes do not explain the bubble, they neglect to fully explore the impact of the decline in underwriting standards. *See, e.g.,* Edward L. Glaeser *et al.,* "Can Cheap Credit Explain the Housing Boom?" at 1, 2–3, Nat'l Bureau of Econ. Research, Working Paper No. 16230, 2010. Glaeser *et al.* examine underwriting in a very cursory fashion; their finding that loan approval rates were constant during the bubble ignores the dramatic rise in loan-application volume. *See ibid.* at 6, 26. This problem is also discussed in Charles Himmelberg *et al.,* "Assessing High House Prices: Bubbles, Fundamentals and Misperceptions," 19 *J. Econ. Persp.* 67, 68 (Fall 2005), which argues that, as of 2004, there was no housing bubble. Although Himmelberg *et al.* note that housing prices are not the same as the annual cost of owning a house, they neglect to consider whether the shift in mortgage-product mix was reducing the (initial) affordability of housing.

80. Between 2004 and 2006, the Federal Reserve forced up the cost of short-term credit, but the effect on mortgage lending was offset by the shift in the product mix and the decline in underwriting standards. Although those at the Federal Reserve could observe rates in real time, neither they nor anyone else could observe, in real time, the decline in underwriting and the shift in product mix. The deterioration in lending standards also left the housing finance system vulnerable to correlated shocks; any decline in housing prices would inevitably result in a market crash because of an increased reliance in the credit model on housing price appreciation.

81. *Cf.* Christopher Mayer *et al.,* "The Rise in Mortgage Defaults," 23 *J. Econ. Persp.* 27, 36 (Winter 2009), which notes that three nontraditional mortgage products "might be responsible for at least part of the delinquency rise."

82. Interest-only mortgages have nonamortized periods during which the borrower pays only interest; the principal balance is not reduced. The interest-only period can range from a few years to the full term of the loan. Once the interest-only period expires, the principal is then amortized over the remaining (shorter) period, meaning that monthly mortgage payments increase substantially on the expiration of the interest-only period, including the possibility of requiring a bullet payment of the entire principal balance at the end of the mortgage term.

83. Payment-option mortgages permit borrowers to choose among monthly payment options. Typically, the choices are payments based on fifteen- and thirty-year amortizations of the mortgage, a nonamortizing interest-only payment, and a negative-amortization payment that does not even cover the interest accrued in the past period. Because of the negative-amortization option, the balance owed on a payment-option mortgage can actually increase. Payment-option mortgages generally have a negative-amortization limit; once too much negative amortization has accrued, the loan resets to being fully amortized over the remaining term. Likewise, the pick-a-pay-period option is often restricted to a limited number of years, after which the loan resets to being

fully amortized over the remaining term. Both types of resets can result in significant increases in monthly payments.

84. A forty-year balloon mortgage, or "40/30," is a thirty-year loan that is amortized over forty years, meaning that there is a balloon payment due at the end of the thirtieth year. The mismatch between the term and the amortization periods reduces the monthly payments before the balloon payment.

85. A hybrid ARM has an initial fixed-rate period, usually at a teaser rate that is lower than those that are available on standard FRMs. After the expiration of the fixed-rate teaser period, the loan resets to an adjustable rate. Typically, these loans were structured as 2/28s or 3/27s, with two- or three-year fixed-rate periods and twenty-eight- or twenty-seven-year adjustable-rate periods. The new rate after the expiration of the teaser can result in substantial increases in monthly payments.

86. Curiously, average credit scores did not significantly change during the bubble years. This may relate to the endogeneity of credit scores to the overall state of the economy; a rising economy might boost credit scores.

87. Nontraditional mortgage products are subprime, Alt-A, and home equity loans. From 2008 to 2017, home equity loans comprised the majority of nontraditional mortgages.

88. *See* Peek, "A Call to ARMs," at 56.

89. Freddie Mac, "Quarterly Refinance Statistics," *at* http://www.freddiemac.com /fmac-resources/research/docs/Fq1_refinance_2019.xls.

90. Some nontraditional mortgages, especially payment-option ARMs, remained on the balance sheets.

91. A jumbo mortgage is a loan that is larger than the conforming loan limit, which is the maximize size the GSEs are permitted, by statute, to purchase.

92. This may be the reason why homeownership actually peaked early in the bubble, in 2004. *See* Paul S. Calem *et al.*, "Implications of the Housing Market Bubble for Sustainable Homeownership," in *The American Mortgage System: Crisis and Reform* 87 (Susan M. Wachter & Marvin M. Smith, eds., 2011). On the contribution of fraud to the bubble, *see* Thomas Herndon, "Liar's Loans, Mortgage Fraud, and the Great Recession," Pol. Econ. Research Instit. working paper no. 440, August 2017; Atif Mian & Amir Sufi, "Fraudulent Income Overstatement on Mortgage Applications during the Credit Expansion of 2002 to 2005," 30 *Rev. Fin. Studies* 1832 (2017); John M. Griffin & Gonzalo Maturana, "Did Dubious Mortgage Origination Practices Distort House Prices?" 29 *Rev. Fin. Studies* 1671 (2016); John M. Griffin & Gonzalo Maturana, "Who Facilitated Misreporting in Securitized Loans?" 29 *Rev. Fin. Studies* 384 (2016); Tomasz Piskorski *et al.*, "Asset Quality Misrepresentation by Financial Intermediaries: Evidence from the RMBS Market," 70 *J. Fin.* 2635 (2015); and Atif Mian & Amir Sufi, "House Prices, Home Equity–Based Borrowing, and the US Household Leverage Crisis," 101 *Am. Econ. Rev.* 2132 (2011).

93. *See* Himmelberg *et al.*, "Assessing High House Prices," at 74.

5. The Bubble Bursts

1. Bankruptcy Abuse Prevention and Consumer Protection of 2005, P.L. 109-8, §§ 901(b)–(c), 907, 119 Stat. 23, 147–49, 152–54, 171–74, (Apr. 20, 2005), *codified at* 11 U.S.C. §§ 101(47)(A), 741(7)(A) (2018), *and* 12 U.S.C. §§ 1787(c)(8)(D)(ii), 1787(c)(8)(D)(v), 1821(e)(8)(D)(ii), 1821(e)(8)(D)(v) (2018).

2. Moody's, *Structured Finance Special Report: Early Defaults Rise in Mortgage Securitizations*, Jan. 18, 2007, *at* https://fcic-static.law.stanford.edu/cdn _media/fcic-docs/2007-01-18%20Early%20Defaults%20Rise%20in%20 Mortgage%20Securitization%20(Moody%27s%20Special%20Report) .pdf.

3. Lingling Wei, "Subprime Mortgages See Early Defaults," *Dow Jones*, Aug. 30, 2006, *available at* http://www.ocala.com/article/LK/20060902/news/60424 1432/OS/.

4. Disclosure Statement, *In re* Ownit Mortgage Solutions, Inc., No. SV-06-12579-KT (Bankr. C.D. Cal., July 25, 2007), at 14–16.

5. Keren Gabay, "A Closer Look at 2006's Early Payment Defaults," *Mortgage Banking* 37, 38–39, May 2007.

6. *Ibid.; see also* Kate Berry, "Ownit Said to Have Sought a Bailout from Merrill Lynch," *Am. Banker*, Dec. 20, 2006; John Blakely, "Ownit v. Morgan, Merrill," *Daily Deal*, Sept. 17, 2007.

7. Disclosure Statement, *In re*: Mortgage Lenders Network USA, Inc., No. 07-10146 (PJW) (Bankr. D. Del. Mar. 12, 2008), at 12–13.

8. "Two Firms File Bankruptcy Due to EPDS," *Origination News*, Mar. 2007.

9. Moody's, *Structured Finance Special Report*.

10. Inside Mortgage Finance, "Non-Agency MBS Issuance by Type," *2019 Mortgage Market Statistical Annual*.

11. Inside Mortgage Finance, "Mortgage Originations by Product," *2019 Mortgage Market Statistical Annual*.

12. *Ibid.*

13. Moody's, "Moody's Downgrades Subprime First-Lien RMBS," Jul. 10, 2007.

14. 12 U.S.C. § 4612(a) (2018).

15. Housing and Economic Recovery Act, P.L. 110-289, § 1124, 122 Stat. 2654, 2691–93 (Jul. 30, 2008).

16. *Ibid.*, § 1402, *codified at* 12 U.S.C. § 1715z-23(m) (2018).

17. FHA, "FHA Single-Family Outlook," reports from FY 2009, *at* https://www .hud.gov/sites/documents/DOC_16576.PDF (2009); FHA, "FHA Single-Family Outlook," reports from FY 2010, *at* https://www.hud.gov/sites /documents/DOC_16575.PDF (2010); FHA, "FHA Single-Family Outlook," reports from FY 2011, *at* https://www.hud.gov/sites/documents/OL_2011 .PDF (2011).

18. FHA, "FHA Single-Family Outlook," reports from FY 2008, *at* https://www .hud.gov/sites/documents/DOC_16577.PDF (2008); FHA, "FHA Single-Family Outlook," reports from FY 2009, *at* https://www.hud.gov/sites/documents /DOC_16576.PDF (2009).

19. Housing and Economic Recovery Act, § 1101.
20. In December 2009, the funding commitments were changed from a fixed dollar amount to a formulaic approach that became a fixed amount when it ended at the end of 2012. *See* Congressional Research Service, "Fannie Mae and Freddie Mac in Conservatorship: Frequently Asked Questions," R44525, updated May 31, 2019, at 7. Under that final figure, the cumulative funding cap for Fannie Mae was set at $233.7 billion and the cumulative funding cap for Freddie Mac was set at $211.8 billion. *See ibid.*, at 7 n.34.
21. Fannie Mae, Certificate of Designation of Terms of Variable Liquidation Preference Senior Preferred Stock, Series 2008-2, § 2(c), Sept. 7, 2008; Freddie Mae, Certificate of Creation, Designation, Powers, Preferences, Rights, Privileges, Qualifications, Limitations, Restrictions, Terms and Conditions of Variable Liquidation Preference Senior Preferred Stock, § 2(c), Sept. 7, 2008.
22. Federal National Mortgage Association, Warrant to Purchase Common Stock, Sept. 7, 2008, at 3, *at* https://www.fhfa.gov/Conservatorship/Documents /Senior-Preferred-Stock-Agree/FNM/warrant/Fannie-Mae-Warrant.pdf; Federal Home Loan Mortgage Corporation, Warrant to Purchase Common Stock, Sept. 7, 2008, at 3, *at* https://www.fhfa.gov/Conservatorship/Documents /Senior-Preferred-Stock-Agree/FRE/warrant/FRE-Warrant.pdf.
23. Senior Preferred Stock Purchase Agreement, dated Sept. 7, 2008, between the US Department of Treasury and the Federal National Mortgage Association, § 5.3, *at* https://www.fhfa.gov/Conservatorship/Documents/Senior-Preferred -Stock-Agree/FNM/SPSPA-amends/FNM-SPSPA_09-07-2008.pdf; Senior Preferred Stock Purchase Agreement, dated Sept. 7, 2008, between the US Department of Treasury and the Federal Home Loan Mortgage Corporation, § 5.3.
24. Senior Preferred Stock Purchase Agreement, dated Sept. 7, 2008, between the US Department of Treasury and the Federal National Mortgage Association, § 5.7, *at* https://www.fhfa.gov/Conservatorship/Documents/Senior-Preferred -Stock-Agree/FNM/SPSPA-amends/FNM-SPSPA_09-07-2008.pdf; Senior Preferred Stock Purchase Agreement, dated Sept. 7, 2008, between the US Department of Treasury and the Federal Home Loan Mortgage Corporation, § 5.7.
25. Third Amendment to Senior Preferred Stock Purchase Agreement, dated Aug. 17, 2012, between the US Department of Treasury and the Federal National Mortgage Association, § 3, *at* https://www.fhfa.gov/Conservatorship/Documents/Senior-Preferred-Stock-Agree/FNM/SPSPA-amends/FNM -Third-Amendment-to-the-Amended-and-Restated-SPSPA_08-17-2012.pdf, which provides that the dividend amount shall be amended to equal the amount by which Fannie Mae's net worth exceeds zero; Third Amendment to Amended and Restated Senior Preferred Stock Purchase Agreement, § 3, dated Aug. 17, 2012, *at* https://www.fhfa.gov/Conservatorship/Documents /Senior-Preferred-Stock-Agree/FRE/SPSPA-amends/FRE-Third-Amend-to -the-Amended-Restated-SPSPA_08-17-2012.pdf, which provides that the dividend amount shall be amended to equal the amount by which Freddie Mac's net worth exceeds zero.
26. Senior Preferred Stock Purchase Agreement, dated Sept. 7, 2008, between the US Department of Treasury and the Federal National Mortgage Association,

§ 5.7, *at* https://www.fhfa.gov/Conservatorship/Documents/Senior-Preferred -Stock-Agree/FNM/SPSPA-amends/FNM-SPSPA_09-07-2008.pdf, *as amended by* Third Amendment to Amended and Restated Senior Preferred Stock Purchase Agreement, § 6, dated Aug. 17, 2012, *at* https://www.fhfa.gov /Conservatorship/Documents/Senior-Preferred-Stock-Agree/FNM/SPSPA -amends/FNM-Third-Amendment-to-the-Amended-and-Restated-SPSPA_08 -17-2012.pdf; Senior Preferred Stock Purchase Agreement, dated Sept. 7, 2008, between the US Department of Treasury and the Federal Home Loan Mortgage Corporation, § 5.7, *as amended by* Third Amendment to Amended and Restated Senior Preferred Stock Purchase Agreement, § 6, dated Aug. 17, 2012, *at* https://www.fhfa.gov/Conservatorship/Documents/Senior-Preferred -Stock-Agree/FRE/SPSPA-amends/FRE-Third-Amend-to-the-Amended -Restated-SPSPA_08-17-2012.pdf.

27. Fannie Mae, Amended and Restated Certificate of Designation of Terms of Variable Liquidation Preference Senior Preferred Stock, Series 2008-2, § 2(c), Jan. 1, 2018, *at* https://www.fhfa.gov/Conservatorship/Documents/Senior -Preferred-Stock-Agree/FNM/Stock-Cert/Second-Amend-FNM-Stock-Cert -as-amended-01-01-2018.pdf; Freddie Mae, Second Amended and Restated Certificate of Creation, Designation, Powers, Preferences, Rights, Privileges, Qualifications, Limitations, Restrictions, Terms and Conditions of Variable Liquidation Preference Senior Preferred Stock, § 2(c), Jan. 1, 2018, *at* https://www.fhfa.gov/Conservatorship/Documents/Senior-Preferred-Stock -Agree/FRE/Stock-Cert/Second-Amend-FRE-Stock-Cert-as-amended_01-01 -2018.pdf.

28. Fannie Mae, Amended and Restated Certificate of Designation of Terms of Variable Liquidation Preference Senior Preferred Stock, Series 2008-2, § 2(c), Sept. 30, 2019, *at* https://www.fhfa.gov/Conservatorship/Documents/Senior -Preferred-Stock-Agree/FNM/Stock-Cert/Third-Amend-FNM-Stock-Cert-as -amended_09-30-2019.pdf; Freddie Mae, Third Amended and Restated Cer- tificate of Creation, Designation, Powers, Preferences, Rights, Privileges, Qual- ifications, Limitations, Restrictions, Terms and Conditions of Variable Liq- uidation Preference Senior Preferred Stock, § 2(c), Sept. 30, 2019, *at* https://www.fhfa.gov/Conservatorship/Documents/Senior-Preferred-Stock -Agree/FRE/Stock-Cert/Third-Amend-FRE-Stock-Certificate-as-amended _09-30-2019.pdf.

29. 83 *Fed. Reg.* 33312, 33330, tbl. 7, July 17, 2018. Under the proposed rule, the GSEs would also have been required, as of September 30, 2017, to have had "total capital," including credit risk transfers, of at least $180.9 billion given the risk-weighting of their assets. *Ibid.* at 33330, tbl. 6.

30. Emergency Economic Stabilization Act, P.L. 110-343, §§ 3(9), 101, 122 Stat. 3765, 3767–68 (Oct. 3, 2008), *codified at* 12 U.S.C. §§ 5202(9), 5211 (2018), which authorizes Treasury to purchase "troubled assets," which are defined to include residential mortgages and MBS.

31. Thomas Herndon, "Punishment or Forgiveness? Loan Modifications in Pri- vate Label Residential Mortgage Backed Securities from 2008–2014," Po- litical Economy Research Institute working paper no. 442, Oct. 17, 2017.

32. CoreLogic, "Negative Equity Q1 2012," *at* https://www.corelogic.com /downloadable-docs/negative_equity_q1_2012.pdf (2012).

33. Figure 5.5 shows that the percentage of mortgages with negative equity steadily declines from 2012 on. Part of that is because of the stabilization of the housing market and increase in home prices, but part is also because many homes with negative equity were foreclosed upon, so those mortgages cease to be part of the calculation.

34. US Treasury, *Making Home Affordable: Program Performance Report through the Fourth Quarter of 2017,* at 4 (Mar. 16, 2018).

35. *Ibid.*

36. FHFA, *Refinance Report, Fourth Quarter 2018,* at 3.

37. Wells Fargo Bank, *Minnesota, Nat'l Ass'n v. Tamis,* No. BER-F-20770-04, (N.J. Superior Court, Chancery Division, Bergen County, Sept. 7, 2007).

38. *See supra* Introduction, note 50.

39. Larry Cordell *et al.*, "The Cost of Foreclosure Delay," 43 *R. E. Econ.* 916 (2015).

40. Adam J. Levitin & Tara Twomey, "Mortgage Servicing," 28 *Yale J. Reg.* 1, 5–6 (2012). *See also* Ingrid Gould Ellen *et al.*, "Do Foreclosures Cause Crime?" 74 *J. Urban Econ.* 59 (2013).

41. Levitin & Twomey, "Mortgage Servicing," at 6, which correlates outbreaks of the West Nile virus and foreclosures with abandoned swimming pools as the likely nexus.

42. Adam J. Levitin, "The Politics of Financial Regulation and the Regulation of Financial Politics," 127 *Harv. L. Rev.* 1991, 2005–7 (2014).

43. Inside Mortgage Financial, "Outstanding Mortgage Securities," *2018 Mortgage Market Statistical Annual.*

44. Herndon, "Punishment or Forgiveness?" estimates that there was $600 billion in foreclosure losses to PLS, a figure broadly in accord with Mark Zandi *et al.*, "Who Bears the Risk in Risk Transfers?" *Moody's Analytics*, Aug. 2017, *at* https://www.economy.com/mark-zandi/documents/2017-08-02-who-bears -the-risk.pdf. Figure 5.9 shows a spike in subprime foreclosures in 2001–2002, but subprime mortgages were a much smaller market at that time than during the period following 2007.

6. Timing the Bubble

1. In this book, we sidestep the question of whether there even was a bubble. For many readers, the question of whether there was a bubble may seem laughable. It's conventional wisdom that there was a devastating housing bubble in the United States in the early part of the twenty-first century. And yet the concept of bubbles is deeply troubling to classical economic thinking, in which asset prices are, by definition, the proper prices. This tautology leaves no room for a bubble; there are only market fluctuations, and not bubbles. Indeed, as economist John Cochrane has said: "Crying "bubble" is empty unless you have an operational procedure for . . . distinguishing them from rationally low-risk premiums." *See* John H. Cochrane, "How Did Paul

Krugman Get It So Wrong?" 31 *Econ. Affairs* 36, 37 (2011). Even now there continue to be scholars who question whether there was a bubble. We have addressed this frankly academic question in other work, Adam J. Levitin & Susan M. Wachter, "Why Housing?" 23 *Housing Pol'y. Debate* 5, 7–9 (2013).

2. Joseph E. Stiglitz, "Symposium on Bubbles," 4 *J. Econ. Perspectives* 13 (1990), which states,

> If the reason that the price is high today is only because investors believe that the selling price is high tomorrow—when 'fundamental' factors do not seem to justify such a price—then a bubble exists. At least in the short run, the high price of the asset is merited, because it yields a return (capital gain plus dividend [here, the housing price appreciation plus consumption value of housing]) equal to that on alternative assets.

Stiglitz's definition is not tautological, as it might appear at first glance, because fundamental value is based on the expected discounted value of future cash flows from the asset.

3. Fernando Ferreira & Joseph Gyourko, "Anatomy of the Beginning of the Housing Boom across U.S. Metropolitan Areas," working paper, Feb. 2, 2018.

4. *See, e.g.*, Peter J. Wallison, "Dissenting Statement," *in The Financial Crisis Inquiry Report: Final Report of the National Commission on the Causes of the Financial and Economic Crisis in the United States* 445 (2011), *available at* http://www.gpo.gov/fdsys/pkg/GPO-FCIC/content-detail.html; Edward Pinto, "Op-Ed.: Acorn and the Housing Bubble," *Wall Street Journal*, Nov. 12, 2009, http://online.wsj.com/article/SB10001424052748703298004574459763052141456.html, which states, "Most agree that the housing bubble started in 1997"; and Dean Baker, "East Asia's Economic Revenge," *Manchester (UK) Guardian*, Mar. 9, 2009. Robert Shiller argues that there were regional housing bubbles as early as 1998, but how these regional bubbles would have become national bubbles is not clear; *see* Robert J. Shiller, "Understanding Recent Trends in House Prices and Homeownership," *Proceedings, Fed. Res. Bank of Kansas City* 89 (2007).

5. *See, e.g.*, Lawrence H. White, "Federal Reserve Policy and the Housing Bubble," 29 *Cato J.* 115 (2009); Ironman [pseudonym], "A Better Method of Detecting Bubbles," *Seeking Alpha*, Feb. 25, 2010, *at* http://seekingalpha.com/article/190753-a-better-method-of-detecting-housing-bubbles, which dates the bubble back to 2001; and James Hagerty, "Who's to Blame for the Housing Bubble?" *Wall Street Journal*, Nov. 16, 2009, which cites housing economist Tom Lawler, who posited that 2002 was the start of the bubble.

6. *See* Robert J. Shiller, irrationalexuberance.com, *available at* http://www.econ.yale.edu/~shiller/data/Fig2-1.xls. Inflation adjustment is based on the Consumer Price Index; the Housing Price Index is a combination of the S&P/Case-Shiller HPI for 1987 to the present and four other sources for different historical data.

7. From 2000 to 2003, FRMs mortgages made up over 75 percent of conventional loans; *see* Inside Mortgage Finance, "Market Share of Adjustable vs.

Fixed Rate Mortgages, Conventional Loans: 2000–2008," *2010 Mortgage Market Statistical Annual.* In 2004, FRMs dropped to a 66 percent market share.

8. Ferreira & Gyourko, "Anatomy of the Beginning of the Housing Boom."

9. Charles Himmelberg *et al.*, "Assessing High House Prices: Bubbles, Fundamentals and Misperceptions," 19 *J. Econ. Persp.* 68 (Fall 2005) However, Himmelberg *et al.* were ultimately comparing imputed rental costs with ownership costs, which they acknowledge are not the same as housing prices. With a nontraditional mortgage, ownership costs of housing could be quite low, even with high housing prices. *See also* Chris Mayer & Todd Sinai, "Bubble Trouble? Not Likely," *Wall Street Journal*, Sept. 19, 2005. The argument by Himmelberg *et al.* in "Assessing High House Prices" assumes the continuation of housing price appreciation at historic rates. In 2004, it was unlikely that prices would continue to appreciate at historic rates because they were at an all-time high relative to imputed rents, suggesting that a bubble might have already been forming in 2004. *See also* Kristopher S. Gerardi *et al.*, "Reasonable People Did Disagree: Optimism and Pessimism about the U.S. Housing Market before the Crash," in *The American Mortgage System* (Marty Smith & Susan Wachter, eds., 2011), which notes the assumptions in economics writing prior to the bubble.

10. It is possible that a bubble was already forming in 2001–2003; we cannot rule it out conclusively. But to the extent that there was a bubble at that time, it was much smaller than what developed in 2004–2006, and its causes were fundamentally different; if there was a bubble in 2001–2003, it was driven by interest rates and monetary policy, which cannot explain the growth of housing prices in 2004–2006. Thus, while we are skeptical that there was a bubble in 2001–2003 in the sense of asset prices becoming untethered from fundamentals, we believe that if there was a bubble at that time, it was distinct from the much more destructive bubble that followed.

11. It is possible, however, that the bubble actually started in 2003, as mortgage originations predate PLS issuance, and mortgage originations increased significantly in 2003–2004 in regions with heavy subprime concentration; *see* Andrey Pavlov & Susan M. Wachter, "Subprime Lending and Real Estate Prices," 39 *R. E. Econ.* 1 (2010).

7. Demand or Supply?

1. The data does not include nonamortized loans or second-lien loans. *See* FHFA Form #075. Presumably the inclusion of these loans would show that borrowing rose even more.

2. FHFA, "Monthly Interest Rate Survey," tbl. 9 (2019).

3. Levitin-Wachter Subprime PLS Database. For a detailed technical discussion about the Levitin-Wachter Subprime PLS Database, *see* Appendix B.

4. Inside Mortgage Finance, "Mortgage Originations by Product," *2019 Mortgage Market Statistical Annual*, which show a decline in subprime originations from $600 billion in 2006 to $191 billion in 2007).

5. Levitin-Wachter Subprime PLS Database.
6. Arthur Acolin *et al.*, "Homeownership and the Use of Nontraditional and Subprime Mortgages," 27 *Housing Pol'y. Debate* 393 (2017).
7. Adam J. Levitin *et al.*, "Mortgage Risk Premia during the Housing Bubble," *J. R. E. Fin. and Econ.* (2019).
8. *See* Inside Mortgage Finance, "Mortgage Originations by Product," *2019 Mortgage Market Statistical Annual.*
9. We use the seven-year Constant Maturity Treasury because it is the closest match to the typical length of home tenure and mortgage tenure.
10. In other work, we find consistent results using a different dataset, namely, one of the securitized loans for which Wells Fargo serves as trustee. These loans include, but are not limited to, subprime loans, and they cover roughly 10 percent of the PLS market. *See* Adam J. Levitin *et al.*, "Mortgage Risk Premia during the Housing Bubble." Our findings are consistent with those of Alejandro Justiniano *et al.*, "The Mortgage Rate Conundrum," NBER Working Paper No. w23784 (2017). For a discussion on how our findings interface with those of Uday Rajan *et al.*, "The Failure of Models That Predict Failure: Distance, Incentives, and Defaults," 115 *J. Fin. Econ.* 237 (2015), *see* Levitin *et al.*, "Mortgage Risk Premia."
11. *See* Michael Lewis, *The Big Short: Inside the Doomsday Machine* 143 (2010), which states, "There weren't enough Americans with shitty credit taking out loans to satisfy investors' appetite for the end product [emphasis removed]."

8. Theories of the Bubble

1. *See* Robert J. Shiller, *Irrational Exuberance* (2nd ed. 2005). *See also* Edward L. Glaeser *et al.*, "Can Cheap Credit Explain the Housing Boom?" NBER Working Paper, No. 16230, July 2010, which concluded that Shiller's explanation is the most convincing; Ernan Haruvy *et al.*, "Traders' Expectations in Asset Markets: Experimental Evidence," 97 *Am. Econ. Rev.* 1901 (2007), which states. "We find that individuals' beliefs about prices are adaptive, and primarily based on past trends in the current and previous markets in which they have participated. Most traders do not anticipate market downturns the first time they participate in a market, and, when experienced, they typically overestimate the time remaining before market peaks and downturns occur."
2. An alternative psychological theory has been presented by Markus Brunnermeir and Christian Julliard. *See* Markus K. Brunnermeier & Christian Julliard, "Money Illusion and Housing Frenzies," 21 *Rev. Fin. Stud.* 135 (2008). Brunnermeir and Julliard argue that consumers are incapable of sorting between real and nominal changes in interest rates and rents. Therefore, consumers account for low nominal rates when making mortgage decisions, but fail to account for future appreciation of prices and rents falling commensurately with anticipated inflation. The result is that they overestimate the value of real estate when inflation is declining.

    Brunnermeir and Julliard's theory may well be correct, but it too cannot explain the movement in PLS yield spreads during the bubble. Therefore, their theory, like Shiller's, is at best an incomplete explanation of the bubble, as the movement in the yield spread shows that any growth in demand was exceeded by a growth in supply.

3. Edward L. Glaeser *et al.*, "Housing Supply and Housing Bubbles," 64 *J. Urban Econ.* 198 (2008), *available at* http://www.economics.harvard.edu /faculty/glaeser/files/bubbles10-jgedits-NBER version-July 16, 2008.pdf.

4. Randall O'Toole, "How Urban Planners Caused the Housing Bubble," Cato Institute Policy Analysis No. 646 (Oct. 1, 2009).

5. *See* Edward L. Glaeser & Joseph Gyourko, "Arbitrage in Housing Markets," in *Housing Markets and the Economy: Risk, Regulation, and Policy* (Edward L. Glaeser and John M. Quigley, eds., 2009), 113, 124, which notes that the tax deduction for home mortgage interest pushes up housing prices in supply-constrained markets. It is notable, though, that the bubble was more extreme in highly supply–elastic markets such as Phoenix and Las Vegas; *see* Thomas Davidoff, "Supply Elasticity and the Housing Cycle of the 2000s," working paper (Mar. 2, 2010), at 2; *available at* http://ssrn.com/abstract =1562741; Richard K. Green *et al.*, "Metropolitan-Specific Estimates of the Price Elasticity of Supply of Housing, and Their Sources," 95 *Am. Econ. Rev.* 334 (2005).

6. *See, e.g.*, Thomas Sowell, *The Housing Boom and Bust* 30–56 (2009); Financial Crisis Inquiry Commission, *The Financial Crisis Inquiry Report: Final Report of the National Commission on the Causes of the Financial and Economic Crisis in the United States*, at 444 (Peter J. Wallison, dissenting), which stated, "The *sine qua non* of the financial crisis was U.S. government housing policy, which led to the creation of 27 million subprime and other risky loans—half of all mortgages in the United States—which were ready to default as soon as the massive 1997–2007 housing bubble began to deflate. If the U.S. government had not chosen this policy path—fostering the growth of a bubble of unprecedented size and an equally unprecedented number of weak and high risk residential mortgages—the great financial crisis of 2008 would never have occurred"; Edward Pinto, "Acorn and the Housing Bubble," *Wall Street Journal*, Nov. 12, 2009, http://online.wsj.com/article/SB1000142 4052748703298004574459763052141456.html ("The flood of CRA and affordable-housing loans with loosened underwriting standards, combined with declining mortgage interest rates . . . resulted in a massive increase in borrowing capacity and fueled a house price bubble of unprecedented magnitude over the period 1997–2006."); Peter J. Wallison, "Cause and Effect: Government Policies and the Financial Crisis," Amer. Enter. Inst. (Nov. 25, 2008), http://www.aei.org/files/2008/11/25/20081203_1123724NovFSOg.pdf; Peter J. Wallison, "The True Origins of This Financial Crisis," *Am. Spectator*, Feb. 6, 2009, *at* http://spectator.org/archives/2009/02/06/the-true-origins-of -this-finan.

7. Michael S. Barr, "Credit Where It Counts: The Community Reinvestment Act and Its Critics," 80 *N.Y.U. L. Rev.* 513 (2006).

8. 12 U.S.C. § 1831u(b)(3) (2018), which establishes the CRA requirement for interstate mergers; *see also* 12 U.S.C. § 1831y (2018), concerning the CRA

"sunshine requirements"; and § 1843(l)(2) (2018), which sets the CRA requirement for financial subsidiaries engaging in expanded financial activities.

9. Bd. of Gov. of the Fed. Res. Sys., "Staff Analysis of the Relationship between the CRA and the Subprime Crisis," memo from Glenn Canner & Neil Bhutta to Sandra Braunstein, Nov. 21, 2008 [hereinafter" Fed Staff Analysis"], at 2, *available at* http://www.federalreserve.gov/newsevents/speech/20081203_analysis.pdf.

10. Financial Crisis Inquiry Commission, "The Community Reinvestment Act and the Mortgage Crisis," *Preliminary Staff Report*, Apr. 7, 2010; "Fed Staff Analysis," which states that HOEPA lending was less prevalent for institutions that were subject to the CRA than for independent mortgage companies; Glenn B. Canner & Neil Bhutta, "Did the CRA Cause the Mortgage Meltdown?" Fed. Res. Bank of Minnea. *Community Dividend*, Mar. 2009; Ellen Seidman, "No, Larry, CRA Didn't Cause the Sub-Prime Mess," in New America Foundation, *The Ladder*, Apr. 15, 2008; Elizabeth Laderman & Carolina Reid, "CRA Lending during the Subprime Meltdown, Revisiting the CRA: Perspectives on the Future of the Community Reinvestment Act," 115 (Fed. Res. Banks of Boston & S.F., Feb. 2009), which found that institutions subject to the CRA institutions were less likely to make subprime loans in California and that subprime loans made by those subject to the CRA that were in CRA assessment areas outperformed these institutions' subprime loans that were made outside CRA-assessment areas.

11. Robert B. Avery *et al.*, "The 2007 HMDA Data," 94 *Fed. Reserve Bull.* A07, A124, tbl. 11 (2008). Critically, not all financial institutions are subject to the CRA, because only federally insured banks and thrifts fall within its ambit. Depositaries' uninsured subsidiaries and affiliates are not subject to the CRA, but insured institutions are permitted to count their subsidiaries' and affiliates' activities toward CRA credit. Independent mortgage companies are not covered by CRA whatsoever.

The variation in CRA coverage enables a comparison of the mortgage lending of CRA-subject institutions with that of other institutions. Bank regulators do not specifically track subprime lending, but so-called HOEPA (high-interest-rate) loans, as defined by the Home Owners' Equity Protection Act of 1994, 15 U.S.C. § 1639b (2018), and regulations thereunder, 12 C.F.R. §§ 226.32, 226.34 (2018), which have to be reported separately under the Home Mortgage Disclosure Act, 12 U.S.C. §§ 2801–2811 (2018), and its implementing regulations, 12 C.F.R. § 203, App. A, I.G.3 (2018), provide a strong proxy for subprime lending.

Institutions subject to the CRA made only a small percentage of HOEPA loans during the 2004–2006 period. While depositaries made over 40 percent of loans, they made less than 30 percent of HOEPA loans. When their subsidiaries and affiliates are included, the market share of all loans was around 70 percent, but HOEPA loan share was only around 50 percent. In comparison, independent mortgage companies made up about 30 percent of the mortgage lending market but around 50 percent of the HOEPA market. HOEPA lending was concentrated in institutions not subject to the CRA. *See* Avery, *et al.*, "The 2007 HMDA Data."

12. *See* Rachel Beer *et al.*, "Are Income and Credit Scores Highly Correlated?" *FEDS Notes*, Aug. 13, 2018, *at* https://www.federalreserve.gov/econres/notes /feds-notes/are-income-and-credit-scores-highly-correlated-20180813.htm, which found a 27 percent overall correlation between credit scores and income, but somewhat higher correlations for the population age sixty-five and under.

13. *See* Avery *et al.*, "The 2007 HMDA Data," Not all HOEPA loans even qualified for CRA credit. To qualify, a loan must be made to an LTMI borrower in the financial institution's CRA geographic assessment area. In 2006, only 10 percent of all loans made by depositaries and their affiliates qualified for CRA credit, and just 6 percent of HOEPA loans; *see* "Fed Staff Analysis," at 7.

14. Robert B. Avery & Kenneth P. Brevoort, "The Subprime Crisis: How Much Did Lender Regulation Matter?" Bd. of Gov. of the Fed. Res. Sys., Division of Research and Statistics, working paper, Aug. 2010, at 14–16, *available at* http://ssrn.com/abstract=1726192.

15. *Ibid.*, at 21.

16. *See, generally*, Adam J. Levitin & Susan M. Wachter, "The Commercial Real Estate Bubble," 3 *Harv. Bus. L. Rev.* 83 (2013).

17. We address the parallel international residential real estate bubbles in other work; *see* Adam J. Levitin & Susan M. Wachter, "Bubbles International: A Comparison of Global Housing Bubbles," working paper, 2019.

18. Proponents of a CRA-induced bubble must, therefore, date the bubble as of 1997, but this would attribute *any* housing price appreciation to CRA, and clearly not all housing price appreciation is a bubble.

19. We believe that the strongest argument that can be made about the role of the CRA is an indirect and nonfalsifiable one: government policy, including the CRA sent a clear signal to the financial services industry that increases in homeownership were valued. Financial institutions took this as cover to loosen their underwriting standards across the board and develop economies of scale in subprime lending, as they knew regulators were cheering on looser lending practices. This sort of role for the CRA in the housing bubble is quite different from the "government made banks lend to unqualified borrowers" sort of argument. In this argument, CRA provides the cover for activities that financial institutions wished to engage in themselves.

20. Federal Housing Enterprises Financial Safety and Soundness Act of 1992 (the "GSE Act"), 102 P.L. 550 § 1331, 106 Stat. 3672, 3956 (Oct. 28, 1992), *codified at* 12 U.S.C. § 4561 (2018). From 1993 to 2008, the affordable housing goals were supervised by the HUD secretary. Starting in 2009, they came under the supervision of FHFA. *See* Housing and Economic Recovery Act of 2008, July 30, 2008, P.L. 110-289, § 1128(b), 122 Stat. 2700 (July 30, 2008), which transferred authority from HUD to FHFA.

21. Xudong An & Raphael W. Bostic, "GSE Activity, FHA Feedback, and Implications for the Efficacy of the Affordable Housing Goals," 36 *J. R. E. Fin. & Econ.* 207, 207–208 (2008).

22. GSE Act, §§ 1341, 1344, 1345, *codified at* 12 U.S.C. § 4566 (2018).

23. 12 U.S.C. §§ 4562–65 (2018).

24. 15 U.S.C. §§ 1601–1606 (2018). A HOEPA loan is a closed-end, nonpurchase money mortgages (excluding reverse mortgages) secured by a consumer's principal residence that either have an APR of more than 800 basis points above comparable maturity Treasury securities (for first liens) or 1,000 basis points above comparable maturity Treasury securities (for junior liens), or that have total points and fees payable by the consumer at or before closing that exceed the greater of 8 percent of the total loan amount or an annually adjusted dollar amount. *See* 12 C.F.R. § 226.32(a) (2018) (Reg Z). HOEPA loans must be separately reported in Home Mortgage Disclosure Act data. *See* 12 C.F.R. § 203.4(a)(13) (2018).

25. *See* 24 C.F.R. §§ 81.16(b)(8), 81.16(b)(12), 81.2 (2018), which defines "HOEPA mortgage" and "unacceptable terms."

26. 60 *Fed. Reg.* 61846, 61893, Dec. 1, 1995, *codified at* 24 C.F.R. § 81.16(c)(2) (2018). Fannie Mae did not believe that it had such authority. *See* Bethany McLean, *Shaky Ground: The Strange Saga of the U.S. Mortgage Giants* 30 (2015).

27. 24 C.F.R. § 81.17(a)(1) (2018).

28. 24 C.F.R. § 81.15(b) (2018).

29. 24 C.F.R. § 81.15(c) (2018).

30. U.S. Dept. of Housing and Urban Development, *Overview of the GSEs' Housing Goal Performance, 1996–2003* (2005).

31. H. L. Bunce, "The GSEs' Funding of Affordable Loans: A 2000 Update," in U.S. Dept. of Housing and Urban Development, Housing Finance Working Paper Series HF-013 (2002), H. L. Bunce &. M. Scheessele, "The GSEs' Funding of Affordable Loans," U.S. Dept. of Housing and Urban Development, Research Report, No. HF-001 (1996); Paul B. Manchester, "Characteristics of Mortgages Purchased by Fannie Mae and Freddie Mac, 1996–97 Update," U.S. Dept. of Housing and Urban Development, Housing Finance Working Paper Series HF-006 (1998).

32. Xudong An & Raphael W. Bostic, "Policy Incentives and the Extension of Mortgage Credit: Increasing Market Discipline for Subprime Lending," 28 *J. Pol'y. Analysis & Mgmt.* 340 (2009); David L. Listokin & Elvin K. Wyly, "Making New Mortgage Markets: Case Studies of Institutions, Home Buyers, and Communities," 11 *Housing Pol'y. Debate* 575 (2000); Kenneth *et al.*, "The Impact of Secondary Mortgage Market Guidelines on Affordable and Fair Lending: A Reconnaissance from the Front Lines," 28 *Rev. of Black Pol. Econ.* 29 (2001).

33. Stuart A. Gabriel & Stuart S. Rosenthal, "Government-Sponsored Enterprises, the Community Reinvestment Act, and Home Ownership in Targeted Underserved Neighborhoods," in *Housing Markets and the Economy: Risk, Regulation, and Policy*, 202, 205 (Edward L. Glaeser & John M. Quigley, eds., 2009), which found "essentially no evidence" that GSE affordable housing goals increase lending or homeownership; An & Bostic, "Policy Incentives and the Extension of Mortgage Credit"; An & Bostic, "GSE Activity, FHA Feedback," at 207–8; Raphael W. Bostic & Stuart A. Gabriel, "Do the GSEs Matter to Low-income Housing Markets?" 59 *J. Urban Econ.* 458 (2006); Brent W.

Ambrose & Thomas G. Thibodeau, "Have the GSE Affordable Housing Goals Increased the Supply of Mortgage Credit?" 34 *Regional Sci. & Urban Econ.* 263–73 (2004).

34. An & Bostic, "GSE Activity, FHA Feedback," at 207–8.

35. 24 C.F.R. § 81.16(c)(2) (2018).

36. The reduction of PLS products in the GSE portfolios is partially attributable to consent agreements with OFHEO after the revelation of GSE accounting irregularities. *See* Financial Crisis Inquiry Commission, "Government Sponsored Enterprises and the Financial Crisis," *Preliminary Staff Report*, Apr. 7, 2010, at 13.

37. Therefore, the 2005 increase in GSE affordable housing goals did not result in an increase in the size of the GSEs' subprime MBS portfolio. Data is not available on GSE alt-A MBS holdings, but based on available evidence, affordable housing goals do not appear to have driven GSE investment strategy.

38. Robert B. Avery & Kenneth P. Brevoort, "The Subprime Crisis: How Much Did Lender Regulation Matter?" Bd. of Gov. of the Fed. Res. Sys., Division of Research and Statistics, working paper, Aug. 2010, at 21, *available at* http://ssrn.com/abstract=1726192.

39. Rubén Hernández-Murillo *et al.*, "Did Affordable Housing Legislation Contribute to the Subprime Securities Boom?" Working Paper 2012-005D, rev. Mar. 2014, *at* http://research.stlouisfed.org/wp/2012/2012-005.pdf.

40. *Ibid.*

41. Prospectus Supplement, CWABS Trust 2005-AB5 (Dec. 23, 2005), at S-8, *available at* https://www.fanniemae.com/resources/file/mbs/pdf/UDD_2007 _101/CWL_2005-AB5_prospectus.pdf.

42. John B. Taylor, "Discretion versus Policy Rules in Practice, "39 *Carnegie-Rochester Conference Series on Public Pol'y.* 195 (1993).

43. John B. Taylor, "Housing and Monetary Policy," NBER Working Paper Series 13682 (2007); John B. Taylor, *Getting off Track: How Government Actions and Interventions Caused, Prolonged, and Worsened the Financial Crisis* (2009).

44. Taylor, *Getting off Track. See also* Andrey Pavlov & Susan M. Wachter, "Subprime Lending and Real Estate Prices," 39 *R. E. Econ.* 1 (2010), which shows how housing price increases can result from either the removal of constraints on access to capital for borrowers via lower underwriting standards, the decline in the cost of credit via interest rates, or the decline in the cost of the mortgage put option (the availability of nonrecourse credit) and demonstrating how these factors affected different geographic regions differently.

45. Glaeser *et al.*, "Housing Supply and Housing Bubbles," at 2–6; Jane Dokko, *et al.*, "Monetary Policy and the Housing Bubble," Finance and Economics Discussion Series, Federal Reserve Board, Dec. 22, 2009; Marek Jarocinski & Frank R. Smets, "House Prices and the Stance of Monetary Policy," 90 *Fed. Res. Bank of St. Louis Rev.* 339 (2008); Marco Del Negro & Christopher Otrok, "99 Luftballons: Monetary Policy and the House Price Boom across U.S. States," 4 *J. Monetary Econ.* 1962 (2007).

46. Ben S. Bernanke, "Monetary Policy and the Housing Bubble," 100 *Am. Econ. Rev.* (2010), *available at* http://www.federalreserve.gov/newsevents/speech /bernanke20100103a.htm; Alan Greenspan, "The Crisis," Brookings Papers on Economic Activity 38–40, *available at* http://www.brookings.edu/~/media /Files/Programs/ES/BPEA/2010_spring_bpea_papers/spring2010_green span. pdf. Bernanke also contests Taylor's counterfactual regressions and argues that the Fed actually adhered closely to the Taylor rule as it should be applied, accounting for anticipated, rather than actual inflation. *See* Bernanke, "Monetary Policy and the Housing Bubble."

47. Depending on the application of the Taylor rule, during this period the Fed Funds rate was either too low or more or less correct during; *see* Bernanke, "Monetary Policy and the Housing Bubble."

48. Edward L. Glaeser *et al.*, "Did Credit Market Policies Cause the Housing Bubble?" Harvard Kennedy School Pol'y Brief, May 2010, at 4. A 1 percent decline in the long-term rate results in roughly an 8 percent increase in housing prices. As ten-year Treasuries fell from a height of 6.66 percent in January 2000 to a low of 3.33 percent in June 2003, that would predict a 26 percent increase in housing prices (the actual increase was 38 percent). And Taylor cannot explain the further 52 percent price increase that occurred once long-term rates started to rise (to 4.99 percent at the peak of the bubble).

49. Bernanke, "Monetary Policy and the Housing Bubble."

50. Adam J. Levitin *et al.*, "North Star: Lessons for the U.S. from the Canadian Housing Finance System," working paper, 2010.

51. Richard Green *et al.*, "Housing Finance in Developed Countries in a Time of Turmoil," working paper, Aug. 2010, which examines why some developed countries experienced housing bubbles, but not others.

52. The Financial Crisis Inquiry Commission, *The Financial Crisis Inquiry Report: Final Report of the National Commission on the Causes of the Financial and Economic Crisis in the United States* 417, 419–20 (2011) (Hennessey, Holtz-Eakin & Thomas dissenting).

53. Ben S. Bernanke *et al.*, "International Capital Flows and the Returns to Safe Assets in the United States, 2003–2007," Feb. 2011, *at* http://www .federalreserve.gov/pubs/ifdp/2011/1014/ifdp1014.htm; Ben S. Bernanke, "Global Imbalances: Recent Developments and Prospects," the Bundesbank Lecture, Berlin, Germany, Sept. 11, 2007; Ben S. Bernanke, "The Global Savings Glut and the U.S. Current Account Deficit," the Sandridge Lecture, Va. Ass'n of Economists, Richmond, VA, Mar. 10, 2005.

54. Bernanke, International Capital Flows"; *see also* Ricardo Caballero & Arvind Krishnamurthy, "Global Imbalances and Financial Fragility," 99 *Am. Econ. Rev. Papers & Proceedings* 584 (2009).

55. Bernanke, "International Capital Flows."

56. *Ibid.*

57. Lloyd Blankfein, "Do Not Destroy the Essential Catalyst of Risk," *Fin. Times* (London), Feb. 8, 2009, at 7.

58. Bernanke, "International Capital Flows."

59. Susan M. Wachter, "The Ongoing Financial Upheaval: Understanding the Sources and the Way Out," ILE Working Paper 09-30, Aug. 2009, *at* http://ssrn.com/abstract=1464791.

60. Atif Mian & Amir Sufi, "Household Debt and Defaults from 2000 to 2010: The Credit Supply View," in *Evidence and Innovation in Housing Law and Policy* 255, 278–79 (LeeAnn Fennell & Benjamin J. Keys, eds. 2017); Atif Mian & Amir Sufi, *House of Debt: How They (and You) Caused the Great Recession, and How We Can Prevent It from Happening Again* 86 (2014); Atif Mian & Amir Sufi, "House Prices, Home-Equity Based Borrowing, and the U.S. Household Leverage Crisis," 101 *Am. Econ. Rev.* 2132 (2011); Atif Mian & Amir Sufi, "The Consequences of Mortgage Credit Expansion: Evidence from the U.S. Mortgage Default Crisis." 124 *Q. J. Econ.* 1449 (2009).

61. Christopher L. Foote *et al.*, "Cross-Sectional Patterns of Mortgage Debt during the Housing Boom: Evidence and Implications," Fed. Res. Bank of Cleveland working paper 19-19 (Oct. 2019) at 2, 25. *See also* Manuel Adelino *et al.*, "Loan Originations and Defaults in the Mortgage Crisis: The Role of the Middle Class," 29 *Rev. Fin. Studies* 1635 (2016), which shows that mortgage originations increased for borrowers at all income levels and credit scores, as did defaults; and Stefania Albanesi *et al.*, "Credit Growth and the Financial Crisis: A New Narrative," NBER Working Paper No. 23740 (Aug. 2017), *at* https://www.nber.org/papers/w23740, which found that most credit growth during the bubble period was concentrated in the prime sector.

62. Foote *et al.*, "Cross-Sectional Patterns of Mortgage Debt during the Housing Boom," at 2.

63. Jack Favilukis *et al.*, "The Macroeconomic Effects of Housing Wealth, Housing Finance, and Limited Risk Sharing in General Equilibrium," 125 *J. Pol. Econ.* 1 (2017).

64. *See, e.g.*, Kathleen C. Engel & Patricia A. McCoy, *The Subprime Virus: Reckless Credit, Regulatory Failure, and Next Steps* (2011); Patricia A. McCoy *et al.*, "Systemic Risk through Securitization: The Result of Deregulation and Regulatory Failure," 41 *Conn. L. Rev.* 493 (2009), which argues that the ability to pass off risk allowed lenders who lowered standards to gain market share and crowd out competing lenders who did not weaken credit standards; Kurt Eggert, "The Great Collapse: How Securitization Caused the Subprime Meltdown," 41 *Conn. L. Rev.* 1257 (2008–2009), which argues that securitization encouraged market participants to weaken underwriting standards; Giovanni Dell'Ariccia *et al.*, "Credit Booms and Lending Standards: Evidence from the Subprime Mortgage Market," Int'l. Monetary Fund Working Paper (2008), at 1, which notes that "lending standards declined more in areas with higher mortgage securitization rates"; Yuliya Demyanyk & Otto Van Hemert, "Understanding the Subprime Mortgage Crisis," 24 *Rev. Fin. Studies* 1848–80 (2008); Geetesh Bhardwaj & Rajdeep Sengupta, "Where's the Smoking Gun? A Study of Underwriting Standards for U.S. Subprime Mortgages," Federal Reserve Bank of St. Louis Working Paper No. 2008-036A; and Christopher Peterson, "Predatory Structured Finance," 28 *Cardozo L. Rev.* 2185 (2007).

65. *See, e.g.*, Benjamin J. Keys *et al.*, "Financial Regulation and Securitization: Evidence from Subprime Mortgage Loans," 56 *J. Monetary Econ.* 700 (2009); Benjamin J. Keys *et al.*, "Did Securitization Lead to Lax Screening? Evidence from Subprime Loans," 125 *Q. J. Econ.* 307 (2010); Atif Mian *et al.*, "The Political Economy of the US Mortgage Default Crisis," 100 *Am. Econ. Rev.* 1967 (2010), which found a correlation between the increase in mortgage securitization and the expansion of mortgage credit in subprime ZIP codes, which was unassociated with income growth; Atif Mian & Amir Sufi, "The Consequences of Mortgage Credit Expansion: Evidence from the U.S. Mortgage Default Crisis," 122 *Q. J. Econ.* 1449 (2009), which found that home equity borrowing accounts for a large share of the rise in household leverage during the bubble as well as defaults; and Atif Mian & Amir Sufi, "Household Leverage and the Recession of 2007 to 2009," 58 *IMF Econ. Rev.* 74 (2010). *But see* Ryan Bubb & Alex Kaufman, "Securitization and Moral Hazard: Evidence from a Lender Cutoff Rule," 63 *J. Monetary Econ.* 1 (2014), which argues that securitization did not result in riskier lending.

66. *See* Susan M. Wachter, "Housing and Credit Bubbles in the US and Europe: A Comparison," 47 *J. Money, Credit & Banking* 37 (2015), which shows that securitization is not the only path to a credit-fueled bubble. Securitization provided only a small share of Irish housing finance prior to the very end of the housing bubble; it never exceeded 10 percent of outstanding mortgages until 2007; *see* Irish Central Bank," Credit and Banking Statistics, Table A.6. Loans to Irish Residents—Outstanding Amounts (Including Securitised Loans)." The Asset Covered Securities Act of 2001 facilitated securitization in Ireland, but it was still slow to take off. Instead, most of the funding for Irish mortgage lending was done through wholesale deposits; *see* Padraic Kenna, "Milestones in 25 Years of Housing Finance in Ireland," in *Milestones in European Housing Finance* 259, 261–62 (Jens Lunde & Christine Whitehead, eds., 2016). A similar story was true for the United Kingdom, which saw a massive expansion of mortgage lending by banks such as Northern Rock, which was funded through wholesale deposits; *see* Kathleen Scanlon & Henryk Adamczuk, "Milestones in Housing Finance in England," in *Milestones in European Housing Finance* 152, 157; Christine Whitehead & Kathleen Scanlon, "Europe's Selective Housing Bubble: The UK," in *Global Housing Markets: Crises, Institutions and Policies* 173, 181 (Ashok Bardhan *et al.*, eds., 2012).

9. The Wall Street Securitization Bubble

1. *See, generally*, Adam J. Levitin & Susan M. Wachter, "The Commercial Real Estate Bubble," 3 *Harv. Bus. L. Rev.* 83 (2013).

2. *See* Susan M. Wachter, "The Market Structure of Securitisation and the US Housing Bubble," 230 *Nat'l Instit. Econ. Rev.* 34 (2014), which shows that a monopolist will internalize systemic risk externalities.

3. *See* Mark Adelson, "MBS Basics" *Nomura Fixed Income Research*, (2006) at 24, *available at* http://www.markadelson.com/pubs/MBS_Basics.pdf (illus-

trating a six-pack deal with over 94 percent of the bonds being AAA-rated A-tranche bonds). Larry Cordell, Yilin Huang, and Meredith Williams, however, found 23 percent average subordination supporting of the AAA-rated bonds in subprime PLS. *See* Cordell *et al.*, "The Role of ABS CDOs in the Financial Crisis," 25 *J. Structured Fin.* 10 (2019). Other data indicates an 18 percent average subordination for AAA-rated subprime mortgage securitization tranches, a 9 percent average subordination for AAA-rated alt-A mortgage securitization tranches, and a 5 percent subordination for AAA-rated prime mortgage securitization tranches. *See* Juan Ospina and Harald Uhlig, "Mortgage-Backed Securities and the Financial Crisis of 2008: A Post-Mortem." NBER Working Paper 24509, Apr. 2018, at 26, tbl. 5 (quotients for each securitization type of sum of principal amounts of Investment Grade Ex-AAA Securities and Non-Investment Grade Securities over All Securities). These figures are not the average of subordination percentages by deals, but of the percentage of non-AAA bonds in deals, but they are a good proxy for subordination levels.

4. *See* Yves Smith, *Econned: How Unenlightened Self-Interest Undermined Democracy and Corrupted Capitalism* 247 (2010), which states, "There was little appetite for the AA through BBB layers of a subprime mortgage bond, which accounted for nearly 20 percent of the total value. There was a cohort of sophisticated investors that were interested. But the small size of this group limited the amount of subprime that could be securitized, and consequently made these investors fairly powerful."

5. Economist Manuel Adelino has found that buyers of subordinated PLS often demanded a premium for investing in riskier deals based on ultimate performance. *See* Manuel Adelino, "Do Investors Rely Only on Ratings? The Case of Mortgage-Backed Securities," at 27, unpublished manuscript, Nov. 24, 2009, *available at* https://fisher.osu.edu/supplements/10/9861/01132010 -Manuel%20Adelino.pdf.

6. Conceivably, overcollateralization of the PLS could also be used to produce higher yields without increasing the yields on individual mortgages, but this would make securitization less profitable.

7. *See* Stephen A. Ross, "The Arbitrage Theory of Capital Asset Pricing," 13 *J. Econ. Theory* 341, 341–43 (1976).

8. We use the term "CDO" to refer to structured-finance CDOs of PLS, but it is important to recognize that not all CDOs were structured-finance CDOs. CDO is simply a generic term for a resecuritization of other securities (or leveraged loans). Many CDOs were resecuritizations of other things, such as Real Estate Investment Trust (REIT) securities, trust preferred securities, high yield debt, leverage loans, and synthetic bank regulatory capital relief (Broad Index Synthetic Trust Offering or BISTRO) deals. Structured finance CDOs were less than half of the CDO market. From 1995 to 2008 there were some 2,280 CDO deals undertaken in the United States, with total collateral of $1.39 trillion. Of these, only 837 deals, totaling $657 billion were structured-finance CDOs. Cordell *et al.*, "Collateral Damage," at 47, App'x 1. Despite the fact that structured-finance CDOs comprised only a minority of the CDO

market, they have been the sector that has received the most attention, such that "CDO" has become synonymous with "structured-finance CDO."

9. We have found the same phenomenon to exist in the commercial real estate market, where, excluding multifamily units, it is an entirely private securitization market. *See* Levitin & Wachter, "The Commercial Real Estate Bubble." The first-loss position in commercial mortgage-backed securities (CMBS) was traditionally held by a small number of sophisticated "B-piece" buyers. Beginning in 2004, these B-piece buyers were outbid by CDOs. With the advent of the CDO in the CMBS B-piece market, underwriting standards declined precipitously, resulting in a bubble that closely tracks the housing bubble.

10. *See* Mark H. Adelson & David P. Jacob, "The Subprime Problem: Causes and Lessons," 14 *J. Structured Fin.* 12, 12–17 (Spring 2008).

11. Cordell *et al.*, "Collateral Damage," at 34, tbl. 6 (2012).

12. *Ibid.*, at 33, tbl. 5.

13. The yields on credit default swap protection (a synthetic long position) on PLS did go up in the second half of 2006, but by that point it was too late—housing prices had already peaked.

14. Sergey Chernenko, "The Front Men of Wall Street: The Role of CDO Collateral Managers in the CDO Boom and Bust," 72 *J. Fin.* 1893, 1897 (2017).

15. Cordell *et al.*, "Collateral Damage," at 31, tbl. 2 (identifying one deal in 1999).

16. We reach this number by taking the quotient of our estimate of CDO real PLS assets over non-AAA-rated PLS issued. We arrive at the numerator by assuming CDOs had $378 billion of real assets, *see ibid.*, at 33, tbl. 4, and that 69 percent of these real assets, or $261 billion, were PLS. *See ibid.*, at 30, tlb. 1. We get the denominator by starting with $3.9 trillion of PLS issued between 2004 and 2007. Inside Mortgage Finance, *2019 Mortgage Market Statistical Annual*. We then assume that 92 percent of this issuance was AAA-rated, so there would be $313 billion of non-AAA-rated PLS. The resulting quotient is 67 percent.

17. *See* Anna Katherine Barnett-Hart, "The Story of the CDO Market Meltdown: An Empirical Analysis," at 10–11 (Mar. 19, 2009) (unpublished B.A. thesis, Harvard College), *available at* http://www.hks.harvard.edu/m-rcbg/students /dunlop/2009-CDOmeltdown.pdf.

18. *See* Securities Industry and Financial Markets Association, *Global CDO Issuance* (2012).

19. See Adam J. Levitin & Susan M. Wachter, "The Commercial Real Estate Bubble," 3 *Harv. Bus. L. Rev.* 83 (2013).

20. Michael Lewis, *The Big Short: Inside the Doomsday Machine* 141 (2010).

21. CDOs originated in Michael Milken's scheme to create artificial demand for poorly rated debt securities. For a history of the origins of the CDO, *see* William W. Bratton & Adam J. Levitin, "A Transactional Genealogy of Scandal: From Michael Milken to Enron to Goldman Sachs," 86 *S. Cal. L. Rev.* 783, 794–811 (2013).

22. Chernenko, "The Front Men of Wall Street," at 1895, 1910, 1926.

23. CDOs indentures limited the amount of collateral that could have a single servicer, usually at 7.5 percent of collateral volume by par dollar amount. *See*

ibid., at 1917. If the sponsor was part of a vertically integrated operation with an affiliated servicer, the single-servicer restriction would limit how much of the sponsor's own PLS could be sold to the CDO.

24. Daniel Beltran *et al.*, "Asymmetric Information and the Death of ABS CDOs," Bd. of Gov. of the Fed. Res. Sys., Int'l Fin. Discussion Paper No. 1075r, 6 (Nov. 2016).

25. Cordell *et al.*, "Collateral Damage," at 44, app. 1; Inside Mortgage Finance, *2019 Mortgage Market Statistical Annual*. To be clear, the $28 billion here is the total issuance of CDO^2, not merely the equity tranche. Note that the figures here all assume par issuance, but that was most affirmatively not the case. With discounted issuance, the leverage is even more extreme.

26. Cordell *et al.*, "Collateral Damage," at 5, 31, tbl. 2.

27. *See* Arthur Acolin *et al.*, "Borrowing Constraints and Homeownership," 106 *Am. Econ. Rev.* 625 (2016); Irina Barakova *et al.*, "Borrowing Constraints During the Housing Bubble," 24 *J. Housing Econ.* 4 (2014).

28. Atif Mian & Amir Sufi, "The Consequences of Mortgage Credit Expansion: Evidence from the U.S. Mortgage Default Crisis." 124 *Q. J. Econ.* 1449 (2009). *See also* Tim Landvoigt *et al.*, "The Housing Market(s) of San Diego," 105 *Am. Econ. Rev.* 1371 (2015), which shows that mortgage credit expansion resulted in a home price increase, particularly in neighborhoods with a disproportionate number of residents who had been previously denied credit.

29. Christopher L. Foote *et al.*, "Cross-Sectional Patterns of Mortgage Debt during the Housing Boom: Evidence and Implications," Fed. Reserve Bank of Cleveland working paper 19-19 (Oct. 2019) at 2, 25. *See also* Manuel Adelino *et al.*, "Loan Originations and Defaults in the Mortgage Crisis: The Role of the Middle Class," 29 *Rev. Fin. Studies* 1635 (2016), which shows that mortgage originations increased for borrowers at all income levels and credit scores, as did defaults; Stefania Albanesi *et al.*, "Credit Growth and the Financial Crisis: A New Narrative," NBER Working Paper No. 23740 (Aug. 2017), *at* https://www.nber.org/papers/w23740, which shows that most credit growth during the bubble period was concentrated in the prime sector; Arthur Acolin *et al.*, "Homeownership and Nontraditional and Subprime Mortgages," 27 *Housing Pol'y Debate* 393 (2017), which shows that homeownership did not increase more in low-income or in minority areas, but instead increase through 2004 across the income spectrum.

30. Christopher L. Foote *et al.*, "Why Did so Many People Make so Many Ex Post Bad Decisions? The Causes of the Foreclosure Crisis." *Fed. Res. Bank of Boston Pub. Pol'y. Discussion Paper Series* 12-2 (2012).

31. Christopher L. Foote *et al.*, "Cross-Sectional Patterns of Mortgage Debt during the Housing Boom: Evidence and Implications," Fed. Res. Bank of Cleveland working paper 19-19 (Oct. 2019).

32. Andrew Haughwoort *et al.*, "Real Estate Investors, the Leverage Cycle, and the Housing Market Crisis," Fed. Res. Bank of N.Y. Staff Report no. 514 (Sept. 2011); Alex Chinco & Chris Mayer, "Misinformed Speculators and Mispricing in the Housing Market," 29 *Rev. Fin. Studies* 486–522 (2016); Albanesi *et al.*, "Credit Growth and the Financial Crisis: A New Narrative"; Charles G. Nathanson & Erik Zwick, "Arrested Development: Theory and

Evidence of Supply-Side Speculation in the Housing Market," 73 *J. Fin.* 2587 (2018).

33. Haughwoort *et al.*, "Real Estate Investors, the Leverage Cycle, and the Housing Market Crisis"; Albanesi *et al.*, "Credit Growth and the Financial Crisis."

34. *See* Freddie Mac, *Annual Report 2005, Consolidated Financial Statements, Note 3: Variable Interest Entities, at* http://www.freddiemac.com/investors/ar /2005/05_11_06_03.htm.

35. FHFA, *Conservator's Report on the Enterprises' Financial Performance, Second Quarter 2010*, Aug. 26, 2010, at 6, 12.

36. The proximate cause of the GSEs' failure was not poor underwriting on the guaranty business for their securitizations, but rather downgrades on PLS in their investment portfolios that left the GSEs undercapitalized and therefore unable to carry on their MBS guaranty business. They were simply too highly leveraged to handle a major market downturn. The GSEs were already in conservatorship by the time losses began to mount from their guaranty business. Given the decline in GSE underwriting standards, however, losses from the guaranty business would have been sufficient to lead to conservatorship.

37. Fannie Mae Trust 2007-101 was a resecuritization of senior tranches of some twenty-two PLS. Fannie Mae guarantied the CDO securities.

38. We do not attempt to formally model GSE behavior here, but merely note that under the Cournot model of duopolistic competition, each duopolist takes the other's output as a given and then behaves like a monopolist.

39. Another possibility, which itself is consistent with the competition story but not "provable," is that the GSEs weakened their underwriting standards in a "gamble on resurrection," as they attempted to recapitalize themselves after being devastated by the refinancing wave of 2001–2003.

Prior to 2001, most GSE corporate debt was noncallable, meaning that the GSEs did not have the right to prepay the debt if interest rates fell. GSE mortgages, however, are prepayable. Thus, when interest rates plummeted in 2001, the GSEs found themselves facing an enormous problem. Their assets were refinanced to pay a lower rate, but they could not refinance their debt. The result was the impending decapitalization of the GSEs.

The GSEs' accounting scandals that emerged in 2004 prevent us from having the full picture of what happened, but if the GSEs were significantly decapitalized, they might have been tempted to "gamble on resurrection," meaning that they might have been tempted to assume greater risks in order to recapitalize themselves. The increased risk profile of the GSEs' business during the bubble could have been the result of a "doubling down" of their bets in an attempt to recapitalize after the refinancing wave of 2001–2003.

10. The Key Market Failure

1. *See* Stephen A. Ross, "The Arbitrage Theory of Capital Asset Pricing," 13 *J. Econ. Theory* 341, 341–43 (1976).

2. *See* Andrey D. Pavlov & Susan M. Wachter, "Mortgage Put Options and Real Estate Markets," 38 *J. R. E. Fin. Econ.* 89 (2009). *See also* Andrey Pavlov &

Susan M. Wachter, "Subprime Lending and Real Estate Prices," 38 *R. E. Econ.* 1 (2011).

3. *See* Jack Favilukis *et al.*, "The Macroeconomic Effects of Housing Wealth, Housing Finance, and Limited Risk Sharing in General Equilibrium," 125 *J. Pol. Econ.* 1 (2017) for an alternate explanation of why risk premia can drop efficiently as constraints are eased.

4. *See* Pavlov & Wachter, "Mortgage Put Options and Real Estate Markets."

5. *Ibid.*

6. We describe negative equity here as being negative equity relative to the market value of the property *plus the costs of sale*. Thus, we use the term negative equity to also cover "near negative equity," when the property has positive market value, but not enough to cover the sales costs as well.

7. 15 U.S.C. § 1681c(a) (2018).

8. Andrew Haughwoort *et al.*, "Real Estate Investors, the Leverage Cycle, and the Housing Market Crisis," Fed. Res. Bank of N.Y. Staff Report no. 514, Sept. 2011; Stefania Albanesi *et al.*, "Credit Growth and the Financial Crisis: A New Narrative," working paper Sept. 10, 2017.

9. Adam J. Levitin, *Consumer Finance: Markets and Regulation* 695 (2018); 15 U.S.C. §§ 1671 *et seq.* (2018).

10. Pavlov & Wachter, *Mortgage Put Options and Real Estate Markets.*

11. *Ibid.*

12. *Ibid.*

13. *Ibid.*

14. *Ibid.*

15. *Ibid.*

16. *See* Haughwoort *et al.*, "Real Estate Investors, the Leverage Cycle, and the Housing Market Crisis"; Albanesi *et al.*, "Credit Growth and the Financial Crisis."

17. We have also undertaken a similar analysis with similar results using a different data source. *See* Adam J. Levitin *et al.*, "Mortgage Risk Premiums during the Housing Bubble," 58 *J. R. E. Fin. & Econ.* (2019).

18. *See* Xavier Gabaix & David Laibson, "Shrouded Attributes, Consumer Myopia, and Information Suppression in Competitive Markets," 121 *Q. J. Econ.* 505, 506–7 (2006), which argues that firms can sometimes reveal exploitation by other companies "and win over customers"; Marisa J. Mazzotta & James J. Opaluch, "Decision Making When Choices Are Complex: A Test of Heiner's Hypothesis," 71 *Land Econ.* 500, 513 (1995), which found that individuals resort to simplified decision-making rules when choices reach a certain level of complexity; Xavier Gabaix & David Laibson, "Competition and Consumer Confusion," unpublished paper presented to the 2004 North American Summer Meeting of the Econometric Society, at 1 (Apr. 30, 2004), which argues that firms with lower intrinsic quality utilize excess complexity to confuse consumers and thereby increase market share.

19. *See* Levitin *et al.*, "Mortgage Risk Premiums during the Housing Bubble."

20. The development of the ABX index, discussed at the end of this chapter, addressed this issue problematically.

21. *See* Adam J. Levitin & Susan M. Wachter, "Second-Liens and the Leverage Option," 68 *Vand. L. Rev.* 1243 (2015).
22. *Ibid.*, which discusses 12 U.S.C. § 1701j-3(d)(1) (2018). We believe that a determined lender could likely structure around the statutory provision, but we are not aware of any having done so, in part because of path dependence and reliance on common loan documentation, in part because of legal uncertainty, and in part because of failure to recognize the risk of the leverage option.
23. *Ibid.*
24. *Ibid.*
25. The LTV and CLTV data come from different datasets, which may explain why the CLTV ratio is slightly lower than the LTV for some years. The LTV data is again from the FHFA's Monthly Interest Rate Survey, while CLTV data is from Intex, a commercial database of securitized loans. The Intex database has CLTV data for loans at origination only if such data are provided by securitization trustees. While the Intex data is likely to include "piggyback" second mortgages—that is, second mortgages made at or around the same time as the first-lien loan—it is unlikely to include "subsequent" seconds, made at some point after the first-lien loan. Thus, the CLTV ratio data we have almost assuredly understate CLTV ratios on a market-wide basis. Nonetheless, the overall picture is unmistakable.
26. The problems created by second liens should not have been surprising. In 1936, Marriner S. Eccles, the chairman of the Board of Governors of the Federal Reserve System, wrote that "the second mortgage is unsound from the point of view of the borrower, unsound from the point of view of the first-mortgage lender, and unsound from the point of view of the mortgage system as a whole." *See* Letter from Marriner S. Eccles to Edward E. Brown, President, The First Nat'l Bank of Chi., dated June 25, 1936, at 3, *appended to* Memorandum to Mr. Daiger, Box 27, Folder 10, Item 7, Marriner S. Eccles Papers, *available at* https://fraser.stlouisfed.org/archival/1343/item/466845, accessed on November 26, 2019. Unfortunately, many of the lessons of the pre–New Deal mortgage market were forgotten during the housing bubble. *See* Adam J. Levitin & Susan M. Wachter, "The Public Option in Housing Finance," 46 *U. C. Davis L. Rev.* 1111, 1170 (2013).
27. Laurie Goodman *et al.*, "Second-liens: How Important?" 20 *J. Fixed Income* 19, 20 (Fall 2010).
28. Michael LaCour-Little *et al.*, "The Role of Home Equity Lending in the Recent Mortgage Crisis," 42 *Real Est. Econ.* 187 (2014).
29. Michael LaCour-Little *et al.*, "What Role Did Piggyback Lending Play in the Housing Bubble and Mortgage Collapse?" 20 *J. Hous. Econ.* 81, 82 (2011).
30. Again, we believe the CLTV data in Figure 10.1 understate the true market-wide CLTV.
31. Economists John Geanakoplos and Lasse Heje Pedersen claim that "monitoring leverage is 'easy'" in that there are clear, observable measures such as loan-to-value ratios, that do not depend on models; *see* John Geanakopolos & Lasse Heje Pedersen, "Monitoring Leverage," Cowles Found., Discussion Paper No. 1838, at 2 (2013). We are less sanguine. Measures such as LTV

ratios are dependent on valuations and appraisals, which are often model-dependent. But more importantly for our purposes here, even if leverage metrics are less manipulatable than other metrics, they are not necessarily observable.

32. There are four major mortgage datasets used commercially: CoreLogic, McDash, Intex, and ABSLoanNet. There are differences in the makeup of the loans in each database, but a common feature is that they all lack reliable and complete CLTV data. For example, CoreLogic's database is missing CLTV data for 65 percent of prime loans and has no CLTV data whatsoever for subprime loans; e-mail from Dr. Laurie Goodman, Dir., Hous. Fin. Pol. Ctr., Urban Inst., to Professor Adam J. Levitin (Dec. 31, 2014) (on file with authors); e-mail from Dr. Sam Khater, CoreLogic, to Professor Adam J. Levitin (Jan. 7, 2015) (on file with authors). Likewise, the McDash loan-level database has the most complete coverage of the Agency market (loans owned or guaranteed by Fannie Mae, Freddie Mac, or Ginnie Mae), but lacks CLTV data; e-mail from Larry Cordell, Vice President, RADAR Grp., Fed. Reserve Bank of Phila., to Professor Adam J. Levitin (Jan. 3, 2015) (on file with authors). The Intex database, which is primarily a tool for conducting valuations of structured securities, has CTLV data, but only for securitized loans (agency and nonagency), and it has limited coverage of subprime securitizations. *See ibid.*; *see also* Global Regions, INTEX, http://www.intex.com/main/solutions_markets.php (http://perma.cc/W26Q-3YFA), accessed Jul. 6, 2015. Similarly, ABSNet Loan HomeVal had CLTV data, but only for nonagency securitizations; *see* ABSNET LOAN HOMEVAL, http://www.lewtan.com/products/absnetloan_homeval.html (http://perma.cc/6VED-VE5R]) accessed Jul. 6, 2015.

It is possible to match data from credit-reporting bureaus with mortgage databases, but this is a difficult task, which federal regulators have only done postcrisis, and this data matching still does not show a complete market-wide picture. Moreover, it is necessarily inexact because credit reports do not indicate collateral property locations or lien priority. Thus, a borrower could have two mortgages, and it would be impossible to tell from a credit report, whether they were a first and second lien on the same property or both first liens on different properties.

33. Thus, a study by economists John Griffin and Gonzalo Maturana finds that over 13 percent of loans securitized in PLSs between 2002 and 2007 were incorrectly reported as having no second lien; *see* John M. Griffin & Gonzalo Maturana, "Who Facilitated Misreporting in Securitized Loans?" 29 *Rev. Fin. Studies* 384 (2016). Many of these unreported second liens were in fact made by the first-lien lender!

While 13 percent may not appear to be a particularly high percentage, these liens increased leverage on a dollar-for-dollar basis. Moreover, the article only addresses PLSs. However, PLSs are not where one would expect to find large numbers of undisclosed second liens. Many second-lien loans were piggybacks, undertaken to enable GSE purchase of the first-lien loan. Thus, the economy-wide incident of undisclosed second liens is likely substantially higher than in Griffin and Maturana's sample.

Griffin and Maturana's article shows that it is possible to discover the existence of second liens, but it also demonstrates how difficult it is. Griffin and Maturana had to "marry" two separate databases, which do not use the same unique loan-level identifier. This meant that they had to engage in an address-matching protocol with the data. Even if one can do such matching well, the data is not available in real time. The second-lien data comes from a database drawn on county real estate records. These records are often recorded with a significant lag, thus frustrating any sort of real-time analysis. Moreover, by definition, a second lien is recorded after the first lien. Thus, the first-lien lender can never know before lending with certainty about the extent of second liens that will be subsequently placed on the property. Most importantly, Griffin and Maturana's data was not available during the bubble.

We have been able to identify only one source in the entire literature that indicates an awareness of rising CLTV prior to 2008. The source is a chart reprinted in several sources that attribute it to an April 2007 "Lunch and Learn" presentation given by Thomas Zimmerman at UBS. We have been unable to track down the original source. This chart indicates that there was rising CLTV on adjustable rate mortgages along with a decline in other indicators of the quality of mortgage lending declined. While the reprinted chart indicates that the data is from Loan Performance (now CoreLogic), this database does not have CLTV data for subprime loans, and has it for only about two-thirds of prime loans. Most importantly, by the time this data started to become available, the housing market was already in decline; this data was too late to foster market discipline.

34. See William W. Bratton & Michael L. Wachter, "The Case against Shareholder Empowerment," 158 *U. Pa. L. Rev.* 653, 717–26 (2010).

35. 12 U.S.C. § 1701j-3(d)(1) (2018). For a history of this provision, see Levitin & Wachter, "Second-Liens and the Leverage Option."

36. Lenders are not expressly forbidden from taking other steps, such as having interest rates adjust with a junior lien or from having a fee attach when a second lien is created, but such steps might be implicitly forbidden by the penumbra of the Garn–St. Germain prohibition against due-on-sale clauses.

37. 12 U.S.C. § 1454(a)(2) (2018) (Freddie Mac); 12 U.S.C. § 1717(b)(2) (2018) (Fannie Mae).

38. Michael LaCour-Little, Wei Yu, and Libo Sun have found that a substantial part of the growth of junior mortgages were home equity lines of credit (HELOCs), but that these HELOCs were used to fund down payments on investment properties, rather than to pay down other higher interest rate debts; *see* Michael LaCour-Little *et al.*, "The Role of Home Equity Lending in the Recent Mortgage Crisis," 42 *R. E. Econ.* 153, 187 (2014).

39. *See* Manuel Adelino, "Do Investors Rely Only on Ratings? The Case of Mortgage-Backed Securities," (Nov. 24, 2009) (unpublished manuscript), *available at* https://fisher.osu.edu/supplements/10/9861/01132010-Manuel%20Adelino.pdf, at 13, 44.

40. *See ibid.*, at 31–34.

41. *See ibid.*, at 33–34.

42. *See ibid.*, at 14–15, 43.
43. *See, e.g.*, Jerome S. Fons, "Rating Competition and Structured Finance," *J. Structured Fin.*, Fall 2008, at 7, 11–14; Joseph R. Mason, "The (Continuing) Information Problems in Structured Finance," *J. Structured Fin.*, Spring 2008, at 7, 7–11; Joseph R. Mason & Joshua Rosner, "Where Did the Risk Go? How Misapplied Bond Ratings Cause Mortgage Backed Securities and Collateralized Debt Obligation Market Disruptions" at 8–15, *available at* http://ssrn.com/abstract=1027475 (May 3, 2007); Matthew Richardson & Lawrence J. White, "The Rating Agencies: Is Regulation the Answer?" in *Restoring Financial Stability: How to Repair a Failed System* 101, 104–15 (Viral V. Acharya & Matthew Richardson, eds., 2009).
44. See generally Mason & Rosner, "Where Did the Risk Go?," at 34–66, which discusses the unique problems that MBS pose for the bond-rating model.
45. *Ibid.*, at 13. The ratings agencies also made their models available to investment banks, which then designed their products to game the ratings models. See Gretchen Morgenson & Louise Story, "Rating Agency Data Aided Wall Street in Deals," *New York Times*, Apr. 24, 2010, at A1.
46. *See* Mason & Rosner, "Where Did the Risk Go?" at 25–28.
47. Larry Cordell *et al.*, "The Role of ABS CDOs in the Financial Crisis," 25 *J. Structured Fin.* 10 (2019).
48. *See ibid.*, at 25. Another problem was that mortgage-servicer ratings were included as a component of RMBS ratings, but servicer performance and RMBS performance are inexorably intertwined. The costs of servicing rise with defaults. Servicer performance also depends heavily on servicer liquidity, which may itself be tied to mortgage-market performance. Many servicers have mortgage-origination affiliates. If the origination business is in trouble, it can impact the liquidity of the servicing business and hence the performance of the servicer. This, then, impacts risks for other lenders whose loans are serviced by the servicers. Using servicer rating as part of the RMBS rating process has an endogeneity problem and effectively double counts servicer risks. *See ibid.*, at 27.
49. *See, e.g.*, Gary Shorter & Michael V. Seitzinger, "Credit Rating Agencies and Their Regulation," Cong. Research Serv., R40613, at 5–6, 11 (2009). Ratings methodologies changed frequently for structured-finance products and were not always consistent between existing and new issues. Mason & Rosner, "Where Did the Risk Go?" at 19, 21, 22 n.75. These models also failed to incorporate much of the available mortgage data (or lack thereof), such as debt-to-income ratio, appraisal type, and lender identity. *See ibid.*, at 23–24.
50. *See* James Grant, *Mr. Market Miscalculates: The Bubble Years and Beyond* 183 (2008).
51. *See* Gretchen Morgenson, "Debt Watchdogs: Tamed or Caught Napping?" *New York Times*, Dec. 7, 2008, at A1; Joshua D. Coval *et al.*, "The Economics of Structured Finance," 4 Harvard Bus. Sch., Working Paper 09-060 (2008), *available at* http://www.hbs.edu/research/pdf/09-060.pdf.
52. *See* Vasiliki Skreta & Laura Veldkamp, "Ratings Shopping and Asset Complexity: A Theory of Ratings Inflation," 56 *J. Monetary Econ.* 678 (2009).

53. *See* Michael Lewis, *The Big Short: Inside the Doomsday Machine* 27–28 (2010), which notes that Mike Burry was only starting to figure out the overpricing of the market in late 2004 and early 2005.

54. *See* Richard Herring & Susan Wachter, "Bubbles in Real Estate Markets," Zell/Lurie Real Estate Ctr., Working Paper No. 402, at 4 (2002), *available at* http://realestate.wharton.upenn.edu/newsletter/bubbles.pdf. Shorting real estate should not be confused with a short sale, in which a mortgage lender agrees to let a borrower sell property for less than the full amount due on the mortgage and forgives the deficiency.

55. Similarly, the uniqueness of real estate is a reason that specific performance is generally available as a remedy for breach of real-estate sales contracts. *See* Restatement (Third) of Prop. (Servitudes) § 8.3 cmt. b (2000).

56. It is also possible to short housing-related stocks, such as those of major homebuilders or banks with large real-estate portfolios, but this applies only indirect market pressure and is an expensive and risky strategy because of the indirect connection with real-estate prices.

57. Insurance conceivably would have provided market discipline. If private mortgage insurance were required on all high LTV loans, as is the case in Canada; *see* David Min, Ctr. for Am. Progress, "True North: The Facts about the Canadian Mortgage Banking System," at 9 (2010), *available at* http://www .americanprogress.org/issues/2010/08/true_north.html, then insurance premiums could have maintained discipline on underwriting standards. *See also* Susan Wachter, "Procyclicality and Lending Standards Through-the-Cycle," unpublished paper (Aug. 2010) (on file with authors). The collapse of the GSEs itself was arguably an insurance failure because the GSEs failed to reserve countercyclically for losses on their guaranty business and found themselves in a rate war (for risk-adjusted rates) with PLS credit enhancements, including monoline bond insurers.

58. *See, e.g.*, Vinod Kothari, *Securitization: The Financial Instrument of the Future*, at 524–25 (2006); and David Mengle, "Credit Derivatives: An Overview," *Econ. Rev.*, Fourth Quarter 2007, at 1, 1–2.

59. CDS can, in theory, be written on a collection, or bucket, of assets, but more often this takes the form of a CDS on a CDO rather than a CDS on a bucket of individually selected assets.

60. The New York State Insurance Department issued a pair of opinion letters opining that a CDS on corporate bonds is not insurance when the payment is not dependent upon the protection buyer having suffered a loss. Opinion of the Office of General Counsel of the NYSID (unnumbered) (June 16, 2000); Opinion of the Office of General Counsel of the NYSID (unnumbered) (May 2, 2002).

61. Dodd-Frank Wall Street Reform and Consumer Protection Act of 2010, Pub. L. 111-203, § 722(b), 124 Stat. 1376, 1673 (Jul. 21, 2010), *codified at* 7 U.S.C. § 16(h) (2018).

62. Commodity Futures Modernization Act of 2000, P.L. 106-554, App. E, § 408, 114 Stat. 2763A-461 (Dec. 21, 2000).

63. *Ibid.*, §§ 101, 103.

64. Larry Cordell *et al.*, "Collateral Damage: Sizing and Assessing the Subprime CDO Crisis," Fed. Reserve Bank of Phila., Working Paper No. 11-30 (2011),

at 34 tbl. 6, *available at* http://papers.ssrn.com/sol3/papers.cfm?abstract_id
=1907299.

65. *Ibid.*, at 33 tbl. 4, *available at* http://papers.ssrn.com/sol3/papers.cfm?abstract
     _id=1907299.

66. Those tranches with original (noninvestment grade) ratings of BB/B were not
     as heavily targeted as the BBB rated tranches, presumably because they were
     always assumed to be vulnerable to losses.

67. Yves Smith, *Econned: How Unenlightened Self-Interest Undermined Democracy and Corrupted Capitalism* 295 (2010).

68. See Jesse Eisinger & Jake Bernstein, "The Magnetar Trade: How One Hedge
     Fund Helped Keep the Bubble Going," *ProPublica*, Apr. 9, 2010, *available at*
     http://www.propublica.org/article/all-the-magnetar-trade-how-one-hedge
     -fund-helped-keep-the-housing-bubble.

69. *See* Smith, *Econned*, at 256–61.

70. This is a distinct type of leverage than that which is usually considered in the
     case of CDOs, namely, the leverage of the protection seller who does not have
     to commit full funding of its position upfront, enabling it to deploy those
     funds elsewhere; *See* Erik F. Gerding, "Credit Derivatives, Leverage, and Financial Regulation's Missing Macroeconomic Dimension," 8 *Berkeley Bus.
     L. J.* 102, 113–14 (2011). It is also distinct from a third type of leverage in
     the CDO space, namely, the leveraging of a limited number of PLS tranches
     into a much greater systemic financial exposure through synthetic securitization. Synthetic CDOs also greatly amplified the financial risk on a set group
     of mortgages. Thus, Larry Cordell *et al.* have found that between 1999 and
     2007, 5,496 BBB-rated PLS were references some 36,901 times in 727 publicly traded CDOs, which had the effect of "transforming $64 billion of BBB
     subprime bonds into $140 billion of CDO assets." *See* Cordell *et al.*, "Collateral Damage," at 2, 10, 34 tbl. 6.

71. *See* Smith, *Econned*, at 261 (emphasis removed).

72. *Ibid.*, at 260; *see also* Eisinger & Bernstein, "The Magnetar Trade," which
     discusses Magnetar's business practices.

73. *See* Smith, *Econned*, at 259.

74. *See* Ingo Fender & Martin Scheicher, "The ABX: How Do the Markets Price
     Subprime Mortgage Risk?" *BIS Q. Rev.*, Sept. 2008, at 67, 68. The ABX was
     launched on January 19, 2006; *see* "CDS IndexCo and Markit Announce Roll
     of the ABX.HE Indices," *Bus. Wire*, Jan. 19, 2007, 8:00 a.m., *at* http://www
     .businesswire.com/news/home/20070119005133/en/CDS-IndexCo-Markit
     -Announce-Roll-ABX.HE-Indices. For details on the ABX index methodology,
     see MarkIt, "Press Release, Index Methodology for the ABX.HE Index for
     the Sub-Prime Home Equity Sector ['ABX.HE Index Rules]" (Sept. 5, 2008),
     at http://www.markit.com/assets/en/docs/products/data/indices/structured
     -finance/ABX%20rules%20revised%209-9-08.pdf.

75. John Geanakoplos, "Solving the Present Crisis and Managing the Leverage
     Cycle," *FRBNY Econ. Pol'y. Rev.*, at 101, 110–11, Aug. 2010, *available at*
     http://www.ny.frb.org/research/epr/10v16n1/1008gean.pdf.

11. Postcrisis Reforms and Developments

1. The 2017 Tax Cuts and Jobs Act reduced the home mortgage interest deduction for the period of 2018–2025. An Act to provide for reconciliation pursuant to titles II and V of the concurrent resolution on the budget for fiscal year 2018 (Tax Cuts and Jobs Act), Pub. L. No. 115-97, § 11043(a), 131 Stat. 2054 (Dec. 22, 2017). The deduction, which allowed a deduction on interest on up to $1 million in home acquisition debt and $100,000 in home equity debt, is now limited to $750,000 solely for acquisition debt, but only for mortgages taken out after December 15, 2017. *Ibid.* Older mortgages are grandfathered into the old deduction, and in 2026, the old deduction caps will again apply to all mortgages. *Ibid.* Additionally, the previously unlimited deduction for state and local taxes (including real estate taxes) is now capped at a $10,000. *Ibid.* § 11042.

   While these changes attracted substantial headlines, they are unlikely to have a significant effect on the housing market overall as many homeowners do not utilize these deductions, which requires filing a return with itemized deductions. For example, historically the home mortgage interest deduction was used by only about 20 percent of tax return filers. *See* Sarah O'Brien, "Tax Bill Will Slash by Half the Number of Homeowners Using the Mortgage Deduction," CNBC.com, Apr. 23, 2018, *at* https://www.cnbc.com/2018 /04/23/tax-bill-will-slash-the-number-of-homeowners-claiming-the -mortgage-deduction.html. The 73 percent of the beneficiaries of the home mortgage interest deduction are homeowners with incomes of over $100,000. *See* Scott Eastman & Anna Tyger, "The Home Mortgage Interest Deduction," Tax Foundation, Oct. 15, 2019, *at* https://taxfoundation.org/home-mortgage -interest-deduction/. However, it is important to note that many homeowners at the higher end of the real estate market pay the alternative minimum tax and therefore do not take itemized deductions. At most, the scaling back of the deduction resulted in limited downward pressure on home prices—a change in fundamentals, but not a large one. *See also* Kamila Sommer & Paul Sullivan, "Implications of US Tax Policy for House Prices, Rents, and Homeownership," 108 *Am. Econ. Rev.* 241, 261 (2018), which estimated that a complete elimination of the deduction would result in a 4.2 percent drop in home prices but a 5 percent increase in homeownership.

2. Dodd-Frank Wall Street Reform and Consumer Protection Act of 2010, Pub. L. 111-203, § 1011, 124 Stat. 1376, 1964 (Jul. 22, 2010), *codified* at 12 U.S.C. § 5491 (2018).

3. Adam J. Levitin, "Hydraulic Regulation: Regulating Credit Markets Upstream," 26 *Yale J. Reg.* 143, 159–60 (2009).

4. Dodd-Frank Wall Street Reform and Consumer Protection Act of 2010, Pub. L. 111-203, § 1411, *codified* at 15 U.S.C. § 1693c(a) (2018).

5. 15 U.S.C. § 1639c(a)(1) (2018).

6. 15 U.S.C. §§ 1639(a)(3), (a)(6), (a)(7) (2018).

7. 15 U.S.C. § 1640(a) (2018).

8. 15 U.S.C. § 1640(e) (2018).

9. 15 U.S.C. § 1640(k) (2018).

10. 12 C.F.R. § 1026.43(e)(1)(i) (2018).

11. 12 C.F.R. § 1026.43(b)(4) (2018).

12. Economic Growth, Regulatory Relief, and Consumer Protection Act, P.L. 115-174, § 101, 132 Stat. 1296 (May 24, 2018).

13. Bing Bai *et al.*, "Did the QM Rule Make It Harder to Get a Mortgage?" Urban Institute, Mar. 1, 2016, *at* https://www.urban.org/research/publication/has-qm -rule-made-it-harder-get-mortgage.

14. *Ibid.*

15. Patricia A. McCoy & Susan M. Wachter, "The Macroprudential Implications of the Qualified Mortgage Debate," 2019 *Law & Contemporary Problems.*

16. Bing Bai *et al.*, "Did the QM Rule Make It Harder to Get a Mortgage?"

17. 15 U.S.C. § 1639c(c)(1)(A) (2018).

18. 15 U.S.C. § 1639h (2018).

19. 15 U.S.C. § 1639e (2018).

20. 15 U.S.C. §§ 1639b(c) (2018).

21. Having equity in the property, however, ensures that the consumer can sell the property and avoid a foreclosure in the event of a disruption to income.

22. Dodd-Frank Wall Street Reform and Consumer Protection Act of 2010, § 941, *codified* at 15 U.S.C. § 78c (2018).

23. In any case, given the moribund state of the private securitization market, the QRM rule has no meaningful effect on mortgage markets.

24. 15 U.S.C. § 1639e (2018).

25. Adam J. Levitin & Tara Twomey, "Mortgage Servicing," 28 *Yale J. Reg.* 1, 4, 28 (2012).

26. *Ibid.*

27. *Ibid.*

28. David Dayan, *Chain of Title: How Three Ordinary Americans Uncovered Wall Street's Great Foreclosure Fraud* (2016); Hearing before the House Financial Services Committee Subcommittee on Housing and Community Opportunity, "Robo-Signing, Chain of Title, Loss Mitigation, and Other Issues in Mortgage Servicing," Nov. 18, 2010 (testimony of Adam J. Levitin).

29. *In re Stewart*, 391 B.R. 327, 355 (Bankr. E.D. La. 2008).

30. 12 C.F.R. § 1024.41 (2018).

31. 12 C.F.R. § 1024.37 (2018).

32. 17 C.F.R. §§ 229.1110, 1111(a)-(b) (2006).

33. 17 C.F.R. § 229.1105 (2006).

34. 17 C.F.R. §§ 229.1111(h)(1), 229.1125 (2018).

35. 17 C.F.R. §§ 229.1111(h)(2), 232.11, 232.301 (2018).

36. SEC Release No. 33-6964 (Oct. 22, 1992).

37. 17 C.F.R. § 230.424(h).

38. US Securities and Exchange Commission, "Asset-Level Disclosure Requirements for Residential Mortgage-Backed Securities," Oct. 30, 2019, *at* https://www.sec.gov/news/public-statement/clayton-rmbs-asset-disclosure.

39. 12 U.S.C. §§ 1455g (2018) (Fannie Mae); 1723c (2018) (Freddie Mac); 15 U.S.C. §§ 77c(a)(2), 78c(a)(12) (2018) (Ginnie Mae).

40. Jonathan R. Laing, "Banks Face Another Mortgage Crisis," *Forbes*, Nov. 20, 2010.

41. 17 C.F.R. § 239.45(b) (2018).

42. *See supra* note 38.

43. Senior Preferred Stock Purchase Agreement, dated Sept. 7, 2008, between the US Department of Treasury and the Federal National Mortgage Association, § 5.7, *at* https://www.fhfa.gov/Conservatorship/Documents/Senior-Preferred-Stock-Agree/FNM/SPSPA-amends/FNM-SPSPA_09-07-2008.pdf, *as amended by* Third Amendment to Amended and Restated Senior Preferred Stock Purchase Agreement, § 6, dated Aug. 17, 2012, *at* https://www.fhfa.gov/Conservatorship/Documents/Senior-Preferred-Stock-Agree/FNM/SPSPA-amends/FNM-Third-Amendment-to-the-Amended-and-Restated-SPSPA_08-17-2012.pdf; Senior Preferred Stock Purchase Agreement, dated Sept. 7, 2008, between the US Department of Treasury and the Federal Home Loan Mortgage Corporation, § 5.7, *as amended by* Third Amendment to Amended and Restated Senior Preferred Stock Purchase Agreement, § 6, dated Aug. 17, 2012, *at* https://www.fhfa.gov/Conservatorship/Documents/Senior-Preferred-Stock-Agree/FRE/SPSPA-amends/FRE-Third-Amend-to-the-Amended-Restated-SPSPA_08-17-2012.pdf.

44. The TBA market is legally possible for Agency MBS only because they are exempt from Securities Act registration. Absent a registration exemption, a forward sale of an MBS without delivery of a prospectus to the buyer would be a Securities Act violation entitling the buyer to rescind the transaction if the MBS's price were to fall. A TBA market is theoretically possible for MBS that qualify for a private placement exemption, but it would necessarily constrain the size of the market.

45. SIFMA, "TBA Market Fact Sheet," 2015, *at* https://www.sifma.org/wp-content/uploads/2011/03/SIFMA-TBA-Fact-Sheet.pdf.

46. *Ibid.*

47. *Ibid.*

48. *Ibid.*

49. If the lender were to sell the mortgage loan to Fannie Mae, it would get paid in Fannie Mae MBS (unless it utilized the cash window option). The MBS it would receive would reflect the coupon on the mortgage loan.

50. James Vickery & Joshua Wright, "TBA Trading and Liquidity in the Agency MBS Market," *FRBNY Econ. Pol'y. Rev.* 8 (May 2013).

51. Parties other than lenders can utilize dollar roll financing.

52. FHFA, "Uniform Mortgage-Backed Security," 84 Fed. Reg. 7793, Mar. 5, 2019.

53. 12 C.F.R. Part 1248 (2018).

54. FHFA, *FHFA Credit Risk Transfer Progress Report, Fourth Quarter 2018*, at 5.

55. *Ibid.*

56. FHFA, *2019 Scorecard for Fannie Mae, Freddie Mac, and Common Securitization Solutions*, at 4, Dec. 2018.

57. Freddie Mac's STACR-SPI program involves the issuance of subordinated junior, nonguaranteed, cash MBS, rather than a credit-linked note.

58. FHFA, *FHFA Credit Risk Transfer Progress Report*, at 5.

59. In the first five years of synthetic credit risk transfer transactions, from 2013 to 2018, the GSEs themselves would issue unsecured notes to investors, rather than have the issuer be a bankruptcy-remote trust. Payment on the notes, however, was based on the performance of a reference pool of loans that have been securitized into a GSE MBS. Such a pool might contain 120,000 loans. As principal was repaid on the loans in the reference pool, the GSE would repay a corresponding amount of principal to the note-holders. If there were losses in the reference pool, those losses were absorbed by the GSE, but the GSE's obligation to pay on the unsecured notes was also reduced.

60. Freddie Mac, "Investors by Transaction," at https://crt.freddiemac.com/_assets/docs/investors-by-transaction-0619.xlsx.

61. Fannie Mae, "Lender Announcement 07-16," Nov. 6, 2007; Freddie Mac, "Single-Family Seller-Servicer Guide," *Bulletin*, Nov. 15, 2007.

62. Fannie Mae, *Selling Guide, B7-1-02, Mortgage Insurance Requirements* (Aug. 7, 2018).

63. Fannie Mae, "Lender Announcement 07–21," Dec. 6, 2007; Freddie Mac, "Single-Family Seller-Servicer Guide," *Bulletin*, Dec. 11, 2007.

64. *See* Fannie Mae, "Selling Guide," Announcement SEL-2013–09, Dec. 16, 2013.

65. *See* Fannie Mae, "Selling Guide," Announcement SEL-2015-04, Apr. 17, 2015; Freddie Mac, "Single-Family Seller-Servicer Guide," *Bulletin* 2015–6, April 17, 2015.

66. *See PHH Corp. v. Consumer Fin. Prot. Bureau*, 839 F.3d 1, 39–41 (D.C. Cir. 2016), *rev'd in part, PHH Corp. v. Consumer Fin. Prot. Bureau*, 881 F.3d 75 (D. C. Cir. 2018), *en banc*.

67. Hearing before the United States Senate Committee on Banking, Housing and Urban Affairs, "Principles of Housing Finance Reform, "June 29, 2017, written testimony of Mr. Michael D. Calhoun, President, Center for Responsible Lending.

68. *See, e.g.*, MGIC, "Rate Sheet, 71–61284," June 7, 2018, which lists additional charges for loans with DTI greater or equal to 45 percent).

69. This is based on a 2.75 percent LLPA for the credit score and LTV and another 1.25 percent LLPA for the minimum PMI coverage, with a PMI premium of 0.37 percent; *see* Fannie Mae, "Loan-Level Pricing Adjustment Matrix," Apr. 8, 2019, *at* https://www.fanniemae.com/content/pricing/llpa-matrix.pdf (LLPAs); MGIC, "Borrower-Paid Monthly Premiums," effective July 9, 2018, *at* https://www.mgic.com/-/media/mi/rates/rate-cards/71-61284-rate-card-pdf-bpmi-monthly-july-2018.pdf, which lists PMI rates.

70. Mark Morial *et al.*, "Senate GSE Reform Proposal: A Blow to Affordable Housing and Harmful to the Overall Housing Market," National Urban League and Center for Responsible Lending, at 5, Mar. 2018.

71. CoreLogic, Press Release, "CoreLogic Reports the Negative Equity Share Fell to 3.8% in the Second Quarter of 2019," Sept. 20, 2019, *at* https://www.corelogic.com/news/corelogic-reports-the-negative-equity-share-fell-to-3.8-percent-in-the-second-quarter-of-2019.aspx.

72. Urban Institute, "Monthly Chartbook," at 9, Oct. 2019, *at* https://www.urban
.org/sites/default/files/publication/101274/october_chartbook_2019_1.pdf.

73. Urban Institute, "Monthly Chartbook," at 8, May 2019, *at* https://www
.urban.org/sites/default/files/publication/100299/may_chartbook_2019.pdf.

74. *Ibid.*

75. Brad Finkelstein, "Why Fannie and Freddie May Need More Treasury Bailout
Cash," *Am. Banker*, Jul. 12, 2018, which argues that a change to the accounting rule requiring earlier loss reserving may require GSEs to draw on
their Treasury lines.

76. You Suk Kim *et al.*, "Liquidity Crises in the Mortgage Market," Brookings
Paper on Economic Activity, Spring 2018.

77. Urban Institute, "Monthly Chartbook," at 12, Oct. 2019, *at* https://www
.urban.org/sites/default/files/publication/101274/october_chartbook_2019
_1.pdf.

78. You Suk Kim *et al.*, "Liquidity Crises in the Mortgage Market."

79. Hal Bundrick, "The 20% Mortgage Down Is All But Dead," *L.A. Times*, Jul.
1, 2017.

80. Arthur Acolin *et al.*, "Borrowing constraints and homeownership," 106 *Am.
Econ. Rev.* 625 (2016).

81. US Census Bureau, Homeownership Rate for the United States [RHORUSQ
156N], retrieved from FRED, Fed. Res. Bank of St. Louis, *at* http://fred.stlouisfed
.org/series/RHORUSQ156N, Jan. 31, 2020.

82. Wendy K. Tam Cho *et al.*, "The Tea Party Movement and the Geography of
Collective Action," 7 *Q. J. Poli. Sci.* 105, 126 (2012).

83. *Ibid.*, at 105, 122, 126.

84. Michelle Zonta *et al.*, "The Role of Midwestern Housing Instability in the
2016 Election," Nov. 29, 2016, *at* https://www.americanprogress.org/issues
/economy/news/2016/11/29/293816/the-role-of-midwestern-housing
-instability-in-the-2016-election/.

85. *Ibid.*

86. *Ibid.*

87. US Department of the Treasury, "Housing Reform Plan, Pursuant to the Presidential Memorandum Issued March 27, 2019," Sept. 2019, *at* https://home
.treasury.gov/system/files/136/Treasury-Housing-Finance-Reform-Plan.pdf.

88. Fannie Mae, Amended and Restated Certificate of Designation of Terms of
Variable Liquidation Preference Senior Preferred Stock, Series 2008-2, § 2(c),
Sept. 30, 2019, *at* https://www.fhfa.gov/Conservatorship/Documents/Senior
-Preferred-Stock-Agree/FNM/Stock-Cert/Third-Amend-FNM-Stock-Cert-as
-amended_09-30-2019.pdf; Freddie Mae, Third Amended and Restated Cer-
tificate of Creation, Designation, Powers, Preferences, Rights, Privileges,
Qualifications, Limitations, Restrictions, Terms and Conditions of Variable
Liquidation Preference Senior Preferred Stock, § 2(c), Sept. 30, 2019, *at*
https://www.fhfa.gov/Conservatorship/Documents/Senior-Preferred-Stock
-Agree/FRE/Stock-Cert/Third-Amend-FRE-Stock-Certificate-as-amended
_09-30-2019.pdf.

89. 83 Fed. Reg. 33312, 33330, tbl. 7, July 17, 2018. Under the proposed rule,
the GSEs would have been required on September 30, 2017, to have core cap-

ital (equity value plus retained earnings) of at least $103.5 billion under one proposed alternative and $139.5 billion under another alternative. Moreover, the GSEs would have been required as of September 30, 2017, to also have "total capital," including credit risk transfers, of at least $180.9 billion given the risk-weighting of their assets. *Ibid.* at 33330, tbl. 6.

90. There is potential upside to the chair of the House Financial Services Committee or Senate Banking Committee in terms of putting GSE reform on the agenda as a way of attracting campaign donations and attention from the housing finance industry, but being successful with reform would actually shut down this donation stream.

12. Principles for Reform

1. *See* Patricia A. McCoy & Susan M. Wachter, "Why Cyclicality Matters to Access to Mortgage Credit," 27 *B.C. J. L. & Social Justice*, 261 (2017).

2. *See* Thorstein Veblen, *The Theory of Business Enterprise* 105–6, 112–13 (1904), which identifies a cycle in which an increase in collateral value increases credit availability, which then further increases collateral value; Nobuhiro Kiyotaki & John Moore, "Credit Cycles," 105 *J. Pol. Econ.* 211, 212–13 (1997), which theorizes a cycle in which increasing collateral value increases credit availability, which then further increases collateral value; and Atif Mian & Amir Sufi, "The Consequences of Mortgage Credit Expansion: Evidence from the U.S. Mortgage Default Crisis," 124 *Q. J. Econ.* 1449, 1490–92 (2009), which finds support for the Kiyotaki & Moore model in the growth of housing prices and credit.

3. *See* Andrey D. Pavlov *et al.*, "Price Discovery in the Credit Default Swap Market in the Financial Crisis," working paper, Sept. 26, 2019.

4. Today, there is competition for credit risk among the major financial intermediaries that insure against credit risk. In particular, the GSEs' back-end synthetic credit risk transfers, have shifted substantial second-loss risk to private investors, although taxpayers are exposed to catastrophic risk. Similarly, the taxpayer is entirely on the hook for Ginnie Mae mortgage risk, and FHA/VA mortgage insurance is in the first-loss position up to the coverage limitation. Any further losses lie on the seller/servicer. (FHA/VA insurance does not pay out immediately upon a default; Ginnie Mae guarantees the timely payment of principal and interest on MBS, meaning that the federal government is ultimately holding the residual credit risk; if a seller or servicer fails, losses move over to Ginnie Mae. *See* You Suk Kim *et al.*, "Liquidity Crises in the Mortgage Market," Brookings Paper on Economic Activity, Spring 2018.)

5. 12 U.S.C. § 1701j-3(d)(1) (2018).

6. *See* Adam J. Levitin & Susan M. Wachter, "Second-Liens and the Leverage Option," 68 *Vand. L. Rev.* 1243 (2015).

7. Mark Morial *et al.*, "Senate GSE Reform Proposal: A Blow to Affordable Housing and Harmful to the Overall Housing Market," National Urban League and Center for Responsible Lending, Mar. 2018.

8. H.R. 2767 113th Cong. (2013) and, in an amended form, H.R. 6746 115th Cong. (2018).

9. Peter J. Wallison *et al.*, "Taking the Government Out of Housing Finance: Principles for Reforming the Housing Finance Market," *AEI*, Mar. 24, 2011, reprinted December 2016, *at* https://www.aei.org/publication/taking-the -government-out-of-housing-finance-principles-for-reforming-the-housing -finance-market-3/.

10. Partnership to Strengthen Homeownership Act of 2015, H.R. 1491, 114th Cong. (2015).

11. *See* Rep. John K. Delaney, "Press Release: Hensarling-Delaney-Himes Announce Bipartisan Housing Finance Reform Act," Sept. 6, 2018, *at* https:// delaney.house.gov/news/press-releases/hensarling-delaney-himes-announce -bipartisan-housing-finance-reform-act.

12. Michael Bright & Ed DeMarco, "Toward a New Secondary Mortgage Market," Milken Institute, Sept. 2016, *at* https://assets1b.milkeninstitute.org /assets/Publication/Viewpoint/PDF/Toward-a-New-Secondary-Mortgage -Market.pdf.

13. Kim *et al.*, "Liquidity Crises in the Mortgage Market."

14. Housing Finance Reform and Taxpayer Protection Act of 2014 S.1217, 113th Cong. (2014).

15. MBA, "GSE Reform: Creating a Sustainable, More Vibrant, Secondary Mortgage Market," Apr. 20, 2017, *at* http://mba.informz.net/z/cjUucD9taTo2M DcyMzAoJnA9MSZ1PTgoMDM1NTc3OCZsaTooMjU4MDMxMQ /index.html.

16. *See* Susan M. Wachter, "The Market Structure of Securitisation and the US Housing Bubble," 230 *Nat'l Instit. Econ. Rev.* 34 (2014), which shows that a monopolist will internalize systemic risk externalities.

17. Jim Parrott *et al.*, "A More Promising Road to GSE Reform," Mar. 2016, *at* https://www.economy.com/mark-zandi/documents/2016-03-22-A-More -Promising-Road-To-GSE-Reform.pdf.

18. Richard Cooperstein *et al.*, "A Vision for Enduring Housing Finance Reform," National Association of REALTORS®, (Feb. 2019). *See also* Andrew Davidson & Richard Cooperstein, "Is There a Competitive Equilibrium for the GSEs?" Sept. 2017, *at* http://d1c25a6gwz7q5e.cloudfront.net/reports/2017 -10-19-GSEs_ADavidsonRCooperstein.pdf. Davidson and Cooperstein envision between one and three GSEs, but in any event, a highly restricted number.

19. Libby Cantrill *et al.*, "U.S. Housing Finance Reform: Why Fix What Isn't Broken?" Feb. 2018, *at* https://www.pimco.com/en-us/insights/viewpoints/us -housing-finance-reform-why-fix-what-isnt-broken.

20. Having several regulated entities does not preclude the potential for additional entities to enter and to help ensure cost containment.

A. The Pre–New Deal Farm Finance System

1. Federal Farm Loan Act of 1916, Pub. L. 64–158, § 18, 39 Stat. 360, 375 (July 17, 1916).

2. *Ibid.*, § 5, 39 Stat. 364–65.

3. Raymond J. Saulnier *et al.*, "Agricultural Credit Programs," in *Federal Lending and Loan Insurance* 152 (1958), *available at* http://www.nber.org

/chapters/c2574.pdf. Only shares purchased by the US government and special National Farm Loan Associations were allowed to vote. *See* Federal Farm Loan Act of 1916, § 5, 39 Stat. 364–65.

4. *Ibid.*, § 21.

5. Federal Land Banks were restricted to making loans at no more than 6 percent. *See ibid.*, § 12. The interest rate of Federal Land Bank bonds was restricted to 5 percent. *See ibid.*, § 20.

6. *Ibid.*, § 9.

7. *Ibid.*, § 8.

8. Jonathan D. Rose, "A Primer on Farm Debt Relief Programs during the 1930s," *Fed. Res. Bd. Finance and Economic Discussion Series*, No. 2013-33, Apr. 22, 2013, at 4, *at* https://www.federalreserve.gov/pubs/FEDS/2013/201333/201333pap.pdf.

9. Federal Farm Loan Act, § 10.

10. *Ibid.*, § 9.

11. *Ibid.*, § 10.

12. *Ibid.*, § 9.

13. *Ibid.*, § 8.

14. *Ibid.*, § 7.

15. *Ibid.*, § 9.

16. *Ibid* § 9.

17. *Ibid.*, § 25.

18. *Ibid.*, § 10.

19. *Ibid.*

20. *Ibid.*, § 12.

21. *Ibid.*, § 12. There was some disagreement, however, as to what the cultivation requirement actually entailed. *See* C. W. Thompson, "The Federal Farm Loan Act," 7 *Am. Econ. Rev., Supplement, Papers & Proceedings of the 29th Annual Meeting of the American Econ. Ass'n.* 115, 123 (1927).

22. Federal Farm Loan Act, § 12.

23. *Ibid.*, § 12.

24. *Ibid.*, §§ 9, 12.

25. Walter B. Palmer, "The Federal Farm Loan Act," 15 *Publications of the Am. Statistical Ass'n.* 292, 293 (1916). Farmers also needed shorter-term credit for equipment and operating capital. The Federal Intermediate Credit Bank system, founded in 1923, was meant to meet this need.

26. Federal Farm Loan Act, § 12.

27. *Ibid.*, § 12. *See also* Palmer, "The Federal Farm Loan Act," at 293.

28. Thompson, "The Federal Farm Loan Act," at 124.

29. *Ibid.*, at 125.

30. Victor W. Bennett, "The Joint Stock Land Banks in Retrospect," 20 *J. Farm Econ.* 857 (1938).

31. Saulnier *et al.*, "Agricultural Credit Programs," at 152.

32. The Joint Stock Land Banks were subject to the same term restrictions as the Federal Land Banks. *See* Federal Farm Loan Act, § 16.

33. *Ibid.*

34. *Ibid. See also* Bennett, "The Joint Stock Land Banks in Retrospect," at 858.

35. Bennett, "The Joint Stock Land Banks in Retrospect," at 858.
36. By the late 1920s, the NFLAs owned 98 percent of the Federal Land Bank stock. *See* Rose, "A Primer on Farm Debt Relief Programs," at 6, n.7.
37. Federal Farm Loan Act, § 26.
38. *Ibid.*, § 27.
39. Bennett, "The Joint Stock Land Banks in Retrospect," at 863.
40. Saulnier *et al.*, "Agricultural Credit Programs," at 159.
41. Farm Credit Administration, "History of FCA and FCS," Sept. 22, 2014, *at* https://www.fca.gov/about/history/historyFCA_FCS.html.
42. *See generally* Rose, "A Primer on Farm Debt Relief Programs."
43. *Ibid.*
44. Pub. L. 72-3, § 2, 47 Stat. 12, 13 (Jan. 23, 1932); Rose, "A Primer on Farm Debt Relief Programs," at 6.
45. Saulnier *et al.*, "Agricultural Credit Programs," at 152–53. These capital injections were set up as revolving accounts in case future draws were needed. *Ibid.* at 153.
46. Bennett, "The Joint Stock Land Banks," at 857.
47. Saulnier *et al.*, "Agricultural Credit Programs," at 152.

B. The Levitin-Wachter Subprime PLS Dataset

1. We caution nonexpert readers not to read too much into this technical point. Our sample may well be statistically significant, but we cannot determine this based on the information we have, and the conclusions we draw are not dependent on an assumption of statistical significance.
2. The Intex database, which is considered one of the most comprehensive, lists 1,907 subprime PLS deals from 2000 to 2008. This suggests a slightly lower number for 2001–2007, which indicates that our sample likely represents about 20 percent of subprime PLS in terms of the number of deals for the 2001–2007 period.
3. Inside Mortgage Finance, *2015 Mortgage Market Statistical Annual: Mortgage Originations by Product*, sum of subprime mortgage originations for 2001–2007.
4. *See* Adam J. Levitin *et al.*, "Mortgage Risk Premiums during the Housing Bubble," *J. R. E. Fin. & Econ.* (2019).

C. CDO Manager Compensation

1. Sergey Chernenko, "The Front Men of Wall Street: The Role of CDO Collateral Managers in the CDO Boom and Bust," 72 *J. Fin.* 1893, 1888 (2017).
2. *Ibid.*, at 1902.
3. *See ibid.*, at 1903, tbl. 3.
4. *Ibid.*
5. *Ibid.*, at 1899.
6. *Ibid.*
7. *See ibid.*, at 1903, tbl. 3.

8. The exception would be if certain overcollateralization and interest coverage triggers were hit, which would result in funds being shifted to pay off investors, resulting in a decline in AUM or, in an extreme case, in the liquidation of the CDO; *see* Chernenko, "The Front Men of Wall Street," at 1898–99. Overcollateralization, however, was calculated based on the par value of AUM, so to the extent that the CDO manager purchased discounted securities, the CDO would appear substantially more overcollateralized than it really was.

9. Joachim Keller, "Agency Problems in Structured Finance—A Case Study of European CLOs," National Bank of Belgium Working Paper, No. 137, Aug. 2008, at 5, *available at* http://aei.pitt.edu/10995/1/wp137En.pdf.

10. The example of CDO manager Wing Chau, described in Michael Lewis's *The Big Short: Inside the Doomsday Machine* 138–144 (2010), would seem to fit this description.

11. *See* Keller, "Agency Problems in Structured Finance," at 12, which states, "The high proportion of performance-based components (subordinated and incentive fees) should provide sufficient incentives to the managers to exert effort to maintain the quality of the portfolio, *unless bad portfolio quality can go undetected for several years during which the manager receives the subordinated management fee* [emphasis added]."

12. Chernenko, "The Front Men of Wall Street," at 1924.

13. *Ibid.*

14. We thank Bill Frey for sharing historical PLS offering pricing figures with us.

15. To understand why all the MBS issued against a pool of mortgages with different interest rates must have the same coupon, imagine a pool containing just three mortgages, each for $100,000, but with interest rates of 5%, 6%, and 7%. The pool has a weighted average coupon of 6%. It is not possible to issue a set of 6% bonds against this pool, however. (For this example, we will ignore servicing and other costs that are taken off the top.) If investors purchase a bunch of 6% bonds, what will happen when market interest rates drop? The 7% mortgage is the one most likely to refinance. Once it refinances, it is no longer part of the pool, and the weighted average coupon of the remaining mortgages in the pool will fall to 5.5%, making the remaining mortgages insufficient to cover the 6% coupon payments due on the bonds. In other words, a prepayment begets a credit risk in pools with differentiated underlying mortgage rates.

   The solution to this problem is to create weighted average coupon interest-only (IO) and weighted average coupon principal-only (PO) bonds from specific mortgages or groups of mortgages. Thus, the 7% mortgage will be bifurcated into a regular $100,000 loan at 6% and a $100,000 IO obligation at 1%, while the 5% loan will be bifurcated into an $86,000 6% loan and a $14,000 PO obligation with a 0% interest rate. Accordingly, the loan pool now consists of what can be conceived of as $286,000 in 6% loans, a $14,000 PO obligation with no interest, and a 1% IO obligation on a $100,000 nominal balance. Against this will be issued $286,000 in 6% bonds, a $14,000 weighted average coupon PO bond, and a $100,000 weighted average coupon IO bond.

Thus, if the actual 7% mortgage is refinanced, the weighted average coupon IO bond will be paid off and there will be a prepayment of $100,000 on the 6% bonds, whose balance will be reduced to $186,000. The weighted average coupon PO bond will be unaffected. In contrast, if the 5% mortgage defaults with 50% credit loss, the loss will be borne by the weighted average coupon PO bond (losing $7,000), and the 6% bonds (losing $43,000), but the weighted average coupon IO bond will be unaffected. An if there is a loss on the 6% mortgage, the weighted average coupon IO and weighted average coupon PO bonds will be unaffected, as they are specifically tied to the 7% and 5% mortgages respectively.

The point of this illustration is that when securitizations pool mortgages of different interest rates, the higher interest rate mortgages have a greater prepayment risk, all else being equal, and this necessitates a structure in which all of the MBS have the same normalized interest rate, excluding the weighted average coupon IO and PO bonds, which are tied to specific mortgages. While one might expect the subordinated junior bonds to have a higher coupon than the senior bonds, this is actually not possible. Consider what would happen if our 6% weighted averaged coupon were divided into senior bonds with a 4% rate and junior bonds with an 8% rate. What would happen if there was a default that wiped out the junior bonds? The remaining underlying mortgages would still have a 6% coupon rate. Where would the remaining 2% of the coupon be allocated after the 4% coupon was paid out on the senior bonds? The complications posed here are such that junior tranches in PLS must have the same coupon as the senior tranches: they will all be 6%.

The credit subordinated tranches of PLS were not, as is often assumed, compensated with higher interest rates. Instead, they had the same coupon as the senior tranches, but they had higher yields that were achieved through issuance at deep discounts from par. The deeply subordinated tranches of PLS sold at substantial discounts from par—as little as 15¢ or 20¢ on the dollar. Given that most of the bonds issued in PLS were from senior tranches, the amount of money at stake from the deeper discounting was not prohibitive.

The twist is that *among* the senior tranches with the same credit risk there will often be reallocation of the coupon, such that some senior bonds are at 4% and others are at 8%, but this is based on prepayment risk, not on credit risk. There was never reallocation of interest among tranches of different credit priority. Thus, imagine a deal with six A tranches and six B tranches. The A tranches are all of the same priority in terms of credit losses, and are senior to all of the B tranches, which bear credit loss in sequential order. If the weighted average coupon on the mortgages in the deal is 6%, that would be the weighted average coupon of the A tranches and the B tranches. The B tranches would be compensated for their credit risk with original issue discount that would increase their yield. The A tranches would sell at par, but might reallocate that 6% weighted average coupon among themselves, however, to reflect differences in prepayment risk. Thus, some A tranches might be "front-pay" bonds that receive any principal prepayments on the mortgages until the bonds are paid off, which means that they are shorter-duration bonds than the "back-pay" bonds, and thus less risky than the back-pay bonds. The back-pay bonds might be compensated for this risk with a slice of the interest normally due to the front pay bonds.

16. Bob Ivry & Jody Shenn, "How Lucido Helped AIG Lose Big on Goldman Sachs CDOs," *Bloomberg*, Mar. 31, 2010.

17. Beltran *et al.*, "Asymmetric Information and the Death of ABS CDOs," at 5.

18. Michael C. Jensen & William H. Meckling, "Theory of the Firm: Managerial Behavior, Agency Costs and Ownership Structure," 3 *J. Fin. Econ.* 305 (1976).

Acknowledgments

We have many people to thank for helping see this book to fruition.

Our thinking in this area was greatly advanced by conversations with Laurie Goodman, Julia Gordon, David Min, Jannecke Ratcliffe, Sarah Rosen, Ellen Seidman, and Barry Zigas, and other participants in the Center for American Progress's Mortgage Finance Working Group. We have also benefited from insights from academic colleagues and coauthors, most notably Arthur Acolin, Raphael Bostic, William Bratton, Paul Calem, Richard Cooperstein, Larry Cordell, Ken Fears, Anna Gelpern, Pat McCoy, and Andrey Pavlov, and the participants in the American Law Institute's $10 Trillion Question conference. William Frey was uniquely helpful to us in explaining the dynamics of the B-piece market. Andrew Davidson's work has also been instrumental in furthering our thinking. Additionally, K-Sue Park provided helpful comments on the final manuscript, and we have been greatly aided by the research assistance of Alexander Canahuante, Kimberly Chan, Desen Lin, Melanie Miller, Anthony Orlando, Eric Pfeifer, and Aidan T. Thornton. We are also thankful to Ian Malcolm and Olivia Elizabeth Woods at Harvard University Press and the production team at Westchester Publishing Services for all their help turning our manuscript into this book.

Some of the ideas in this book were first developed in articles published in various scholarly journals. In particular, Chapters 6–8 build on ideas first discussed in an article we published as "Explaining the Housing Bubble," *Georgetown Law Journal* 100, no. 4 (2012): 1177–1258. Likewise, Chapter 10 builds on ideas first discussed in an article we published as "Second Liens and the Leverage Option," *Vanderbilt Law Review* 68, no. 5 (2015): 1243–1294. We are grateful to this journal, as well as to the *Harvard Business Law Review*, *Housing Policy Debate*, *U.C. Davis Law*

Review, and *Yale Journal on Regulation*, which gave us the opportunity to publish in their publications. Our research has also benefited from a trio of grants from the Georgetown Law Reynolds Family Fund, and Susan gratefully acknowledges financial support from the Zell-Lurie Real Estate Center at the Wharton School of the University of Pennsylvania.

Finally, there are our families, who have been subjected to hearing more about mortgages and securitization than anyone should have to endure. In Adam's home, Sarah, Amalia, and Kalman bore this burden with a smile and occasional eyeroll (and Isaac was added along the way, substantially delaying the completion of the manuscript but providing a delightful distraction). To this day, Adam has never succeeded in explaining to his children what Fannie Mae does, but it is a mark of some progress that they inevitably ask questions about "Frannie Mae and her friend Farmer Mac" whenever they drive past Fannie's old headquarters on Wisconsin Avenue.

Susan's grandchildren are still too young to ask, but their parents, Susan and Michael's adult children Jessica Wachter and Jonathan Wachter, don't need to, as they know more about finance than almost anyone. Mostly, Susan would like to thank her husband, Michael Wachter. Without his wisdom and loving support, this and a lifetime of work would not have been possible.

This book is dedicated to our spouses, who have long suffered our work in its production and whose presence makes our houses our homes.

Index

Deal, 16. *See also* housing finance system; mortgages
loans, bullet. *See* bullet loans
loans, low- or no-documentation, 175, 190
loans, nontraditional, 223–224, 225. *See also* mortgages, nontraditional
loan sizes, during housing bubble, 142–143
loan-to-value (LTV) ratio, 13, 19, 25, 187, 190, 211, 213, 222, 223, 225, 227, 241, 248, 298n29, 300n78, 305nn155,157, 312n64, 319n76, 342n25, 343n32; during bubble, 143, 145, 147, 192–193, 195; after bubble, 121; in Dodd-Frank, 208–209; in Federal Farm Loan Act, 267, 269; Federal Home Loan Banks and, 44; Federal Housing Administration insurance and, 49, 58; Government Sponsored Enterprises and, 76, 91, 180; during Great Depression, 39; Home Owners Loan Corporation and, 45, 46, 48; Hope for Homeowners program and, 118; jumbo mortgages and, 98; lack of regulation for, 208, 209; limits on, 26, 29, 91; nontraditional mortgages and, 106, 175; postwar mortgages and, 60; on pre–New Deal mortgages, 19–21, 22; regulation and, 59; risk-based pricing and, 248
Loewenstein, Lara, 161
long-short strategy, 201–202
low-income housing, 48–49. *See also* Federal Housing Administration (FHA); low- to moderate-income (LTMI) borrowers; public housing
low- or no-documentation loans, 175, 190
low- to moderate-income (LTMI) borrowers, 151, 153, 154, 161, 175, 177, 178. *See also* Community Reinvestment Act (CRA)
LTMI (low- to moderate-income) borrowers, 151, 153, 154, 161, 175, 177, 178. *See also* Community Reinvestment Act (CRA)
LTV (loan-to-value) ratio. *See* loan-to-value (LTV) ratio

Magnetar hedge fund, 202
maintenance/improvements of properties, 9
margin calls, 89
market: federal interventions to support, 117–121. *See also* housing finance markets; housing market
Market Condition Delivery Fee, 224
market developments, postcrisis, 216–225; growth of risk-based pricing, 223–225;

GSE credit risk transfer programs, 218–223
market discipline, 95, 134, 162, 196, 258, 344n33
market efficiency, 167–168; theories about housing bubble and, 165 (*see also* market failure)
market failure, 165; failure to price default put option, 186–190; short selling housing and, 198–203. *See also* information failures; risk, mispricing of; shorting housing
market fragmentation, 239–240, 253
market freeze, 106, 110, 115, 117
markets, housing finance. *See* housing finance markets
Mayer, Chris, 134
MBS (mortgage-backed securities). *See* mortgage-backed securities (MBS)
Merrill Lynch, 114
Mian, Atif, 161, 176–177
middle-class households, effects of crisis on, 228–229
Millennials: effects of crisis on, 229; homeownership rates of, 10; underwriting standards and, 229
minority communities: subprime lending and, 86. *See also* race/ethnicity
mobility: housing needs and, 34; labor market migrations, 32–33
monetary policy, 5, 37, 68, 230; refinancing boom, 158; in supply-side theories of bubble, 149, 157–161
money market instruments, 68, 78
moral hazard: in existing reform proposals, 235, 254; in securitization, 67, 162, 209
mortgage, thirty-year fixed. *See* thirty-year fixed-rate mortgage (American Mortgage)
mortgage-backed securities (MBS), 70, 241; exempt from registration, 213; in Franny Meg structure, 260; Freddie Mac and, 73, 74–75; Ginnie Mae and, 74; lack of standardization of, 75–76; in multi-issuer/multi-guarantor model, 251; in multi-issuer/single-guarantor model, 251; private-label MBS, 230; safety of as asset class, 88; spread of housing market crisis and, 115; Uniform MBS structure, 75, 216–218. *See also* Agency MBS; Fannie Mae; Freddie Mac; Ginnie Mae; securitization
Mortgage Bankers Association, 252
mortgage banks, 77–78